T0355168

Separate But Faithful

When Bad Policy Makes Good Politics: Running the Numbers on Health Reform
Robert P. Saldin

Citizenship By Degree: U.S. Higher Education Policy and the Changing Gender
Dynamics of American Citizenship
Deondra Rose

Politics at Work: How Companies Turn Their Workers into Lobbyists
Alexander Hertel-Fernandez

The Cities on the Hill: How Urban Insitutions Transform National Politics
Thomas K. Ogorzalek

Framing Inequality: Media, Public Opinion and the Neoliberal Turn
in U.S. Public Policy
Matthew Guardino

Mobilized by Injustice: Criminal Justice Contact, Political Participation, and Race
Hannah L. Walker

Short Circuiting Policy: Organized Interests in the American States and the
Erosion of Clean Energy Laws
Leah Cardamore Stokes

The Rise of Political Action Committees: Interest Group Electioneering and the
Transformation of American Politics
Emily J. Charnock

Separate But Faithful: The Christian Right's Radical Struggle to Transform
Law & Legal Culture
Amanda Hollis-Brusky and Joshua C. Wilson

Separate But Faithful

The Christian Right's Radical Struggle to Transform Law and Legal Culture

AMANDA HOLLIS-BRUSKY AND JOSHUA C. WILSON

OXFORD
UNIVERSITY PRESS

Oxford University Press is a department of the University of Oxford. It furthers
the University's objective of excellence in research, scholarship, and education
by publishing worldwide. Oxford is a registered trade mark of Oxford University
Press in the UK and certain other countries.

Published in the United States of America by Oxford University Press
198 Madison Avenue, New York, NY 10016, United States of America.

Library of Congress Cataloging-in-Publication Data
Names: Hollis-Brusky, Amanda, author. | Wilson, Joshua C., author.
Title: Separate But faithful : the Christian Right's radical struggle to
transform law & legal culture / Amanda Hollis-Brusky, Joshua C. Wilson.
Description: New York, NY : Oxford University Press, [2020] |
Series: Studies in Postwar American political development |
Includes bibliographical references and index.
Identifiers: LCCN 2020010426 (print) | LCCN 2020010427 (ebook) |
ISBN 9780190637262 (hardback) | ISBN 9780190637286 (epub)
Subjects: LCSH: Church and state—United States. |
Christianity and politics—United States. | Religion and law—United States. |
Conservatives—United States. | Freedom of religion—United States. | Conservatism.
Classification: LCC KF4865 .H65 2020 (print) |
LCC KF4865 (ebook) | DDC 349.73—dc23
LC record available at https://lccn.loc.gov/2020010426
LC ebook record available at https://lccn.loc.gov/2020010427

1 3 5 7 9 8 6 4 2

Printed by Sheridan Books, Inc., United States of America

To
Bob Kagan,
Our teacher, mentor, and friend

CONTENTS

ACKNOWLEDGMENTS

This book is dedicated to Robert A. Kagan or, as he is known to his friends, colleagues and students, Bob. In addition to serving separately as a dissertation advisor and mentor to both of us at the University of California, Berkeley, Bob is responsible for us meeting, for us collaborating, and for putting the wheels in motion for this project. The story of this book and our collaboration begins in 2011. Josh was just finishing up his first book project, *The Street Politics of Abortion*, and in the course of that research had come across a set of newish law schools with a very specific and peculiar mission—to recruit and train students according to what we would eventually learn is called a "Christian Worldview" perspective. Intrigued but unsure of how to think about these Christian Worldview law schools, Josh relayed this interesting tidbit to his former advisor Bob Kagan. Without missing a beat, Bob said, "You have to talk with Amanda Hollis-Brusky. Her work on the Federalist Society could be helpful for how you think about these law schools and their potential impact."

As is usually the case, Bob's instincts were right-headed. After Bob's introduction, we met for coffee at a conference and came away with a plan to co-author a single article. That article, "Lawyers for God and Neighbor," which appeared in *Law and Social Inquiry* in 2014, raised additional questions about law schools and their relationship to legal mobilization, so we agreed to write another article. In researching that second article, we realized that what we were finding and the questions we were raising were too big for an article or even two. We had unwittingly started a book project and an eight-year scholarly partnership.

As it has taken shape and in its various iterations, this book has benefited from the feedback, careful attention, and review of dozens of scholars across political science and sociolegal studies. Susan Sterett encouraged us to first pursue a grant with the National Science Foundation and worked with us again in her capacity as editor of *Law and Society Review*. Jon Gould gave this project his attention and interest at the National Science Foundation and continues to be a model of engaged scholarship and academic citizenship. We owe a huge debt—both scholarly and professionally—to Charles Epp, who developed the support structure framework in 1998 and who was singularly helpful and encouraging to us as we updated, refined, and deployed the framework for this project. Steven Teles took an early interest in the project and encouraged us to pursue an advanced contract with Oxford. Our editor David McBride saw potential early on in the project, gave us a contract and trusted us to complete it. Ann Southworth continues to be a mentor to both of us. In addition to her comments and conversations at very early stages of this project, she organized a thrilling conference at the Center for Empirical Research on the Legal Profession at the University of California, Irvine, Law School in April 2019 where we received feedback from an interdisciplinary group of brilliant scholars including Bryant Garth, Mark Graber, Sandy Levinson, Neal Devins, Lawrence Baum, Leah Litman, Jane Schacter, and Swethaa Ballakrishnen.

We also benefitted from feedback received at the Inaugural Conference on Right Wing Studies organized by Christine Trost and Lawrence Rosenthal at the Center for Right Wing Studies at the University of California, Berkeley. In the same vein, we received valuable feedback on this project from invited talks at Lund University in Sweden and The University of Paris-Sorbonne. The project has also been improved from conversations with scholars doing exciting work in the field of religion and politics—Andrew Lewis, Daniel Bennett, Mary Ziegler, and Nancy Wadsworth in particular. Paul Collins, Jeffrey Dudas, Renee Cramer, Jill Weinberg, Colin Beck, Jennifer Merolla, Rachel VanSickle-Ward, Abby Wood, Heidi Haddad, Anil Kahlan, Liz Chiarello, Catherine Albiston, John Bliss, Rick Hasen, Jack Balkin, Nancy Reichman, Lynn Mather, Christopher Schmidt, Laura Beth Nielsen, and Robert Nelson each served as sounding boards at critical points in the project's development. We are thankful for their time and friendship.

We want to emphasize that this list is nowhere near exhaustive—it does not include the dozen anonymous reviewers on article manuscripts, the three reviewers of our book manuscript, and the countless comments and conversations during conference panels, over coffees, over drinks, etc. Please know that if you reviewed any version of this project at some stage, we are so grateful for your thoughts and comments. We are confident they only made the manuscript better.

We also want to thank the eighteen student research assistants who worked on this project over the course of seven summers and academic years, gathering, coding, organizing, and hunting down difficult-to-find data: at Pomona College, Larkin Corrigan, Mollie Cowger, Joanmarie DelVechio, Sarah Dupree, Hutchinson Fann, Carly Grimes, Roger Huddle, Sarah Laws, Adam Revello, Ani Schug, Hannah State, Tena Thau, Jerry Yan, and Olivia Zalesin; at the University of Denver, Lauren Yehle, Jaser Alsharhan, Stephen Preisig, and Marnier LeBlanc.

Scholarly projects this big cannot happen without a robust support structure of their own. For their patronage and financial support, we first and foremost want to acknowledge the National Science Foundation Law and Social Sciences Division (Award Numbers 1551863 and 1551871) for providing approximately $254,000 in combined funding for this project between 2016 and 2019. The funding allowed us to travel for fieldwork and interviews, to hire our three excellent project consultants—Seth Masket, Jason Renn, and David Glick—and to provide research opportunities for the students listed.

At the very early stages of this project, Amanda also received a Hirsch Research Initiation Grant through Pomona College and received support for student research from Pomona College's Summer Undergraduate Research Program (SURP). Amanda would also like to thank Pomona College for its generous sabbatical support and for her colleagues in the Politics Department who afforded her the time and space to write up six years' worth of research, fieldwork, and findings over the course of the 2018–19 academic year. Similarly, Amanda owes a debt of gratitude to Kevin Dettmar and the Humanities Studio at Pomona College, where she served as a fellow for the 2019–20 academic year. Finally, she would like to give a shout out to Evelyn Khalili, Politics Department coordinator, who helped with paperwork, hiring of students, reimbursements, and all of the maddening Workday things.

Similarly, Josh would like to thank the University of Denver for its various forms of support over the life of this project. This support has been financial, in the form of the Professional Research Opportunities for Faculty (PROF) grant, the Faculty Research Fund (FRF) grant, the Sabbatical Enhancement Award, and the Rosenberry Fund Grant Award. It has come in the form of creating the time needed to write, as enabled by the sabbatical and mini-sabbatical programs. It has been in the form of administrative support, with particular thanks going to Corinne Lengsfeld, Daniel McIntosh, Jeff Quinlisk, Jennifer Collum, Doug Booth, Noelle Strom, and Megan Whitman. Finally, it has come in various forms of support from his incredible, and very supportive, department colleagues, with particular thanks going to Seth Masket, Lisa Conant, and Nancy Wadsworth.

We would also like to acknowledge our families and friends. Amanda would like to thank her extended family back on the East Coast who keep her grounded and up-to-date on Boston sports news and the VIPs of her "family band"—Sean, Annabelle, and Eloise. Amanda would also like to thank coffee, without which this book would not have been produced; her big teddy bear of a dog Hank, who sat at her feet to make sure she did not get up and take too many writing breaks; the hundreds of hours of reruns of *Star Trek TNG*, *DS9*, and *Voyager* that she watched with her daughters at night to decompress; Ladies Rock Camp, which allowed her to transform into an actual rock star two weekends a year; and her friends in Claremont and across the globe who bring her joy and help her stay sane in this politically tumultuous world.

Josh would like to thank his family and friends who expressed just the right amount of interest in this project, which is to acknowledge that it was going on, occasionally ask questions, but to mainly focus on so many other things to discuss, plan, and do. If Amanda is thanking coffee, then Josh is thanking tea (both hot and iced) and lap swimming pools, as well as his too-early-departed writing partner,

Purrcila. Josh would especially like to thank Elisha, Lila, and Reed, his parents, and the state of Colorado that provides them with an awe-inspiring place to live and regularly get away from work.

Finally, for their time and their confidence, we thank the forty-two students, faculty, and administrators who agreed to be interviewed in conjunction with our research. We are also thankful for the dozens of others who allowed us to sit in and engage in participant observation of classes and campus life, and still others who took the time to respond to our alumni survey. They entrusted us with their stories and their experiences. We have done our best to accurately and carefully represent those stories and experiences in the following pages. We hope the finished product does them justice.

Introduction

As America's legal standards have crumbled in the hands of those trained in the nation's law schools, Christians have awakened to the opportunity to equip men and women to restore justice to America. In the 1970's and 1980's several efforts have been made to raise up law schools with godly standards to restore American law to its original Biblical foundation . . . [these efforts] have met with vigorous opposition from the American Bar Association, the national law school accrediting agency. Not one of these law schools with a nationwide vision has received full accreditation . . . As America enters into the final fifteen years of the twentieth century, we face the frightful prospect of having no Christian law school serving the nation as a whole that is committed to a curriculum based upon the law of God and infused by the Holy Spirit of truth. CBN University has a unique opportunity to fill this void, and provide a quality legal education to deserving Christian men and women who desire to be equipped to serve the cause of justice in our land.

—Herbert W. Titus and Gerald R. Thompson,
"CBN University Proposed School of Law
Feasibility Study." May 17, 1985.

Ten years prior to penning this call to action for "Christian men and women who desire to be equipped to serve the cause of justice in our land," Herbert W. Titus, a Harvard-educated JD and tenured law professor, was teaching criminal law at the University of Oregon. Moved by his recent conversion to Christianity and seeking to align his newfound faith with his longtime study of the law, Titus announced one day in class to his students, "If you want to understand criminal law historically, you have to know that man is who Jesus says he is in Mark Chapter 7 [of the Holy Bible]." Titus then quoted the Holy Gospel to his students. According to his memory of the events, "when I tried to get that discussion in the classroom . . . I had people screaming at me. I had people say, 'You can't bring the Bible into a law school classroom!'" (Titus 2016). At that moment, Titus said he realized that there was an "irreconcilable conflict between what I now believed was true and what I could teach." He would need to reconcile his presuppositions about his faith and law, or he would need to leave the legal profession altogether.

Separate But Faithful. Amanda Hollis-Brusky and Joshua C. Wilson, Oxford University Press (2020). © Oxford University Press. DOI: 10.1093/oso/9780190637262.001.0001

Titus left the University of Oregon and took a sabbatical year in Switzerland. There, in what he describes as a sign from God, Titus crossed paths with two students from Oral Roberts University, a charismatic evangelical Christian university founded by the televangelist Oral Roberts in Tulsa, Oklahoma, in 1963. The students informed Titus that Oral Roberts intended to open a law school "rooted in charismatic Christian belief" with the aim of "train[ing] the next generation of legal minds to 'integrate their Christian faith into their chosen profession' and to 'restore law to its historic roots in the Bible'" (Stolberg 2011). Herb Titus, after a lot of praying, made the decision to leave his tenured position at the University of Oregon to become one of three full-time faculty members at what would become the O. W. Coburn School of Law at Oral Roberts University. Titus's dean at the University of Oregon warned him that he was throwing his career away and that a charismatic Christian evangelical law school could never be accredited by the American Bar Association. As Titus recounts, "God's call was so strong, it didn't faze me." He responded, "We'll be accredited. I'm not going to worry about that" (Titus 2016).

As Titus's dean predicted, accreditation was an uphill battle for O. W. Coburn School of Law. A significant departure from religiously founded or affiliated law schools of the past, O. W. Coburn School of Law had a tight religious filter for screening faculty and students, a filter that was key to maintaining the evangelical Christian character and culture of the law school. The requirement that students and faculty "take an oath of religious faith" was considered contrary to the American Bar Association's requirement at that time (Standard 211), which stated that a law school "shall foster and maintain equality of opportunity in legal education, including employment of faculty and staff, without discrimination on the basis of race, color, religion, national origin, gender of sexual orientation, age or disability" (Winter 1981, 1095–96). In the eyes of many members of the American Bar Association, including the head of its Accreditation Group, Jim White, what Oral Roberts University was proposing with its law school amounted to a license to discriminate on the basis of religious belief, which would set "a precedent for future exclusionary practices by other law schools" (Barbash 1981).

After a protracted fight with the American Bar Association complete with litigation, O. W. Coburn School of Law won provisional accreditation in 1981. Most significantly, after a "spirited debate," the American Bar Association delegates voted to amend Standard 211 to include the following phrase:

> Nothing herein shall be construed to prevent a law school from having a religious affiliation and purpose and adopting policies of admission and employment that directly relate to such affiliation and purpose so long as notice of such policies has been provided to applicants, students, faculty and employees. (Winter 1981, 1095–96)

Though O. W. Coburn School of Law would struggle financially and close within five years of this victory, Oral Roberts and his great experiment bequeathed two major gifts to the fledgling Christian conservative legal movement (CCLM). First, in a deal brokered by Herb Titus, Oral Roberts gifted his law library and resources to fellow televangelist and lawyer Marion "Pat" Robertson, who had long dreamed of adding a law school to his Virginia Beach, Virginia–based Christian Broadcasting Network University (CBNU). The CBNU law school would be renamed Regent Law School. Herb Titus would become its founding dean.

Secondly, the forty-eight-word amendment to the American Bar Association's Standard 211 that Oral Roberts's great experiment in legal education gave birth to opened the door for other like-minded patrons to follow suit, investing in and building their own distinctly Christian, biblically oriented, religiously controlled law schools. As mentioned above, with Oral Roberts's gift and blessing, televangelist and attorney Pat Robertson founded Regent Law School in Virginia Beach, Virginia, in 1986, as part of his global Christian Broadcasting Network (CBN) empire. The founding vision for the law school was articulated clearly by Titus and his legal assistant in the feasibility study that laid the groundwork for acquiring the law school from Oral Roberts: "The vision for the Law School includes not only quality education in legal analysis and skills, but quality education which will re-establish the Law of God, rediscover America's constitutional faith, reclaim truth in education, and restore liberty and justice for the nation" (Titus and Thompson 1985, 2).

Roughly a decade and a half later in 2000, responding to a group of disgruntled law faculty at the University of Detroit Mercy Law School who approached him about the lack of "true Catholic" options for legal education, Domino's Pizza mogul and conservative Catholic patron Thomas "Tom" Monaghan welcomed the first class of law students at his newly established Ave Maria School of Law in Ann Arbor, Michigan. The school, which was described by the *National Catholic Reporter* as having "a more conservative religious orientation than any existing Catholic law school in the nation" and as "militantly religious" (Schaeffer 1999), would relocate to Naples, Florida, in 2009.

In 2004, Jerry Falwell, Christian Right political activist and founder of the Moral Majority, opened Liberty Law School as the latest addition to his Liberty University in Lynchburg, Virginia. Falwell erased any doubts about the purpose of Liberty Law by stating that it was created with the "belief that we needed to produce a generation of Christian attorneys who could, in fact, infiltrate the legal profession with a strong commitment to the Judeo-Christian ethic" (Anderson 2007).

Not every New Christian Right patron followed the Oral Roberts approach to institution building, however. In 2000, patron Alan Sears launched the Blackstone Legal Fellowship as the educational arm of Alliance Defending Freedom (ADF), the largest and most heavily resourced New Christian Right public interest law firm (Hollis-Brusky and Wilson 2017). Like the other patrons, Sears built the

Blackstone Fellowship to create "intellectual balance" in the presentation of law and legal foundations and to make sure that conservative Christian law students across the country knew that they were not alone. But, as we describe in greater detail in the chapters that follow, the Blackstone approach is distinct from the high-cost legal institution building approach of the other patrons. The three-phase Blackstone summer program held at ADF headquarters in Scottsdale, Arizona, is an attempt to train, educate, and socialize law students from all over the country in the natural law and then to place them into internships where they can draw on this distinctly Christian training in their legal practice.

Beyond simply providing Christian students and faculty with fellowship, a faith-friendly environment, and an opportunity to integrate the Bible into the study of law, each of these institutions understands itself as transformative in purpose, and radically so. Each seeks to promote and reinforce a vision of law rooted in Christianity and biblical principles, a vision of law that at minimum challenges, and at times directly rejects, the widely shared premises of "secular legalism" that both legal liberals and mainstream legal conservatives in American law and most of the Western world have embraced since the nineteenth century.

Recalling the opening excerpt in this chapter from the CBNU feasibility study, the animating belief of each of these patrons is that legal education, once it is properly aligned "with godly standards," will produce lawyers equipped and motivated to "restore American law to its original Biblical foundation" (Titus & Thompson 1985). This forms the common denominator across the otherwise open idea of pursuing law via a "Christian Worldview"—a term frequently deployed by those affiliated with these institutions.

Seen with this ultimate reformative end in mind, these law schools can be understood as adding to the ranks of institutions meant to enable the Christian Right to pursue both its short- and long-term policy goals in a broader set of political venues. As multiple historians and political scientists have noted, the conservative ascent within the Republican Party is marked, in part, by the building of "alternative institutions to train its own set of elites," with the concept of training being broadly defined (Grossman & Hopkins 2016, 92). While alternative institution building started with secular conservative organizations, the Christian Right has intentionally pursued this means since, arguably, the creation of the Moral Majority in 1979.

The first wave of culturally conservative, political, organizational creation focused on electoral politics, enabling the Christian Right to simultaneously wage the "culture war" and meaningfully insert itself into Republican Party leadership (Layman 2001; Baylor 2017; Conger 2018; Grossman & Hopkins 2016; Layman & Brockway 2018; Lewis 2019). As will be described in the following chapters, the Christian Right's institution building also came to include litigation and judicial politics in the 1990s and 2000s, and the scope of this undertaking reached beyond creating new public interest legal organizations meant to counter the American Civil Liberties Union. By creating law schools and legal training programs, the Christian Right has created institutions that in and of themselves stand as statements of defiance. They also aim to equip the Christian Right with a new set of movement resources.

Scholarship has shown how law schools and legal training programs, functioning as "gatekeepers to the profession" (Teles 2008, 13), are positioned to provide various forms of essential capital for movements interested in transforming law. They attract, socialize, and credential lawyers (*human capital*) (Teles 2008); establish or provide inroads to networks for group advancement (*social capital*) (Southworth 2008); and create, spread, and legitimate ideas within the legal, political, and wider publics (*intellectual* and *cultural capital*) (Balkin 2001; Teles 2008; Hollis-Brusky 2013, 2015).

Scholarship also corroborates the proposition that law schools and legal education are an important part of the broader "support structure" (Epp 1998) for legal and constitutional development. From the New Deal Revolution in the 1930s and '40s and the birth of legal liberalism (Irons 1993; Teles 2008) to the "Rights Revolution" of the mid-twentieth century (Epp 1998; Johnson 2010; Kluger 2004; Tushnet 1987) to the conservative counterrevolution currently underway on the Supreme Court (Teles 2008; Southworth 2008; Hollis-Brusky 2011, 2013, 2015), we see how sweeping changes in law, policy, and legal culture originated in changes in law schools, legal training, and education. Moreover, recent high-profile investments in legal education by conservative patrons and donors such as the Koch brothers, the Olin Foundation, and the Scaife Foundation to establish conservative "beachheads" in the legal academy for conservatives who reject the liberal legal orthodoxy (Teles 2008; Mayer 2016; Miller 2006) demonstrate the widely held belief that American law schools are a critical linchpin in the battle for control over the law.

But while this scholarship establishes law schools and training programs as a precondition for legal mobilization and change, it leaves open an important question. Namely, are different types of supporting institutions more or less effective at producing and facilitating the transfer of these valuable resources among and within movements? Relatedly, are there types of supporting institutions that best facilitate the transfer of resources between movements and policymakers? This book, an in-depth, comparative study of the burgeoning "support structure" (Epp 1998) for Christian conservative legal mobilization, will directly address this open question in the literature and provide important lessons and insights for scholars and practitioners of social movements, legal mobilization, and constitutional development.

As we explain in Chapter 2, because of the "radical" and "transformative" (Scheingold & Sarat 2004, 101–103; Wilson and Hollis-Brusky 2018) nature of the New Christian Right's project and because of its history with building separate cultural and educational institutions (see, e.g., den Dulk 2006; Williams 2010), these early patrons decided not to invest in existing law schools—an approach we refer to as *infiltration* throughout this book. Instead, as we show, emboldened by

Oral Roberts's victory against the American Bar Association, these patrons largely pursued what we refer to in this book as a *parallel alternative* approach to legal education by building new, separate law schools dedicated to promoting a "Christian Worldview" within the law: Regent Law School, Ave Maria School of Law, and Liberty Law School.

But movement patrons did not exclusively pursue a *parallel alternative* approach. Blackstone Legal Fellowship represents a third approach to institution building within our study: what we call the *supplemental* approach. Blackstone, as we introduced earlier, is a competitive summer program that accepts students from law schools across the country, brings them to Scottsdale, Arizona, for a three-week, intense boot camp in the Christian foundations of the law and then plugs them into internships and networking opportunities with like-minded conservative Christian legal professionals. Similar to the summer fellowship opportunities offered by conservative think tanks and organizations like the Hertog Foundation, which are focused on traditional politics (Grossman & Hopkins 2016, 185; Levin 2016), and the Federalist Society for Law and Public Policy Studies in the legal arena, which provides alternative educational programming and network connections for conservative and libertarian law students (Southworth 2008; Teles 2008; Hollis-Brusky 2015), Blackstone's summer program provides an alternative legal education and curriculum and social and professional networking connections for Christian conservative law students attending (mostly) non-Christian law schools. While distinct from the Federalist Society in important ways that we explain in Chapter 1, both of these institutions represent the *supplemental* approach to building support structures for a movement.

We take this variation in strategies for building support structure institutions by the Christian Right as a jumping-off point and ask the following questions in our study:

1. Why did these New Christian Right patrons reject the lower-cost, lower-risk, *infiltration* approach to support structure building in favor of a mix of *parallel alternative* and *supplemental* approaches?
2. What are the consequences of these strategic choices in terms of support structure efficacy and viability?

In other words, analyzing our cases through the lens of Support Structure Theory (SST) (Epp 1998), we ask, what are these institutions' relative and collective abilities to create the resources required to support and effect legal and political change? Are these institutions producing or poised to produce valuable resources (*human capital, intellectual capital, social capital, cultural capital*) for litigators, advocacy organizations, judges, and policymakers?

To answer these questions, our research design employed a mixed-methods approach to data collection and analysis. We detail our data collection methods in Appendices A, B, and C. In brief, we conducted forty-two semi-structured interviews with faculty, staff, students, and alumni at our four primary institutions (Regent Law, Ave Maria School of Law, Liberty Law School, Blackstone Legal Fellowship) and at one of our secondary sites, Notre Dame Law School. We also engaged in participant observation at each of these sites. Additionally, we engaged in interpretive data analysis (Yanow 2003) of publicly available and solicited archival documents and artifacts from each institution, constructing a database of over 800 primary documents, which were collected and coded using Atlas.ti qualitative data management software. We also use hand-collected and Web-scraped data on faculty scholarly output, litigation participation and impact, involvement in professional networks such as the Federalist Society, media appearances and mentions, and alumni employment in order to better understand the flow of movement capital. Drawing on this specific mix of methods enabled us to triangulate data sources (Bowen 2005; Creswell et al. 2003; Tarrow 1995) and tell a more robust and complete narrative of the rise, purpose, and influence of these potentially transformative legal institutions.

Chapter 1 introduces the theoretical approach we use to analyze the case of the CCLM, an approach which draws on a refined understanding of Support Structure Theory (SST) (Epp 1998; Hollis-Brusky 2011). Introduced by Charles Epp in his canonical work, *The Rights Revolution,* SST reflects a conditional theory of constitutional change, emphasizing that getting the right judges and Justices on the court—the key variable for judicial politics and political scientists—is a "necessary but not sufficient condition" for constitutional change, development, or revolution (Epp 1998). To enact sweeping changes in the law, Epp and others emphasize, judges and Justices still require the right cases, framed properly, asking the right legal questions, supported by legal arguments that are deemed at least somewhat credible to the broader legal community (Epp 1998; Hollis-Brusky 2011, 2015). As we explain in Chapter 1, this is where the "support structure" comes in, providing four types of vital capital for legal change and development: *human, social, cultural*, and *intellectual*. Aggregating insights from two decades worth of literature engaging with SST, we introduce our key theoretical contribution to this field—the Support Structure Pyramid—as a way of visualizing and organizing our thinking about different kinds of support structures and their potential for capital production and transmission. Chapter 1 also introduces our typology of support structure strategies, identifying three ways movements can engage in institution building of support structures (*infiltration* approach, *supplemental* approach, *parallel alternative* approach) and, as we outlined earlier, situates our case study institutions within this typology.

Chapters 2 and 3 provide background on our case study institutions. Chapter 2 provides a detailed history of the Christian Right political movement and situates the rise of the CCLM within the broader history, behavior, and strategy of the Christian Right. In doing so, Chapter 2 also provides a detailed and persuasive answer to the question of why the patrons of the CCLM rejected the *infiltration* model of support structure building in legal education and training in favor of a mix of *parallel alternative* and *supplemental* strategies. Chapter 3 constitutes a deep dive into the founding visions and missions of our case study institutions. We look at the intentionally transformative missions of each institution and then examine how those missions have changed or evolved over time. Importantly, Chapter 3 also previews some of the constraints and challenges each institution faces in attempting to realize its transformative mission: principally, constraints surrounding finances and patronage, accreditation, and financial aid.

Chapters 4–7 analyze the actual and potential capital outputs of each institution as support structures for the CCLM. We organize and structure our analysis using the four forms of capital we identify in Chapter 1 as being vital for law schools and legal training programs to produce—*human, social, cultural,* and *intellectual.*

Chapter 4 begins with *human capital*—lawyers and legal professionals—as perhaps the most important output of these support structure institutions. We first look at how each institution recruits "mission-oriented" faculty and students. We then examine how each institution attempts to shape and develop future lawyers through its curriculum and training. According to Gary Becker, the economist who coined the term *human capital* (Becker 1962), "[e]ducation and training are the most important investments in human capital" (Becker 1994, 17). Finally, we evaluate the outputs of these efforts: how many graduates are licensed attorneys, what kind of law do they go on to practice, are they going on to become "culture warriors" (Wilson and Hollis-Brusky 2014) for the movement, fulfilling their founding patrons' missions and visions? Drawing on a mix of data from a Web-based survey of Ave Maria School of Law alumni and data gathered from LinkedIn and Web-based searches, we provide an initial evaluation of the actual and potential contributions of these institutions' alumni toward the ambitious goals of the Christian Right. Put another way, if the goal of these transformative legal institutions is (borrowing Falwell's expression) "to produce a generation of Christian attorneys who could, in fact, infiltrate the legal profession with a strong commitment to the Judeo-Christian ethic" (Anderson 2007), then this chapter evaluates their efforts at doing so thus far.

Chapter 5 combines an analysis of our institutions as generators of *social capital* (networks) and *cultural capital* (cultural recognition and prestige). We combine these two forms of support structure capital under the umbrella of what one of our interviewees at Blackstone Legal Fellowship referred to as "credibility capital": the need to be taken seriously by mainstream actors and to avoid the "crazy Christian" stigma. For a movement to be taken seriously, its ideas have to be part of the conversation and the debate. In order to get into the conversation, these ideas and the actors that espouse them cannot be viewed as totally "off-the-wall" (Balkin 2001; Teles 2008; Hollis-Brusky 2015). So we ask how well-integrated these faculty and their ideas are into (1) more mainstream conservative networks and (2) more mainstream conservative media. To answer the first question, we track both the quantity and quality of faculty participation in Federalist Society events, an influential organization that represents the mainstream conservative legal movement (Southworth 2008; Teles 2008; Hollis-Brusky 2015). To answer the second, we track media participation by faculty at each institution, categorizing the outlet and the topic and qualitatively examining how each actor speaks about the law in the media.

Chapters 6 and 7 look at *intellectual capital*, examining the impact of these institutions as purveyors of transformative ideas about law. In Chapter 6 we examine the quality and quantity of faculty publications (how often they publish, where they publish, who cites them, and how often they are cited) and the quality and impact of each institution's in-house law review publications (e.g., *Regent University Law Review*, *Ave Maria Law Review*, etc.). In Chapter 7 we look at the higher-impact area of litigation—where legal ideas can have significant "consequences" (Hollis-Brusky 2015). We ask who is participating in litigation as counsel of record or *amici curiae* (friends of the court), what areas of litigation they are involved in, and who is citing their scholarship in briefs or judicial opinions.

Our concluding chapter aggregates insights from the book and asks what the CCLM as a case study tells us about (1) the strategic options available to patrons looking to bolster the "support structures" for their movement and (2) the consequences of those choices—both broadly and for the specific case studies examined here. In addition to summarizing our findings, this chapter revisits SST and the Support Structure Pyramid we introduce in Chapter 1 and brings it into conversation with social movement theory, and scholarship on legal mobilization and the legal profession to suggest areas for future development, integration, and inquiry based on the insights generated from our case study. Finally, we close the book by returning to our case studies and asking how we can understand them in relation to the Christian Right and contemporary conservatism, more generally.

The Frankfurter Adage (or, Why Legal Movements Need Support Structures)

> In the last analysis, the law is what the lawyers are. And the law and the lawyers are what the law schools make them.
> —Felix Frankfurter, May 13, 1927[1]

Movements and movement patrons create and design institutions and employ specific strategies that they believe will help them best achieve their goals (Edwards & McCarthy 2007; Meyer 2004). But, in bringing these institutions into existence, they confront what one scholar has called the "Frankenstein problem" (Guzman 2013, 1000). Institutions are costly, complex, dynamic, living entities that are difficult to control (Walker 2012; Edelman et al. 2010). They are embedded in shifting social, legal, and political contexts and realities that are outside of the control of those who establish and intend to use them. Institutions also create new leaders and, thus, the possibility for competing interests—both within an institution and/or between an institution's leaders and other movement actors. Perhaps most importantly, the resources produced by these institutions can change the very movements they are meant to serve in ways both desirable and undesirable for their founding leaders and patrons. Hence, the Frankenstein problem.

So why invest costly resources in institution building at all? The answer is: because we know that certain types of legal institutions are a necessary (albeit not sufficient) condition for litigation-based movements seeking to achieve their goals (Epp 1998; Teles 2008; Southworth 2008; Hollis-Brusky 2015). As we describe in great detail in the section that follows, legal institutions are at the core of what political scientist Charles Epp called the "support structure" for legal mobilization and change (Epp 1998). Support Structure Theory (SST) is critical to understanding longer-term developments in law and legal change because it shines a spotlight on the "supply side" of legal and constitutional change (the resources necessary to produce sustained litigation campaigns that result in court cases) rather than focusing

Separate But Faithful. Amanda Hollis-Brusky and Joshua C. Wilson, Oxford University Press (2020). © Oxford University Press. DOI: 10.1093/oso/9780190637262.001.0001

exclusively on the "demand side" (judges and judicial decisions), which captures the attention of most judicial politics and law and courts scholars (Hollis-Brusky 2011).

To return to the Felix Frankfurter quote at the beginning of this chapter, the law is "what the lawyers are," and the lawyers are "what the law schools make them." This perhaps overstates the role of law schools alone as agents of legal change but nicely foregrounds their vital role as part of the support structure for legal change overall. As Epp and others have shown, because building and maintaining a robust support structure is a "necessary" though not "sufficient" condition for achieving meaningful change within the American legal system (Epp 1998), understanding the creation, composition, and efficacy of a movement's support structure is important for predicting its potential future impact.

This chapter proceeds, first, by reviewing SST as it has been developed and deployed in the law, courts, and sociolegal literature. As we will see, a movement's support structure not only is the Frankfurter-spotlighted "lawyers" and the "law schools" that produce them but also encompasses other institutions vital to producing other kinds of resources critical to bringing about legal change. Aggregating insights from SST and introducing others based on our own original research, we next introduce the Support Structure Pyramid—a model for conceptualizing litigation-based movement support structures, institutions, and their relationship to legal change. Finally, we suggest three support structure types or strategies—*infiltration, supplemental,* and *parallel alternative*—each of which represents a different way to approach the aforementioned Frankenstein problem (Guzman 2013, 1000) of organizational or institutional creation. We introduce this typology of strategies as a way of understanding and contextualizing the choices and initial decisions of Christian Right movement leaders and patrons when they decided to consciously invest in institution building as a means of bolstering the legal support structure for their movement, choices we describe in great detail in Chapter 2.

Support Structures: What They Are and Why They Matter

The concept of a "support structure" for legal mobilization was first introduced in Charles Epp's now-canonical work, *The Rights Revolution* (1998). In this book, Epp seeks to understand why the Warren Court's so-called rights revolution happened in the United States when it did. In other words, he asks, "What conditions encouraged the Supreme Court to regularly hear and support individual rights cases after largely ignoring or spurning them for 150 years?" (Epp 1998, 2). Isn't the answer to this question simply "activist judges"? Not exactly, Epp explains. Receptive judges are a necessary but not sufficient condition for dramatic legal change or revolution. After all, as Epp notes, judges cannot make cases appear before them "as if by magic" (Epp 1998, 18).

The rights revolution, Epp answers, was prompted by sustained litigation brought by lawyers and made possible only after the creation of a robust "support structure" for legal mobilization. This support structure, according to Epp, consisted of rights advocacy lawyers, rights advocacy organizations, and financial aid and funding for these lawyers and organizations (3). These three elements comprise what we will refer to as the *thin* conception of support structures. Several scholars who have built upon Epp's work, applying his model inside and outside of the American context, have done so in a way that limits their support structure inquiry to these three elements (e.g., Morton & Allen, 2001; Gauri & Brinks, 2008; Sanchez Urribarri et al. 2011; Staszak, 2015).

The *thick* understanding of the concept, what we advocate for in this book, comes from asking the follow-up question: what prompted these three structures to come to life? Epp describes several conditions that enabled these structures to come to life in the American context: the creation and rise of the modern law school, which resulted in the diversification of the legal profession as well as the creation of a legal academic class charged with thinking deeply about the law (recall the Frankfurter Adage); the reorganization of legal practice, which produced legal expertise, professional organization, and efficiencies that created space for pro bono work; and changes in government policy and legal rules that both increased litigant access and created sources for funding new types of cases (Epp 1998, 44–69).

While Epp himself deploys the *thin* definition of support structures in his case studies throughout the book (rights advocacy lawyers, rights advocacy organizations, and financial aid and funding), several other scholars have applied a broader understanding of support structures in their work regarding activists' efforts in the United States and abroad. For example, Galligan and Morton note the importance of law schools, legal academics, and changes in legal practice to the "Australian rights experience" (2013, 17). Similarly, in their analysis of South Africa's support structure, Marcus and Budlender expand their understanding of support structures to include organizations that make "use of social mobilization and advocacy to ensure that communities are actively involved in asserting rights inside and outside the legal environment" (2008, 94).

In the United States context, scholars building on Epp's work have expanded and refined SST in fruitful ways, suggesting that one should also look at the degree to which support structure organizations and actors are successfully able to: access stable, deferential funding sources that allow them to maintain and pursue their mission (Teles 2008); effectively network actors and organizations that connect various support structure institutions (Southworth 2008); and positively affect the perception of their legitimacy and authority and, thus, their reception and incorporation by both elite and public audiences (Teles 2008; Hollis-Brusky 2011, 2015).

The necessity of having a support structure for legal change is intuitive once revealed, but that does not mean that it is without criticism. One recurring critique of SST is that it is too vague and difficult to operationalize. For example, in their five-country volume *Courting Social Justice*, Gauri and Brinks note that "[I]t is difficult if not impossible to characterize the requisite support structures in the abstract" (2008, 16). Similarly, another group of scholars note that "[support structure theory's] inherent difficulties become apparent when one tries to operationalize a country's support structure" (Sanchez Urribarri et al. 2011, 395).

Another criticism is that SST does not sufficiently address the significance of other factors that are part of the greater political context within which real change occurs (Southworth 2000; Marcus & Budlender 2008). Such critics want to know how support structures inform our understanding of why movements implemented court strategies and/or how employing litigation relates to activism in other government branches and forums (Silverstein 2009); why judges and Justices accepted the cases and/or decided them they ways that they did; and which cases resulted in realized change, versus producing "hollow" (Rosenberg 2008) or "myth of rights" outcomes (Scheingold 2004). Additionally, SST does not address whether or not a country's laws allow for one to bring a case in the first place (Scheingold 2004; Staszak 2015; Cichowski 2016).

Epp has responded to these sorts of critiques by emphasizing that SST "reflects a *conditional* theory of causality, positing that a support structure is a *necessary condition* for sustained judicial attention to rights, making such attention possible" (2011, 406–7). This is a far narrower interest than many may want to read into the theory. The narrowness, however, insulates the theory from many of the above critiques while still affirming their value in more fully understanding legal change. Like Epp, our book adheres closer to the theory's original interest in understanding what enables movements to enter the legal arena in a serious, sustained way.

The Support Structure Pyramid

As noted, Epp and subsequent scholarship have established an interrelated "*conditional* theory of causality" between movement support structures and successful litigation-based change efforts. Movements must have support structure institutions that effectively generate and transfer recognized capital among movement members, and between the movement and decision makers who can access and pull the levers of power. In the pyramid and throughout the book, we identify the following kinds of capital as vital to movement success and efficacy: *financial* (patronage and monetary support), *human* (e.g., lawyers to bring cases and staff institutions), *intellectual* (e.g., legal arguments and related support to make convincing arguments), *social* (e.g., professional networks to share resources and serve as a judicial audience indirectly checking judges), and *cultural* (e.g., mechanisms to increase the perceived legitimacy and authority of a movement within various publics).

Support structure and movement success are then determined by the ability to create "sustained judicial attention" as measured not only by court victories, but also by the repeated raising and normalization within elite and/or public circles of issues and issue frames related to the movement's policy goals. As noted in the work of sociolegal scholars, movements don't just succeed when they win the cases they litigate. Rather, sustained litigation—even when cases are lost—can be counted as success by such litigation introducing new conceptual frames, changing the public or elite discussion of a topic, raising a movement's profile, increasing institutional resources, etc. (McCann 1994; NeJaime 2011; Polletta 2000). We expand upon the idea of sustained litigation, then, by looking for the ways that these support structure institutions seek to both facilitate sustained litigation and to meet the ends of introducing conceptual frames, etc., via means other than litigation (e.g., via scholarship, media, and presentations).

Aggregating these insights from the relevant literature, Figure 1.1 proposes a model that we call the "Support Structure Pyramid." Starting from the "base," attention is first given to funding sources to highlight the importance that funding (or lack thereof) can have on the entire model of legal change. We have opted to use the

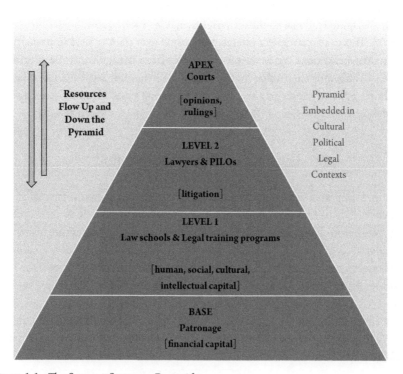

Figure 1.1. The Support Structure Pyramid.

term *patronage* broadly here in an effort to capture and add to points made by Epp (1998) and Steven Teles (2008). The former draws attention to the point that organizations and lawyers need financial resources in order to work toward legal change. The latter develops this by noting that for support structures to function well they not only need financial resources, but also need those resources to be delivered in a way that maximizes deference to the organization's visionary "entrepreneurs" and increases institutional stability.

It is not, however, assumed that deference always produces stability, valuable products, and success. Rather, it is an understanding derived from Teles's case studies regarding interference and conflicts of interest in the first generation of conservative public interest law (2008). It also notices that patrons can choose to fund either or both Level 1 and Level 2 organizations and actors. Finally, the use of the term *patronage* is not meant to limit conceptualizing support structure funding to big money donors. Rather, funders come in a range of forms—large and small, institutional and individual—and support structure institutions can acquire substantial financial resources and needed stability from a combination of these sources.

What's more, the placing of patronage at the base of the model does not assume that funding is not an ongoing point of concern, conflict, and maintenance for organizations and movements. Rather, support structure organizations often need to continue to compete for, cultivate, and protect funding sources. The patronage step and the ripple effects that it has on the rest of the model should thus be seen as dynamic. This is especially true when like-minded institutions have to compete for a particularly scarce pool of resources, or when the reliability of future funding is uncertain (Bennett 2017). If issues at the base become too problematic, the whole model is destabilized and can collapse.

Moving up the pyramid, "Level 1" comprises law schools and training programs. Law schools and training programs produce these forms of capital by attracting, creating, and credentialing professionals (*human capital*); establishing or being tied to networks for group advancement (*social capital*); and creating, spreading, and legitimating ideas within the legal, political, and wider publics (*intellectual* and *cultural capital*). Level 1 actors and institutions thus stand to influence broader publics, from the legal and policy communities to the general public, by putting new ideas and elites into circulation. Relatedly, but more narrowly, they also stand to influence judicial outcomes by making judges receptive to new legal arguments, and by supplying the means by which they can write and defend changes in the law. Specifically contributing to that end, Level 1 actors and organizations also access the pyramid's apex by training law clerks who assist judges, producing academic literature consumed and employed by judges, and hosting or staffing training programs and conferences attended by judges. In the longer run, these institutions can also influence the law by staffing the judicial bench with graduates.

While judges sit atop the pyramid, as we have sought to emphasize, they are far from the only important audience if one is interested in more fully understanding and evaluating the place of support structures within legal and policy change. That is, Level 1 actors and institutions are not only seeking to put capital into circulation up the pyramid, but they are also seeking to otherwise influence the broader cultural and political contexts that the pyramid is embedded in. They should, thus, be studied with an eye toward evaluating whether they are performing these valuable tasks. The same is also true for actors and institutions at the pyramid's next level.

Level 2 of the pyramid, occupied by lawyers, legal organizations, and litigation, captures the transition to the more visible parts of the support structure. Since litigation provides the first potentially highly visible part of the legal change process, it is here and at the judicial level that most scholarly and popular attention has been paid. That said, Level 2 produces a mix of products, only some of which are commonly noticed and only one that is exclusive to Level 2 suppliers, that is, litigation.

Levels 1 and 2 can be bound together by networks such as the Federalist Society (Hollis-Brusky 2015). Lawyers and legal organizations can also independently produce *intellectual* and *cultural capital* through developing novel legal claims and engaging in public relations work. For example, Brown (2002) describes how conservative Christian lawyers fundamentally changed their strategies and First Amendment jurisprudence by innovatively moving from the establishment to the free speech clause (47, 58–77). In the same vein, Teles (2008, 244–49) and Den Dulk (2008) both highlight the importance of public interest law organizations (PILOs) framing legal issues to both win in litigation and to alter public discussion. Finally, the importance of seeing how broader, non-elite audiences understand legal change efforts and law is also seen in Wilson's (2013) and Lewis's (2017) work on abortion politics.

One can even see Level 2 actors and organizations engaging in producing (or at least refining, modifying, altering) *human capital* in the training of lawyers new to a movement or legal practice. Finally, individual actors can simultaneously occupy space within both Level 1 and 2 organizations, as seen in the case of law professors who continue to practice, or Level 1 organizations that maintain clinical training programs or close relationships with public interest law organizations. In spite of these connections, education's centrality in Level 1 and litigation's centrality to Level 2 justify their separation within the model. The separation also makes the model more transferable to countries outside of the United States where patrons and others might have fewer opportunities to influence Level 1 institutions.

Focusing on litigation, Level 2 includes both high- and low-profile legal actions. In his discussion of the secular conservative legal movement, Teles notes the importance of a "B Team" of lawyers that can handle the more mundane tasks involved in litigation efforts. He notes that it is relatively easy to get lawyers for high-profile cases, but it is another matter to get lawyers to be on the watch for and take on the smaller cases that are likely settled out of court and that never garner public attention. This imbalance means that potentially fruitful cases—including those that might be of interest to higher courts or that provide the opportunity to learn and develop new legal strategies—are missed, and that much of the follow-up work of enforcing major case rulings is left untouched (2008, 254–55). As scholars of the Christian Right have emphasized, this is not ignored in the contemporary CCLM (Christian Conservative Legal Movement). Alliance Defending Freedom (ADF) (Wilson 2016), Freedom of Conscience Defense Fund, and Pacific Justice Institute (Bennett 2017) intentionally staff lawyers in these "B Team" roles.

Judges and other court actors, such as clerks, sit at the apex of our Support Structure Pyramid as they ultimately decide cases born and influenced through the combined—though not necessarily coordinated—efforts of Level 1 and 2 actors. Their role in the pyramid is initially defined by litigation, but their function within this model is not limited to the content of judicial decisions.

As with all of the levels of the pyramid, the direction of the flow in this model is not just upward and direct. Level 1 not only provides goods for Level 2 and courts, and Level 2 not only supplies cases and arguments to courts. It is important to note that these lower tiers also stand to *receive* goods from those above them and that this can give rise to cyclical feedback loops. For example, the attention and involvement of judges and prestigious lawyers with Level 1 institutions (through talks, appearances, and visiting positions) can provide these institutions with legitimacy, credibility, and authority (i.e., *cultural capital*), creating a means of attracting and securing patronage. The same is true in terms of Level 2 actors when they win in court, or when judicial decisions cite their work. Perhaps most importantly, a judicial decision—even when the movement did not win in the case—can send capital back down and outside of the pyramid.

Judicial opinions can provide salience for a set of issues (*cultural capital*) that might result in attracting or securing additional patronage. Further, the reasoning and written opinions of judges and Justices can legitimate (or delegitimize) a movement's capital by drawing on it (or rejecting it) in their legal reasoning. In a similar vein, these written opinions can also open up and inspire new avenues for the development of *intellectual capital* by Level 1 and Level 2 actors. As the standing and resources of those who constitute Level 1 and 2 grow through this downward and outward flow, the benefits can flow back upstream in the form of better resources and increased or more effective access to the pyramid's higher tiers. It seems reasonable to assume that this process can accelerate as it gains momentum, and that networks connecting actors and institutions positioned along the pyramid can meaningfully assist in this cyclical and contextually embedded process.

The Federalist Society serves as an example of the sort of dynamic and varied relationships that can exist between the model's tiers. This organization not only connects Levels 1 and 2 as they supply intellectual resources for lawyers to deploy and judges to consume, but it also facilitates policing those same judges by creating a "judicial audience" (Baum 2006; Hollis-Brusky 2015, 155–8). That is, Level 1 and 2 actors are part of a broader group that observes and comments on judicial decisions, and because of their *cultural capital*, these comments carry weight within and beyond the legal sphere. This, in turn, creates a means of encouraging judicial decisions aligning with the movement's interests and, thus, is a good example of diverse interactions that can occur between the pyramid's levels.

Again, it should be stressed that this pyramid exists within broader social and political contexts. That is, the recognized value of the capital and resources produced at each level as well as its ability to flow up and down the pyramid are affected by wider social and political conditions. Returning to the Federalist Society as an example, its efficacy is clearly increased under conservative administrations that give it more direct access to traditional avenues of power. This, subsequently, increases the organization's perceived prestige, which can, in turn, increase its funding base, the power of its judicial audience, its standing within the legal academy, its ability to influence public discussions and opinion, etc.

Correspondingly, changing political and social contexts can also decrease a support structure's efficacy. Previewing the lessons learned from our case studies, Regent Law supposedly placed 150 graduates with the George W. Bush administration—a clear boon for the school. Regent, however, also came under fire when one of those graduates—Monica Goodling—became embroiled in a very public scandal (see e.g., Lithwick 2007; Savage 2007; Neil 2007; Krugman 2007). This hurt Regent's reputation and presumably its ability to continue to place graduates in high-profile positions of influence. When the subsequent Obama administration came to power, Regent's effectiveness as a support structure was further decreased, showing the ways that the value of capital can fluctuate dramatically on account of changes in the political or cultural context.

That said, the most effective movement organizations can attempt to, at least partially, insulate themselves from changing greater contexts. Organizations such as the Federalist Society can seek to take advantage of favorable political conditions by suggesting judicial appointments to friendly administrations and governments, creating favorable future political conditions that will outlast such administrations and governments (see, generally, Hollis-Brusky 2015). The anti-abortion movement provides another example by transitioning their efforts away from federal politics, and toward friendly state political arenas, where their efficacy was greater and where the movement could build capital while waiting for increased federal political opportunities (see, e.g., Conger 2018; Wilson 2016). Such steps, however, cannot fully insulate movements from the greater contexts within which movements, movement actors, and movement institutions exist.

While not wholly inclusive of every concern or facet noted in the sampling of support structure and law and social change literatures, the pyramid model provides a far more detailed, explicitly organized conceptual understanding of support structures than what has existed thus far. Furthermore, it includes multiple variables that can be tested individually or collectively. Finally, while the model is primarily rooted in the observations from studies of legal advocacy within the United States, from looking at the work of other scholars with more international and comparative focuses (Galligan & Morton 2013; Marcus & Budlender 2008; Gauri & Brinks 2008; Cichowski 2016), we believe that the core of the model can travel across borders and be tailored for specific variations.[2]

To be clear, our model does not seek to explain a movement's decision to engage in or avoid litigation campaigns. It does, however, allow scholars to analyze the achievements of litigation campaigns (defined by sustained and/or successful litigation) by prompting close attention to questions surrounding the configuration, embeddedness, and subsequent productivity of their support structure institutions. As at least two decades of scholarship have illustrated, sustained litigation is the product of considerable work *outside* of the court to generate, normalize, and institutionalize ideas (Epp 1998; Hollis-Brusky 2015; Teles 2008).

Thus, the proposed model prompts researchers to ask whether movements have access to institutions and actors at each level of the Support Structure Pyramid. Do the institutions and actors produce the forms of capital outlined in the pyramid? Are those forms of capital able to move up, down, and beyond the pyramid and bear weight, or do they fail to enter the legal, political, and public marketplaces or hold much recognized value within them once they are produced? And how are all of these factors influenced by the larger contexts within which the institutions exist and operate?

Our work in this book concentrates on demonstrating the utility of this model, and the questions it raises, through our case studies of Christian conservative legal education. The CCLM presents a unique opportunity to study the efficacy of these Level 1 support structure types. Before turning to them, however, another factor needs to be introduced that should help us contextualize the initial strategic support structure decisions of the CCLM leaders and patrons and what consequences these choices have had and will continue to have for support structure efficacy moving forward.

Categorizing Support Structure Strategies and Strategic Choices

By our estimation, there are three general strategies for developing Level 1 and 2 movement support structures, each of which carries distinct costs and benefits (see Table 1.1). While they are listed here as distinct from one another, those looking to develop such support structures can engage in one, two, or all three strategies if interested and able. We define each approach next and then discuss in more detail how these strategies bear out and interrelate in our case studies. As will be shown, the choices made in terms of deciding which strategy, or strategies, to invest in have direct bearing on some of the contextual factors that will influence the institution's form and future development.

Table 1.1. **Support Structure Strategies**

	Infiltration Strategy	*Supplemental Strategy*	*Parallel Alternative Strategy*
Approach	Invest in preexisting institutions	Work to supplement existing institutions	Create wholly new institutions
Cost	Low	Moderate	High
Degree of Control	Low	Moderate	High

The *infiltration* strategy involves investing in or attempting to infiltrate preexisting institutions. *Infiltration* is a relatively lower-cost approach to developing support structures, since the start-up costs associated with building something from scratch are not present. That said, it also involves a lower degree of control for those seeking to create support structures. Applying this model to Level 1 institutions, this strategy might involve, for example, endowing one or more chairs in an academic department, providing money for a resident scholar or clinic, or working to place sympathetic academics or administrators on the faculty of institutions in order to change the political or intellectual character of that institution. Infiltrating and influencing hiring practices is also an option, but it is one that involves long-term calculations and an uncertain payoff.

The Koch brothers' funding of existing educational institutions presents an example of this approach, and its risks, within the broader contemporary conservative movement (Levinthal 2015). In terms of the existing literature on legal education, Teles's discussion of the Olin Foundation's approach to spreading the Law and Economics movement—a movement centering economic and social choice theory in the study of law—represents the *infiltration* approach (2008, 181–207). For reasons explained in the next chapter, the patrons and other leaders driving the creation of the CCLM largely steered away from investing in the *infiltration* strategy.

The *supplemental strategy* is a true middling strategy in this typology—it involves more resources and a bigger investment than *infiltration*, but significantly less than the *parallel alternative* strategy. The *supplemental* strategy affords those creating institutions more control than the *infiltration* approach, but because this approach involves working alongside existing institutions, one lacks full control. While its range of functions and membership spans multiple levels of the pyramid, the Federalist Society offers one way of thinking about the *supplemental* strategy. It provides a *supplemental* education, training, and a network for right-of-center law students and academics but is housed primarily within mainstream or existing law schools.

In terms of the CCLM, the movement has made increasing inroads into the Federalist Society. For example, one can cite the Federalist Society's Religious Liberties Practice group generally, or, more specifically, the February 12, 2018, hosting of a nationwide "teleforum" on the U.S. Health and Human Services' newly created Conscience and Religious Freedom Division within its office of Civil Rights. This forum was headed by the division's leader, the former chief operations officer and legal counsel for the Becket Fund for Religious Liberty, Roger Severino.[3] While such access to the Federalist Society is obviously increasing, it is still true that the organization has a significant libertarian orientation, which can cause problems for the CCLM. Given this, ADF's Blackstone Legal Fellowship—a summer training program for Christian law students—represents the *supplemental* strategy in our fieldwork.

The *parallel alternative* strategy—creating brand-new institutions—comes with the highest price of the three options, but it also affords the greatest amount of control over the shape, content, and culture of the institution. That, however, does not mean that these institutions are wholly unconstrained. Law schools, for example, still have to operate within the norms of the American Bar Association if they want to be accredited, and accreditation is presumably a significant factor in attracting respected faculty, quality students, and many patrons. It is also undoubtedly a significant factor in a school's ability to be taken seriously within the greater legal community.

Within the existing scholarship on contemporary law schools, Teles's detailing of Henry Manne's development of George Mason University School of Law arguably fits this strategy, but it straddles the line between the *infiltration* and *parallel alternative* strategies to developing support structures (2008, 207–19). Deeper and unambiguous roots to the *parallel alternative* strategy are seen in Howard University School of Law's multiple connections to the Civil Rights Movement (Johnson 2010; Kluger 2004; Tushnet 1987). While created in response to segregation and the need for African Americans to be able to access the law, Howard Law came to see itself in the 1930s as explicitly working to get the "accepted devices of the law adapted to peculiar Negro problems" (Tushnet 1987, 31). As such, Howard Law came to possess an explicit orientation toward social change and, as will be explored in the book's final chapter, it explicitly functioned as a *parallel alternative* institution fueling legal change.

In terms of our research, the *parallel alternative* strategy is represented in Regent, Liberty, and Ave Maria Schools of Law—all of which were created with explicitly religious missions in mind by leading activists within the Christian Right. As evidenced by the number, the *parallel alternative* strategy has become the primary means of creating Level 1 support structure institutions for the CCLM. As will be shown in Chapter 2, while this is clearly the highest cost strategy, various factors led patrons and other CCLM leaders to see it as the best potential strategy to pursue.

Thinking about these strategies in relation to building a movement, it should be noted that they can reinforce, as well as conflict with, one another. For example, the *supplemental strategy* can help train and credential lawyers and place them in a position to better infiltrate existing Level 1 and 2 institutions (*infiltration strategy*). The Federalist Society has effectively played this role within the secular conservative legal movement, that is, helping to socialize and train law students from elite law schools and working to place them on law faculties through the Olin Fellows program and/or through its more informal academic and professional networks (Teles 2008; Hollis-Brusky 2015).

On the other hand, these strategies can also work against one another. The decision to invest in *parallel alternative* institutions, for example, will have the consequence of redirecting resources and personnel from existing institutions. In other words, if we assume that *human capital* is a limited resource, then the decision to deploy that capital in service of building a *parallel alternative* institution necessarily works against and weakens the *infiltration* strategy. If the lawyers produced all gravitate to newly created Christian law schools, there are fewer who are able to spread their view of the law to those outside of Christian conservative institutions.

What's more, such complementary, competitive, and possibly detrimental relationships can not only happen between, but also within, support structure types. Thinking again in terms of limited resources, one can foresee that *parallel alternative* or *supplemental* institutions, with their higher demand for all types of resources, will compete with one another for funding, desirable students, and top faculty. The same can be seen with the creation of Level 2 PILOs. Alternatively, one can also imagine ways in which such institutions complement one another through their proliferation. For example, the more Christian conservative law schools or PILOs there are, the more they are able to network among one another, supplying a means for increased cooperation, intellectual exchange, and broader perceived legitimacy.

Finally, when used in conjunction with the Support Structure Pyramid, these typologies present a means to better understand movement choices, constraints and opportunities, and support structure efficacy in resource production. They prompt asking why a movement chose one, or various, means to create support structures. Once created, one can ask how existing institutions relate to one another, as well as to the subsequent choices made regarding movement strategies.

Restated, these different types of Level 1 and 2 institutions will exist within somewhat different contexts, will have somewhat different relations to the other pyramid tiers, will stand to produce somewhat different resources for movements, and the combination of these things will produce costs and benefits that need to be understood. The reasons for choosing one versus another, or why one may appear to work better for a given movement, are thus important things to be determined if we are to understand specific movements, as well as the efficacy of movements more generally.

The Conservative Christian Legal Movement as a Case Study in Support Structure Theory

The CCLM provides a unique opportunity to study the efficacy of the different support structure strategies and types we introduced and described. On account of developments we explore in great detail in Chapter 2, the CCLM has, since the mid-1980s, invested to varying degrees in support structure institutions representative of each of these three types. We use this variation to help assess whether these different support structure strategies are more or less efficacious at facilitating the production and transfer or resources to movements, within movements, and between movements and policymakers.

Conservative interests have always had a voice in law and courts, but the creation of a formal conservative Christian legal movement is both a relatively recent event and one that required significant effort. As we detail in the next chapter, prior to the mid-1980s and 1990s, conservative Christian lawyers existed around the country, but they were overwhelmingly independent actors. When they did organize into firms, they were generally small and poorly funded, and most were located far from the seat of national power (Diamond 1998; Brown 2002). The lack of organized engagement with law and courts significantly changed when high-profile leaders in the New Christian Right responded to the need to both strengthen and diversify their political resources. In doing so, however, these patrons largely rejected the lower-cost, lower-risk *infiltration* approach—the approach that had been used by most other movements to build their support structures for legal mobilization. We explore the reasons for this decision in depth in the next chapter and examine the paths and opportunities not taken by examining the more well-established Notre Dame Law School, Baylor Law School, and Pepperdine Law School.

Instead of investing in these existing conservative Christian law schools, these leaders decided to invest in a new set of Christian Right legal institutions. Pat Robertson, who had helped start the Christian Coalition, established Christian Broadcasting Network University Law School (later to be renamed Regent Law School) in 1986. Noted conservative Catholic activist and Domino's Pizza mogul Tom Monaghan founded Ave Maria School of Law in 1999. And Jerry Falwell, who was at the center of the Moral Majority, fulfilled his long-time dream of adding a law school to his Liberty University empire in 2004 with the establishment of Liberty Law School. This constellation of schools represents the *parallel alternative* approach to support structure building within the CCLM and forms the core of our primary case studies for the book.

As Table 1.2 and the Introduction previewed, not every Christian Right patron viewed the *parallel alternative* approach to support structure building as the most appealing strategy. In 2000 conservative and culture war veteran Alan Sears founded the Blackstone Legal Fellowship, a conservative Christian training program for law

Table 1.2. CCLM Level 1 Institutions: Institutional Facts

	Date Est.	Founder	Faith Tradition	Example of Founder's Connection to Christian Right	Location	IL 2014 Class	Affiliated PILO
Regent University Law School	1986	Marion "Pat" Robertson	Evangelical Protestant	Christian Coalition of America	Virginia Beach, VA	106	American Center for Law and Justice
Liberty University School of Law	2004	Jerry Falwell	Evangelical Protestant	Moral Majority	Lynchburg, VA	85	Liberty Counsel
Ave Maria School of Law	1999	Tom Monaghan	Conservative Catholic	Operation Rescue, Thomas More Law Center	Naples, FL	112	Thomas More Law Center (1999–2009)
Blackstone Legal Fellowship	2000	Alan Sears	Conservative Christian	Alliance Defending Freedom	Scottsdale, AZ	154	Alliance Defending Freedom

students supported by and run within ADF. The three-phase Blackstone summer program, which represents the *supplemental* strategy to support structure building in this study, is an attempt to train, educate, and socialize law students from all over the country in the natural law, and then to place them into internships where they can draw on this distinctly Christian training in their legal practice. As such, it completes the book's core of case studies. Additionally, because the Blackstone Legal Fellowship and these schools entered the legal market within a decade and a half of one another, we are able to examine their efforts and efficacy as support structures for the Christian Right holding broader political and professional variables (more or less) constant.

It is important to note here that the three laws schools sitting alongside the Blackstone Legal Fellowship were not the only conservative Christian law schools founded within the last two decades. As will become evident in Chapter 3, however, these three law schools were selected because of their direct connection to these Christian Right movement patrons and their ties to prominent Christian Right PILOs (Level 2 support structures), and on account of their transformative missions and open touting to serve as engines of legal and political change. These qualities and connections to the Christian Right make these law schools ideal to study within the support structure framework and distinguish them from other conservative Christian law schools founded around the same time (e.g., University of St. Thomas School of Law in Minnesota).

Animated by SST and organized in large part by the Support Structure Pyramid, we ask: What are these institutions' relative and collective abilities to create the resources required to support and effect legal and political change? Are they producing valuable resources for public interest law firms, advocacy organizations, funding organizations, and/or for policy demanders (judges/Justices/policymakers)? Before we answer these questions, in the next chapter we review the history and creation of the Christian Right, situate the conservative Christian legal movement within it, and answer a more foundational question: namely, why did these Christian Right patrons reject the *infiltration* strategy in favor of the higher cost *parallel alternative* approach to support structure building?

The Genesis of the Christian Conservative Legal Movement and the Road Not Taken

The Christian Right, like much of the contemporary conservative coalition, is the product of a range of social and political conflicts and changes spanning the twentieth century that eventually, and powerfully, combined in the 1970s and '80s in a way that structures politics to this day. In brief, many of the institutions and constituencies that now define the conservative coalition—from the National Rifle Association, to Christian educational institutions and their governing bodies, to the Republican Party establishment at the state and national levels—had decades-long internal fights between their more moderate and more conservative wings. By the 1980s, though, conservatives had prevailed in these battles, and additional conservative institutions had been built (Lewis 2017; Hollis-Brusky 2015; Winkler 2013; Schuman 2010; Teles 2008; Ringenberg 2006). The story of the Christian Right is one that runs parallel to, is entangled with, and in many ways reflects, the broader creation of modern conservatism. Surveying these historic contours not only helps one understand the Christian Right's place in contemporary politics, but it also clarifies the Christian conservative legal movement's position within the Christian Right, and the reasons its support structures have developed how and when they have.

A highly abbreviated version of the contemporary Christian Right's history can start in the first half of the twentieth century with the creation of conservative Christian institutions—distinctly Christian schools, colleges, bookstores, media, and networked churches. Self-identifying fundamentalists and evangelicals were united in their rejection of what they saw as the liberalizing and secularizing trajectories of social norms, established institutions, mainline Protestantism, and the nation as a whole. In spite of this, they were hamstrung in their abilities to effectively fight these changes. Fundamentalists and evangelicals were split along political policy lines, geographically disbursed, variously invested in engaging with the public sphere, and spread across the two political parties.[1] As a result, they were unidentifiable and ineffective as a political constituency for much of the twentieth

Separate But Faithful. Amanda Hollis-Brusky and Joshua C. Wilson, Oxford University Press (2020). © Oxford University Press. DOI: 10.1093/oso/9780190637262.001.0001

century (Brint & Schroedel 2009a, 2009b; Dochuk 2007, 2012; Hall 2009; Moreton 2010; Schulman & Zelizer 2008; Williams 2010).

Unable to change the wider world, and scattered by events such as the Dust Bowl, the Great Depression, and increased popular mobility, conservative Christians held on to control of their immediate communities by creating institutions built with the idea of rejecting larger societal changes. Christian schools sheltered white evangelicals from Darwinism, the removal of Bible reading and prayer from public schools, and racial integration (Ringenberg 2006, 178). Christian colleges were established as means of mobility that would not come with the threat of "the many reports of how many students from Christian families left home to study in college . . . and then returned without their faith and/or their purity" (175).[2] Finally, bookstores, media, and networked churches created a sense of community among those who came to see themselves as an embattled minority diffusely spread across the nation (Dochuk 2007, 2012; Moreton 2010; Williams 2010). What these institutions also did, however, was to form the foundation for what would become the Christian Right's infrastructure.

Evangelical cultural institutions created a network spanning the country, but the Cold War, fueled by a fear of "Godless communism" and magnified by the Soviet Union's nuclear capabilities, provided the context within which the evangelical movement could grow in size and influence. A young Billy Graham and others harnessed this fear, along with a collection of anxieties stemming from the social isolation and dislocation of modern life, to drive a nationwide revival movement (Dochuk 2012; McGirr 2002; Moreton 2010). The previous decades had seen a dramatic reduction in "the numbers and influence of evangelical Protestants in the cultural-producing institutions," and regular church attendance was low in the pre-War period, shrinking the emergent evangelical community's size, potential, and influence (Brint & Schroedel 2009, 4; Gallup n.d.). This mid-century revival, however, did the opposite. Regular church attendance rates rose in the 1950s, evangelicals continued to create their own culture-producing institutions, and national political forces began to see the potential power of a mobilized evangelical community.

As the South transformed from a Democratic to a Republican stronghold from the 1950s through the '80s via racialized politics, it exported its political interests to the rest of the country with the help of the Western Sunbelt and the rural Midwest—all regions well networked by the evangelical diaspora (Dochuk 2007, 2012; McGirr 2002; Moreton 2010; Schickler 2016). The combination of forces not only transformed the politics of these regions but also transformed the GOP as they brought together various strands of conservatism that came to define the modern Republican Party. The far-right asserted their identity of being the last defenders of freedom by blending aggressive anti-communism, small-state and anti-government aid attitudes, racialized anxiety, and conservative Christianity. They then used this potent cocktail to marginalize the moderate, Northeastern Eisenhower/Rockefeller

Republicans (Glenn & Teles 2009; Goldwater 2007; Lowndes 2009; McGirr 2002). In the process of doing so, they also worked to create the identifiable, mobilized constituency that we know as the Christian Right, and to securely consolidate it within the GOP. While arguably reductionist, these changes can be marked as finally coming together with the Presidential nomination and election of Ronald Reagan and the creation of identifiable Christian Right political organizations.

The Road from Electoral Politics to Litigation

According to Paul Boyer (2008), "As early as 1975, Representative John Conlan ... met with Bill Bright of Campus Crusade for Christ and other evangelicals to craft an electoral strategy that would turn worried evangelicals into voters" (4). With this attention came the development of overtly political institutions meant to finalize the creation of the Christian Right. The Moral Majority, under the leadership of Jerry Falwell and mobilized to elect Ronald Reagan, became the first major political institution for the newly formed Christian Right. That said, it would eventually fall victim to long-standing tensions that exist within this constituency, high-profile scandals, and the movement's own political naiveté. In spite of this specific failure and these limitations, a brief surveying of the histories of selected Christian Right institutions helps to show how movement actors clearly learned from their experiences in the political sphere, solidifying the Christian Right's place in both American conservatism and politics.

The Moral Majority, on its face, was open in its membership. Falwell, however, had held onto the term "fundamentalist" to describe himself, as opposed to the more open "evangelical" description employed by Graham and others. He had also stated that he "didn't even get along very well with other kinds of Baptists, let alone with Methodists, Presbyterians, or Catholics"; he attacked other popular televangelists as "religious phonies raping America"; and, relatedly, he noted that he was "uneasy just being around those he considered less devout" (Williams 2010, 173). Given this, one can question how open the Moral Majority was to natural allies who would come to compose the modern Christian Right.

Self-inflicted wounds also came in the form of high-profile missteps and scandals. Reminiscent of his earlier opposition to the American Civil Rights Movement, Falwell attacked South Africa's Bishop Tutu as a "'phony' and [defended] the white apartheid South African government" (Williams 2010, 222). Local state chapters of the Moral Majority launched campaigns that embarrassed the organization, prompting Falwell to have to publicly come out against them (Williams 2010, 199). The late '80s also saw the televangelists Jim and Tammy Faye Bakker, followed by Jimmy Swaggart, become mired in very public scandals (Johnson 2014). The cumulative effect of such coverage added to a criticism of the movement as hypocritical and intolerant.

Finally, the early Christian Right was burned by an oversized faith in the power of the presidency and the federal government. While they had worked to elect Reagan to the nation's highest office, abortion remained legal and school prayer was still not permitted. Eight years later, George H. W. Bush's election did nothing to improve meaningful Christian Right access to the presidency or the federal legislature. Evangelical disillusionment with national politics festered, and many activists were drawn to the more radical street-level activism of the 1980s and '90s anti-abortion movement, continuing to harm the Christian Right's public image (Wilson 2013).

Floundering on the national level, the leaders of the Christian Right turned to the less seen and arguably more significant sources of political power found in local and state policy venues. Their disillusionment with public, national politics also helped them to recognize the value of the nation's courts. That is, as they learned that they were not championing the causes of the nation's majority, and thus that their effectiveness in the majoritarian branches of government was limited, they turned their attention to the primary venue for minority politics—courts. All of this can be seen through the transition of power within the Christian Right from Jerry Falwell to Marion "Pat" Robertson.

The Christian Right's disillusionment, and its evolving strategic range, is evident in Paul Weyrich's 1999 admission that "I no longer believe that there is a moral majority. I believe that we have probably lost the culture war. That does not mean the war is not going to continue and that it isn't going to be fought on other fronts." Joining Weyrich, fellow Moral Majority veterans Cal Thomas and Ed Dobson admitted that they were not able to meet their political ends because, "we lacked the power" to achieve their ends "exclusively, or even mainly, through the political process" (Brown 2002, 4). These comments are remarkable for at least two reasons. First, they clearly illustrate the Christian Right's change in political perspective from silent majority to silenced minority. Second, while they allude to continuing the fight elsewhere, their defeatist tone belies the fact that the shift to "other fronts" was long since underway in the Christian Right.

Just over a decade earlier, in 1988, the depth of Jerry Falwell's disillusionment was far greater. Having recently stepped down from his leadership of the Moral Majority, the prospect of the Christian Right continuing to develop in the face of his institution's demise appeared bleak. Sounding defeated, Falwell claimed that "We are the last minority . . . You can no longer attack a man's color, but right today you can refer to fundamentalists as Bible-bangers" (Williams 2010, 223). While variously problematic in its assertion about discrimination, the pivot from claiming to be a "moral majority" to a minority holds the means to the Christian Right's expansion into the courts as a political forum.

The following year, 1989, would see Pat Robertson and Ralph Reed's founding of the Christian Coalition. This new political institution offered a fusion of a more genuine big-tent, traditional Republican Party approach to politics, with the conservative religious and political views of Falwell, as well as his recently voiced feelings of belonging to a persecuted minority.[3] This persecuted minority frame had mobilizing effects for those identifying with the movement—they saw themselves as now fighting for their very survival in the face of a grave and outnumbering domestic threat. It also opened the door to the Christian Right engaging in the "politics of rights" alongside majoritarian politics (Scheingold 2004). By embracing the "politics of rights," the Christian Right would gain access to new rhetorical resources in the public sphere, as well as a wholly new venue: the courts. By utilizing courts, the movement could defend themselves and also potentially go on the offensive against their adversaries.

Progressives, via the rights revolution, were arguably the first to enter the courts to pursue variably coordinated campaigns aimed at advancing the political and social rights of newly mobilized groups (Epp 1998). Conservatives initially protested these advances by mounting ad hoc defensive stands, arguing that the courts were being used in inappropriate ways, and criticizing "activist judges" who they saw as overstepping their institutional boundaries. In doing so, though, they were exposing that they had not noticed and adjusted to fundamental changes in the ways that politics and governance were now being effectively conducted (Teles 2008; Glenn & Teles 2009). Secular conservatives, however, began to change their approach to courts and politics over the course of the 1970s and '80s.

Crying foul about liberal "activist judges" persists as a mainstay of conservative rhetoric, but secular conservatives have been developing their resources and capacity to go on the offensive in courts for decades. To this end they developed public interest law firms that could pursue principled litigation campaigns, academic movements that could supply much needed *intellectual capital* for conservatives, and networks that created *social* and *human capital* to drive the movement (Teles 2008; Southworth 2008; Hollis-Brusky 2015). Initially excluded from, or simply not yet seeing the value in, the rising conservative legal movement, religious conservatives waited roughly a decade to follow their secular correlates in developing these resources.

As Andrew Lewis notes, the turn to the courts and rights claiming "is monumental" in terms of both conservatism generally, and the Christian Right specifically (2017, 2). Modern American conservatism had largely been defined by fighting, rather than advancing, the rights claims asserted by various minority groups in court. The movements comprising the progressive American rights revolution (e.g., the Civil Rights, the prisoner and accused, women's, LGBTQIA+, disability, Latinx, indigenous peoples, and other rights movements) are credited with driving party realignment and propelling conservatives to power in the modern GOP (Glenn & Teles 2009; Lowndes 2009; Schickler 2016). Conservative politicians and public intellectuals have for decades heralded states' rights in their fight against the individual rights claimed in the rights revolution, and conservative academics such as Mary Ann Glendon (1993) cite America's push for individual rights as a source of the country's decline (Dudas 2017). Finally, as discussed in the previous section, reactions to the rights revolution and its accompanying cultural changes are specifically cited as instrumental in the creation of the Christian Right as a political force. The desire to roll back such changes, and stifle and defeat future ones, is thus at the core of the conservative movement.

It is this wider context, then, that makes it both astounding and revolutionary that, as Lewis's book *The Rights Turn in Conservative Christian Politics* convincingly demonstrates,

> Conservatives are now using typically liberal arguments, promoting *individual rights*. Conservatives are now wielding these rights arguments with increasing frequency in the judicial courts and the courts of public opinion. And religious conservatives . . . are at the helm, winning political victories and gaining legal protection . . . In the process [the Christian Right] has shifted from protecting community morality to embracing certain liberties . . . Evangelicals, and their Christian Right allies, have become baptized into political liberalism. (2017, 1)[4]

Not surprising given the Christian Coalition's cultivation of the persecuted minority self-perception, Pat Robertson is located squarely in the middle of the Christian Right's pivot to taking their fight to the courts. In 1990, one year after founding the Christian Coalition, Robertson funded the establishment of the American Center for Law and Justice (ACLJ) and hired attorney Jay Sekulow to run it. The ACLJ is arguably the first modern Christian conservative legal organization (CCLO). According to his thorough book on CCLOs, *Defending Faith*, Daniel Bennett notes that the ACLJ has recent revenue of $17.5 million while it also receives additional revenue from Christian Advocates Serving Evangelism, which has its own recent revenue count of $53 million (2017, 20). The ACLJ actively litigates a range of Christian Right interests, but reflecting the organization's closeness to the Republican Party, it is also "one of the most politically oriented CCLOs," and thus it engages in a range of cases and also partisan political activities that one might associate with the broader conservative coalition beyond just the Christian Right (22).[5]

Since its founding, the ACLJ has been joined by other similarly well-funded CCLOs including Mat Staver's Liberty Counsel (initially established as a minor player in 1989, but fundamentally changed in 2000 by becoming a part of Jerry Falwell's network of institutions), Alliance Defending Freedom (ADF; originally established as the Alliance Defense Fund in 1994 but changing their name to reflect their change in strategies in 2012), the Becket Fund for Religious Liberty (1994), First Liberty (1997), and Thomas More Society (1997).

As the CCLOs with the greatest budgets (individually, they all have revenue ranging from $3.1 to $48.3 million), they collectively represent a formidable, politically savvy legal force developed in a remarkably short period of time. Through their founders, leadership, and organizational structure and composition, each of these CCLOs has conservative Protestant or Catholic roots that are followed by an openness to working with other religiously oriented conservatives in a way that is representative of much of the post–Christian Coalition movement (Bennett 2017, 20).[6] Finally, with cases such as *Lamb's Chapel v. Center Moriches Union Free School District*, 508 U.S. 384 (1993), *McCullen v. Coakley* 573 US 464 (2014), *Burwell v. Hobby Lobby Stores, Inc.* 573 US 682 (2014), and *National Institute of Family and Life Advocates v. Becerra* (2018), they have a proven record of being effective in the nation's highest court.

These CCLOs do not represent Christian conservatives' first entry into the court. Christian conservative lawyers had long existed in the United States, as had some conservative religious legal organizations. For example, William Jennings Bryan, in 1925, litigated on behalf of the evangelical cause against evolution in the popularly named "Scopes Monkey Trial." Decades later, Jay Sekulow ran his own small CCLO called Christian Advocates Serving Evangelism before Robertson tapped him to run the ACLJ. That said, these legal elements were seriously lacking before Robertson launched the Christian Right's broader effort to earnestly invest in them. In other words, there may have been identifiable Christian conservative lawyers over the course of the twentieth century, but there was little to suggest a Christian conservative legal movement (CCLM) until that century's close.

Robertson had made an earlier move toward developing the Christian Right's legal resources by providing financing for the establishment of the National Legal Foundation (NLF) in 1985 (Brown 2002, 38). His early interest in including judicial politics alongside the Christian Right's electoral politics is likely linked, in part, to Robertson being a Yale Law School graduate. The perspective gained from this training arguably made him well positioned to see what other actors in the Christian Right may not have seen until later. Creating NLF was, however, a half-hearted initial entry into the judicial realm.

The group formally split from Robertson three years after its founding when he ran for president, but NLF is still in existence today, and it still shows indirect connections to Robertson. Its three current attorneys are all graduates from Robertson's Regent University School of Law, and it is listed on the ADF's website as an allied organization along with Robertson's ACLJ and other CCLOs.[7] In the words of Daniel Bennett, however, "[c]ompared to other CCLOs, the NLF's activities are relatively lackluster" (2017, 28).

As noted, the organization is recently listed as having only three lawyers on staff, a perusal of its history does not show it to have had more than that, and at times it was limited to just one attorney on staff.[8] What's more, Robertson's initial investment appears to pale in comparison with his investment in creating the ACLJ, and the loss of his support as a patron surely stunted the organization's ability to grow. According to Bennett's research, the NLF's recent revenue is listed at $236,000— a fraction of ACLJ's $17.5 million (20). Finally, given the shortage of financial and legal resources, it is not surprising that "most of its work is confined to filing

supportive amicus briefs"—a strategy that Teles cites as a sign of public interest organization ineffectiveness (Bennett 2017, 28; Teles 2008).

In its size, limited budget, and emphasis on filing amicus briefs over investing in
its own litigation efforts, the NLF represents what much of the Christian Right's
legal landscape looked like prior to the infusion of resources in the 1990s and early
2000s.[9] In fact, compared with what is found in much of the Christian Right's response to the litigation emerging from the street politics of abortion, the NLF can
in some ways be seen as advanced for its time.

As anti-abortion activists took to the streets in the 1980s and '90s, they were
met by a series of injunctions, followed by state and federal laws that regulated
their activities in front of abortion clinics. Even though groups such as Operation
Rescue were able to organize massive protests around the country, they were not
equipped to supply legal support for individuals who they spurred to action and
who were subsequently arrested when they ran afoul of these regulations. It was not
uncommon to find anti-abortion activist leaders searching their congregations for
lawyers of any sort who could file motions for arrested activists.

Those lawyers who were found often worked pro bono, far outside of their legal
specializations, and without substantial legal resources to pull from beyond what they
already had in their offices. There may have been multiple lawyers working on related
issues around the country, and some of them were even working on these issues as part
of their formal professional careers, but they were not effectively networked together.
Given this, these lawyers were largely outmatched by their opponents, who, while of-
tentimes also volunteers, were able to pull from national legal networks working to defend abortion rights. As a result, the anti-abortion activist wing of the Christian Right
was largely limited to ad hoc legal defenses and they were delayed in their ability to go
on the offensive in court against their adversaries (Wilson 2013, 2016). The CCLM
would have to wait until collections of these veteran Christian attorneys, along with
emerging legal talent, could be pulled together and organized institutionally.

Alliance Defense Fund (later Alliance Defending Freedom) represents one such
effort to aggregate and coordinate the Christian Right's growing litigation efforts.
In the ADF's own words, "Recognizing the need for a strong, coordinated legal defense . . . our Founders saw a battlefield in disarray with inadequate resources to
win. There were allies, but no alliances. There was limited unity of effort and limited
common strategy."[10] While created to coordinate efforts, the ADF largely scrapped
this mission in 2012 in favor of increased central control. In the statement explaining
their corresponding name change, the organization announced that

> For some time, many within our organization have been concerned that
> our name, Alliance Defense Fund, does not sufficiently, accurately convey
> who we are and what we do. It was the name chosen by our Founders,
> for good reasons at the time. Back then . . . we provided legal and finan-
> cial resources for other Christian attorneys. So, the term "fund" was very

appropriate. Nowadays, though, we do our own litigating. We actively defend clients and engage the opposition . . .

. . . We do not want [people] thinking of us as a "fund." . . . We want them to know that we are passionate about defending freedom . . . that defending it is the mission of our lives.[11]

In redefining themselves, the ADF moved from being a clearinghouse to capturing the lion's share of CCLM funding to drive their own litigation efforts.[12] Bennett (2017) lists the ADF as having the greatest budget among the major CCLOs, and the ADF defended their move, arguing that the "nature of the work we do requires us to secure resources" (Alliance Defending Freedom, "Our New Name").

As an extension of their newly claimed finances, the ADF simultaneously gained even greater control over the Christian Right's litigation efforts and hobbled other CCLOs that were dependent upon the ADF's funding—groups that could make the same claims about the nature of their work and the necessity of resources. Instead of allies needing to be brought together in an alliance, such CCLOs were now positioned as "a hindrance to our ministry . . . making it unworthy of the God who has given us our mission" (Alliance Defending Freedom, "Our New Name"). Not surprisingly, the ADF's changes aggravated divisions between Christian Right leaders and their organizations. It also established the CCLM's present litigation field with the ADF at the top, followed by a select few CCLOs with secure independent funding bases, sitting well above all other CCLOs. Alliances are, thus, hard to see, but hierarchies and the desire for individually controlled institutions continue to be clear.

This conflict shows the persistence of tensions and fractures within the Christian Right, and the subsequent CCLM. It also helps illuminate one reason for the CCLM's modern form. In relation to the former, the ADF represents the Christian Right's penchant for creating institutions that, no matter their size, are arguably the extension of a strong central leader who seeks to maximize control.[13] Such leaders and their institutions are wary of collaborating with others. When these inherent apprehensions cannot be overcome, it is no surprise that these leaders marshal their resources to create institutions of their own that they can better control, and that they subsequently—directly or indirectly—mobilize against their competitors/would-be-allies.[14] As will be seen below, this pattern will continue into the creation of the CCLM's later support structures.

Understanding the Early Thinness of the CCLM's Support Structures

Although leaders within the Christian Right were able to create CCLOs by consolidating lawyers who had found their way to Christian litigation—from

Sekulow's early legal representation of Jews for Jesus, to lesser known lawyers drawn in through the street politics of abortion and other movements—they were still hampered by a broad, longer-term capital supply problem. The full range of *intellectual, cultural,* and *social capital,* as well as a persistent source of increased *human capital,* all of which are essential in building and sustaining a successful litigation-based change campaign, were not evident at the time. In other words, there were standing inefficiencies in the existing Christian conservative legal movement.

Restated in terms of the Support Structure Pyramid, which we introduced in Chapter 1, Christian Right patrons had established Level 2 organizations in CCLOs, and those organizations had given them increased access to the nation's courts. This effectively establishes the CCLM as defined by the thin conception of support structures—the Christian Right now had identifiable rights advocacy lawyers, legal organizations, and funding. Their prima facie effectiveness in driving legal change, however, was incomplete. They could now bring more cases and start to stoke demand for more cases, but their court and cultural resources were shallow. As the progressive rights revolution and the more recent rise of the secular conservative legal movement evidenced, they would continue to be hobbled until they could establish themselves within Level 1 of the Support Structure Pyramid.

Two problems, however, combined to seriously impede the CCLM's progress and their entry into Level 1 of the Support Structure Pyramid. First, much like fundamentalists' and early evangelicals' aversions to public engagement and politics, conservative Christians had a long-standing mistrust of lawyers, and there was an established belief that it was difficult, if not impossible, to be both a good lawyer and a good Christian (Baker & Floyd 1997; den Dulk 2006; Southworth 2008; Wilson and Hollis-Brusky 2014). Exacerbating and intertwined with this was a persistent, parallel mistrust of the nation's colleges and universities that helped create the institutional landscape that threatened the emergent CCLM's prospects (Ringenberg 2006).

In addressing these problems, we see parallels to moves made in the 1970s to allow Christian conservatives to enter politics. In that earlier period, Francis Schaeffer, a Swiss-based American evangelical theologian, helped bring Christian conservatives into the public square (Hankins 2008). Alongside Graham's efforts, Schaeffer's books, lecture tours, and films helped to give theological reasons—even a duty—for orthodox Christians to engage in politics. Decades later, institutions within the CCLM did the same for the practice of law, reframing law from a profession to a religious calling (Wilson & Hollis-Brusky, 2014). The ADF's statement regarding their name change reflects such a shift. In the organization's words, their legal work is directed by "God who has given us our mission" (Alliance Defending Freedom, "Our New Name"). Seen as a religious calling, legal practice and, by extension, law schools were thus able to become more visible and realistic options for Christian conservatives.

Reframing the practice of law, however, is not enough on its own to fully supply the CCLM with the capital that it needs to thrive. The reframing of legal practice may provide Christian conservatives with a new means of understanding lawyers and the possibilities of their work, but it was hard to see an avenue to becoming such a Christian attorney if law school still seemed unwelcoming and possibly posed a threat to one's Christian identity. At best, the overwhelming majority of existing law schools presented three years of being an outsider and/or keeping one's Christian identity private, something many of our interviewees spoke about. At worst, they stood as a means of leading the devout away from what they could now see as their calling.

Relatedly, even if aspiring Christian lawyers were able to accept law school's perceived risks, existing law schools did not readily provide a means to create the other forms of capital that such institutions stand to provide legal movements. Mainstream law school faculty were not seen as advantageously engaging the topics that motivated the Christian Right, producing needed scholarship and raising the profile and legitimacy and their various legal interests. Securing and cultivating these resources and providing a clear, welcoming, and safe way to become a lawyer were problems still needing to be addressed.

While evangelical and fundamentalist Christian conservatives have long had ample options in terms of pursuing elementary through college education in their own institutions, the prospects for graduate and professional training outside of the ministry were—and still are—scant in comparison. A brief review of the history of Christian conservative higher education helps explain the contemporary dearth of evangelical and fundamentalist graduate and professional education options, the institutional and cultural changes that enabled CCLM leaders to create new law schools that could feed their movement, and the forms that these new law schools have subsequently taken.

Reactions to what Christian conservatives saw as the combined threats of secularization and liberalization in American culture and education in the last quarter of the nineteenth century, and into the first decades of the twentieth, produced the "Bible College Movement" (Ringenberg 2006, Chs. 5–7). This movement helped lay the foundation for popular fundamentalist and evangelical higher education. It also, however, arguably helped create the scarcity of professional education options that constrained the CCLM at the end of the twentieth century.

Seeking to counter secularization while responding to the increased public interest in, and importance of, formal educational training and achievement, "early Bible schools . . . usually listed some courses in the liberal arts and a large amount of work in biblical studies, theology, and practical Christian training" (Ringenberg, 160). While some of these schools went on to increase their liberal arts offerings, their missions have largely remained and, thus, "they have usually [expanded their offerings] by increasing the length of their programs rather than by reducing the Bible requirements" (Ringenberg, 161). By virtue of their focus on religious training above more generalized higher education, Bible schools held limited prospects for eventually evolving to offer graduate and professional training beyond formal ministry positions. As fundamentalist and evangelical populations changed in the twentieth century, though, so did their educational offerings.

The Bible schools were joined in responding to liberalization and secularization in higher education by "new liberal arts colleges . . . founded [in the twentieth century] by new evangelical denominations or independent groups that separated from the mainline denominations in protest over the latter's growing liberal theological orientation" (Ringenberg, 185). These new institutions seemed better positioned as more complete liberal arts schools, rather than the more limited Bible colleges, to eventually produce graduate offerings that would appeal to and serve Christian conservatives. They were, however, often hobbled by weak financial foundations. As new denominations or independent groups, they were correspondingly starting anew financially and had little support to offer their new liberal arts schools. The result was that "in too many cases, limited resources have caused institutions to hire inadequately trained professors to direct courses whose quality was defended because of the Christian character of the teachers" as opposed to their academic rigor (Ringenberg, 182). Flawed from their inception, then, such faculty hires, courses, and graduates did not serve as a substantial means for building or spurring demand for professional and graduate programs in the Christian conservative sphere.

The future prospects for fundamentalist and evangelical post-graduate education changed in the mid-twentieth century. The combined creation of a parallel Christian conservative institutional world and the more broad-based revival movement initially spearheaded by Billy Graham led to significant wealth creation for a handful of Christian ministerial leaders. A select collection of such leaders used their wealth to create Christian colleges that offered more than the early Bible colleges and were on far better financial footing than the bulk of newly created liberal arts schools. They were also adamant about creating institutions that would stand as highly visible markers in the fights against liberalization, secularization, and communism in the academy, the culture more generally, and in the greater world. Some of the most prominent and important of these new major Christian conservative colleges were John Brown University (est. 1920), Bob Jones University (est. 1927), Oral Roberts University (ORU; est. 1965), Pepperdine University (est. 1937), Liberty University (est. 1971), and Regent University (est. 1977, fittingly originally named Christian Broadcasting Network University after Pat Robertson's media network).

These schools were not only the products of the wealth generated by their founders' varied institutional domains, they were also formed in ways that reflected, helped sustain, and developed the collective institutions in realizing their founders' visions for the world—an impulse that follows through to the creation and form of the eventual law schools. To this end, "[i]n the late twentieth century the fastest-growing program of the large fundamentalist churches—as well as many conservative Protestant churches—was the Christian day-school movement.

Consequently, the fastest-growing program in fundamentalist colleges was that of preparing teachers" (Ringenberg, 178). Not surprisingly, the leading Christian conservative universities also boast significant theater arts programs that feed Christian evangelical entertainment ministries. As Oral Roberts himself said in relation to his university's sports programs, but with an underlying logic that clearly relates to these schools' collective interests in forwarding their leaders' larger visions for the world, "For us to be relevant, we had to gain the attention of millions in a way that they understood and they would then tune us in on TV to hear us preach the gospel" (Ringenberg 2006, 187).

With a similar instrumental view, students and faculty at these institutions are often regulated in ways reflective of their founders' desires to fend off what can be seen as competing, and possibly corrupting, influences. Their experiences are also cultivated in ways that serve the founders' larger vision. Ringenberg notes that Liberty, for example, "required each student to complete one Christian service assignment each semester," much of which was done at Falwell's Thomas Road Baptist Church (163). What's more, "all first-year students took classes in Christian evangelism, in which they learned the basic techniques and ethos of personal soul winning" (178). At Oral Roberts, "students are required to take three three-credit courses in religion, one each in Old Testament, New Testament, and charismatic life and healing ministry. Students (as well as faculty) are also required to attend chapel twice weekly." ORU students, and formerly faculty, are also required to meet physical fitness requirements in line with Roberts' vision (Schuman 2010, 167).

Finally, reflecting the pervasiveness of centralized control, these schools often regulate academic freedom in ways that are taboo at other institutions. As Bob Jones III stated, "We're unusual in our objective to teach the students what he [Jones] believes . . . we don't throw out a bunch of theories to them about religion of the world and philosophy and this sort of thing." As the founding Bob Jones put it, "if you don't like it here you can pack up your dirty duds and hit the four-lane highway" (Ringenberg 2006, 180).

By combining their founders' interests in changing the world with their ample financial resources in historically demonstrable ways, these new schools held the means to address the professional and graduate education needs for their communities once such needs were identified by their leaders. Regent, in fact, "operates almost totally as a graduate institution. Pat Robertson . . . sought to found a graduate professional program to train Christian leaders in areas that could have the greatest impact in changing society" (Ringenberg 2006, 220). While "the visions of . . . a 'Christian Johns Hopkins' remained in the dream stage," it is in some ways no wonder, then, that ORU, Liberty, and Regent developed law schools— the details of which will be fully developed in the following chapter (Ringenberg 2006, 192).

Strategies for Adding Thicker Support Structures

Creating a new law school is an incredibly high financial investment, and the costs stand to persist for years since it can be difficult for educational institutions to become wholly self-sufficient. Such costs dwarf those of endowing faculty chairs, funding clinics, and creating centers at existing law schools as seen in the *infiltration* strategy. What's more, a newly created law school faces the challenges of developing the less tangible, but highly important, *cultural capital* that existing law schools already possess. Building such capital is difficult, and typically something done over significant time, seriously impeding a new school's ability to produce broadly recognized *cultural capital*. While the *parallel alternative* strategy offers more control over all aspects of an institution, and the potential to produce higher volumes of needed capital, these risks and costs are so great that CCLM leaders' decisions to choose it over an *infiltration* strategy, or a combined *infiltration* and *supplemental* strategy, are remarkable even when the law schools are seen as extensions of their existing institutions.

The specific context of the Christian Right adds to both the risks and the questions regarding the choices that were made to primarily pursue the *parallel alternative* strategy to create support structures. Returning to the idea of producing *cultural capital*, as noted earlier in this chapter, the Christian Right is saddled with a negative popular stigma. As Ann Southworth's book on conservative lawyers makes clear, this stigma extends into the conservative legal world as well (2008). If Christian conservative lawyers have trouble building capital with groups with which they share interests, it is hard to see how Christian conservative schools would effectively generate broader *cultural capital* in ways that would benefit conservative Christians and the CCLM.

Similar concerns extend to the prospects for producing quality *human* and *intellectual capital*. Top law school student prospects and aspiring or existing faculty face significant risks in coming to newly established law schools. For students, there should be concerns about the abilities of new schools to be able to tap into professional networks that help them secure jobs. For possible faculty, there should be concerns about the long-term stability of a new institution and possibly how joining such an institution might affect their professional standing. Finally, accreditation should be a concern for both groups.

Given these collected concerns, the pools of possible interested students and faculty are limited—a condition exacerbated in these cases by the centrality of these schools' Christian conservatism—and they run a real risk of bringing in a lower quality of both students and faculty. If this were to happen, it would weaken the institutions' abilities to produce quality capital of all sorts for the associated movement.

Schools can try to assuage such concerns by signaling their stability and prospects via financial security and subsequent prestigious administrative and faculty hires. With these newly formed religious law schools, these concerns might also be mitigated by the particularly attractive nature of the mission for the devout and, as some interviewees cited, a faith that God will see them and these institutions through. This all said, new institutions are still at an overwhelming disadvantage in relation to existing schools when it comes to acquiring the resources they need to be maximally, and possibly even minimally, effective as law schools and support structures.

Considering all of this, one must ask why leaders in the emergent Christian conservative legal movement, with the exception of the ADF, primarily chose the highest risk and highest cost option for obtaining thick support structure institutions. The answer to this question returns us to the themes seen in the histories of the Christian Right and Christian conservative education.

Rejecting the *Infiltration* Strategy

As just described, one path for the CCLM to create and acquire needed capital and avoid the aforementioned risks was to work with and within existing law schools. While the *"infiltration"* title we have chosen for the strategy may connote a degree of hostility—an existing institution being invaded and overrun by an outside force—this does not have to be the case. Rather, movement actors can appeal to potentially sympathetic existing institutions in developing support structure resources, and such options appeared readily existent for the Christian Right.[15]

As noted by Ringenberg, "among the intentionally Christian universities, those with the broadest range of major professional and graduate programs are Baylor and Pepperdine. Baylor and Pepperdine also both have highly regarded law . . . schools" (2006, 219–20). The same is clearly true for Notre Dame when broadening "intentionally Christian universities" to include Catholic institutions. What's more, each of these institutions is demonstrably conservative. While other institutions could be seen as infiltration candidates for the CCLM, these conservative, "critical mass" religious institutions lead the list with their established histories, networks, faculty, and traditions.[16] As such, these schools stood to provide the CCLM with rich and immediate access to all of the forms of capital that they needed.[17]

The presumably attractive possibilities presented by these institutions heighten the need to explain why movement leaders would choose the more costly and risky *parallel alternative* strategy and completely avoid the *infiltration strategy*. In the interests of space, and considering various similarities between the Baylor and Pepperdine stories, we will limit our discussion to the broadly illustrative examples of Baylor and Notre Dame below.

Baylor

As evangelical and fundamentalist Protestants were being organized into an identifiable—and identifiably conservative—political constituency, the changes enveloped all related institutions, including the nation's Southern Baptist colleges and universities. "Beginning in 1979, the insurgent conservative party [within the Southern Baptists] . . . gradually secured control of the denomination, including the right to select trustees of the major seminaries" (Ringenberg 2006, 235).[18] The institutional fights continued through the 1980s, producing literal breaking points in the 1990s.

Baylor University in Texas, the nation's flagship Southern Baptist university, was among those that attempted to carve out a moderate position within the faith: "in 1991 Baylor altered the terms of its charter, through the Texas legislature, seeking a moderate bulwark against the apparent threat of a fundamentalist takeover" (Schuman 2010, 83). In that same year, Texas Baptists as a whole split into a conservative faction—the Southern Baptists of Texas Convention—and a more moderate faction—the Baptist General Convention of Texas (Schuman 2010, 83). Again signaling its desire to be politically moderate within the context of Southern Baptists, Baylor University became affiliated with the latter convention. Finally, in what can be seen as a direct response to the conservative takeover of Southern Baptist seminaries, Baylor received a charter to create its own seminary in 1991, and they enrolled their first class in 1994.

The timing of these events is helpful in understanding why Baylor and other prominent Southern Baptist institutions, with law schools such as Wake Forest and the University of Richmond, were not the targets of *infiltration* investment. The leaders of the CCLM were firmly on the side of the conservative takeovers of American evangelical and fundamentalist institutions specifically, and the GOP more generally. Baylor and the other schools that broke away from the conservative takeover were, thus, clearly in the opposition. That said, Baylor remains deeply committed to education from a Christian perspective. As Ringenberg details, Baylor has committed to becoming "the unquestioned premier Christian research university in the Protestant tradition in America" (236). Instead of leaving the faith altogether or surrendering its conservative (though *not* fundamentalist) values, Baylor has been described as "fighting a two-front war . . . against anti-intellectual fundamentalism in the church on one hand and secular trends in the academy on the other" (Ringenberg 2006, 235).

Supportive of Baylor's religious and conservative commitments, "all first-year [undergraduate] students are required to attend chapel twice weekly, and there is a six-credit-hour religion requirement (one course in the Christian scriptures, one in the Christian heritage)" (Schuman, 84). While the law school does not have such requirements, its mission statement opens by declaring that "Baylor Law shares in the University's mission to educate men and women by integrating academic excellence and Christian commitment within a caring community" (Baylor University n.d.).

In addition to this, "Baylor has an explicit faculty hiring religious hierarchy" that privileges "Baptists, other evangelicals, mainline Protestants, Catholics, Greek-Orthodox, and Jews" and disqualifies other faiths and non-believers. Faculty applicants are also questioned about their faith as part of the formal interview process, and "tenure is accompanied by a reaffirmation by both the candidate and the institution of the centrality and importance of religious beliefs and behavior" (Schuman, 84).

Along with Baylor's moves in the 1990s to insulate itself from and push back against the ascendant conservative forces within Southern Baptist organizations, though, the decision to "become the unquestioned premier Christian research university in the Protestant tradition in America" further puts it at odds with the more conservative elements within the Christian Right. A 2012 collection of speeches, titled *A Higher Education: Baylor and the Vocation of a Christian University*, is telling here.

Baylor President Ken Starr writes in the foreword that the purpose of inviting a range of speakers to campus whose talks are collected in *A Higher Education* was to set the tone for Baylor's future development. Picking up after President Starr, the then Provost Elizabeth Davis ended her introduction to the collection by stating, "We hold firmly to the conviction that the world needs a preeminent research university that is unambiguously Christian. *A place where such a commitment does not imply a lack of scholarly inquiry . . .*" (Noll et al. 2012, 4–5).[19] As this statement implies, the collected speeches are replete with their authors noting both the virtues, as well as what they see as the very real perils of being dedicated to a religious identity. The statement and the collection also give life to the idea that Baylor is locked in a two-front war with secularism on one side, and fundamentalism on the other.

In the words of Mark Noll, a prominent scholar of Christian history based at Notre Dame, who closes the collection, truly adhering to "Christian intellectual life . . . requires an exercise in tightrope walking." He goes on to state that

> In the current American scene we have several obvious examples of falling off the wire into a crass biblicism . . . zealous adherents to Scripture simply toss the baby of well-grounded learning with the bathwater of learning abused for God-denying purposes. These examples include manic single-issue public advocacy that claims to represent "biblical politics"; runaway Americanism that depicts our nation's early history as the land of the converted and the true-blue evangelical; and the cruder forms of "intelligent design" that repeat William Paley's error of using God to fill in the gaps of contemporary scientific knowledge. (96–97)

To avoid joining those falling off of the wire, then, Noll implores Baylor to use the Baptist "spirit of independence to welcome academics from all the major historical Christian traditions . . . And if Baptists demonstrate their traditional Baptist courage in the face of powers that be—whether those powers are unexamined local traditions, national political enthusiasms, or the conventions of elite American academia—then Baylor University would be doing both Christian and academic worlds the greatest service possible" (111).

As perhaps the collection's most overt examples of Baylor's rejection of the contemporary Christian Right and their associated fundamentalist colleges and universities, Noll's words capture why Baylor may at first appear to be an infiltration candidate, but in actuality, it was anything but. In other words, while Baylor was dedicated to being demonstrably Christian and conservative, it was going to be far more open, it would directly engage with the wider world, and it would have a far more traditional adherence to academic freedom than the institutions that laid claim to evangelicalism and fundamentalism in higher education and contemporary politics.

Returning to the law school specifically and its mission statement, the opening regarding their shared Christian commitment is immediately followed by two sentences echoing the above sentiment: "Baylor University is dedicated to the traditional responsibilities of higher education: dissemination of knowledge, transmission of culture, search for new knowledge, and application of knowledge. Moreover, within the context of a culturally diverse community, Baylor University strives to develop responsible citizens, educated leaders, dedicated scholars, and skilled professionals who are sensitive to the needs of a pluralistic society" (Baylor, n.d.). As such, the values advocated for by Noll have been enacted in the law school's vision of its duties and place in the world.

Given this, another reason, and a persistent one at that, for the CCLM's lack of interest in investing in Baylor is abundantly clear. In brief, by leaders within the movement, Baylor can be seen as part of the problem, and not part of their solution to it. While their specific stories are different, the Baylor story also gives the framework for understanding why other existing, established Protestant institutions were also unattractive options for the CCLM *infiltration* investment.

Notre Dame

Notre Dame stands as another major institution that would seem to be a high-profile target for the *infiltration* strategy, especially for conservative Catholics. The arguable opening of the Christian Right to increasingly include Catholics, combined with what will be discussed here and further developed in subsequent chapters regarding Notre Dame's academic prestige as well as its connections to powerful conservative networks, suggests more than this.[20] That is, Notre Dame is arguably the nation's *best* option for an *infiltration* strategy. In brief, Notre Dame's law school has done significant work not only to become one of the nation's elite law schools, but also to become arguably the nation's elite *conservative* law school. Furthermore, as this section will show, Notre Dame offers access to the highest quality of all of the forms of capital sought by a movement in a Level 1 support structure.

In 1999 Patricia O'Hara became the law school dean, and she undertook the literal rebuilding of the law school.[21] According to one interviewee, she also undertook its figurative rebuilding with an eye toward attracting and retaining leading conservative legal scholars. "Her first set of people she recruited to the school were very invested in that idea. Then it becomes self-replicating because those people have invested." Almost two decades into this "self-replicating" process, the same interviewee tallied its effectiveness, "We don't have a [constitutional] law person who's not an originalist and we have like 14 [constitutional] law people . . . I would put it this way, everyone who gets hired here who doesn't fit that [conservative] mold is an accident . . . There's an explanation for everyone" (Notre Dame Faculty 1 2016).

As a marker of the success in realizing this vision, multiple faculty interviewees freely listed the signs of Notre Dame's elite conservative legal capital. As one interviewee noted, "[w]atching my colleague Bill Kelley serve in the White House a few years ago, and play an instrumental role in both John Roberts and Sam Alito getting on the Supreme Court, I think was an impressive thing" (Notre Dame Faculty 2 2016). Similarly, another faculty member noted, "I just bumped into John Roberts on Saturday. Literally my wife almost tackled him. Then [House Speaker] Paul Ryan was over there" (Notre Dame Faculty 3 2016). Portraits of conservative Supreme Court Justices hung in many of the faculty interviewees' offices. They served as visual reminders of the various faculty members' time spent as clerks for these Justices, and the corresponding prestige that such service brought to these members and to Notre Dame.

This elite faculty conservatism has resulted in attracting a higher percentage of academically elite conservative students. "I think our students are the best part of the place. I mean they all come here because they have a sense of there's something interesting going on . . . Now probably compared to most law schools in the country we get a bigger percentage of conservatives but I think that's in part because a lot of elite law schools, their representation of conservatives is still pretty small" (Notre Dame Faculty 1 2016).

What's seen here are various themes repeated in the student and faculty interviews: a self-conscious awareness of the law school's majority ideological positioning, the acknowledgment that a degree of political diversity still exists within the school, an understanding that Notre Dame has occupied a unique space within the legal academy, and a belief that it possesses a corresponding prestige that is not fully captured by its *U.S. News* ranking.

One faculty member put it this way:

> we regularly punch way above our weight in terms of [judges] hiring ex-
> students, placing federal clerks . . . where do they go to look for sharp,
> conservative kids? They come to Notre Dame. On our faculty we have 13
> former Supreme Court clerks . . . These guys remain tied in, they remain
> completely connected . . . They totally maintain those networks . . . Those
> networks are strong, and they're tight. When [faculty member] gets
> on the phone and tells somebody this guy's good, he gets the clerk-
> ship . . . [W]here else are you going to go if you're looking for prestigious,
> conservative faculty? We are the place . . . It's kind of like the Federalist
> Society distilled in the sense of that's the place you go for your judges, and
> this is where you go for your clerks. (Notre Dame Faculty 3 2016)

Given the 2017 appointment of Notre Dame Law Professor Amy Barrett to the
Seventh Circuit Court of Appeals, and her consideration for Justice Kennedy's
2018 vacated Supreme Court seat, it appears that Notre Dame might also unsurprisingly be becoming a place where "you go for your [conservative] judges"
as well.

It is important to also note that the University of Notre Dame as a whole
represents a broad spectrum of political ideology, and various interpretations of
Catholic teaching and both the university's and the law school's missions. As a faculty interviewee related, "your local experience at Notre Dame matters enormously
in terms of how you experience what people understand our mission to be in terms
of the politics of it" (Notre Dame Faculty 1 2016). Within this established range
of understandings, however, the law school has clearly staked out its place on the
political right. As a result, the law school is regarded "as being kind of a more conservative outpost on campus" (Notre Dame Faculty 3 2016). That said, faculty and
student interviewees also strongly emphasized that it was still an open and outwardly
oriented place.

Given the insularity and mistrust that runs through much of the Christian
Right's history, as well as the specific anti-Catholic themes seen, these qualities of
openness can be viewed with suspicion by leaders within the Christian Right and
the CCLM. What's more, as the interviews made evident, the desire for openness
and an outward orientation are realized in the law school in a variety of ways, potentially alienating members of the CCLM. One self-identifying Protestant faculty
member stated, "We're going to hire atheists and Jews and Muslims, and that's going
to be okay" (Notre Dame Faculty 3 2016). Similarly, another noted that "there is
no statement of faith [for faculty and students]. The only kind of criteria we have is,
we're looking for people who are interested in the conversation, and who can kind
of contribute to it in some respect, but that allows for a lot of different perspectives,
and you see them here" (Notre Dame Faculty 2 2016).[22] Such openness in hiring

exceeds that of Baylor and definitely reaches beyond what is seen at Liberty, Regent, and Ave Maria's law schools.

In discussions of the school's academic orientation, faculty interviewees were keen to point out how they fundamentally differed from newly created Christian conservative law schools in these terms. One faculty member asserted that, "Notre Dame is trying to be excellent and Catholic. Regent and Liberty, for whatever it's worth, they're not going to get to excellent anytime soon, in the sense that we're talking about . . . engag[ing] with the world around us, at the highest level" (Notre Dame Faculty 2 2016). As will be further shown in quantified detail in later chapters, Notre Dame offers the unique combination of academic prestige that translates to influence within the legal academy and profession (i.e., *intellectual* and *cultural* capital); professional network connections (i.e., *social capital*); highly credentialed graduates (i.e., *human capital*); clearly demonstrable religious commitment; and, again, demonstrable conservatism. Collectively, these virtues allow Notre Dame to "regularly punch way above [its] weight," and it has "an opportunity to try to engage with the world . . . at the highest level" (Notre Dame Faculty 3 2016; Notre Dame Faculty 2 2016). If the CCLM is genuinely invested in creating not only Christian lawyers but also a greater movement that can fundamentally change the culture, such engagement and recognized respect is, if not required, clearly advantageous.

In spite of this, the CCLM did not directly invest in Notre Dame as a support structure.[23] As will be seen later, however, Notre Dame is not wholly outside of the CCLM. Leaders within the ADF have recognized Notre Dame's value as they built and continue to run the Blackstone Legal Fellowship. This is not surprising since, as will be seen, the ADF shares a mainstream view of credentialing, engagement, and effectiveness that Notre Dame faculty have expressed. That is, they share a view that, "if our distinctiveness is going to be important, we have to be able to engage the rest of the world . . . and be excellent at doing it" Notre Dame Faculty 4 2016). To this end, select Notre Dame faculty teach in Blackstone, recognizing and using the school's *intellectual capital*.[24] Student interviewees reported that the ADF regularly hosts a recruitment dinner at Notre Dame, showing that the organization recognizes and actively courts the valuable *human* and *social capital* that Notre Dame offers, and that Blackstone and the CCLM can then benefit from. Finally, completing the cycle, faculty interviewees recall writing letters of recommendation for Blackstone applicants, and interviewed students either know others who have applied and/or attended, or they had themselves been through the Blackstone program.[25]

The ADF's working with Notre Dame, however, is unique within the CCLM. As such, it previews some of the divisions to be explored in how CCLM actors conceive of themselves, their movement, and their institutions, and what stands to best advance their goals—differences and divisions that will animate this book's subsequent chapters.

The Roads Taken and Not Taken

As this chapter has demonstrated, the decisions to create law schools and alternative legal training over investing in existing ones reflects a larger pattern repeated over the duration of the Christian Right's existence. As seen in the institutional histories of earlier Christian Right organizations, "[m]ost of the schools were founded . . . by unusually aggressive and dynamic men who then continued to lead the schools they founded. Their followers often deferred to them more completely than they would to the leaders of a college that existed for a century or longer" (Ringenberg 2006 178). While this statement was originally made in reference to Christian colleges and universities, the next chapter will show how it directly applies to Christian conservative law schools as well. Thus, just as with earlier Christian Right political institutions, big personalities with defined views of the world's problems and their solutions form the base for the Christian conservative legal movement and its support structures. Institutional creation is, thus, not just about some idea of efficiency in adding to what one already has, or even advancing a collective vision for the world. It is about maximizing control at every level in bringing one's specific vision to life. *Infiltration* strategies don't meet these collective ends as well as *parallel alternative* approaches do, a realization that helps explain the course of the CCLM support structure development.

What's more, given the continued presence of Jerry Falwell and Pat Robertson, we see not only a repeated pattern of leadership styles, but also repeated central leaders. Their individual political institutional histories show that these are not leaders who are content to work behind the scenes, in collaboration with others, or in a part of or alongside existing institutions. These are men who have a history of creating their own institutions where they can try to exercise maximum control with the aim of maximizing their impact. When they determined a need for traditional political resources, they created their own. When they determined the need for litigation resources, they created their own. When they determined the need for support structures for each they, again, created their own.

Along with the general desire for creating, and further developing, one's own institutions and exercising the highest degree of control, the specific histories of prominent preexisting educational institutions serve as examples of another reason for the lack of adequate post-graduate degree programs generally, and law schools specifically, to serve the Christian conservative population. As such, they help explain why Baylor and Notre Dame, which would appear to be highly attractive options for an *infiltration* approach to creating CCLM support structures, were not meaningfully pursued. Their stories also provide a more general explanation for why *other* preexisting Protestant and Christian law schools were also not targets for *infiltration* investment. Whether they were seen as not being truly religious, or otherwise lacking the diversity and quality of capital possessed by the three schools explored, such criticisms likely reinforced the other impulses expectedly driving the creation of wholly new institutions.

If this chapter has helped contextualize and explain the choices the CCLM did not make in terms of investing in existing Level 1 support structures—the roads not taken by its patrons—the next chapter explores the roads they did take and the consequences of those choices for building support structures for their movement.

In the Beginning: Creation Stories

Having rejected the *infiltration* approach to support structure capacity building, three high-profile patrons of the Christian Right opted to follow in Oral Roberts's footsteps, building their own distinct and distinctly Christian conservative law schools between 1986 and 2004. These *parallel alternative* support structure institutions are, to recall: Regent Law School in Virginia Beach, Virginia, founded in 1986 by Christian Broadcasting Network creator and lawyer Marion "Pat" Robertson; Ave Maria School of Law (AMSL), founded by Domino's Pizza mogul and conservative Catholic patron Thomas Monaghan in Ann Arbor in 1999 but relocated to Naples, Florida, in 2009; and Liberty Law School in Lynchburg, Virginia, founded by Moral Majority leader Jerry Falwell Sr. in 2004.

As we teased in the beginning of the book, not every Christian Right patron followed the Oral Roberts *parallel alternative* approach to institution building. In 2000, patron Alan Sears launched the Blackstone Legal Fellowship as the educational arm of Alliance Defending Freedom (ADF), the largest and most heavily resourced New Christian Right Public Interest Law Firm (Hollis-Brusky & Wilson 2017). Blackstone's summer program provides an alternative legal education and curriculum and social and professional networking connections for Christian conservative law students attending (mostly) non-Christian law schools and represents the *supplemental* approach to support structure building in our study.

In this chapter, we outline the visions for the intentionally transformative missions of each of these support structure institutions. We also preview some of the constraints and challenges each institution faced initially (and continues to face) in attempting to realize its transformative mission: principally, constraints surrounding finances and patronage, accreditation, financial aid, and licensing requirements for attorneys.

Separate But Faithful. Amanda Hollis-Brusky and Joshua C. Wilson, Oxford University Press (2020). © Oxford University Press. DOI: 10.1093/oso/9780190637262.001.0001

Founders, Founding Visions, and Missions

Regent Law School
Founded in 1986 in Virginia Beach, Virginia
Christian Right patron: Marion "Pat" Robertson

"Pat had always wanted to start a law school" (Titus 2016). Marion "Pat" Robertson is a lawyer by training, having graduated near the top of his class from Yale Law School in 1955. But the turning point in his life—one that would direct him initially away from the practice of law—was the religious conversion he underwent shortly thereafter. In the 1960s, following his newfound calling from God, Robertson launched himself full-time into the business of evangelizing and building political and cultural advocacy institutions in service of his conservative evangelical vision. Most notably, Robertson founded the Christian Broadcasting Network (now seen in 180 countries and broadcast in seventy-one languages), the Christian Coalition of America, a conservative Christian advocacy non-profit and voter turnout organization launched in the afterbirth of Robertson's failed bid for the American presidency in 1988, and Christian Broadcasting Network University (CBNU), which would be renamed Regent University in 1990. According to a plaque that hangs outside of the Regent University Administration Building, Robertson founded then–Christian Broadcasting Network University after receiving divine inspiration from God:

> The inspiration for a school at CBN came in August 1975 as Pat Robertson prayed over lunch in Anaheim, California, about purchasing a small parcel of land for CBN. He was suddenly overwhelmed by a sense of God's presence. "Don't buy just five acres," the Lord seemed to say. "Buy the entire tract of land and build a headquarters and school for My glory."[1]

Divine origins aside, Robertson's founding of CBNU, the motto of which is "Christian Leadership to Change the World," also represents a recognition that higher education is a critical component to training and placing future foot soldiers for his movement (*human capital*) into positions of power and influence: leaders in government, public policy, business, and education. Robertson was a savvy politician. But he also recognized a deficit. He was not directly involved in the training and education of future lawyers, the single group Tocqueville recognized as far back as the 1830s as the most influential civic and political group in America (Tocqueville 1835).

So, as we previewed in the Introduction, when fellow Christian televangelist Oral Roberts, who had grown weary from his extended battle for law school accreditation with the American Bar Association and finding himself in difficult financial straits, called Robertson and offered him the law library, Robertson jumped at the chance. He commissioned Herb Titus, who had moved from Oral Roberts to CBNU a few years prior to lead the public policy school, to write a feasibility study and present it to the board of trustees. Titus's blandly titled "Proposed School of Law Feasibility Study" is, in fact, a dramatic read, sweeping in its indictment of American legal education and polemic in its recommendations and call to action. The document's "Introduction" begins with a retelling of America's founding period and the close connection between the founders' natural law philosophy and biblical law:

> Not only did America's founding fathers base their claim for recognition of the United States of America among the family of nations upon the Bible but they sought to build the internal legal and political system of each state and of the United States upon Biblical law . . . In light of this Biblical legacy, America's earliest efforts to educate its people for leadership in law and politics focused upon the laws of God. Not only did law students study Blackstone's Commentaries, itself based upon an analysis of the true meaning of law as contained in the book of Genesis, but they studied the Bible, before they tackled the legal texts, the treatises, and the oases on property, tort, contract, and criminal law. (Titus and Thompson 1985, 1)

But, as Titus continues, American legal education took a wrong turn in 1870, moving "away from its Biblical foundation" and substituting "God's law for 'man's law.'" The chief architect of this decline, Titus asserts, was C. C. Langdell, who, upon assuming the deanship of Harvard Law School, introduced the "case method" of teaching law, which took as its primary assumption the fact that principles of law and legal standards evolved over time as judges applied rules to new cases. In other words, under this new method of legal education, judges and lawyers did not see their job as "discover[ing]" God's law, which was unchanging and rooted in biblical standards, but, rather, judges and lawyers came to see themselves as the "creator(s)" of law and legal standards. As a result, Titus laments, "almost all of today's lawyers have come to believe that man can make whatever law he chooses to govern society," resulting in the "crumbling" of "legal standards" and the "erosion of law and liberty" at the hands of a legal profession steeped in moral and legal relativism (Titus and Thompson 1985, 1, 9).

The need for a law school dedicated to restoring American law to its biblical foundations and to providing a much-needed corrective for the disastrous turn in American legal education is described in equally dramatic terms by Titus: "As America enters into the final fifteen years of the twentieth century, we face the frightful prospect of having no Christian law school serving the nation as a whole that is committed to a curriculum based upon the law of God and infused by the Holy Spirit of truth." Titus continues, "CBN University has a unique opportunity to fill this void, and provide a quality legal education to deserving Christian men and women who desire to be equipped to serve the cause of justice in our land" (Titus and Thompson 1985, 2). Titus then proceeds to outline the "Vision" for the law school in four parts: (1) Re-establish the Law of God ("the Law School will seek to influence the restoration of America's legal and political systems upon the law of God as revealed in the Bible, and thus foster a reformation in American jurisprudence"); (2) Rediscover the National Covenant ("[a]mong but a handful of nations, such as England and Israel, the United States is a covenant people, a free society governed by the consent of that people in national covenant before God"); (3) Reclaim Truth in Education ("[t]he Law School's goal is to produce . . . Biblically grounded law textbooks [which can be] distributed nationwide for the purpose of presenting a truly Christian law text alternative . . . in the hope of influencing other educators to reconsider their teaching materials"); (4) Restore Liberty and Justice ("[t]hrough the careers of its graduates and the dissemination of legal thought by its faculty and students, the Law School proposes to restore justice and liberty to America") (Titus and Thompson 1985, 11–13).

In Titus's study, we clearly see the intentional and intentionally transformative founding vision of what would become Regent Law School. The goal, as we can see, is not simply to provide fellowship and a welcoming campus culture for Christian-identifying law students. The goal is transformative (or restorative if one adheres to Titus's vision): to rebuild the foundations of American law and jurisprudence from the bottom up, beginning with legal education. In his "Vision" statement, Titus articulates the important place law schools occupy as transformative institutions. In points 3 and 4 in particular, Titus references the importance of *human capital* and *intellectual capital* as valuable currency in the battle for the control of the law more broadly. We also see the theme of American exceptionalism, links to the founding period, and the belief that America is unique as a "covenant people" and, thus, has a special responsibility to and place before God. The biblical heritage of America's founding and of its laws, according to Titus, is stated most prominently in the Declaration of Independence, which references the "Creator" and "the laws of nature and nature's God," which, as Titus insists, "were well known terms denoting the Law of God as revealed through God's created order and God's Word" (Titus and Thompson 1985, 1).

More than thirty years since its founding as Christian Broadcasting Network University School of Law, many of these same ideas that inspired the founding vision are visible in the architecture and physical structures on the Regent Law campus. Several architectural elements connect the campus to the American founding period. The architecture of the campus buildings is Colonial Revival, recalling the Georgian architecture of the founding period. The bricks, as our campus tour guide informed us, were manually aged and weathered to give the campus an older, more authentic appearance. The interior paint inside the administration building is a colonial blue-gray, selected because of its connection to America's founding period. The Founders Inn located on Regent campus celebrates the founding generation with rooms such as the Jefferson Amphitheatre, and the Harrison, Franklin, Patrick Henry, and Madison rooms. The Cape Henry Cross and the Eternal Gospel Flame, prominent features on the Regent campus, connect this

American exceptionalism with a broader, global Christian project. The plaque in front of the former reads: "April 29, 1607 *Act One, Scene One of the unfolding drama that became the United States of America.* The first English settlers landed at Cape Henry, planted a wooden cross and claimed the land for God."[2] The plaque in front of the Eternal Gospel Flame—a dramatic, perpetually burning flame encircled by a black and white map of the globe—celebrates the global reach and aspirations of the Christian Broadcasting Network while highlighting the centrality of the United States of America to carrying out its mission.[3]

Despite this apparent continuity between the founding vision of Regent Law and its campus environment, there have also been changes that reflect a tempering of that vision due, in part, as we explain in our constraints sections, to the realities of the legal market, law student recruitment, accreditation, etc. These changes, slight over time but significant when viewed cumulatively, can be seen in the messaging Regent Law has communicated through its "Message from the Dean," the place on the Regent law website where the dean lays out the mission and vision of the law school in an attempt to attract likeminded students. In 1997, for example, the dean's message read like a CliffsNotes version of Titus's 1985 polemic:

> Given the crisis in our legal system and our society, it is not a coincidence that many men and women of all denominations and backgrounds are being called to the legal profession. Regent University School of Law exists for such a time as this. I challenge you to consider our times and to consider your destiny. At Regent you will not study law for law's sake, but for strengthening the remarkable and purposeful relationship that can be found between Judeo-Christian principles and the Constitution given to us by our founding fathers (as cited in Wilson and Hollis-Brusky 2014, 426).

It is important to note here that Titus was removed by Robertson in 1993 in a controversial move we discuss at greater length later in this chapter. However, as we can see, the 1997 dean's message still resembles Regent Law's founding vision and mission. Compare this with the 2018 message from then-Dean Michael Hernandez:

> You are bright, motivated, and interested in law, and you want to pursue an education that will prepare you to be an attorney with a passion for justice who will make a lasting impact on the world. So, why Regent Law? Of the more than 200 fully accredited law schools in the United States, Regent Law offers a unique combination of a Christ-centered mission, a first-rate faculty and academic program, and high levels of student satisfaction.[4]

Apart from the phrase "Christ-centered," this reads like the welcome message from a dean at any non-Christian, non–mission oriented law school. It reads like the mission statement of a school interested, perhaps by necessity, in casting a wider, worldlier net than Titus and Robertson ever envisioned when founding CBNU Law School in 1986.

The "Mission" articulated in the 2018 Dean's Message—"Old and New, National and Global"—also indicates a break from the founding vision of Regent Law and its architectural components. As we explained previously, Regent's founding vision and architecture elevate the "Old" by emphasizing Regent's biblical mission, the "National" by drawing a line connecting the Bible and the American Founding and emphasizing American exceptionalism, and the "Global" by connecting America to the world through its ministry and Christ-centered mission. But what is the "New," and how does this square with Regent's founding mission and vision? After all, Titus and Thompson explicitly rejected the "New" legal training and thinking, an approach that had, he argued, resulted in a descent into moral and legal relativism and the crumbling of our legal system. *Dean Hernandez explains the short-hand mission in the following way:* "Grounded in the best of the old and the new, we lay a foundation of first principles of law, the Western Legal and Common Law traditions, and American Constitutionalism, while equipping students with the contemporary knowledge base and skills necessary to thrive in any law-related discipline."[5] References to "biblical" and "Judeo-Christian" principles have been replaced with the more secular-sounding "first principles," and Regent is also emphasizing its mission to equip students with a "contemporary knowledge base" and provide them with the "skills" they need to be a lawyer. As further evidence of Regent Law casting a wider net beyond the "Old" and trying to appeal to the "New," the recently revamped motto of Regent Law, "practice-ready, purpose-driven,"[6] replaced its longtime motto of "Law is more than a profession. It's a calling" (as cited in Wilson and Hollis-Brusky 2014, 426). As we have argued elsewhere, this "calling" language is a significant feature across Christian faiths and immediately signals to and would attract the members of that community (Wilson and Hollis-Brusky 2014). Regent Law's new motto emphasizes the professional aspects of law ("practice-ready") and replaces the Christian vocational language of "calling" with the more encompassing "purpose-driven." This change, as we explore in the constraints section later in this chapter, reflects a shift in priorities from the mission-central goals and objectives highlighted in the Titus study to the non-mission-related realities of having to operate within the legal profession.

Another important aspect of Regent Law that was not present at the founding but that has become an important part of the appeal of Regent for potential students is its relationship with the American Center for Law and Justice (ACLJ). Founded by Robertson in 1996—the same year Regent Law won full accreditation from the American Bar Association—the ACLJ is a public interest law and litigation organization designed to counterbalance the liberal, anti-Christian, anti-religious influence of the American Civil Liberties Union (ACLU). Returning to the Support Structure Pyramid, we can see the appeal of shaping and producing *human* and *intellectual capital* in Level 1 and then having an immediate pipeline for that *human* and *intellectual capital* into Level 2 litigation efforts. Indeed, as evidence that this relationship was understood and pursued purposefully by Robertson, the ACLJ was initially housed on the upper floor of the law school. But while this relationship would seem like an overwhelmingly positive feature in terms of the Support Structure Pyramid, there is also potential for the law school mission to be coopted or contracted into a narrow focus on litigation and policy while neglecting the broader purposes and functions of institutions of legal education—the production and generation of *social capital, cultural capital*, and *intellectual capital* outside of litigation. We examine the perils and possibilities of this relationship in greater detail in Chapter 5.

Ave Maria School of Law
Founded in 1999 in Ann Arbor, Michigan; Relocated in 2009 to Naples, Florida
Christian Right patron: Thomas Monaghan

"Ex-Pizza Magnate Builds Law School for God," is just one of several sensational headlines communicating Domino's Pizza founder Thomas "Tom" Monaghan's decision to spend $50 million to establish a distinctly Catholic and unabashedly conservative law school in Ann Arbor, Michigan (Hyde 1999, C1). Monaghan, who had been a long-time donor to and supporter of conservative Catholic causes, committed himself full-time to these causes in 1998, selling the majority of his stake in Domino's Pizza for a reported $1 billion (Prud'Homme 1999), which he pledged to use to "promote[ ] his faith" (Suhr 2000). And he has made good on that promise. Monaghan has financed a network of Catholic primary and secondary schools, donated to politicians who oppose abortion, used his newspaper (*Credo*) and the radio station he owns (WDEO) to promote his conservative Catholic agenda, and co-founded The Thomas More Law Center, an anti-abortion public interest law firm (Prud'Homme 1999). Among all of these, Monaghan said that building the law school was "one of the most exciting things I've been involved in in my life . . . one of the most important" (Hyde 1999, C1).

In media reports covering the news at the time, Monaghan cited his disappointment with Catholic education, including Catholic legal education, saying that "much of it has become secularized," as impetus for his new law school (Hyde 1999, C1; Suhr 2000). Monaghan pointed to "[t]he lack of God in our society, the breakup of families, the low legitimacy rate, abortion" as the result of the secularization of legal education (Suhr 2000). AMSL would, according to Monaghan, cure these social and political ills and fill a real Catholic leadership void, becoming "the West Point for Catholic laity in the years to come" (Troy 1999).

Monaghan's law school project attracted more than sensational headlines. It also attracted the attention and support of prominent conservative Catholic political

leaders, legal minds, and jurists. Former federal judge Robert Bork signed on as one
of Ave Maria's first faculty members. Then–Supreme Court Justice Antonin Scalia
helped consult on the design of the curriculum along with conservative legal scholar
and Notre Dame professor Charles Rice (Hyde 1999; Bullard 2000). The founding
board of governors of Ave Maria Law School included U.S. Representative Henry
Hyde, the most "fervently anti-abortion" national legislator; Helen Alvare, who
worked for the Pro-Life Secretariat of the National Conference of Catholic Bishops;
the archbishop of New York, Cardinal Edward Egan; Princeton professor Robert
George; Kate O'Beirne of the prominent conservative *National Review* magazine;
and conservative activist Alan Keyes. Surveying its founding faculty and board, the
National Catholic Reporter assessed AMSL as having "a more conservative religious
orientation than any existing Catholic law school in the nation" and went so far as to
label the school as "militantly religious" (Schaeffer 1999).

Monaghan's announcement was not received as welcome news in other cor-
ners of the Catholic community. The move prompted some head-scratching from
Catholic leadership and administrators at the time who thought his "money would
have been better spent on any of the more than 20 existing Catholic law schools nationwide" (Suhr 2000). Other Catholic legal leaders responded more defensively.
Monika K. Hellwig, executive director of the Association of Catholic Colleges and
Universities, insisted that "Catholic law schools, and the Jesuit schools in particular,
have been offering legal clinics for the poor and addressing Catholic social teachings
for years. They pride themselves in being extremely Catholic" (Fitzgerald 2014,
246). Some Catholic law professors called Monaghan's project "presumptuous" and
part of a thinly veiled conservative "political agenda" rather than his professed devo-
tion to Catholic legal education (Suhr 2000). In the parlance of Support Structure
Theory, these Catholic leaders saw Monaghan's decision to reject the *infiltration*
path as a missed strategic opportunity at best and a move motivated by political
hubris at worst.

Ave Maria's early success in recruiting quality students and faculty seemed to put
these criticisms from the Catholic community on pause. Like Regent Law's "first-in"
positioning (after the collapse of Oral Roberts) within the evangelical law school
space, AMSL could claim "first-in" for a distinctly conservative Catholic law school,
as a haven for faculty and students who believed that the Catholic legal education at
Notre Dame, Georgetown, Detroit Mercy, and other Catholic law schools was not
"true" Catholic legal education (Fitzgerald 2014, 289–291). Bernard Dobranski, a
graduate of Notre Dame and University of Virginia Law School, left his deanship
at the law school of the Catholic University of America in Washington, D.C., to become the founding Dean of AMSL. In Monaghan's words, the hire of Dobranski
provided "immediate credibility in the legal community."[7] The six founding full-
time teaching faculty of AMSL also had elite legal training and credentials. Four of
the six received their JD from Notre Dame Law School (Richard Myers, Stephen
Safranek, Joseph Falvey, and Mollie Murphy), and the other two were Harvard Law

(Howard Bromberg) and University of Chicago Law (Robert Bork) graduates. As for student recruitment, thanks to generous financial aid and scholarship packages made possible by the initial Monaghan gift, AMSL appeared to be hitting way above its entering weight class. Its first graduating class in 2003 had an almost "unheard of bar passage rate of 93% for first-time takers" for the Michigan bar exam. The second class upped the bar passage rate to 100%, and in 2006, 96% of graduates from AMSL who took the Michigan bar exam passed (Newton 2008). Its application for full accreditation with the American Bar Association was approved in a non-controversial vote in 2005.

This early track record of success was, however, interrupted (some would argue derailed entirely) when Monaghan and the AMSL Board of Governors announced plans in February 2007 to relocate the law school from Ann Arbor, Michigan, to southwest Florida. Monaghan had purchased a tract of land in Florida that would become Ave Maria Town, a planned conservative "Catholic paradise" (Taylor 2016), where he was also building his undergraduate university (Ave Maria University). In the interim, the plan was to relocate the law school to Naples, Florida, while construction and permitting was underway in the township of Ave Maria.

The announcement of the plan to relocate AMSL provoked swift and serious opposition from faculty and alumni. A majority of the faculty issued a vote of no confidence in Dean Dobranski, passed a resolution opposing the move to Florida, and lodged a complaint with the American Bar Association (Schultz 2007). Three of the faculty most vocally opposed to the move filed a whistleblower lawsuit against AMSL after two were denied tenure and the third, founding faculty member Stephen Safranek, was suspended (Schultz 2007). The alumni board backed the faculty, issuing a vote of no confidence in the leadership of AMSL and calling for the resignations of both Dobranski and Tom Monaghan (Schultz 2007). A news report of their statement reads:

> "The Alumni Association Board of Directors believes our alma mater's early success counsels against a decision to close the school in Michigan," says the statement. "We have difficulty believing that Ave Maria School of Law's amazing success is sufficiently likely to recur after " 'relocation.' "[8]

In the end, the lawsuits, complaints, and opposition to the move failed to dissuade the board or Monaghan to change their plans, and the law school relocated to Naples, Florida, in 2009.

Those who moved with the school from Michigan to Florida, a group that included founding Dean Dobranski and only two of the core group of six founding faculty (Myers and Murphy, who are married to one another), insist that the mission and identity of AMSL remain the same. One administrator, who has been with AMSL since the Michigan days, noted that "the move of the school really was difficult" because most of the "core group" of "original faculty" did not come. This administrator noted that the "curriculum" and the focus remain the same and that the reconstituted Naples faculty is "as committed to the mission as it ever has been" (Ave Maria Administrator 1 2015). The mission itself, as articulated by AMSL, has not changed at all over time. An examination of online mission statements over time, courtesy of the "Wayback Machine,"[9] corroborates this. Unlike Regent, whose mission statement has evolved dramatically since the founding days of Herb Titus, AMSL's founding mission statement[10] and its current mission (below) statement are nearly identical.

> Ave Maria School of Law is a Catholic law school dedicated to educating lawyers with the finest professional skills. Inspired by Pope John Paul II's encyclical *Fides et Ratio*, Ave Maria School of Law offers a distinctive legal education—an education characterized by the harmony of faith and reason. Formed by outstanding professional training and a distinctive educational philosophy, Ave Maria's graduates are equipped for leading positions in law firms, corporate legal offices, the judiciary, and national, state, and local government.[11]

The only difference between the founding and current mission statements is the verb tense. The founding mission statement used the future tense ("will be") while the current mission statement uses the present ("are"). This consistency in mission and branding likely explains why, when asked to describe the school's mission in interviews, students, faculty, and administrators could, and sometimes did, recite the mission statement by heart, or could at least recall the shorthand in Latin, *Fides et Ratio* ("faith and reason"). One 1L (first year) law student was even asked to put it as an extra credit answer on an exam.

Faculty and administrators interviewed at AMSL also seemed to have a clear sense of how their institution could and hopefully would contribute to the broader support structure for legal and constitutional development. A top AMSL administrator said that "[o]ur mission is to develop, instill, cultivate, produce lawyers that will go out into society and practice law in a way that they see it as a vocation, as a calling from God. That they will bring to their practice natural law and the teachings of the Catholic Church" (Ave Maria Administrator 2 2015). And in an excerpt that recalls Monaghan's "West Point for Catholic laity" (Troy, 1999) vision from the founding period, another administrator articulated the impact of AMSL in the following manner:

> Some of our early alums are just starting into that mid—or early mid—career stage, but once we have more of those who become judges, who become legislators, who become leaders in law firms and organizations that lead throughout the country. My hope is that you'll start to see . . . a more transformative influence on the legal profession as a whole. (Ave Maria Administrator 3 2015)

Again, putting this in terms of Support Structure Theory, AMSL is conscious about how it is producing *human capital* and aspirational in terms of the transformative effect that capital will have on the broader legal profession.

There is at least one way in which the realization of Monaghan's founding mission and vision for AMSL has been compromised by the move to Naples, Florida. While in Ann Arbor, Michigan, students had direct access to the Thomas More Law Center, the Monaghan-founded and funded conservative Catholic public interest law firm. Located in the same Monaghan-owned office complex as AMSL ("Domino's Farms"), the Thomas More Law Center gave students direct access to and experience with conservative Catholic litigation. The Thomas More Center was co-founded by Monaghan in 1988. Like Robertson and Regent Law's ACLJ, the litigation firm was founded to "restore and defend America's Judeo-Christian heritage" and to counter "the destructive impact of organizations like the ACLU."[12] Also recalling the relationship between the ACLJ and Regent Law, AMSL was built a mere stone's throw away from the Thomas More Law Center, making the ties between the two—and the *human, intellectual, cultural, social capital* transfer—easy and easily identifiable. By moving the law school away from Domino's Farms and into southwest Florida, Monaghan effectively severed the pipeline between AMSL and Thomas More Law Center, a fact that, among many other factors, has hurt recruitment of true-believing mission students for whom this opportunity would have been attractive.

Visiting the Naples, Florida, campus today, one is immediately struck by the juxtaposition of old, traditional Catholicism and Catholic symbols with the "Floridification" of the law school. The palm tree–lined Naples campus is located in a converted nursing home. Stucco exterior, Spanish red-tile roofs, and pools around campus create a resort-style feel to the exterior. Inside, however, the décor clearly communicates and centers the law school's Catholicism. In addition to the "Respect Life Garden" and courtyard, the interior halls feature crucifixes, pictures of Catholic cardinals and bishops, statues of saints, and other standard Catholic decor. The law school also clearly broadcasts its conservative credentials. In a nostalgic nod to its founding location, AMSL's "Michigan Room" features pictures of prominent conservative figures who have spoken at the law school: Supreme Court Justice Clarence Thomas, former Republican governor of Florida Jeb Bush, former Reagan attorney general and Heritage Foundation fellow Edwin Meese III, and former Chief of Staff to George W. Bush Karl Rove.

Interview data with current faculty, administrators, and students confirms that the school does not attempt to water down its mission orientation or political orientation in its recruiting materials or self-presentation and marketing. AMSL is proud of its status as Number 1 in National Jurist Pre-law Magazine's "Best Law Schools for the Devout" (this appears in recruiting flyers, and the plaque hangs prominently in the main campus building) and also touts on its website main page its "Most Conservative" honorific from this same magazine.[13] Speaking with faculty and administrators, AMSL believes that its distinctly conservative Catholic brand is one that sets it apart from other law schools, one that it is proud to promote.

Blackstone Legal Fellowship of Alliance Defending Freedom
Founded in 2000 in Scottsdale, Arizona
Christian Right patron: Alan Sears

"Obviously, we're not here to play games or put in time—we are here to win, seeing a day when our legal systems and our cultures, now in so many ways so set against the Truth of God, are transformed to protect the sacredness of life, marriage, family, and religious liberty" (Carosa 2014). This is how Alan Sears, a longtime culture warrior and veteran of the Reagan administration, where he worked closely with Attorney General Edwin Meese as the chairman of his infamous pornography commission (Lewis 1986), described his motivation for founding Alliance Defending Freedom (ADF; formerly Alliance Defense Fund), which has grown to be the largest and best funded Christian conservative public interest law firm in the United States (Hollis-Brusky & Wilson 2017; Bennett 2017). In 2000, with Sears at the helm, ADF launched its Blackstone Legal Fellowship to provide training and education for Christian law students throughout the country, training and education that ADF believed would better position it "to win" the longer-term battles Sears cites against a legal profession and culture "set against the Truth of God."

Located at ADF's headquarters in Scottsdale, Arizona, the competitive fellowship program has grown from 24 fellows in 2000 to 158 fellows in 2015.[14] According to ADF's 2017 public tax filings, the Blackstone program has trained 1,962 law students from 227 law schools.[15] Phase I of Blackstone Fellowship is a two-week educational boot camp in the natural law with a rotating set of faculty who lead seminars and devotionals designed to address "challenges facing Christians in the legal profession." According to a top Blackstone administrator, the readings and topics of these seminars vary according to what is currently of interest to fellows and faculty (Blackstone Administrator 1 2015). Phase II is a six-week internship and Phase III is a one-week, end-of-the summer career development seminar designed to help fellows "develop a deeper vision of their professional calling."[16]

According to our interviews with Blackstone leaders, the program came to be as a result of "the negative experience that Alan Sears had when he was in law school, that he was alone, that the other side was not articulated, except to be perhaps ridiculed or caricatured" (Blackstone Administrator 1 2015). Similar to the law schools' statements, Sears built the Blackstone Fellowship to create "intellectual balance" in the presentation of law and legal foundations and to make sure that conservative Christian law students across the country knew that they were not alone. (Blackstone Administrator 1 2015). ADF's public tax filings in 2001 articulate the purpose of the Blackstone Legal Fellowship in more explicit, support structure–oriented terms:

This summer-long leadership development program in law and servant ministry is unlike any other legal internship program ever offered. As a rigorous internship for exceptionally capable and highly motivated law students, the Blackstone Fellowship inspires a distinctly Christian world-view in every area of law, and particularly in the areas of public policy and religious liberty. With this ongoing program, it's ADF's goal to train a new generation of lawyers who will rise to positions of influence and leadership as legal scholars, litigators, judges—and perhaps even Supreme Court Justices—who will work to ensure that justice is carried out in America's courtrooms.[17]

Echoing this language but muting the "Christian worldview" aspect, a Blackstone administrator explained to us in an interview that influencing the law and judicial outcomes needs to start from the bottom up: "Unless you're dealing with the law profession culture, you're not going to influence the Court, you're not going to have the right decisions, so to speak" (Blackstone Administrator 1 2015). While this is similar to statements we heard at the law schools, Blackstone's approach to changing legal culture and precedent is distinct in a few important ways.

Evidence from interviews suggests that Blackstone was explicitly designed to respond to and supplement perceived deficiencies not only in mainstream legal education but also in distinctly Christian conservative education:

We weren't opposed to Christian Law Schools, heaven forbid, but . . . that's just not the only game in town nor should it be . . . I'm all for distinctively Christian education but we have to think that through when you're talking about a profession . . . I went to a top 10, top 15 law school because I knew that it provided the capital, the credentialing point to allow me to have many options versus no options or minimal options. (Blackstone Administrator 1 2015)

This quote illustrates a consistent thread of concern we heard throughout our interviews with Blackstone staff and alumni about avoiding what we will paraphrase as "the crazy Christian" stigma: concerns with having proper "credentialing" (Blackstone Administrator 1 2015) and having enough "credibility capital" (Blackstone Administrator 2 2015) to influence the legal profession and the wider world. The founders and current leadership of Blackstone are intentional about the kinds of faculty and students they recruit for participation in the fellowship (increasingly drawing their participants from top-10, top-20 law schools), and while they offer a distinctly Christian training and curriculum for their summer interns, there is a strong focus on networking and professional development. As one of the media-focused administrators at Blackstone put it to us in our interview, you need "credibility capital" to be taken seriously in the legal profession:

Because you can have the money, you can have the people, and you can have your own institutions, but the fact is . . . you have to play on the field that's there. You don't show up at a stadium where there's no game. You have to go to the institutions of influence so you can influence those institutions. Because otherwise you're staying in the corner by yourself. (Blackstone Administrator 2 2015)

Here we see how the Blackstone leadership identifies the limitations of the *parallel alternative* approach to producing *human* and *social capital*, and the virtues of a *supplemental* approach. Initially drawing more heavily from mission-oriented schools like Regent and Ave Maria for its students, Blackstone now primarily recruits from and attracts JD candidates from Ivy League and top-50 law schools (Blackstone Administrator 3 2015). Its faculty, while variable from year to year, typically includes those who graduated from and now teach at nationally prestigious institutions. A list we obtained of past Blackstone faculty includes five Notre Dame Law School Faculty—Amy Coney Barrett, Richard Garnett, John Nagle, Charles Rice, and O. Carter Snead—as well as faculty from George Mason University School of Law,[18] Baylor University,[19] and University of Texas at Austin.[20]

Blackstone also rotates in non-academics to demonstrate the real-world applicability of its education and programming and to facilitate networking opportunities between leading Christian Right actors and its interns. Past faculty have included David French of *National Review Magazine*, Kyle Duncan, General Counsel of the Becket Fund (and now a Trump-appointed federal judge), Christian commentator and media personality Hugh Hewitt, Jennifer Marshall of the Heritage Foundation, Jennifer Roback Morse of The Ruth Institute and Timothy Goeglein of Focus on the Family. As one Blackstone alum noted, the program "takes it beyond the academic to the practical. You're talking about these world views of these theories, but then, 'Okay, well, how's that affect how we look at social issues, how we approach the role of government, how we approach our role in society?'" (Blackstone Alum 1 2015).

This programmatic focus on the practical application of a Blackstone education in government and in society further illustrates the leadership's emphasis on being taken seriously by mainstream elites. Again, in our interview, administrators repeatedly emphasized the importance of image and "credibility capital" with "elites" and "elite institutions," saying that ADF and Blackstone sought to steer the movement away from the stigma of the crazy Christian so that "[i]t's not just Bayou Bill Bob saying, 'God's law over Man's law!'" (Blackstone Administrator 2 2015). Echoing the same sentiment, another top administrator emphasized that the goal is to persuade the broader public that "We're not from Cookville" and that they are not "the Bible thumping loud obnoxious fools" (Blackstone Administrator 1 2015). By engaging with the mainstream institutions and actors in a serious way, by not "staying in a corner by yourself" (Blackstone Administrator 2 2015), ADF and Blackstone hope to pull the mainstream toward them rather than pushing the mainstream (and the wider world) away from them.

Reinforcing its aspirations to avoid the crazy Christian stigma, ADF's and Blackstone's public-facing visage has been scrubbed of much of the Titus-esque, "Christian Worldview," culture wars polemic language we pulled from the organization's 990 filing form in 2001. For example, ADF and Blackstone are located in a sleek office park in Scottsdale, Arizona. As we toured the building with an employee of ADF, there were virtually no visible tells that we were, in fact, in the belly of the Christian Right litigating beast. Two weeks shy of Christmas, a large, tastefully decorated tree adorned the lobby as we waited for our hosts to greet us, but absent from sight were any crucifixes, statues, paintings, or the other religious symbolism we had been accustomed to seeing at the law schools we visited. During our tour, we saw a few crosses in individual cubicles of attorneys and other employees at work, but nothing ostentatiously or aggressively Christian. Most memorable from our tour was the media bullpen, a room with half a dozen televisions, each broadcasting a different cable news network. Our tour guide noted that his team at ADF and Blackstone receives extensive media training and then said something to the effect of (and we paraphrase) "we train them so they don't go on TV and confirm the crazy Christian image." We will return to this when we discuss Blackstone's leveraging of and production of *cultural capital* in Chapter 5.

Along with its media and messaging savvy as an organization, Blackstone recognizes the importance of networking. Blackstone, through internships, has an intentional and explicit focus on networking or providing *social capital* for the CCLM (Conservative Christian Legal Movement). As articulated in ADF's public tax filings, once law school students complete the Blackstone Fellowship program, "they've gained practical experience, forged relationships with likeminded attorneys, and caught a vision for how God can use them as judges, law professors, and practicing attorneys to help keep the door open for the spread of the Gospel in America."[21] While the Christian law schools we visited aspire to do the same, the evidence of being well positioned to do so was often unclear at best. Students at Liberty and Ave Maria, for example, were not readily able to identify such networks beyond a broader statement regarding the quality of their faculty. Blackstone's internship program, thus, illustrates how it both pulls from and stands to affect the other layers of the pyramid. Blackstone's capital is increased by its connection to Level 2 institutions (including but not limited to ADF), it uses its internship program to transfer this capital to the fellows, and the fellows are then positioned to use this capital—along with that from their mainstream law schools—in order to successfully pursue high-status careers from which they stand to change law, policy, and culture.

Liberty Law School
Founded in 2004 in Lynchburg, Virginia
Christian Right patron: Jerry Falwell

"We certainly are training Christian activists . . . We're turning their attention to understand the Bible is the infallible word of God, that the American Constitution is a sacred document and that the Christian worldview is their matrix of service" (Schwartz 2004). This is how Jerry Falwell, long-time Christian Right political activist and patron, explained the purpose of Liberty Law School, founded in 2004 at Falwell's Liberty University in Lynchburg, Virginia. Liberty Law School's creation story includes familiar threads from those of Regent, Ave Maria, and Blackstone— a politically savvy and well-resourced Christian Right patron disgruntled with the shrinking role of religion in the public square, a belief that higher education in general and legal education in particular had become secularized and captured by liberals, and the desire to train a generation of Christian attorneys who could work to restore law and America to its biblical heritage and foundations. A televangelist and pastor at the Thomas Road Baptist megachurch, Falwell was also the co-founder and leader of the Moral Majority, a group of conservative pastors and televangelists who became organized and politically active in the late-1970s to counter what they characterized as attacks on religious values and religious institutions by government. While many cite the Supreme Court's decision in *Roe v. Wade* (1973) as a catalyst for the Moral Majority, as Randall Balmer has documented, the IRS decision in 1974 to remove tax-exempt status from Bob Jones University for its refusal to allow interracial dating (for professedly religious or biblical reasons) played a key role in activating the Moral Majority (Balmer 2014). Viewing this decision as an attack on the autonomy of Christian institutions and on Christian higher education specifically, Falwell complained, "In some states it's easier to open a massage parlor than to open a Christian school" (Wertheimer 2006).

The Moral Majority started as a rag-tag group of preachers, according to Falwell: "When we started Moral Majority, we were novices. You could have gotten most of our preachers who were interested in public policy in a phone booth at the time" (CNN 2007). As we describe in some detail in Chapter 2, this rag-tag group grew and quickly became a force in American politics, claiming credit for turning out thousands of first-time voters to elect President Ronald Reagan in 1980 and for electing Republicans down-ticket. As Falwell has said, "We just got everybody registered. We got them to the polls. And they pulled an R and went on down with Rs and 12 liberal senators went out of business" (CNN 2007).

Before Falwell created the Moral Majority, he had founded and served as president of Liberty Baptist College in Lynchburg, Virginia. After his successful first foray into politics in 1980, Falwell grew his college to university status and changed its name to Liberty University. Like Pat Robertson, Falwell's experience in the public square affirmed the importance of building institutions that would train, socialize, and credential the next generation of leaders in fields outside of theology; fields such as government, business, education. Liberty University's long-time motto is "Training Champions for Christ," and there is an overt emphasis on leadership development with an eye toward "reclaiming the world" for Christ.[22] The

Liberty University website connects this motto to founder Jerry Falwell's vision and legacy: "In 1971, Rev. Jerry Falwell Sr. dreamed about world change. He envisioned a generation of professionals in every field who loved God, served others, and were the best at whatever they were called to be. He saw a university on a mountain where this training could happen—and he started to build it."[23] Falwell's influence and imprimatur on the culture of Liberty University has been strong and long-lasting. Speaking to reporters after Falwell's death in 2007, Liberty University students cited Falwell's call to be "Champions for Christ" as providing meaning and inspiration for them and talked about the importance getting out of "the Christian bubble" so they can "change the world" (Santos and Stallsmith 2007).

Before he died, Jerry Falwell fulfilled what several sources confirmed was his long-time dream of building a law school at Liberty University. As a pamphlet obtained during a campus tour describes, "When Dr. Falwell founded Liberty University in 1971, he envisioned that the first professional school of the University would be a law school."[24] According to Herb Titus, Falwell and Liberty University president A. Pierre Guillermin had brought him in as a consultant on the feasibility and design of a law school at Liberty University in the early 1980s when Titus was starting the Public Policy School at CBNU (Titus 2016). For reasons we were told relating to the finances of Liberty University, it took Falwell thirty-four years to make his vision a reality (Liberty Faculty 3 2015). In a prepared statement for the opening of Liberty Law, Falwell put the importance of the founding of Liberty Law School on par with the Liberty Seminary in terms of fulfilling the Christian mission:

> The opening of the LU School of Law in 2004 compares in importance with the establishment of our Seminary in 1973. The training of pastors, missionaries, evangelists and theological teachers enables us to fulfill our calling to be "the light of the world," as we evangelize the nations for Christ. The new School of Law enables us to fulfill our calling as "the salt of the earth," confronting the culture and raising a standard for righteousness. This is a historic occasion and I am very excited.[25]

Falwell's use of the phrase "historic occasion" in this prepared statement is more than marketing. He believed that founding Liberty Law School was a pivotal moment in the history of law writ large, one that would help reorient America and the world back to its Christian foundations and principles.

That Falwell believed that the founding of his law school was a "historic occasion" is vividly illustrated in a series of six large commissioned paintings displayed prominently in Foundations Hall, the main hallway of Liberty Law School. The series of paintings by the Lynchburg, Virginia–based artist Paul Dinwiddie is called the *History of the Rule of Law* and depicts six of the allegedly most important moments in the history of the rule of law. Painting 1 depicts the Christian creation myth from the Book of Genesis, with God as "Creator and Source of Law." Painting 2 in the series, *The Judeo-Christian Foundation for Law Is Laid*, shows Moses receiving the Ten Commandments. Painting 3 depicts the signing of the Magna Carta in England, while Painting 4, *A New Nation Is Born—Under God and the Rule of Law*—is a scene from the birth of the United States of America. The Founding Fathers are standing together around a desk in a wheat field with language from the Declaration of Independence, the preamble to the Constitution, and the Bill of Rights scrawled across it, and the brochure language emphasizes the Declaration's reference to rights coming from "our Creator" as evidence of the biblical foundations of America's founding documents.

Painting 5, *Breakdown in the Rule of Law*, is the most dramatic in the series. It portrays the outside of the United States Supreme Court encircled in dark, ominous clouds with protestors holding signs for and against abortion, for and against school prayer, for and against the Ten Commandments being posted in public spaces. In the lower right hand corner we can barely make out an overturned police car and in the upper left hand corner we see swirling around in the dark clouds copies of Charles Darwin's *The Origin of Species*, Alfred Kinsey's book, *Sexual Behavior*, the *Humanist Manifesto*, and Sidney Simon's textbook on *Values Clarification*. The brochure description recounts the moral and legal decline of America on account of removing God from schools and the public square and embracing evolution, moral relativism, and the sexual revolution. With the Supreme Court at "the epicenter" of this seismic shift in law and culture, the brochure laments that "America has become a nation that has tried to uncouple its destiny from the Divine and turned from absolute Truth and the transcendental values of our forebears. But it is not too late. There is still hope for recovery and restoration of the rule of law."

Painting 6, the final in the series, is called *Restoration of the Rule of Law*. The painting shows Jerry Falwell, eyes closed, kneeling in prayer in front of an empty courtroom of the United States Supreme Court. Above Falwell's head we see the seal of Liberty Law School emerging from blindingly bright light and clouds, as if it were God's answer to Falwell's prayers. In the upper right hand corner, we see an ethereal rendering of Liberty Law's graduating class, who also appear to be heads down in prayer, hovering over the Supreme Court. Finally, the marble Lady Liberty who adorns the exterior of the Supreme Court is inside the courtroom with her blindfold and the scales of justice. The brochure describes the founding, mission, and vision of Liberty Law in this grand historical context and affirms the historic importance Falwell ascribed to his role and to Liberty Law's role in returning law to its proper foundations:

> Our motto is *ad fontes*, which is Latin for "back to the sources." Law is a manifestation of God's character. When the foundation of law is properly understood and applied, law is designed to protect life over death, exalt liberty over tyranny, and bring order out of chaos. But, when the foundation is destroyed or distorted, law has the opposite effect. It promotes death

over life, elevates tyranny over liberty, and creates chaos instead of order. The mission of Liberty is to restore the foundations of law by grounding it in transcendent principles in the context of the Christian intellectual tradition in honor and conformity to the higher law of our Creator.

The Christian Worldview message is clear: Falwell and Liberty Law are an integral part of the restoration of law to its biblical and Christian foundations.

Liberty Law's mission statement and Dean's messages have also been framed in these transcendent terms. While more muted in its call-to-arms than Regent Law's original mission statement described earlier, Liberty Law's original mission statement has a distinctly Christian character and moral or normative content. Here is an excerpt from Liberty's original "About us" description from 2003:

> We believe the rule of law is rooted in transcendent principles and objective moral order and, as a result, law places an extrinsic restraint on people's actions, especially morally deficient people. We believe that law should not be wielded as an instrument of political, social, or personal change, but that it should serve the common good of mankind. We believe there exists a foundational moral law that, by its very nature, is fixed, uniform, and universal, and thus applicable at all times, to all people, in all places. It transcends men and women and forms the proper basis for all human laws.[26]

Like we saw with Regent, Liberty Law's "About us" or mission statement has also evolved dramatically over time. It is now more about "skills" or professional training and opportunity and is more descriptive of the law school experience than about the broader importance of law's transcendence, moral character, and universality.[27] However, it still maintains and broadcasts its distinctly Christian and biblical orientation. For example, while highlighting its lawyering skills program (a program we heard about repeatedly during interviews with students and faculty), Liberty still promotes the Christian roots of its training: "Because our rigorous legal skills program is taught from a Christian worldview, we'll not only prepare you with the core competency skills you'll need to practice law, we'll teach you how to integrate faith and reason into your field."[28]

While, as we see, the vision and mission of Liberty Law have been framed in very historically significant and even transcendent terms, the physical space in which the law school is housed, a recently remodeled building acquired from a cell phone manufacturing plant that left Lynchburg (Schwartz 2004), does not reflect these historic and transcendent aims. When we visited Liberty Law, the windowless, converted-factory campus, which is removed from the broader main campus of Liberty University, had the feeling of an isolated compound or a bunker. If Falwell wanted his students to break out of the "Christian bubble," and to interact with the wider world, the physical space in which they are trained and incubated as lawyers is one that promotes the opposite—isolation and seclusion from the wider world. One reporter who visited the campus described what he saw as the disconnect between Liberty Law's grandiose mission and marketing and its physical space:

> Liberty School of Law's catalog features photos of grandiose cathedrals, stone-carved passageways, gothic spires, and starkly lit columns. The school itself sits in a corner of a building surrounded by a metal fence and connected to an 800,000-square-foot industrial compound. The complex used to house an Ericsson cell phone plant. Located just outside Lynchburg, Va., a historic river town, Liberty Law is flanked by strip malls, the roar of the highway, and radio towers that dot the hills of the Blue Ridge Mountains. Inside, where the school occupies a single long floor, the décor is Best-Western-meets-dentist's-office. (Gagnon 2004)

As that same reporter put it, "The school's factory-like setting isn't a bad fit for its mission. From the pulpit, Falwell recently said that Liberty Law is in the business of manufacturing 'junkyard dog lawyers who believe in God and the Bible'" (Gagnon 2004). Similarly, Falwell told one audience in 2004 that Liberty Law was going to "train a few thousand Christian attorneys who are just as radical as the preachers" (Americans United 2004).

As the last entrant into the Christian Right legal education market of the three law schools in our study—entering 18 years after Regent Law and 5 after AMSL— Liberty Law has benefited from and faced distinct challenges on account of this last-in positioning. Being a later entrant into the Christian conservative legal market, Liberty benefited from the accreditation battles earlier schools had fought and won. Liberty also benefited by being able to hire Regent graduates and faculty who had the right training and orientation. For example, Bruce Green, Liberty's founding dean, was a Regent Law graduate, and Jeffrey Tuomala, Liberty's original Dean for Academic Affairs, was a Regent Professor and had worked closely with Herb Titus. Roger Bern had also worked with Herb Titus to develop the curriculum for the O. W. Coburn School of Law at Oral Roberts University as an original faculty member there before moving to Regent Law and eventually helping to launch Liberty Law in 2003 as part of its inaugural faculty (Titus 2016). As we discuss in greater detail in the next chapter, Liberty's later entrance into the market, though, may have disadvantaged it in terms of attracting faculty with more broadly recognized legal capital.

Until very recently, Liberty Law could also offer its students a direct pipeline into litigation—a way to transfer their Level 1 training into Level 2 advocacy, in the parlance of the Support Structure Pyramid. In a 2003 deal brokered by Jerry Falwell, Liberty Law formed a partnership with the Orlando, Florida–based Liberty Counsel, a Christian Right public interest law organization (PILO) founded and led by Mathew Staver. The terms of the partnership included Staver opening up a branch of Liberty Counsel in Lynchburg, Virginia, and establishing the Center for Constitutional Litigation and Policy (later renamed the Liberty Center for Law and Policy) on Liberty Law's campus to "train law students in all aspects of constitutional litigation, with a particular emphasis on the defense of religious liberty, the sanctity of human life, and traditional family values."[29] The partnership with Staver and Liberty Counsel is a clear manifestation of Jerry Falwell's vision for Liberty Law—a place where radical "junkyard dog lawyers" would be trained and then take their battles directly before the Supreme Court. Speaking of Staver, his colleague Rena Lindevaldsen said he is someone who is "committed to 'fighting the cultural battles' to restore prayer in schools and to overturn *Roe v. Wade*" (Hammack 2012). Staver became the second Dean of Liberty Law in 2006, serving eight years before resigning in October 2014 over what many speculate was a precipitous decline in bar passage rates for graduates (Walls 2014).

Staver's deanship and the prominent presence of Liberty Counsel on campus was controversial among some of the faculty we interviewed, who viewed his single-minded, one-track focus on litigating the culture wars as myopic in a broader law school environment. According to one faculty member who wished to remain anonymous, Staver "had this school so focused on religious liberty public interest law and Liberty Counsel specifically that I think at times it was hard to recruit students if they didn't have that vision." Continuing, this faculty said that during Staver's deanship "there were some dark days here" that forced some faculty out. Another faculty member said Staver's recruitment of the "culture war sort" of faculty and his intense focus on Liberty Counsel resulted in "the law school [being] neglected." For all its advantages in terms of recruiting policy-minded students and plugging them directly into litigation, this partnership, which was effectively dissolved after Staver's departure from Liberty Law, illustrates the perils of Level 2 institutions and agendas co-opting Level 1 institutions and losing sight of the broader education and preparation of its students, what Herb Titus referred to in our interview as "the tail wagging the dog" (Titus 2016).

Contextual Realities and Constraints in Realizing the Mission

The *parallel alternative* and *supplemental* approaches to support structure building each come with a degree of control over the resulting institutional culture and capital production—a degree of control that is higher than that afforded by the *infiltration* approach. But as we emphasized in Chapter 1, because these institutions exist within professional, financial, and political contexts, patrons do not have complete control over their institutional creations. There are known constraints and unknown constraints. In the sections that follow, we focus on the known constraints and contextual realities of building *parallel alternative* and *supplemental* institutions within the context of the legal profession, risks these Christian Right patrons factored in and assumed when they decided to build their institutions. This section raises the broader question of how insurgent movements such as the Christian Right can effect transformative change from within the very profession they are challenging while simultaneously working within its rules and responding to its market forces (Wilson and Hollis-Brusky 2018).

"Unholy Alliance"—The Perils of ABA Accreditation

According to Titus (2016), "Liberty wouldn't be in existence today, neither would Ave Maria be in existence today, except for [Oral Roberts]. Regent wouldn't be in existence . . . he was the one who'd go to battle . . . that's what changed the rule and changed the whole course of the effort." As we recount in the Introduction, the accreditation battle between Oral Roberts University's O. W. Coburn School of Law and the American Bar Association (ABA) did, in fact, change "the whole course of the effort" for these Christian Worldview institutions. O. W. Coburn School of Law was initially denied provisional accreditation by the association because it required students and faculty to take an oath stating that they "will endeavor to exemplify Christ-like character . . . through faithful group worship on and off campus" and "I will yield my personality to the healing and maturing power of the Holy Spirit" (Barbash 1981). The ABA argued that this oath was in clear violation of Standard 211, which stated that that a law school "shall foster and maintain equality of opportunity in legal education, including employment of faculty and staff, without discrimination on the basis of race, color, religion, national origin, gender or sexual orientation, age or disability" (Winter 1981, 1095–96).

Oral Roberts who, in Titus's words, was a "no-compromise guy" (Titus 2016), refused to allow the ABA's initial denial to stand. Roberts and his team of lawyers took the battle to federal court, alleging that the ABA had violated the private law school's right to free exercise of religion under the First Amendment of the U.S. Constitution (Winter 1981, 1095). U.S. District Judge James B. Moran agreed, "saying that because accreditation is a requirement of state laws, ABA decisions become tantamount to government actions penalizing a religious group and interfering with the free exercise of religion" (Barbash 1981). The court order forced the ABA delegates to vote to reverse their decision and grant provisional approval to O. W. Coburn School of Law. More importantly, however, the case prompted the ABA, after a heated debate among the delegates, to adopt a forty-eight-word amendment to Standard 211 that stated:

> Nothing herein shall be construed to prevent a law school from having a religious affiliation and purpose and adopting policies of admission and employment that directly relate to such affiliation and purpose so long as notice of such policies has been provided to applicants, students, faculty and employees. (Winter 1981, 1095–96)

This controversial amendment, which opponents at the time argued made the ABA complicit in "legitimizing discrimination" on the basis of religion (Barbash 1981), opened the door for institutions such as Regent Law, AMSL, and Liberty Law School to employ a religious filter for students, staff, and faculty. This screening process was critical to maintaining the Christian culture, curriculum, and character of these institutions, a character that justified the investment in building separate, *parallel alternative* institutions in the first place.

But being accredited by the ABA is not a one-off process. It involves maintaining certain standards and quality control measures regarding curricular content and offerings, admissions of students and student services, hiring of faculty, staffing of administration, library and information resources, facilities, equipment and technology, bar passage rates for graduates, and employment and placement success, among others.[30] The ABA, while exercising its quality control power, also exerts "monopoly power" over almost all aspects of legal education and training (Shepherd & Shepherd 1998, 2091). If law schools fall out of compliance with any of these standards the ABA will, after a period of warning and probation, revoke accreditation, which means that graduates will not be eligible to sit for the bar exam and become licensed attorneys in most states.[31]

Entering the law school market thus means acknowledging the ABA's initial and continuing authority and "monopoly power" over all these aspects of a law school's operation, a power that limits the control Christian mission-oriented schools would have over their institutions. For these reasons, Herb Titus, the founding Dean of Regent Law School, warned in his 1985 Feasibility Study of the "unholy alliance" that could result between a Christian Worldview law school and the American Bar Association:

> Though sought for and obtained by the vast majority of law schools in America today, A.B.A. accreditation is not something to be pursued without careful reflection. Accreditation represents a submission to the A.B.A.'s authority and thorough scrutiny, and usually signifies that a law school is in accord with the A.B.A.'s view of, and commitment to, legal education. . . . For these reasons, A.B.A. accreditation of a Christian educational institution presents a significant risk of compromise in key areas of Christian principle. Therefore, a decision to apply for provisional accreditation of the Law School by the A.B.A. must be preceded by developing a strategy which will protect the University from participating in an unholy alliance (2 Corinthians 6:14), and which above all else reflects an accurate spiritual discernment of God's will in the matter. (Titus and Thompson 1985, 25)

Titus's warning powerfully illustrates the risks these Christian Right patrons were assuming by getting out of the "Christian bubble" and building their own law schools within a secularized legal profession and association that operates with a different calculus and a different worldview. Specifically, Titus here refers to the perils of submitting the law school's religious mission to a secular authority that might force it to "compromise in key areas of Christian principle" in order to be in compliance. In waring of this potential "unholy alliance" Titus cites 2 Corinthians 6:14 of the Bible, which says, "Do not be yoked together with unbelievers. For what do righteousness and wickedness have in common? Or what fellowship can light have with darkness?"[32]

Yoking themselves together with the unbelievers in the ABA and the wider legal profession has had continuing consequences for each of these law schools. The search for full accreditation at Regent Law—a process that took ten years and multiple attempts—had particularly serious consequences for the harbinger of the perils of the "unholy alliance" himself, Herb Titus. After moving from Oral Roberts University, the ABA denied Robertson and Titus's request to transfer Oral Roberts University's provisional accreditation, saying they would have to start the process anew. In 1987, the ABA then denied the law school accreditation altogether, noting in its report that " 'The Law School does not have the resources necessary to provide a sound legal education and accomplish the objective of its educational program' " (Davis 1995). As one reporter put it, "everything at the new school was suspect . . . [f]aculty salaries were too low, the law library was inadequate, the dean was part-time, the university didn't have enough money" (Davis 1995). And, importantly, CBNU did not appear to offer tenure for faculty, one of the ABA's requirements for accreditation. After Titus and then-CBN (Christian Broadcasting Network) president Bob Slosser sent a letter to the ABA explaining that there was, in fact, tenure at the law school, they were granted provisional approval in 1989. As it would turn out, however, this letter misrepresented the situation either intentionally or unintentionally to the ABA, a fact that would become public through litigation over a series of firings of faculty and administrators in 1993 (Davis 1995).

While Regent Law School was being reviewed for full ABA accreditation in 1993, a high-profile clash between Titus and patron Pat Robertson resulted in Robertson and the board of trustees firing Titus. Media accounts from the time note that the speculation was that Robertson and Regent were "anxious about accreditation" and wanted to "cultivate a more moderate image than the one offered by Mr. Titus," who, as we have detailed throughout the book, was public and polemic in his commitment to the transformative and radical mission of Regent Law School (Margolick 1993). This speculation was later supported by Titus himself, who produced copies of internal memos and reports that claimed his vision for Christian education and the curriculum "were considered a liability by university officials" and were ultimately the grounds for his dismissal (O'Keefe 1994). Titus also said in our interview that he and Robertson clashed over whether or not to accept federal financial aid, which Titus referred to as an "economic trap" that would inevitably result in compromise of the school's Christian mission and principles because of the various conditions the federal government attaches to it (Titus 2016).

The firing of Titus by Robertson and the board of trustees was also accompanied by the firing of three other faculty who were Titus devotees, two of whom claimed to be tenured (Davis 1995). The firing of supposedly tenured faculty prompted eight faculty to file a complaint to the ABA about the lack of tenure and academic freedom at Regent Law (O'Keefe 1994). It also incited student protests. As Robertson himself said at the time, the students "were in open rebellion" (Margolick 1993). Students were seen around campus at the time sporting tee shirts that read " 'Reunite Us With Titus' and quoting St. Paul's Second Letter to the Corinthians: 'I had no peace of mind because I did not find my brother Titus there' " (Margolick 1993; Geroux 1994). The dean who replaced Titus, J. Nelson Happy, described the controversy to a reporter as a "holy war": "It was a religious war, a holy war . . . I had never seen anything like it. To some people, the old system represented God and righteousness and the new one was evil, and that's all there was to it" (Geroux 1994).

Because of the controversy, uncertainty over tenure, and the lawsuits filed by faculty, the ABA refused to grant Regent Law full accreditation that year or the next. Regent did finally earn full accreditation in 1996 (Davis 1996). While Titus said that schools before Oral Roberts's fight with the ABA "either failed or they changed their mission" (Titus 2016), it is clear that practical considerations still force conflict, sacrifice, and compromise within those schools that seek to survive in a competitive legal marketplace. In the case of Regent Law, the conflict led to a "holy war," forcing one of the leading crusaders and visionaries of the Christian Worldview movement out in favor of meeting these mainstream requirements that bring professional legitimacy. This move, in turn, increased the likelihood of the institution being taken seriously within the legal profession, thereby enabling it to produce and send valued capital up the Support Structure Pyramid.

Regent Law is not the only school to have been forced into "compromise" on account of ABA accreditation and oversight. In August of 2016, after being on the ABA's watch list for three years, AMSL was put on sanction by the American Bar Association for its student admissions standards.[33] The association found that AMSL was in violation of Standards 501(a) and 501(b). According to the *ABA Journal*, "Standard 501(a) requires that law schools must have sound admissions policies and practices." and "Standard 501(b) states that a law school should only admit candidates who appear capable of completing a legal education program and being admitted to the bar" (Ward 2016). Because of its admission of "significant numbers of extremely high-risk students . . . defined as students with an LSAT of 144 or below, with correspondingly low grades" (Ward 2018), AMSL was sanctioned and forced to supply a "reliable plan" for remedying the issue and was also required to "supply the accreditation committee with admissions data and methodology, including factors considered besides LSAT scores and undergraduate GPAs" (Ward 2018).

For a Christian Worldview institution that needs to admit a critical mass of dedicated Christian, mission-oriented students to maintain its Christian character, we can see how the admissions requirements coupled with the bar passage rate requirements of the ABA can significantly constrain an institution's ability to hand-pick students for their commitment to Christ and the school's mission. AMSL did, in fact, comply, and by February 2018, the ABA removed its remedial sanctions (Ward 2018). These regulations mean that a Christian Worldview institution might have to weight GPA and LSAT scores more heavily in the admissions selection process than religiosity or commitment to the Christian mission in order to bring their policies into compliance with the ABA. We discuss the consequences of this constraint on the production of *human capital* more thoroughly in the next chapter.

While it has not been formally sanctioned, Liberty Law School has also recently come under scrutiny for its Personal Honor Code, which prohibits "Non-marital sexual relations or the encouragement or advocacy of any form of sexual behavior that would undermine the Christian identity or faith mission of the University constitute morally inappropriate sexual misconduct and constitute violations of this Personal Code of Honor."[34] Some observers have questioned whether this policy violates the ABA's rules for admissions that prohibit discrimination on the basis of sexual orientation. Liberty Law, in particular, was "in the crosshairs" in the wake of a legal controversy surrounding a faith-based Canadian law school's attempt to restrict student conduct "to heterosexual marriage" and revoke privileges to sit for the bar exam for students found in violation of the policy (Kellner 2015). Rena Lindevaldsen, who teaches Family Law at Liberty and who was the interim dean at the time, responded to questions about the Canadian case, saying that because of its Personal Honor Code "it's a concern for [Liberty Law School in] the future" (Kellner 2015).

One of the reasons Christian Right patrons initially rejected the *infiltration* approach was that they viewed other religious, long-established Christian law schools as having succumbed to the secularizing forces of the legal profession. Schools such as Georgetown and Notre Dame were routinely cited in the litany of law schools that did not provide a true Christian Worldview experience because, among other things, they allowed LGBT student clubs and pro-choice speakers and admitted students who espoused these views. These schools had, to recall Titus's formulation, entered into an "unholy alliance" with secular unbelievers. If the ABA should decide to crack down on Liberty Law School's Personal Honor Code and force schools to "compromise key areas of Christian principle" by admitting students and sanctioning student activities that run counter to missions, these schools face the difficult choice of de facto secularizing and submitting to the authority of the ABA, or of losing accreditation entirely. Taken together, these early tensions between these mission-oriented law schools and the association illustrate some of the interconnected, but conflicting, factors that are necessary for both realizing an institution's specific mission and increasing institutional capital in the wider world.

As a fellowship and not a full-fledged law school, the Blackstone Legal Fellowship is, to a significant degree, free from these particular constraints.

Patronage and Financial Stability

Suppose one of you wants to build a tower. Won't you first sit down and estimate the cost to see if you have enough money to complete it?
—Luke 14:28[35]

Patronage and financial stability (or instability)—variables we have located at the base of our Support Structure Pyramid—interact initially and continually with the other levels of the pyramid, shaping, enabling, or constraining these support structure institutions in their abilities to produce and send valuable capital up the pyramid. While we will continue to discuss the base throughout the book—particularly in terms of its noticeable effects on student recruitment (*human capital*)—in this section we briefly review the patron's involvement in and commitment to each of these institutions, their finances, and their revenue streams.

Patron involvement can benefit an institution, especially in terms of executing a mission that is tied to a particular set of ideas embodied in the leader of a movement, but it can also pose a risk for an institution's financial status and stability. For example, according to an analysis by the ratings organization Moody's, Regent's lack of a diverse structure of governance and decision-making was an area of concern for potential lenders and investors:

> The university's 83-year-old founder, Chancellor "Pat" Robertson, remains at the center of its governance and management structure with several family and business ties to other board members. The sudden presidential resignation of an apparent successor in September 2013 underscores the paucity of succession planning at Regent and raises questions about the longer term direction of the university.[36]

We saw Robertson's heavy-handed approach to governance in 1993, which resulted in a swift purge of dissenting faculty and a "holy war" on campus, which delayed Regent Law's accreditation with the ABA. Without a clear plan for succession after Robertson's death and with Robertson remaining "at the center of its governance" structure, which includes mostly Robertson's friends and loyalists, Regent Law's financial security remains uncertain, which impacts its financial status. Moody's has raised similar concerns about Liberty's governance structure, even though it has survived the first succession of leadership from Jerry Falwell to his son Jerry Falwell Jr:

> Governance and management structure and practices are evolving but decision-making remains relatively concentrated with the Chancellor/

President and Liberty has less institutionalization of best practices than more established universities. Governance practices require the board to ascribe to a Liberty University Doctrinal Position, which strengthens the institutional culture but limits diversity of opinion.[37]

Here Moody's points out the tension between maintaining a strong Christian "institutional culture" and practicing good governance, which requires "diversity of opinion" at the helm of an institution. Again, from a financial and investment perspective, having power concentrated in a single patron (or spread nominally among his friends and family) can affect an institution's credit rating and financial prospects.

While tied perhaps too closely to their founding patrons from a good governance perspective, Regent Law's and Liberty Law's connections to larger universities bearing the same names provides a degree of financial benefit and security. For example, Jerry Falwell Jr., who has taken over for his late father, has told the faculty at Liberty Law that the law school was his father's dream and that Liberty University would float it for as long as it needed to become financially self-sufficient (Liberty Faculty 2 2015). And Falwell Jr.'s ability to float the law school has increased exponentially over the past decade thanks to Liberty University's profitable online program. As a long feature in *The New York Times Magazine* reported in 2018, the online program at Liberty University, "one of the most lucrative in the country," has allowed the university to increase its assets "tenfold" over the past decade (MacGillis 2018). Similarly, when Regent Law was undergoing an accreditation review in 1991 and the ABA expressed concern about the school's lack of finances, Robertson granted it $117 million from CBN, Robertson's extremely profitable global media conglomerate (Davis 1996; Robichaux 1996).

As with Regent and Liberty, AMSL's founding patron's orientation significantly affects the school's form and function. The controversial decision to move the law school from Ann Arbor to Naples notwithstanding, Monaghan appears to be a bit more hands-off than his counterparts at Regent and Liberty. When questioned, very few faculty and students recalled seeing him attending a talk or commencement or meeting with student groups. An administrator who has been with the law school since its founding in Michigan said, "Mr. Monaghan has never really been involved in the day to day operations of the law school. He was more involved in [Ave Maria University] . . . He was more present there" (Ave Maria Administrator 1 2015). The administrator did note, however, that Monaghan comes to campus once a year to give the students a presentation about "professional dress." And when it comes to the financing of AMSL, this administrator described Monaghan's hands-off, "sink or swim" approach to patronage:

> [t]he vision was "we will give all of you guys some initial startup money and then it has to sink or swim on its own." . . . [I]n the early years he gave us a huge amount of money and it was a declining amount. We had to

be able to survive on our own and not be dependent on annual subsidies. That's been a big thing. (Ave Administrator 1 2015)

This same interviewee also said that if AMSL were "really in trouble," they could not say whether or not Monaghan would help out financially.

According to the metrics used by the Department of Education (DOE), AMSL has been "in trouble" for most of its existence. In 2016, the DOE's Heightened Cash Monitoring (HCM) watch list was made public, and AMSL was one of three law schools on the list of 540 private colleges and universities.[38] According to the *American Bar Association Journal*, the HCM is "a government list of universities that are being watched to make sure federal student aid is being used in a way that is accountable to students and taxpayers" (Weiss 2016). AMSL has been subject to "level 1" monitoring by the DOE, "which requires schools to submit records of student-aid disbursements before drawing down the federal funds" (Weiss 2016). Further digging by reporters confirmed that AMSL had been on the DOE watch list since 2005 (Hidalgo 2015). When asked to comment, "Ave Maria School of Law Dean Kevin Cieply told the Naples Daily News [when the list first became public] that the school was on the list because it was "a new school, with very few assets, a little bit of debt and not a huge endow-ment" (Weiss 2016). For the time being, AMSL appears to have removed itself from heightened government scrutiny. Based on the reports available on the federal financial aid website, AMSL was removed from the list sometime between September 1 and December 1, 2016.

The fact that AMSL is not attached to a bigger university like Regent and Liberty means it faces different financial challenges, especially as it has entered the market as a new law school. As one legal reporter recently put it, "It's hard out there for an independent law school:

> The number of law campuses that aren't attached to larger universities is slowly dwindling amid closures and mergers, and several stand-alone campuses are fighting for survival. The seven-year downturn in legal ed-ucation, which appears to be coming to an end, hit independent law schools especially hard because they can't tap into university funds to tide them over in lean times. Many independent law schools also experienced sharper enrollment declines than their university-affiliated counterparts. (Sloan 2018)

The reporter contrasts schools like AMSL with the University of Minnesota Law School, which has reportedly received $16 million from the University of Minnesota since 2012 to cover losses (Verges 2016). President Kevin Cieply of AMSL also highlighted the lack of "economies of scale" when operating as an independent law school:

"When you're an independent law school, you have to replicate everything a regular university would have," said Kevin Cieply, dean of the 19-year-old Ave Maria School of Law. "We have to do our own Title IV [compliance], our own human resources, our own counseling for students. "There are no economies of scale. You're doing everything yourself, so costs are higher." (Sloan 2018)

On the flip side of that, the reporter noted in that same article, "being independent means having less oversight or meddling from a University board of trustees, more control over governance, and the ability to be nimble and adaptive without having to get approval from a larger administrative body" (Sloan 2018).

These different financial orientations produced distinct concerns about the ability to attract and produce *human capital* in the form of students, as we discuss in greater detail in the next chapter. While these concerns will exist for any newly created school, their importance is all the more visible given the legal market's ongoing contraction. In the words of an administrator at Regent Law School, this exogenous shock forced many law schools to make tough decisions about quality control versus revenue:

[E]verybody's been hit with the market contraction . . . [So] do you uphold standards of quality or do you just say we're going to have two hundred people in the door no matter what and if you can breathe and walk at the same time, we'll let you in? Some schools have gone in that [open admissions] direction. (Regent Administrator 1 2016)

Given that these schools must fold religiosity into their calculations when responding to this market, shrinking the pool of desired students, the decision is difficult and stakes are amplified.

The importance of financial security is underscored when one looks at how Regent and Liberty have been able to weather the contraction in the legal market. As was noted several times in our interviews, Liberty offers the most attractive financial aid and scholarship packages of any school in Virginia. This can help them compete with Regent for academically solid devout students.

Importantly, this is something that Ave Maria has not been able to do since its move from Michigan, given its unstable base and, arguably, an even more competitive market, given the number of existing and better-established Catholic law schools—even if they are not considered as truly Catholic by Ave Maria's standards. The lack of stable and sufficient funding set a deteriorating cycle into motion, as we discuss more fully in the next chapter. As funding dropped, the quality of students dropped, as did the number of students invested in the mission. This led to AMSL's problem with bar passage and with mission maintenance. This, in turn, reinforces and accelerates the deteriorating cycle by deterring strong potential future students, faculty, and patrons.

Supplemental support structure institutions, while lower cost than the *parallel alternative* institutions we have been discussing thus far, are still enabled and constrained by their patrons and finances. In terms of patronage, Alan Sears, while at the helm of Alliance Defending Freedom (ADF), was the visionary for the Blackstone Legal Fellowship (Blackstone Administrator 1 2015). As we noted earlier, because of his own experiences feeling isolated as an outsider in law school, Sears wanted to create a program to train Christian law students in the biblical foundations of the law and, importantly, to connect them with other likeminded students, faculty, and legal professionals. But Sears, who was busy leading the litigation juggernaut that is ADF, took a minimal role in Blackstone after helping find a full-time director—Jeffrey Ventrella—who has more or less run the program since the beginning. Ventrella tapped Sumi Thomas as his Chief of Staff to work on recruitment and internships, and the two have had almost complete autonomy to shape and reshape the curriculum, recruit faculty and students, and design the Blackstone experience.

As described to us in our interview, Alan Sears provided the "emotional motivation" behind Blackstone but has not micromanaged the program or insisted on being deeply involved. Interviewees noted that ADF is not "personality-driven" and while Sears has to be "the face of the organization," he also "understands succession" (Blackstone Administrator 1 2015). Contrast this with Moody's unfavorable assessment of the lack of succession planning and diffuse governance of Regent Law and Liberty Law—two schools that might fairly be characterized as "personality-driven."

Blackstone Legal Fellowship relies on the revenue stream of ADF to finance its staff, pay its rotating set of faculty, cover costs for its student summer fellows, and pay for marketing and outreach. According to ADF's tax filings in 2017, their total expenses related to "Allied Support and Training" (of which Blackstone is only one part) were $7,585,466.[39] So compared with the costs of running a law school, Blackstone's overhead is relatively much lower. For example, AMSL as a stand-alone law school reported functional expenses of over $14.8 million in 2015.[40] From a financial perspective, Blackstone is on extremely solid financial footing. Since its founding, ADF's budget has grown at an impressive rate, from $4.7 million in 1997 to $18 million in 2003 to just shy of $40 million in fiscal year 2012 (Hollis-Brusky and Wilson 2017, 126). The last reported public filing from ADF in 2017 listed revenues exceeding $55 million.[41] Part of this increase can be explained by a $10 million grant from the National Christian Foundation, a Christian charitable organization that provides around $600 million in grants to churches and religious organizations each year (Hollis-Brusky and Wilson 2017, 126).

Blackstone's reliable revenue stream from ADF means that it can guarantee scholarships to all of its fellows that cover the costs of airfare, lodging, and most meals for Phases I and III. Blackstone estimates that costs are around $6,300 per intern.[42] Attached to ADF and existing outside the scope of ABA regulation,

Blackstone is, thus, insulated from many of the external factors that variably affect the newly created Christian Worldview law schools.

Bringing the Support Structure Pyramid Back In

This chapter has detailed how these four transformative Christian institutions have attempted to position themselves not only as law schools and sites for alternative legal training and fellowship for Christian conservative students, but also self-consciously as support structures for the CCLM, institutions built to manufacture and transmit valuable capital up the Support Structure Pyramid. We have explored the genesis of each, their missions, and their transformative visions for law and legal culture. Importantly, we have also detailed some of the known risks—the known constraints—these patrons assumed when they decided to build their own support structure institutions in lieu of investing in existing ones. Most prominently, these constraints involve regulation and requirements of the legal profession and the American Bar Association (what Titus referred to as an "unholy alliance"), the role of founding patrons in continuing governance and support, and the financial stability (or instability) that forms the base of our Support Structure Pyramid.

The next four chapters will analyze and evaluate these institutions, separately and collectively, in terms of the quality and quantity of capital they have produced or are plausibly poised to produce for the movement. We begin with *human capital* (Chapter 4), then turn to *social* and *cultural capital*, which we discuss together under the umbrella term "credibility capital" (Chapter 5). The next two chapters examine the impact of Christian Worldview institutions' production of *intellectual capital* inside the academy (Chapter 6) and on litigation and judicial opinions (Chapter 7).

Human Capital (or, "A Generation of Christian Attorneys")

How does an institution, to quote Jerry Falwell Sr., set out to "produce a genera-tion of Christian attorneys"?[1] The first step is to recruit the right kind of faculty and students. We explore each institution's efforts and success at recruitment of *human capital*, highlighting the importance of having faculty committed to the mission as well as a critical mass of "mission students" as opposed to "non-mission students" in order not to dilute the Christian mission of the institution. As our interviewees emphasized, they are not looking to have a diverse student body in the traditional sense, which would risk inviting in those who might be hostile to the school's principles and mission. Instead, they emphasize diversity *among* law schools and their distinctiveness within the legal market writ large, as one of only a few schools that provide distinctly Christian legal education to Christians who are also aspiring lawyers.

The next step in producing "a generation of Christian attorneys" is to train them to be lawyers, to educate them about the law within the Christian Worldview mold. Given that, we next examine each institution's core "mission" courses as well as how biblical themes and readings are integrated into other courses throughout the cur-riculum. Finally, we present some initial data on the relative and collective output of *human capital* for the Christian Conservative Legal Movement (CCLM), their re-turn on investment. How many graduates are licensed attorneys, what kind of law do they go on to practice, and are they going on to become "culture warriors" (Wilson & Hollis-Brusky 2014) for the movement, fulfilling their founding patrons' missions and visions?

Separate But Faithful. Amanda Hollis-Brusky and Joshua C. Wilson, Oxford University Press (2020). © Oxford University Press. DOI: 10.1093/oso/9780190637262.001.0001

If You Build It, They Will Come: Recruiting "Mission" Faculty and Students

Faculty Recruitment: The Promise of "Academic Freedom" and a Different Kind of Diversity

One of the biggest challenges Herb Titus described to us in establishing the first Christian Worldview law school of the contemporary era at Oral Roberts University was in finding faculty. He knew there must be faculty like him, Christian-identifying law professors who felt isolated in their mainstream, secularized law schools, but he didn't know how to find them and whether they would be properly trained to teach, for example, Torts or Criminal Law from a distinctly Christian Worldview perspective. As Titus recounted to us, "When we opened at ORU in the fall of 1979, I was the only person who had any experience teaching in law school . . . you couldn't find people. I finally found Roger Bern . . . He's the only person I could find, and I searched long and hard for people who had some teaching experience" (Titus 2016).

But finding these faculty was key to the mission, as Titus noted in his Feasibility Study for Christian Broadcasting Network University (CBNU) Law School. If they were forced to populate the law school with mainstream faculty who held secularized views of law, then "the project is better left undone":

> The only way the CBN University law School can be truly distinctive in American legal education (and thus worth the effort) is by being committed to a diversity among different law schools. If the Law School hires faculty members who hold the same views held by other legal educators, the project is better left undone. Accordingly, the Law School is committed to hiring people who will teach only from a Biblical, or Christian, perspective, in accordance with the University's policies. The law School faculty must speak with one voice to challenge the secularization of legal education in the land today. (Titus and Thompson 1985, 14)

In the parlance of Support Structure Theory, Titus is acknowledging the futility of building a *parallel alternative* institution only to have it infiltrated by the very same faculty who are driving and maintaining "the secularization of legal education in the land today." In order to maintain the purity of the mission, the school would only hire "people who will teach only from a Biblical, or Christian, perspective."

This focus on uniformity, conformity, and the faculty "speak[ing] with one voice" would seem to be at odds with two core values that the American Bar Association (ABA), higher education, and the legal profession writ large have adopted: diversity and academic freedom. The ABA's emphasis and enforcement of its "Diversity and Inclusion" requirement for students and faculty (Standard 206)[2] has long been viewed as an obstacle for a law school that would privilege religiosity over, for example, "[looking] like President Clinton's cabinet" (Shaffer 1993, 1860–61). Moreover, Standard 211 is, at its core, a statement on the value and importance of diversity. And it was the lack of religious diversity, specifically, at Oral Roberts University that prompted the ABA accreditation battle we discussed in the Introduction and Chapter 3. ABA delegates were particularly concerned with the religiosity requirement, saying that this amounted to "an absolute right to discriminate on religious grounds" (Winter 1981, 1096).

Diversity of belief is limited, first and foremost, by the statement of faith or doctrinal statement each institution requires its faculty to sign upon employment. Liberty University's doctrinal statement, for example, is 722 words long and includes passages about faculty "conforming" themselves "to the likeness of Jesus Christ" and being "responsible to live in obedience to the Word of God in separation from sin."[3] Regent University's "Statement of Faith" is considerably shorter than Liberty's at 253 words, but it contains similar normative language about living "righteous and holy lives" in accordance with "the Holy Spirit" who "indwells those who receive Christ."[4] At Ave Maria School of Law (AMSL), an administrator we interviewed confirmed that he and the other Catholic faculty have to "take a profession of faith" and vow to follow "the Catholic teachings, the Magisterium and the Holy Scripture" (Ave Maria Administrator 2 2015). The non-Catholic faculty, of which there are only a few at AMSL, had to take a vow "to respect our mission" (Ave Maria Administrator 2 2015). While drafted broadly as avowals of Christian faith, these statements combined with the schools' reputations for being conservative and devout effectively preclude faculty from the pool who, for example, while Christian-identifying would support LGBTQ rights or who hold pro-choice views on abortion.

Redefining diversity as not within a single institution but, instead, within the legal profession or the law school market more broadly has allowed these institutions to maintain a uniform Christian-believing faculty while still claiming to promote diversity. We saw this formulation of "diversity among" versus "diversity within" in Titus's study: "The only way the CBN University law School can be truly distinctive in American legal education (and thus worth the effort) is by being committed to a diversity among different law schools" (Titus and Thompson 1985, 14). An administrator at Regent Law with whom we spoke also emphasized this "diversity among" position in our interview, stating that this view of diversity writ large in the law school market is set against "what I would call a cookie cutter approach to diversity, which really means every school needs to look exactly like each other and it needs to include these 22 different categories of people" (Regent Administrator 1 2016). Diversity is accomplished by providing a distinct product, a form of legal education that the broader legal market had long excluded from their mainstream curricula.

"Speaking with one voice" as a faculty and as an institution also cuts against traditional notions of academic freedom, widely understood to mean the full freedom to research, teach, and to express spoken or written opinions freely in public.[5] Because academic freedom is considered such a crucial component of higher education, the ABA requires that all law schools have a stated policy on academic freedom.[6] The ABA offers as a template the "1940 Statement of Principles on Academic Freedom and Tenure" of the American Association of University Professors (AAUP):

Academic Freedom[7]

1. Teachers are entitled to full freedom in research and in the publication of the results, subject to the adequate performance of their other academic duties; but research for pecuniary return should be based upon an understanding with the authorities of the institution.

2. Teachers are entitled to freedom in the classroom in discussing their subject, but they should be careful not to introduce into their teaching controversial matter which has no relation to their subject. *Limitations of academic freedom because of religious or other aims of the institution should be clearly stated in writing at the time of the appointment.* (emphasis added)

3. College or university teachers are citizens, members of a learned profession, and officers of an educational institution. When they speak or write as a citizen, they should be free from institutional censorship or discipline, but their special position in the community imposes special obligations. As scholars and educational officers, they should remember that the public may judge their profession and their institution by their utterances. Hence, they should at all times be accurate, should exercise appropriate restraint, should show respect for the opinions of others, and should make every effort to indicate that they are not speaking for the institution.

Importantly, as we note with italics at the end of bullet point two, the AAUP Statement does carve out space for faith-based institutions. According to the AAUP website, this tenet was reinterpreted or clarified in 1970 to account for faith-based institutions while still insisting that the AAUP does not "endorse such a departure" from academic freedom.[8]

Notice of such "limitations of academic freedom because of religious . . . aims" is required to appear on applications for faculty employment so that there is a complete and transparent understanding of the ways in which the religious mission of the school might affect academic freedom as traditionally understood. At Regent, for example, the application for faculty employment contains the following language on academic freedom:

"Academic Freedom" means that a faculty member in teaching is free to convey to students his/her opinions, conclusions, and analysis with regard to the subject being taught, and (*within the accepted academic parameters of the course, consistent with the Statement of Faith, and subject to reason-able University direction and oversight*) to exercise discretion with regard to teaching ..."[9] (italics added)

Here we see from the italicized language in the parenthetical that academic freedom at Regent is bounded by and conditioned on the statement of faith that we explored earlier. Liberty's Statement on Academic Freedom adopts the AAUP language nearly verbatim but adds modified language about speech that accords with Liberty's faith and mission to the point about public citizenship and expression of views: "When they speak or write as citizens, they should be free from institutional censorship or discipline, but their special position in the community *and their relationship with a university whose distinctive mission is defined by its identity with historic Christian faith* imposes special obligations ..." (italics added).[10]

In addition to their ABA-mandated commitments to academic freedom on paper, some faculty with whom we spoke emphasized a different kind of academic freedom these Christian Worldview law schools offered that traditional law schools do not. But academic freedom was defined as being able to harmonize one's faith with one's study and practice of law, about being able to speak truth to power and not having a conflict between one's religious beliefs and professional practice. This revised understanding of academic freedom was most clearly and cogently articulated by Herb Titus in our interview:

> If you read John 8:31–32, John 8:31 says, "If you abide in my Word, then you shall know the truth and the truth shall set you free." What's the lesson? The lesson is that the Word of God, the Bible, is the standard. If you abide in the Bible as the standard by which you determine whether something's true or not, then you're basically free. For a Christian it's academic freedom, of course I think it's academic freedom for anybody, but it is definitely for a Christian. (Titus 2016)

One Regent Law faculty member whom we interviewed was particularly emphatic about the degree of academic freedom she believes she has at Regent Law when compared with other law schools. In fact, this faculty member deployed the phrase six times in our brief interview without being prompted. Academic freedom appears three times in this one excerpt alone:

> So that love of Christ combined with the commitment to a first-rate academic excellence really equals academic freedom because when you are at a school as a person of faith, that is not encouraged or not even allowed. I remember just getting ridiculed as an undergrad in terms of my position on things that were informed by my faith. So we have just so much academic

freedom here . . . Just tons of freedom, academic freedom. (Regent Faculty
1 2016)

Similarly, a Liberty Law professor said he would likely not have the same "academic
freedom" to teach according to his Christian faith at a secular law school and that,
in turn, would mean he could not be "honest with [himself]" (Liberty Faculty
1 2015).

The narrative of being freer at these institutions to express one's beliefs, to teach
and study and speak in accordance with one's Christian faith, and to bring the Bible
into the classroom was a strong draw to these schools for many faculty who had
experiences being "ridiculed" for their beliefs in undergrad or in law school (Regent
Faculty 1). A Liberty Law professor who had attended Regent Law School said that
"My faith, it was never questioned and I was never subjected to any kind of ridicule.
I never thought that I had to keep any view that I had private because it was a religious thing that no one wanted to talk about" (Liberty Faculty 2 2015).

The potential to be surrounded by likeminded Christian, conservative colleagues
and students—the attraction of homophily—is also one of the primary reasons faculty expressed in interviews for choosing to come. One faculty member described
himself as "very conservative" and described his affinity for Liberty Law School, in
part, in those terms (Liberty Faculty 2 2015). Similarly, a professor who teaches the
core Christian jurisprudence courses at AMSL left another Catholic institution in
the Northeast because it had become increasingly liberal and, as he became "more
and more conservative," the environment was "occasionally hostile" (Ave Maria
Faculty 1 2015). An Ave Maria administrator described the appeal of AMSL as a
draw for very conservative Catholic faculty:

> I think the majority of the faculty members are well in the stream of being
> very orthodox, and Christian at least, most of them majority Catholic.
> I think the conservative approach. This is a very conservative Catholic law
> school. I think a lot of them are drawn politically to the conservative ele-
> ment, but also they're deep in their faith, or secure in their faith, and they
> want to come to a place where that's not attacked. It's also they can share
> it without feeling they have to run it though a screen or be reserved about
> it at all. That they're talking to people that have a similar belief system and
> that they're able to also infuse their beliefs into the curriculum, into their
> lectures, and that it's just that kind of situation. (Ave Maria Administrator
> 2 2015)

That conservative culture attracts more faculty members who are conservative, said
one professor who was also an AMSL law student: "It's no secret that Ave Maria has
a reputation as a conservative Catholic law school . . . I think there's probably some

self-selection that goes on, that people who feel comfortable in . . . a conservative environment . . . would consider applying here" (Ave Maria Faculty 2 2015).

The unique requirements and culture of religiosity at these institutions—key to maintaining their missions—obviously limits the potential pool of available and interested faculty. To that end, Regent Law's first-in positioning has given it an advantage in terms of faculty pedigree. For many years it was the only relatively safe, and thus attractive, destination for disaffected Christian law faculty and accomplished Christian lawyers interested in transitioning to academia. This positioning has enabled Regent Law to draw better-credentialed faculty than its later competitors, increasing its *cultural capital* within the wider legal profession. As evidence, 43% of Regent's 2016–17 regular faculty hold JDs from top-20 law schools.[11]

Because of its relative proximity to Regent Law School—just 200 miles separate the two Virginia-based law schools—Liberty Law competes directly for conservative Christian, mission-oriented faculty with the more well-established Regent Law School. This proximity, combined with Liberty Law's late entrance into the market in 2003, has disadvantaged the school in terms of these traditional metrics of faculty pedigree. As Table 4.1 illustrates, Liberty Law has the lowest percentages of faculty in our study with JDs from top-20 (10%) and top-50 (20%) law schools. Liberty Law also had the highest percentage of faculty from unranked law schools (25%, versus Regent's 14% and AMSL's 6%).[12] By comparison, 42% of Ave Maria's faculty attended top-20 law schools. Of the Liberty Law faculty who hold JDs from unranked schools, half earned their degrees from either Regent Law or Liberty Law. The remainder of these faculty members earned degrees from other unranked religious law schools.

Table 4.1. **Percent of Faculty with Law Degrees from Variously Ranked Law Schools**

	Ave Maria	Liberty Law	Regent Law	Blackstone Fellowship	Baylor Law	Notre Dame
1–10 Law Schools	19%	5%	31%	20%	15%	52%
11–20 Law Schools	23%	5%	12%	11%	11%	28%
21–50 Law Schools	11%	10%	16%	2%	18%	5%
51–Unranked Law Schools	31%	45%	25%	9%	52%	6%
Unranked Law Schools	6%	25%	14%	0	4%	0
International Institution Law Degree or No JD	10%	10%	2%	57%	0%	9%

Source: Calculated using *U.S. News & World Report* Law School Rankings 2016.

The explanation for Ave Maria's faculty status is likely similar to Regent's, but with a distinctly Catholic variation to it. While there are numerous Catholic law schools for devout Catholic law faculty to join, they are perceived by many orthodox Catholics to be superficially religious (Arthur 2006; Ringenberg 2006). When Ave Maria was established, these true-believing Catholic faculty flocked to the new law school, as did other conservative Catholics seeking a more orthodox institution than the ones that existed up to that point. As we detailed in Chapter 3, AMSL lost many of its founding faculty when Monaghan made the highly controversial decision to move the campus from Ann Arbor, Michigan, to Naples, Florida. Still, AMSL's active faculty percentages at each level of JD prestige are still more than two times higher than they are for Liberty's lifetime.

While faculty JDs don't explicitly factor into *U.S. News & World Report* rankings, they do feed into the "Quality Assessment" part of the rankings (worth 40% of an institution's score),[13] where fellow legal academics, lawyers, and judges evaluate the overall quality and reputation of an institution. This competitive ranking system determines a law school's broader *cultural capital* within the legal profession and beyond and can either boost or drive down student recruitment, faculty recruitment, fundraising, capital campaigns, and institutional maintenance (Sauder and Espeland 2009), which could, in turn, affect the survival and the mission of these *parallel alternative* institutions.

Looked at as a whole, the initial *cultural capital* that faculty bring to these new schools is given some context by comparing them with the longer established law schools at Baylor and Notre Dame—the schools we reviewed in Chapter 2 as the paths not taken for the *infiltration approach*. Around the turn of the twenty-first century, leaders at Baylor University decided to elevate the school's standing in the academy. To this end, "Baylor developed a plan . . . [to] become the unquestioned premier Christian research university in the Protestant tradition in America" (Ringenberg 2006, 236). Baylor's law school has achieved a standing in the *U.S. News* listing that suggests its seriousness, listed at 51 in the rankings at the time of writing. Its religious hiring and tenure requirements, as well as its undergraduate required church attendance, speak to its dedication to Christian conservative values. As such, it appears to be an institution that should be able to attract serious, Christian conservative faculty. The numbers, however, tell a different story. Regent and Ave Maria actually have more top-20 law graduates on their faculty, as well as more top-50 law school graduate faculty than does Baylor's faculty. When looking at Ave Maria's post-move "active" subset of faculty, the two schools are almost identical in terms of top-20 and top-50 faculty graduates, though Baylor outcompetes Ave Maria in the narrowest top-10 category.

Notre Dame, as the more highly ranked of the comparative case studies, has over half of its faculty graduating from top-10 law schools, and 80% graduating from top-20 law schools. It also has no faculty from unranked American law schools. As such, it possesses an impressive amount of *cultural capital* in the form of its faculty's alma

maters. Notre Dame is, of course, well positioned via its legacy as the nation's premier Catholic research university to attract and retain such a faculty. Both interview
data and secondary research show that Notre Dame did not always occupy this position but, rather, it mobilized its impressive financial resources to attract and retain
prestigious faculty over the last few decades (Arthur 2006).

Though direct comparisons with the Blackstone Legal Fellowship cannot be
drawn for any given year because the faculty as a whole rotates, we can see that in the
aggregate that the majority of Blackstone-invited faculty (57%) do not have a JD.[14]
Advanced degrees within this non–JD holding Blackstone faculty group included
individuals holding master's and PhD degrees in political science, policy, international relations, business, and theology. Theologians and seminarians were by far
the largest sub-group, comprising one-third of the non-JD group (33%). Because
Table 4.1 shows the overall percentages of faculty rather than just JD-holding faculty, Blackstone actually looks like it is outperformed by Regent Law and AMSL in
terms of top-20 and top-50 faculty. These percentages are a bit misleading because
more than half of the Blackstone faculty do not hold JD degrees.

If we focus just on the group of Blackstone faculty members with a JD (43% of
the total population), those numbers look much more favorable for Blackstone with
47% of the JD-holding faculty coming from top-10-ranked institutions and an additional 31% coming from top-50. As with Notre Dame Law School, Blackstone does
not have any faculty participating who earned their JD from an unranked American
law school.

This gap in initial *cultural capital* provided by faculty alma maters between
these *parallel alternative* institutions and their *infiltration* and *supplemental*
counterparts once again points to the questions as to why, when thinking from
a purely strategic sense, a growing and well-funded movement would choose to
spend resources on creating wholly new law schools when existing ones could
provide much more in the way of immediate *cultural capital*. In brief, CCLM
leaders are clearly willing to sacrifice traditional notions of *cultural capital* when
it is replaced by the potential for more control over institutions. This is especially
true when those traditional institutions are not trusted by those leaders, when
they are not believed (rightly or not) to have produced many Christian conservative lawyers, and when those same leaders have well-established histories of
creating their own institutions.

Student Recruitment: "Mission" versus "Non-Mission" Students

One of the more interesting findings at AMSL was the fairly prevalent and casual
deployment of the terms *mission student* and *non-mission student*. Mission students
were identified as those students (mostly from out of state) who were drawn to
the school by the mission, who could have gone elsewhere and perhaps to higher-
ranked law schools, and those who were involved in the leadership of pro-life club

Lex Vitae, Knights of Columbus, attended daily mass, went to the March for Life together, and were involved in "sidewalk counseling," which is how students at AMSL
describe abortion clinic protesting. The mission students, according to one student,
also tended to be from "big families" and were, for the most part "homeschooled."
They also tended to hang out with one another and were referred to by other
students as "the Holy Rollers" (Ave Maria Student 1 2015).

Mission students came to AMSL because the institution and the faculty were
unapologetically conservative Catholic and pro-life. As another AMSL student
explained, "It's quite remarkable to have faculty members that are pretty conservative in their views, and that they all defend life." This same student contrasted her
law school experience with her undergraduate experience in Northern California, "I
don't think I could name a professor in undergrad that was openly pro-life, or pro-
family, or pro-religion in any way" (Ave Maria Student 2 2015). Others described
being explicitly called by God to AMSL, "I chose [AMSL] because I felt called to
come here by God. He said, through prayer, that He's prepared a place for me. I said
if He's prepared a place for me it's got to be good" (Ave Maria Student 3 2015).

Non-mission students were described as being almost all local, they might be
Catholic but they did not consider themselves devout, and/or they chose AMSL
because it was the best school they could get into or it allowed them to remain in
the area. A self-identified "mission" student described the "non-mission" students at
AMSL in the following way:

> We do have a number of students who came because they didn't want
> to leave the region. They got into other schools in Florida, but they have
> families, they're older, they're one of those non-traditional [students].
> Even traditional students who just didn't want to leave the region for what-
> ever reason. They just decided to come here. I would say that a lot of them
> still tend to be at least more politically conservative or possibly Christian.
> They still have usually a commonality, but I have seen some students who
> came here solely from this region or maybe not too far from Miami. (Ave
> Maria Student 1 2015)

A Web-based survey we conducted in 2018 with AMSL alumni (see Appendix C)
provides additional insight into the mission- versus non–mission student divide
within the student body. Students who selected "Fit with Mission" as one of their
responses to the question of what drew them to AMSL were classified as "mission
students." Tracking how these respondents moved through the survey compared
with those who did not check "Fit with Mission" as a reason for attending AMSL
further illustrates the student body divide we heard about in campus conversations.
Mission students, who comprised two-thirds of our respondent pool, were 32 percentage points more likely to identify as Catholic (82.5% versus 50%), 13 percentage points more likely to identify as conservative (68.8% versus 55.3%), and 20

points more likely to approve of President Trump (71.7% versus 51.2%). Also consistent with what we heard on campus, mission students in our survey were 20 percentage points more likely to report having been in the top 25% of their classes than non-mission respondents (47% versus 27%). Only one-third of mission students identified "Location" as a reason for attending AMSL whereas two-thirds of non-mission students emphasized "Location." This reinforces the regional-versus-nonregional divide we heard about in campus interviews.

Everyone had different estimates about the percentage of mission students at AMSL currently—anywhere from 5%–15%—but the consensus seemed to be that the school was attracting fewer since its move from Ann Arbor to Naples. An administrator with whom we spoke speculated that, in addition to geography, the decline in high-quality mission students could be attributed to finances: ". . . when the school was initially started it brought in some real [high quality students], because almost all of the students were on a full ride. Tom Monaghan basically funded everything, and so they got a very high academic caliber of students" (Ave Maria Administrator 2 2015). ABA reports corroborate this assertion. In 2003, for example, Ave Maria reported that 37.1% of its student body were on full-tuition scholarships, while an additional 37.1% received half-to-full tuition (Margolis et al. 2005, 115). By 2011 those numbers had dropped dramatically, with only 7.7% of students receiving full tuition and another 15.6% receiving half-to-full (Margolis et al. 2013, 107). The most recent ABA report shows a bit of a rebound, with 19% of students receiving full tuition and another 23% receiving half-to-full (American Bar Association 2018). Even still, the downturn in AMSL's financial base, which we explored at length in the last chapter, has forced AMSL to cast a wider net for tuition-paying students, which has affected the overall quality of the student body and, as several students confirmed in interviews, has brought to campus a significant percentage of students who are not committed to the mission.

This loss of control over the student body and, as a result, the character and culture of the institution was one of Herb Titus's greatest fears as Dean of Regent Law School in the early days. Titus believed that in order to fully execute the mission of an integrated Christian legal education, Regent needed to maintain strict screening procedures for students. This meant rigorously enforcing the religious standard for students and refusing federal financial aid that, in his words, amounted to an "economic trap" meant to undermine those standards because it required schools to adopt certain policies of non-discrimination in hiring and admissions.[15] Such strict control over the mission, however, comes with costs. Titus explained his disagreement with Robertson on admissions and financial aid in our interview:

> I was much stronger in terms of screening students. I was very much aware
> that if you didn't have a very strong body that was committed to a Christian
> ministry and so forth, it would be endangering the school's future. That
> was Number 1. Number 2 is that I was also someone who believed that

we should maintain our independence from financing by the government, and also by the academic freedom statement. I believed that those were two very crucial elements, which, apparently, Pat [Robertson] didn't consider because after I left they changed them both. (Titus 2016)

While a tight filter for screening students and faculty preserves institutional purity, it is hard to foresee many students who would be willing or able to attend a school that did not offer financial aid. Robertson, a more strategic political player than Titus, decided to compromise and accepted the conditions of federal financial aid in return for the benefits of appealing to a wider base of potential students.

Even with a slight reduction in the absolute control Titus sought over the student population, interviews revealed that Regent Law still manages to attract a significant portion of devout law students who come for the school's unique mission. This sentiment was eloquently expressed by a mission student at Regent Law who spoke of the uniqueness of the student experience, especially vis-à-vis the faculty:

I love the law. I love it. I love Christ. I get to fuse two things that I love at a place that not only would tolerate it, perhaps, but encourage it. It's not [that] there are not Christian faculty members who are at other law schools. There's not many of them. There are, but maybe they're . . . and again I can't speak, but more tolerated than encouraged. Maybe to be in a place where you get to fulfill your passion of wanting to train excellent attorneys and think about the law in depth. Study the law in and out, make sure my students are great lawyers. But getting to do it with Christ in mind, that's unique. That's why I'm here. I know that's why many of our faculty members have chosen to be here making perhaps less money or less prestige, maybe not, I don't know, but I can assume why they're here. (Regent Student 1 2016)

This particular student came to Regent Law from California, specifically because of the school's unique, Christ-centered mission. Unlike AMSL and, as we will discuss in a bit, Liberty Law, Regent Law draws significant numbers of students from what a Regent Law administrator described as the main "feeder states"—Florida, California, Michigan, Texas, and New York (Regent Administrator 1 2016). One way Regent is able to attract students like this, according to this same administrator, is through their Honors Program, which welcomed its first class in 2011:

Our honors program was set up. . . . to say to someone who would want to go to a Christian law school, but has really high credentials, "you shouldn't have to feel like you're making some sacrifice to come here. We want to make sure that your experience rivals whatever that other school is that you got into."

Regent Law's Honors Program comprises anywhere between 20% and 25% of each class (Regent Faculty 1 2016). These relatively higher-caliber students have access to small, Honors-only sections of required classes, special programming, research assistantships with professors, and access to special network opportunities.[16] As a faculty member involved with the program at the time emphasized to us, the Honors students get better placements than their peers post-graduation. To illustrate, this faculty member noted that 28% of the Honors class of 2014 received judicial clerkships, and several others were placed with state attorneys general (Regent Faculty 1 2016).

Liberty Law School has followed in the footsteps of its Virginia neighbor, announcing its new Honors Program in February 2018.[17] While we visited before this program was launched, the website describes the Honors program in very similar terms to Regent's in terms of eligibility and benefits with Honors students gaining access to small seminars, faculty and networking opportunities, invited dinners and lunches with visiting judges and attorneys, and access to research opportunities with faculty.[18] Prior to launching its Honors Program, Liberty Law School attracted mission students by leveraging three resources from Liberty University: its Falwell-centric prestige and recognition within conservative Christian political circles, its undergraduate students, and its finances. An administrator involved with Liberty Law's admissions confirmed in our interview that being connected with Liberty University has allowed the law school to piggyback on the more established institution's reputation: "One of the great things about . . . Liberty Law School is that we are attached to Liberty University, in and of itself being the world's largest Christian school, so we have a great network of marketing opportunities through that" (Liberty Administrator 1 2015).

The connection to Liberty University also provides a direct pipeline of potential students to the law school. Two of the current law students we interviewed on campus had also attended Liberty University as undergraduates and spoke of their desire to continue their education there as a reflection of their positive experiences with Liberty University's Christian Worldview education. As one student noted of his decision to stay at Liberty for law school,

> I've been here for a long time. The reason that I came here initially was for the Christian education . . . part of [my decision to stay for law school] too came down to this is, this is where I'm familiar with and after being at the institution for at that point almost five years, I have a lot of respect for the institution. The Christian values and principles were really important to me and also the faculty here are just unlike any people I've ever met. (Liberty Student 1 2015)

Of the three mission law schools we examine here, Liberty Law is also able to offer the best financial packages. In the early years, the amount of financial aid Liberty offered was astounding. For example, in 2005, the first year it reported data to the ABA, 60% of Liberty's student body had full-tuition scholarships, while another 32% received half-tuition or more (Margolis et al. 2008, 403). That same year, for purposes of comparison, Regent Law granted 5.9% of its student body full scholarships and an additional 18% received half-tuition or more (Margolis et al. 2008, 599). Ave Maria, which was also known for its generous aid packages in the Michigan years, still only granted 24.7% full-tuition scholarships and 16.9% half-tuition or more that same year (Margolis et al. 2008, 111). None of the students we interviewed talked about scholarship money as a deciding factor, but administrators at the two other schools both highlighted Liberty Law's financial aid capabilities as part of its competitive advantage in recruiting students (Ave Maria Administrator 2 2015, Regent Administrator 1 2016).

Undergraduate degree-granting institutions provide some insight into the kinds of students each of these *parallel alternative* schools has been able to successfully attract over time. While not a perfect proxy for "mission students," the percentage of students coming from Christian undergraduate institutions tells us something about the desire for certain students to have a culturally similar and distinctly Christian law school experience. Supporting this, in a 2018 Web-based survey of Ave Maria School of Law alumni, 57% of alumni who we categorized through their responses as "mission" students also attended a Christian undergraduate institution whereas 78% of "non-mission" students attended non-Christian undergraduate institutions.

Seeing the potential importance of the students' undergraduate institutions for understanding the schools' abilities to realize their missions, Figure 4.1 presents data on the percentages of a subset of alumni with Christian undergraduate degrees over time. As we explain in greater detail in Appendix A, because national organizations do not collect this information, we relied on Web searches of known-to-us alumni through LinkedIn, Facebook, Martindale, and Web-based Google searches to identify alumni and collect data on their undergraduate-granting institutions. We were able to find information for roughly half of each of these institutions' graduates using this method, so we must be cautious with any conclusions we draw. Nonetheless, the data is interesting and instructive.

Using this same data set, Figure 4.2 presents the percentage of this subset of the student body coming from the geographic region of "The South,"[19] where each of these institutions is currently located.

Relevant particularly to the AMSL story, we see from Figure 4.2 that, as interviews alluded to, after the move from Michigan to Florida in 2009, Ave Maria's percentage of regional students from the South increases significantly while its percentage of students from Christian undergraduate institutions declines slightly. With regard to Christian undergraduate institutions, with the exception of a few spikes and dips, Regent has tended to attract anywhere between 25% and 45% of its student body from culturally similar Christian institutions and over half of its student body consistently from the regional South with that percentage noticeably increasing once

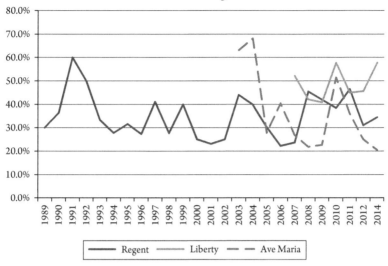

Figure 4.1. Percent of identified alumni who attended Christian undergraduate institutions over time.

Percentages based on subset of alumni identified through LinkedIn, Facebook, Martindale, and name-based Google searches for lists of graduating classes (see Appendix A for more detail). As of 2015, this subset represented ~48% of Regent Law alumni, ~43% of AMSL alumni, and ~52% of Liberty Law alumni.

the last of the Oral Roberts students who moved with the school had graduated. While we have fewer years of data for Liberty, whose first class graduated in 2007, its percentages of students from Christian undergraduate institutions has ranged from roughly 40% to 60%, and its percentages of local students sits even higher, ranging from 60% to 74% for the years for which we have data.

The regional elements of Regent and Liberty are important to recognize. While there is a popular conception that the Christian Right and evangelicals are overwhelmingly concentrated in the South, this is not fully supported by data. It is true that the dominant religious denominations associated with the Christian Right are historically Southern, and that evangelicals make up higher percentages of the population in Southern states. That said, once-Southern religious denominations have spread beyond their old borders, the modern Christian Right has strong founding roots in California (Dochuk 2012), and evangelicals form a substantial percentage of state populations across the geographic majority of the country (Pew Research Center, 2019). What's more, evaluations of the Christian Right's power at the state level exposes its significant presence and influence in states beyond the geographic South (Conger 2010a, 2010b; Conger & Djupe, 2016). Given this, one could expect these schools to draw a more geographically diverse, national student body. As noted, though, the schools still rely heavily on the South.

Figure 4.2. Percent of graduating class who attended undergraduate institutions in the regional South.

Percentages based on subset of alumni identified through LinkedIn, Facebook, Martindale, and name-based Google searches for lists of graduating classes (see Appendix A for more detail). As of 2015, this subset represented ~48% of Regent Law alumni, ~43% of AMSL alumni, and ~52% of Liberty Law alumni. The "South" was determined by the U.S. Census categories and included undergraduate institutions in the following states: Delaware, Maryland, West Virginia, D.C., Virginia, Kentucky, Tennessee, Arkansas, Oklahoma, Texas, Louisiana, Mississippi, Alabama, Georgia, South Carolina, North Carolina, and Florida.

Traditional metrics of LSAT scores (the law school admissions test) and median GPA (undergraduate grade point average) provide a sense of the relative quality of the student body of each of these mission schools and how they relate to the legal market more broadly. All data here appears in American Bar Association published reports from 2003 to 2017. In Figures 4.3 and 4.4, we have included data for the rejected *infiltration* law schools we examined in Chapter 2—Baylor Law School and Notre Dame Law School—for purposes of comparison. Because these institutions are each over 100 years old, it is in one sense unfair to compare their numbers with these newly established and still-establishing law schools. However, it is important to know that these were paths potentially available to the founding Christian Right patrons and ultimately rejected in favor of the difficult, high-cost, higher-control option of building brand new institutions.

In terms of LSAT scores, according to the Law School Admissions Council (LSAC), the national weighted average for all test takers is between 151 and 152.[20] As Figure 4.3 illustrates, Notre Dame and Baylor consistently outperform this national average, signaling a higher-caliber and -quality student body than these newer

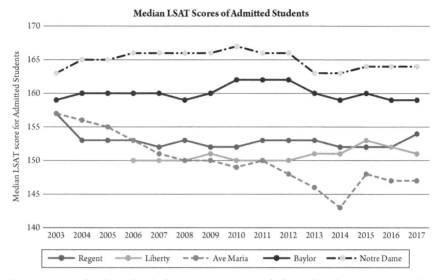

Figure 4.3. Median law school admissions test scores of admitted students over time with comparisons with potential infiltration schools Notre Dame and Baylor. *Source*: American Bar Association Reports 2003–17.

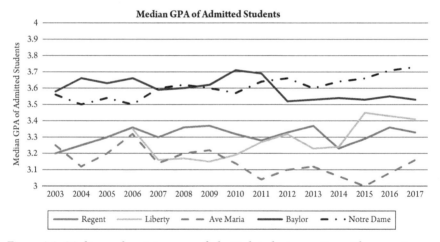

Figure 4.4. Median grade point average of admitted students over time with comparisons to potential infiltration schools Notre Dame and Baylor. *Source*: American Bar Association Reports 2003–17.

mission schools. Regent Law has hovered just around the national weighted LSAT average over time, while Liberty Law has hovered just below.

As depicted in Figure 4.4, undergraduate GPA tells a similar story about the overall and relative strength of each institution's student body, with Notre Dame and Baylor attracting students with GPAs between 3.5 and 3.7 and Regent and

Liberty Law averaging around 3.3 for their incoming classes. Ave Maria's marked downward trajectory in both LSAT and median GPA maps on to what we heard in interviews about the Michigan versus the Florida years. In the beginning, thanks to generous seed funding from Thomas Monaghan and targeted recruiting, AMSL was able to attract students on par with Regent Law's best class historically. As we will explore later, these early classes at AMSL also passed the bar exam with incredibly impressive percentages. However, after the move to Florida in 2009, AMSL has underperformed the national weighted average, tracking in the high 140s for LSAT scores with a low water mark of 143 in 2014. As we examine later, these lower-caliber incoming classes have, unsurprisingly, struggled to pass the bar exam and become licensed attorneys, feeding into the downward cycle of rankings, recruiting, and scrutiny and sanction from the ABA.

The quality and academic caliber of the student body can also positively or adversely affect one's law school experience. A higher-caliber mission student at AMSL confided to us that the class admitted in 2013 was known as "The Party Class" and that their presence and partying was a distraction both in and out of the classroom. Reflecting on her experience, she said, "You know, students who came in with higher LSAT or GPA, I think would have changed the classroom experience a little bit . . . I think with the lowering of the LSAT scores and the GPA . . . you're going to get students who aren't necessarily a good fit to be in law school" (Ave Maria Student 1 2015).

ABA data on overall selectivity—that is, the percentage of applications accepted by the institution—illustrates this point and puts a data-driven exclamation point on the afore-cited AMSL mission student's concerns about the quality and fit of the student body. In Figure 4.5, the more selective and competitive schools are

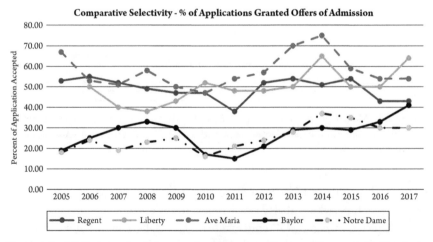

Figure 4.5. Admissions selectivity over time with comparisons with potential infiltration schools Notre Dame and Baylor. *Source*: American Bar Association Reports 2003–17.

at the bottom of the graph, making offers of admission to a smaller percentage of applicants, while those at the top are making offers to a larger percentage of students in their applicant pools (indicating that they are less selective and less competitive).

Beginning in 2011, all schools—including Notre Dame and Baylor—have been accepting a higher percentage of applications as the number of students applying to law school has dropped nationally and the market has contracted (Tamanaha 2012; Barton 2015). However, even in the midst of this market contraction, Notre Dame and Baylor remained at or below the 40% mark for acceptance rate. On the other hand, Regent and Liberty have crept above the 50% mark, with Liberty Law's acceptance rate spiking up to 65% in 2014 and 64% in 2017. AMSL, as we can clearly see, has been the least selective of all the schools, particularly since 2011. In 2013 and 2014, AMSL made admissions offers to 70% and 75% of all applicants, respectively.

In addition to putting institutions at risk of sanction by the ABA (which we saw with AMSL), these numbers can and do affect the recruitment of high-caliber and mission-appropriate *human capital*. For example, incoming LSAT, median GPA, and selectivity together constitute 25% of the overall assessment score for the widely publicized *U.S. News & World Report* rankings of law schools.[21] In 2019, *U.S. News & World Report* ranked Notre Dame Law School 24th and Baylor Law 50th out of 194 total law schools. In comparison, these upstart new mission law schools—Regent Law, Liberty Law, and Ave Maria School of Law—fall in the bottom fourth of all law schools and are correspondingly listed as "rank not published" or "unranked."[22]

These numbers and rankings are published widely in guides for prospective law students across the country and available on hundreds of websites for potential law students making decisions about where to apply (Tamanaha 2012). Perhaps even more importantly, because of the importance the broader legal profession places on credentialing, these numbers also matter in terms of the *cultural capital* assigned to these graduates as they make their way in their careers. If the goal is to be taken seriously, to infiltrate and successfully reshape law, legal culture, and legal institutions, then starting from a position of skepticism because of a lack of *cultural capital* is one more obstacle these Christian lawyers must overcome.

More Than Fellowship: A "Christian Worldview" Legal Curriculum

"You are . . . free to disagree with biblical positions, but you have to have your Bible open and your code book open and your case book open" (Regent Faculty 1 2016).

Once they have recruited students to campus, the primary way these three institutions attempt to shape them is through their distinct law school curriculum. Each institution requires classes in the curriculum that incorporate biblical themes, courses that make explicit the "Christian foundations" of law. At Regent Law, for example, all students take a course in the first year titled "Christian Foundations of Law." The course description reads:

> Jurisprudential survey of the Christian foundations of Anglo American law, including the development of higher/natural law thinking, higher law influence on the development of the common law, the rise of modern legal philosophies and the influence of Christian and secular worldviews on the development of American law.[23]

According to detailed course notes obtained by the authors, the Christian Foundations course (as taught by Jeffrey Brauch, who was Regent Law's dean from 2000 to 2015) juxtaposes "Secular Humanism" with "Christianity" and lays out how each understands key concepts such as "Truth," "Man," "God," and "Law." Mobilizing sources such as Francis Schaeffer's *A Christian Manifesto*, Thomas Aquinas, Sir Edward Coke, William Blackstone, Notre Dame Professor Charles Rice, and Brauch's own textbooks, *A Higher Law* and *Is Higher Law Common Law?*, the key principle reiterated throughout the course is that "Secular Humanism" leads to "chaos, Tyranny, and strong state power" whereas "Christianity" leads to "Form-Freedom Balance," where the "state can't do everything" and in which there's "something above government."[24] To provide some more insight into Brauch's course and its animating purpose, one need only read the "Preface" to the second edition of *A Higher Law*: "Since the first edition of this book was published, I have enjoyed a great privilege. I have joined hundreds of students in a quest. A quest to ask questions that are often ignored in a traditional law school course" (Brauch 2008, xiii).

Similarly, Liberty Law requires two "Foundations of Law" courses—Foundations I and Foundations II—which, taken together, promote and scaffold a "Christian Worldview" perspective on the law. The catalog description for Foundations I describes the course as "[a]n introduction to the theological and philosophical foundations of law, including the . . . Creator/creature distinction; the development of higher/natural law thinking . . . and the biblical basis for the fundamental principles underlying the several courses that comprise the basic curriculum."[25] The description for Foundations II is described similarly but emphasizes "the influence of Christian and secular worldviews on the application of American law, with a particular emphasis on the influences of the Founding Fathers and the drafters of the Declaration of Independence and the Constitution."[26] Course notes from Foundations I as taught by Bruce Green, who was the dean at Liberty from 2004 to 2006, reveal similar topical coverage to Regent's Christian Foundations course. One interesting exception is Green's reliance on Herb Titus's book *God, Man and Law: The Biblical Principles* (Titus 1994) to demonstrate how and when legal education took its wrong turn away from Christian foundations and toward

secular humanism. To illustrate, here is an excerpt from a student's supposedly verbatim transcription of Green's presentation slides on "Legal Education Today" from
September 13, 2005:

1. *In legal education certain fundamental value assumptions by most faculty and
   students may be detected.*
2. *These value assumptions form a <u>framework of thought</u>—almost never openly articulated, they lurk behind everything that is said and done.*
3. *The law student undergoes a <u>process of socialization</u> that involves the identification
   and acceptance of these accepted truths about law and lawyering.*
4. *Cramton used "the ordinary religion of the law school classroom" as a shorthand expression for this value system.*[27]

This effort to reveal the underlying assumptions and presuppositions of contemporary legal education and law is consistent with something we heard repeatedly in
interviews with Liberty Law faculty and students, namely, that secular law schools
and even many purportedly Christian-identifying law schools operate with and in-
doctrinate law students using certain unstated assumptions about the secular, sub-
jective, man-made nature of law. The so-called neutral, case-centric approach to
legal education, faculty and students at our Christian Worldview institutions argue,
are not value-free at all. Rather, they have made the choice to divorce law from its
moral, Christian, and biblical underpinnings, which is a value choice equally as important and consequential as the choice to teach law from a Christian Worldview
perspective.

Notes from Liberty Law's Foundations II course taught in the Spring of 2011
by Rena Lindevaldsen reveals a more topical, culture-wars issue focus. For example, Class 1 is titled "Law and Life (Part 1): The 'Right' to Kill the Unborn."
Classes 2 and 3 are also about abortion; Class 4 transitions to "Law and End of
Life Decisions"; Class 8 is about "Marriage"; and Classes 9 and 10 turn to the
right to "Christian Education," covering hot-button topics such as school prayer
and accommodation of religious exercise in public schools. Other topics covered in the course include capital punishment, and church–state relations more
generally.[28]

Similarly, AMSL requires their students to take three core "mission"
courses. "Moral Foundations of Law," is required for all 1L (first-year) students.
"Jurisprudence" and "Law, Ethics and Public Policy" can be taken in the second
or third years of law school. In addition to these core, required mission courses,
students at AMSL can elect to take religiously inspired or grounded courses such
as "Catholic Social Teaching and the Law," "Canon Law," "Religious Freedom,"
"Church and State," "International Law and the Holy See," and "Papal Teaching
and the Law." The course description in "Papal Teaching and the Law," for example,
highlights just how "unique" AMSL's extensive consideration of Catholic teachings

is for a law school curriculum: "The Holy Fathers through history have provided some of the most profound insights into the law and the human condition. Social encyclicals, as well as those that discuss the value of human life and the law will be considered in this unique course."[29]

Faculty, students, and alumni we interviewed spoke frequently about how biblical and Christian teachings are also woven into non-mission and non–explicitly religious classes on property, family law, international law, contracts, and many others. At Ave Maria, we heard repeatedly that "faculty have some obligation to try when relevant to integrate the natural law perspective into their teaching" (Ave Maria Faculty 1 2015). Regent Law Professor Scott Pryor, reporting on the findings of a university-wide committee exploring how Regent's mission is integrated by faculty in practice, has written that "a faculty member at the Law School should seek to discover the normative 'will of Almighty God' in the Scriptures in dialogue with the Scriptures, within an historical tradition, and as part of a present community" (Pryor 2000, 705). As one Liberty law student conveyed in an interview, the conversation is "very integrated . . . a lot of things that we talk around law, there are biblical examples of . . . we can have these conversations of how do we integrate our faith with this law" (Liberty Student 2 2015). Similarly, a student at AMSL noted that the faculty "try to add a little bit of Catholic reading or Christian reading anyway, some philosophy element. Having to get confronted by all of it sometimes is a little tough, but I do think there's a value to it" (AMSL Student 1 2015). The classes that we sat in on at all three institutions opened with class prayers, and it was common for the faculty to explicitly return to religious or biblical themes as the law was discussed.

Course notes and syllabi we obtained also illustrate how faculty weave religious and biblical perspectives into non-mission courses. Interestingly, many of the textbooks assigned for these core 1L courses such as Criminal Law, Torts, Property, and Contracts are standard textbooks widely assigned outside of these institutions. For example, in their criminal law courses, faculty at Regent Law, Liberty Law, and AMSL all assign Joshua Dressler's *Understanding Criminal Law*, the same textbook assigned by Orin Kerr at George Mason Law, and Richard Garnett at Notre Dame Law School.[30] Additionally, a recent review of criminal law textbooks confirms that Dressler's is among the standard textbooks assigned by law faculty (Ohlin 2016). The course notes we obtained, however, confirm what we heard from our interviews: that faculty actively work to supplement these standard casebooks with material and perspectives that scaffold a natural law or Christian Worldview perspective.

For example, in Liberty Law Professor Jeffrey Tuomala's Con Law I course, the *Holy Bible* is "required" reading alongside more standard constitutional law casebooks,[31] and he cites Matthew 22:44 ("Love the lord your God, love your neighbor as yourself") and the Ten Commandments in exploring the concept of liberty in the "Due Process" clause.[32] At Regent Law, Professor Lynne Marie Kohm's Family Law course begins with an outline of "God's Design for Marriage," citing Bible verses from Genesis, Mark, and Hebrews.[33] Professor Eric DeGroff's Property II course begins by outlining biblically derived and supported principles about the concept of property, including "God Owns the Earth and Everything In and on It" (citing Lev. 25:23, Deut. 10:14; Job 41:11; Psalm 24:1), and "The Christian's Attitude toward Property" (citing Matthew 5:38–42, 19:21–24; Acts 4:32–35; Romans 12:13; 2 Corinthians 8:7–15, etc.).[34] Professor Scott Pryor's Contracts course at Regent Law provides students with the "Biblical view of promises," discusses God as the source of "liberty to execute certain promises enforceable by law," and discusses the importance of "written contracts" in the context of "God's word" expressed in writing in the Ten Commandments.[35]

In 2001 AMSL advertised the intentional efforts that its faculty make to integrate Catholic teachings throughout the curriculum on its website in the following way, saying:

> In addition to these [mission] courses, faculty members address moral and ethical issues that arise naturally throughout the curriculum and explore them in light of the moral and social teachings of the Catholic Church. For example, in Criminal Law the professor might discuss the Catholic teaching on capital punishment, and in Constitutional Law, the Catholic teaching on human rights, society's responsibility to the poor, and the culture of life. In Family Law, the professor might draw on the Church's rich teaching on the nature of the family.[36]

Consistent with this, for example, AMSL Professor Eugene Millhizer's Criminal Law course devotes an entire section to the Catholic teachings about punishment, with a focus on the *Evangelium Vitae* (the papal encyclical) and the teachings of the Catholic Catechism on punishment and retribution.[37] Professor Brian Scarnecchia shepherds students through his Bioethics course—one of the most popular, we were told, by self-identified mission students at AMSL—by assigning his own textbook, *Bioethics, Law and Human Life Issues: A Catholic Perspective on Marriage, Family, Contraception, Abortion, Reproductive Technology, Death and Dying*.

There is ample support for the claim that these Christian Worldview institutions are doing something qualitatively different with their curriculum than traditional law schools. They are, as they advertise, providing "more than Christian fellowship" for students and faculty. As we show in the next section, however, these law schools still need to graduate lawyers who will be prepared to pass the bar exam and to practice law. There is a clear and identifiable tension for these schools between mission and non-mission demands. Some, as we show, have navigated this tension better than the others.

Return on Investment: "A Generation of Christian Attorneys"?

Having shown how these *parallel alternative* institutions recruit students and faculty and having reviewed their curricular efforts to train and produce a distinctly different brand of lawyer, a significant question is: What happens to these students once they graduate? Are they going on to positions of power and influence? Are they drawing on their distinctly Christian legal training to help reshape the foundations of law? While we don't have a complete picture of alumni activity and influence for reasons that have to do both with access (which we describe in greater detail in Appendix A) and their relatively recent establishment and the career stages of their alumni, we can provide some insights into their productivity as support structures for the Christian Right to date. In the sections that follow we track these graduates' relative successes and failures in meeting the licensing requirements to practice law, and we review some general employment data for all three schools.

Meeting the Bar: Will This "Generation of Christian Attorneys" Be Licensed to Practice Law?

Oral Roberts's path-altering legal victory against the American Bar Association opened the door for these Christian Worldview law schools to seek accreditation, which meant that their graduates would be eligible to sit for the bar exam in every state. The state bar agencies are creatures and legal creations of the state that regulate access to legal services principally by controlling the quality and quantity of licensed attorneys in a particular state. The licensing exam tests basic lawyering skills and proficiencies, state-specific knowledge and competencies, as well as the ability to apply legal principles to a series of real-world problems. Given this, these Christian Worldview law schools must balance their commitment to teaching law in a fundamentally distinct, Christian manner—the entire reason for their creation— while also providing students with the general skills and competencies they will need to pass the bar exam and become licensed attorneys in their state of residence.

Striking the right balance has been difficult for these schools, and it is a live and ever-present concern for faculty and administrators we spoke with at each of these schools. Veering too far in one direction or the other, as we illustrate, threatens the ability of these institutions to realize their Christian missions—an overemphasis on skills and basic legal curricula threatens to water down the Christian Worldview aspects of the curriculum, while an underemphasis on these skills affects bar passage, student recruitment, rankings, ABA accreditation, and basic survival as a law school.

The ABA data on combined school average pass rates each year provides insight into how well each of these institutions has performed over time preparing their graduates to pass the bar exam and become licensed attorneys. As in previous graphs, we have also included rejected *infiltration* options Notre Dame Law School and Baylor Law School for purposes of comparison. As we can see, until 2012—the year the market contraction caught up with them—Notre Dame and Baylor were consistently above the 90% mark in average combined annual bar passage. Even after 2012, the lowest each school performed in bar passage was 80%. Each of these new mission schools, by comparison, has struggled at different periods with bar passage. These struggles, in part, a product of their newness and, in part, a product of their unique requirements of religiosity in their student body and their curriculum, and their responses are instructive of some of the broader tensions we outlined earlier between mission-specific and basic legal professional elements of these law schools.

In 2002, the first year for which we have data, we see from Figure 4.6 that under half of Regent Law's graduates passed the bar exam (45%). And that was not the low water mark for Regent. As media accounts detail, in 2000, Regent Law's bar passage rate "had sunk to 36%" (Vegh 2007). This happened to be the year that Monica Goodling, the infamous Regent alumna who took heat in front of Congress for using political criteria to fire U.S. attorneys in the Bush administration, sat for the bar exam. Goodling's politicized antics coupled with Regent's low bar passage rate in her graduating class prompted legislators and pundits to openly question the legitimacy of Regent Law School during the hearings. Representative Steve Cohen (D-Tenn.) asked Goodling if she was "aware that 50 to 60% of the students [in your graduating class] failed the bar the first time" while Jon Stewart of *The Daily Show* referred to Regent Law as being about as rigorous as a "'Jiffy Law' drive-through" (Vegh 2007). Paul Krugman in the *The New York Times* intimated that the bar passage

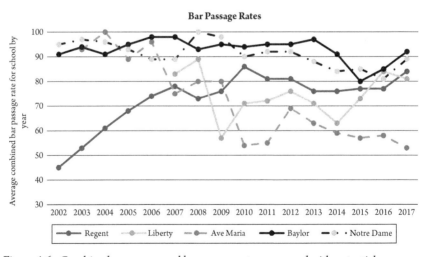

Figure 4.6. Combined average annual bar passage rates compared with potential infiltration options Notre Dame and Baylor. *Source*: American Bar Association Reports 2003–17.

problems had more to do with Regent Law prioritizing the culture wars over academic standards, calling its graduates "extremists" and warning that Goodling was just one part of a larger government "infiltration" strategy of the Christian Right (Krugman 2007).

By the time the Monica Goodling scandal captured national attention in 2007, Regent Law had already rebounded in terms of its bar passage rates, hovering between 75% and 80%. Dean Jeffrey Brauch, who took over in 2000, six years after founding Dean Herb Titus was fired for, among other things, overemphasizing religiosity over student quality and other professional concerns, took a number of steps to address the bar passage issue. As *The Virginian-Pilot* reported, Regent Law added required courses covered in the bar exam, including business and family law, and replaced part-time faculty with full-time faculty in the important skill area of legal writing (Vegh 2007).

As Figure 4.6 demonstrates, over the last five years Regent Law's bar passage rate has held steady and even increased slightly. The school averages just shy of an 80% average combined pass rate annually, and in 2017, Regent Law boasted the number one position in Virginia for graduates passing the Virginia bar exam (94.59%), outperforming highly ranked schools University of Virginia and George Mason (Tubbs 2017). As it achieves more success along these dimensions, Regent Law has turned up the volume on its professional- and lawyering-skills-training messaging and substantially muted the polemic religious language that comprised the core of its public-facing messaging under founding Dean Herb Titus. In the previous chapter we highlighted the stark differences in Regent Law's messaging between 1997 and 2018—with the former laden with religious calling and polemic language surrounding the broader Christian-driven mission of reforming law and legal education and the latter emphasizing the professional development opportunities at Regent Law. Regent Law's new motto, changed in 2018, captures this transition in messaging more succinctly, from "Law is more than a profession. It's a calling" to "Practice-ready, purpose-driven." Once again, this shift away from privileging religiosity and the Christian mission, toward legal and professional preparation—a shift driven both by the demands of the legal market and by the realities of existing in a tightly regulated and controlled professional environment—ensures the survival of the law school as a law school but could have the effect of watering down the distinctly Christian aspects of the school as a support structure for the Christian Right.

Liberty Law has experienced similar struggles balancing its religious mission and purpose with the market and professional considerations of being a full-service and fully accredited law school. New law schools without long-standing reputations and job placement records find it difficult to recruit high-quality students as it is, and when one factors in the fact that Liberty Law is competing against the older, better-established Regent Law for Christian Worldview and regional students, those difficulties multiply. While Liberty Law was always going to face an uphill battle for these reasons, several faculty confided to us that these problems were compounded under the deanship of Mathew Staver, who led Liberty Law from 2006 to 2014. As we examined in the last chapter, Staver brokered the partnership between his policy-oriented public interest law firm Liberty Counsel and Liberty Law School and remained at the helm of both.

Faculty told us in confidence that Staver's narrow focus on the culture wars and on recruiting students and faculty with an interest in public policy resulted in "neglect" of other parts of the law school as a site for professional development and broad legal training. During the eight years Staver was dean, the average bar passage rate was 71%. Two of those years, however, Liberty Law posted its two lowest ever bar passage rates (57% in 2009 and 63% in 2014). The headline of a local newspaper in 2014 shortly after Staver's resignation succinctly illustrated the problem: "Bar exam pass rates a priority as Liberty searches for new law school dean" (Pounds 2014).

A faculty member we spoke with discussed the shift of focus of Liberty Law in the post-Staver era, emphasizing the importance of prioritizing professional preparation over the previously dominant focus on "religious liberty litigation":

> I think we're much more focused now on the things we need to be focused on which is that our students are taking a bar that doesn't care about religious liberty litigation. They have to know torts, contracts, property, and civ pro. We're getting a whole lot more detail oriented and trying to figure out, as we have seen our bar pass rate tumble a little bit, what can be done to turn that around. We're working together as a unit to try to turn that around. We're having very productive discussions in faculty meetings and just faculty members in general talking trying to come up with ideas and solutions. (Liberty Faculty 2 2015)

Chief among the steps Liberty Law has taken to improve the professional training of its students has been investing in its lawyering skills curriculum. Liberty students now take six required lawyering skills classes—one each semester—and the school's "Law School Academics" page makes the "practical skills program" its centerpiece. The program, as it advertises on its website, deploys the same "practice-ready" language that Regent Law has recently integrated into its motto:

> Start developing the skills you need to practice law from day one. Our innovative practical skills program offers you a comprehensive skills curriculum that will prepare you for your career. As a student at Liberty Law, you'll have a minimum of six courses of real-world training through our Center for Lawyering Skills that will equip you to graduate "practice-ready."[38] (quotes in original)

As evidence that this new practice-oriented branding is paying dividends, every student we interviewed emphasized the "lawyering skills" program as one of the most valuable and important pieces of their Liberty Law education.

These investments in skills-training seem to be paying dividends for Liberty, as it has been trending upward since Staver's departure in 2014. In 2016, Liberty was second for bar passage in the state of Virginia, with 89.66% passing the bar, which put them second, behind top-ranked University of Virginia and ahead of their Christian Worldview competitor, Regent Law, which notched a 78.79% pass rate (Liberty University News Service 2016). Liberty Law's bar passage woes under Mat Staver illustrate the perils of running a law school as if it is *only* a support structure institution for a movement rather than a fully functional and full-service law school. It must be both in order to survive and fulfill its unique mission.

As we discussed in the previous chapter, AMSL is a tale of two law schools: the Ann Arbor, Michigan, period from 2000 to 2008, and the Naples, Florida, period from 2009 forward. Figure 4.6 illustrates the stark differences as measured by bar passage rates. The first four classes of AMSL graduates to sit for the bar exam— those students who had received generous financial aid packages—notched an impressive 93%, 100%, 89%, and 96% combined average bar passage rate, putting them in lockstep with Notre Dame and Baylor. Though the school's numbers dropped to 75%, 80%, and 80% in the following three years, prior to the move to Naples, Florida, as Figure 4.6 illustrates, bar passage has been on a steady decline since the move. Since 2010, AMSL graduates have averaged below a 60% combined average bar passage rate.

Visiting AMSL in April 2015, we heard repeatedly about the interconnected bar passage and student recruitment problems from administrators, faculty, and students. As one faculty member put it to us in confidence, "We've got a bar problem. It's affected our recruiting. It's affected our admissions. It's affected everything. It's affected our alumni network . . . we need to get that straightened out" (Ave Maria Faculty 3 2015). Like Liberty and Regent, AMSL has responded to its decline in bar passage by investing more time and attention into lawyering skills and by increasing its coverage of material from the Florida bar exam, where, for example, 81% of its graduates sat for the bar in 2017 (American Bar Association 2018). An administrator at Ave Maria addressed the changes AMSL was implementing in response to poor bar exam performance in our 2015 interview:

> We're bringing in a bar passage director. The faculty has passed to change the curriculum to more match the Florida Bar Exam. We're going to do what's called . . . It's not called a boot camp, but it's essentially a boot camp, during orientation, we're flipping orientation. Instead of just having some academics and making it an administrative week, this is going to be some administration and give them a one credit hour course on how to succeed in law school . . . So critical reading, critical thinking, writing for the law

exam, all of that in the first week and it's a one credit hour course. We're doing a lot of that stuff to try to change, so I do see us academically becoming much, much better, and getting back to I think where the school initially wanted to be, or started off as." (Ave Maria Administrator 2 2015)

Even with all these changes in the works, as we reviewed in the previous chapter, AMSL was still placed on a financial watch list by the Department of Education and in 2016 was formally sanctioned by the ABA for admitting too many students who were at a high risk of not passing the bar exam. As of February 2018, the ABA has removed its remedial sanctions, but the 2017 bar exam results are not encouraging. The school notched a record low 53% overall average pass rate in 2017. The bar passage issue is more than just an annoying distraction from the mission focus of AMSL. It is, as one faculty member put it to us in confidence, a "matter of survival."

The Big Picture: Employment Data for Regent, AMSL, and Liberty

How many of the graduates of these mission-oriented schools are employed within nine months of graduation? What careers do they choose, and what does this reveal about these law schools as both professional training institutions and as mission-oriented support structures for the Christian Right?

Self-reported employment statistics provide a sense of the overall percentages of lawyers employed within nine months of graduation. Figure 4.7 aggregates employment data as reported and published by the American Bar Association from 2003 to 2017.[39] As with student quality metrics and bar passage rate, we see that once again the potential *infiltration* options of Baylor and Notre Dame far outperform their more recently established mission counterparts. The benefits of institutional

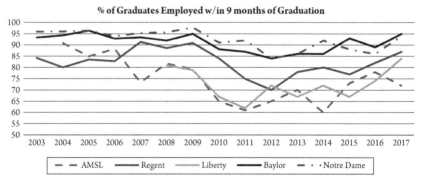

Figure 4.7. Percent of alumni employed within nine months of graduation compared with potential infiltration options Notre Dame and Baylor. *Source*: American Bar Association Reports 2003–17.

stability and reputation are brought into sharp relief when we look at how each of these schools responded to the law market contraction, which began in 2008 and has only started to stabilize. For example, at the bottom of this current market cycle in 2011 (and in the context of more stringent reporting requirements by the ABA), Notre Dame and Baylor still posted employment numbers in the mid-80% range. That same year Regent reported numbers of 72%; AMSL, 61%; and Liberty, 56%.

While all schools have posted more attractive employment numbers on average since 2011, Notre Dame and Baylor are consistently employing anywhere from 10% to 30% more of their own graduates than these newer mission schools. And, it should be noted that Notre Dame and Baylor graduate on average almost twice the number of graduates of each of these mission schools. In 2017, for example, the graduating class at Notre Dame was 207 and Baylor was 130. That same year Regent graduated 78 students, Ave Maria graduated 81, and Liberty graduated 58. Just in terms of raw numbers, in some years the rejected *infiltration* options of Notre Dame and Baylor are *each* producing greater numbers of working lawyers than all three mission schools combined.

The ABA reports also break down annual employment statistics by sector for each institution. These reports show what percentage of each graduating class is employed in which legal sector within nine months of graduation. We averaged fifteen years of this data (2003–17) for each of the mission schools and the comparative case studies of Notre Dame and Baylor and present this data in Table 4.2. For context, the bulk of all lawyers, anywhere from 70%–75%, go into private practice (American Bar Association 2013; Garth et al. 2014, 24–25), about 8% of practicing lawyers are in Government, an additional 8% in Private industry, 1% are

Table 4.2. **American Bar Association Data on Employment by Sector Averaged for Years 2003–17**

% Employed	Ave Maria	Regent	Liberty	Baylor	Notre Dame
Overall w/in 9 months	74.4%	81.6%	72.5%	91%	92.2%
Law Firm	45.9%	42.6%	45.2%	69%	58.3%
Business & Industry	20%	17%	18%	9%	8%
Government	18%	19%	19%	12%	14%
Public Interest	3.8%	7.2%	6.6%	1.2%	4.8%
Clerkships	7.5%	7.6%	7.1%	6.4%	14.3%
Academia/Education	3.8%	4.45%	4.2%	1.7%	1.1%

Sources: American Bar Association Law School Admission Council Official Guide to ABA Approved Law Schools (Margolis et al 2005, 2006, 2007, 2008, 2009, 2010, 2011, 2012, 2013) and American Bar Association Section of Legal Education and Admission to the Bar (https://www.americanbar.org/groups/legal_education/resources/statistics/)

in Education, and another 1% serve in Legal Aid/Public Defender roles (American Bar Association 2013).

With these national practice setting numbers in mind, we see from Table 4.2 that the initial distribution of students from these mission-based schools looks markedly different from the national distribution and from the rejected *infiltration* options of Notre Dame and Baylor. First off, the percentages of students entering government jobs at all three mission schools—AMSL (18%), Regent (19%), and Liberty (19%)—is more than twice the national average and is also significantly higher than Baylor and Notre Dame. These figures align with the data we presented in Chapter 3 about the motivating missions and purposes of these institutions. Recall, for example, that Tom Monaghan said that AMSL would become the "West Point for Catholic laity." Similarly, Jerry Falwell upon founding Liberty Law told reporters that "we certainly are training Christian activists" and that the founding motto of Pat Robertson's Christian Broadcasting Network University (later to be renamed Regent) was "Christian Leadership to Change the World." It would appear that in this critically important support structure category of Government, these institutions are fulfilling their patrons' visions.

Education is another category where the mission schools stand out. Baylor and Notre Dame track the national distribution, placing around 1% of graduates in Education, whereas the mission-based schools are all placing higher percentages of graduates straight into Education—AMSL (3.8%), Regent (4.4%), and Liberty (4.2%). Some of this likely has to do with the dearth of Christian Worldview–trained faculty and the need for this distinct brand of *human capital* to feed back into these institutions. These institutions have tended to hire their own graduates back on as adjunct or full-time faculty. Additionally, as we illustrated in Chapter 3, the newer Christian Worldview schools like Liberty Law benefited from having Regent Law–trained graduates as founding faculty members. It is important to note here that we have very little evidence that any of these graduates are infiltrating the faculty at other institutions. From a support structure perspective, this insularity is not ideal. It likely also reflects a lack of *cultural capital* and a lingering skepticism within mainstream legal education of the Christian Worldview brand of education, something we examine in greater detail in the next chapter.

Finally, while we don't have good national data on the percentage of lawyers engaged in public interest law—the field where most of the high-impact transformative litigation happens—we see that Regent Law (7.2%) and Liberty Law (6.6%) are placing higher percentages of graduates straight into this field than Baylor (1.2%) and Notre Dame (4.8%). We discuss the possible reasons for this in the next chapter. That is, both Regent Law and Liberty Law built their schools in connection with a prominent public interest law firm (the American Center for Law and Justice and Liberty Counsel, respectively). As we also discuss in the next chapter, AMSL had a direct pipeline into public interest law with the Thomas More Law Center, which was all but severed when Monaghan moved the school from Michigan to Florida.

While interesting, this ABA data is limited in a few ways. The categories are broad and do not tell us, for example, which levels of "Government" graduates are working in or what kinds of law firms they inhabit. Additionally, these employment statistics only report the first job straight out of law school and do not capture these same graduates in mid-career or those who are quite advanced. Did the "Clerks" listed in these reports go on to careers in the legal academy, public interest law, or eventually a judgeship later on in their careers? To attempt to answer these questions, we searched for alumni of these mission institutions on the Web. We primarily relied on professional networking sites LinkedIn and Martindale, while also scouring Facebook alumni groups for additional names and then conducting name-based Google searches. After identifying alumni and their occupation, we coded for the type of legal job or sector as well as the location of their employment by region. Additionally, we collected available information about where they obtained their undergraduate degrees and coded for type (Christian or secular) as well as the regional location of their undergraduate institution (see Appendix A for more detail). Through these Web-based searching methods, we were able to find 2015 employment data for 1,580 Regent Law alumni (~ 48%),[40] 649 AMSL alumni (~43%),[41] and 490 Liberty Law alumni (~52%).[42] Clearly, this is not a comprehensive data set, but it does provide greater insight into a sample of alumni at various career stages.

Consistent with ABA reporting and consistent with statistics on the legal profession as a whole, the largest percentage of alumni identified on LinkedIn and Web-based searches for all three mission institutions were working in private practice. For Regent Law, that number was 63%, for AMSL that was just over half at 51%, and for Liberty Law that number was just under half at 48%. Some law firms do bring impact litigation and policy-oriented litigation, and many large law firms allow or even require their associates and partners to do pro bono work on behalf of public interest causes or low-income clients (see, e.g., Granfield and Mather 2009). To corroborate this national data, in the Web-based survey we conducted with AMSL alumni in 2018, 87% of the respondents who indicated that they perform pro bono work were employed in a private law firm. Of these respondents, over two-thirds (66.67%) indicated that they found pro bono work through Alliance Defending Freedom (ADF). As we have indicated throughout the book, in addition to being the home of the Blackstone Legal Fellowship, ADF is the epicenter of culture wars litigation in the United States (see, e.g., Bennett 2017; Hollis-Brusky & Wilson 2017; Wilson 2016). Unfortunately, we do not have data on how many of the lawyers identified in our Web sample are engaging in pro bono work on behalf of Christian Right causes. That being said, we should not discount the possibility that some of these lawyers are supporting these causes through pro bono work.

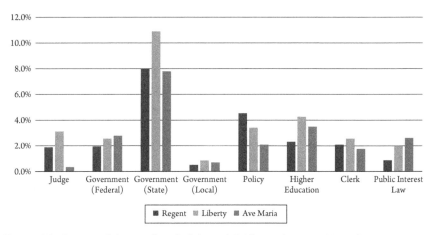

Figure 4.8. Percent of alumni identified through Web searches in 2015 working in support structure–relevant sectors of the legal profession. Percentages based on subset of alumni identified through LinkedIn, Facebook, Martindale, and name-based Google searches for lists of graduating classes (see Appendix A for more detail). As of 2015, this subset represented ~48% of Regent Law alumni, ~43% of Ave Maria Law School alumni, and ~52% of Liberty Law alumni.

Figure 4.8 illustrates the employment breakdowns we have identified as most relevant and important in terms of Support Structure Theory. From the perspective of our animating theory, having direct access to decision-making, that is, placing *human capital* into positions where it can directly pull the levers of power, is the most effective and efficient way to influence law and policy. The categories of "Judge," "Government," and "Policy" reflect the percentages of total alumni identified through our Web search who were employed in these sectors. More indirectly but, nevertheless, important from the perspective of judicial decision-making, "Clerks" help draft judicial opinions and, as political science has demonstrated, serve as important behind-the-scenes influences on judges and their legal reasoning (Hollis-Brusky 2015, 25–26; Peppers 2006; Ward & Weiden 2006). As Support Structure Theory emphasizes, however, having the decision-makers in place is a necessary but not sufficient condition for changing the law (Epp 1998). A movement also needs lawyers to bring cases ("Public Interest Law") and academics ("Higher Education") to provide the ideas or *"intellectual capital"* that scaffold judicial decisions (Hollis-Brusky 2015).

When we examine these high-impact support structure areas of the legal profession, we see that these mission-based schools, even at relatively young ages, are placing alumni in each of these categories, albeit a small overall percentage of graduates identified are working in some of these sectors. The Liberty Law sample population tracks the national average reported by the ABA for the key support structure category of "Judges," which is about 3% of the overall lawyer population

(American Bar Association 2013), while Regent Law and AMSL are slightly under that average in our sample. As in the ABA reports we reviewed earlier, all three mission schools in our sample had a higher percentage of alumni working in "Higher Education" than the national lawyer distribution average of 1%. In the important category of "Public Interest Law," where most of the transformative impact litigation campaigns are initiated (Cummings & Rhode 2009; Southworth 2004; Trubek 1991), we see lower overall percentages in our sample than those fifteen-year averages reported by Liberty Law and Regent Law to the ABA. This could be because our sample did not adequately capture that part of the population or because the reported lawyers who initially went into clerkships or entry-level positions with Liberty Counsel or the American Center for Law and Justice, for example, have since moved into a different sector of the legal profession.

Also fairly consistent with the fifteen-year ABA averages we reported earlier, we see the alumni in our sample overperforming the national lawyer distribution about twofold in the combined category of "Government." Because we had more detailed data to draw on from our Web search, we were able to divide the category of "Government" in Figure 4.8 into "Federal/State/Local." This allowed us to see that the vast majority of the alumni employed in this category for all three mission schools are working at the "State" level. This data aligns well with what we already know about conservative Christian evangelicals.

First, while they have been active in federal politics for decades, there is a longer-standing affinity among Christian conservatives for state and local politics. Evangelicals have invested heavily in infrastructure that helps to enable political mobilization at the state level. Williams notes that while conservative evangelicals had some national television networks and nationally syndicated religious broadcasters since the late 1970s, they also have "a host of local TV preachers [who], filled the airwaves with Christian messages" (2010, 161).

Complementing this are the networks of local churches that can help provide voters and campaign resources that can be especially effective in states with significant evangelical populations. Not surprisingly then, again in spite of significant national-level, evangelical political and legal organizations, Christian conservatives have been far more active and effective in state- and local-level politics than they have on the national level (Mello 2016; Williams 2010; Wilson 2013, 2016). Using abortion politics as one example, the combination of state-level resources, friendly legislatures, and limited political opportunities at the federal level has made the states the primary forum for anti-abortion activism for decades (Wilson 2013, 2016). Beyond abortion, it should not be a surprise that activism at the state and local level has also been central to the Christian Right's influence within the Republican Party as a whole (see e.g., Baylor 2017).

Overall numbers and percentages aside, we know from previous work on influence networks that it only takes a handful of strategically placed actors with access to power and decision-making to exert influence on law and politics (Haas 1992;

Sebenius 1992; Yee 1996; Cross 2013; Hollis-Brusky 2015). To illustrate, Bob McDonnell, who graduated with Regent Law's inaugural class in 1989, served in the Virginia House of Delegates from 1992 to 2006, was elected Virginia's Attorney General from 2006 to 2009 and later became the Governor of Virginia from 2010 to 2014 before he was embroiled in a corruption scandal that ended up as a case before the United States Supreme Court. While in power, not only did McDonnell push the Christian conservative agenda, he also appointed sympathetic Regent Law graduates to serve as political appointees for the state of Virginia.[43]

Similarly, Liberty Law alumnus Matt Krause, who also graduated in Liberty's inaugural class, was elected to the Texas House of Representatives in 2012. Now in his third term, Krause has built his platform around, among other conservative values, "traditional family values and pro-life advocacy."[44] Speaking with his alma mater, Krause said of his public service, "We are on this earth for a very short time and we need to do all we can to maximize our effectiveness and our ability to impact the culture while we are here. Public office is a great way to do that."[45]

There are, no doubt, dozens of stories we could tell about alumni from each of these mission institutions working to bring about the kinds of broad-scale cultural transformations the Christian Right seeks. But what we cannot know at this point is whether the sum total of these efforts justifies the enormous financial investments each of these patrons made when they decided to build their own law schools. Trying to reshape the law and legal culture from the bottom up is a long-term game and the payoffs are uncertain. At this point, what we can do and what we have done is describe in detail the scaffolding each of these Christian Right institutions is building to play this long game and identify the forces that are working with and against them in accomplishing their missions.

Bringing the Support Structure Pyramid Back In

In this chapter we have analyzed the ways these mission institutions are attracting conservative Christian faculty and law students; training *human capital* in a distinctly different, Christian Worldview way; and working to make sure their graduates are both licensed and employed after graduation. We have also examined some of the difficulties or constraints pushing against the accomplishment of this mission— constraints that have to do with reputation, rankings, money, and the requirements of being a fully accredited law school.

Bringing the Support Structure Pyramid back in, recruiting, training, credentialing, and placing *human capital* into the legal profession is a necessary step that movements need to take if they hope to eventually influence the law and the legal culture. While this effort requires an incredible amount of resources, particularly when movements choose to build their own institutions from scratch, the payoffs on these investments are usually decades away. We are here reminded of an Ave Maria administrator's answer to our question about what they see as Ave Maria's current or potential impact:

> Some of our early alums are just starting into that mid- or early mid-career stage, but once we have more of those who become judges, who become legislators, who become leaders in law firms and organizations that lead throughout the country, my hope is that you'll start to see . . . a more transformative influence on the legal profession as a whole. (Ave Maria Administrator 3 2015)

While having sympathetic or, even better, deeply committed movement members with access to power is a necessary step, it is not the only step successful movements can or should take if they hope to have a "transformative influence on the legal profession as a whole." The next chapter looks at the way these institutions create and facilitate the transfer of *human capital* to the Christian Right and the broader conservative legal movement through social networks and relationships (*social capital*). It also examines these institutions as purveyors of *cultural capital*; that is, it evaluates their ability to prime audiences to receive (and to not dismiss out of hand) their transformative and revolutionary ideas, or *intellectual capital*.

Social and *Cultural Capital* (or "Credibility Capital")

> We do think there is a place for our voice, but there's a right way to ex-
> press this and a right way to advocate for God on that basis. . . . Being
> taken seriously by elites, being taken seriously in serious places [is im-
> portant to us]. It's not just Bayou Bill Bob saying, "God's law over Man's
> law!" That's really not what it is.
>
> —Blackstone Administrator 2 2015

We first heard the term *credibility capital* while interviewing Blackstone administrators
at the Alliance Defending Freedom (ADF). One administrator, who handled public
relations and media relations, emphasized time and again in our interviews and
during our visit the value that the ADF places on being taken seriously both by elites
and wider publics. As we wrote in Chapter 3, this desire to play on the elite's turf and
to engage with elites animated founder Alan Sears's desire to launch the Blackstone
Legal Fellowship as "a middle way" (Blackstone Administrator 2 2015) or what we
have referred to throughout this book as a *supplemental approach* to building the
Christian Right's support structure. The Blackstone leadership recognized the difficulty, in particular, of developing credibility capital with elites and wider publics
when pursuing a *parallel alternative* approach. When institutions reject and intentionally exist outside the cultural and legal mainstream, it is far more difficult to
have influence on the mainstream. The leadership of Blackstone likened this kind
of cultural self-separation to a "Holy Huddle" and to "show[ing] up to a stadium
where's there's no game" (Blackstone Administrator 2 2015).

The aim of the credibility capital game, to continue the metaphor, is to influence
elites and to prime wider publics so that both audiences are receptive to the kinds of
transformative ideas the Christian Right is working to develop and disseminate. In
other words, the work involves making sure the movement's ideas are not perceived
to be "positively looney" and "off-the-wall" (Balkin 2001, 1444–45; Teles 2008, 12;
Hollis-Brusky 2015, 159–64) but, instead, are viewed as comfortably within the
bounds of legitimate legal discourse. Of course, as we have discussed throughout

Separate But Faithful. Amanda Hollis-Brusky and Joshua C. Wilson, Oxford University Press (2020). © Oxford University
Press. DOI: 10.1093/oso/9780190637262.001.0001

the book, the legal philosophy and jurisprudence embraced by Regent Law, Liberty Law, and Ave Maria School of Law (AMSL) still occupy an outsider status within the legal academy and are viewed with a certain amount of skepticism even within the conservative legal movement (Southworth 2008). And in the broader public, there is the "crazy Christian" stigma that each of these institutions must overcome, a stigma built up over years by media portrayals of wild-eyed religious extremists speaking for the movement.

This chapter analyzes the actual and potential production of two dimensions of credibility capital—*social capital* and *cultural capital*. To gauge *social capital*, we look at the extent to which our three primary case study institutions are networked both with Christian Right movement institutions and with other more main-stream elite conservative institutions and networks like the Federalist Society. To measure *cultural capital*, we look at print media appearances for the faculty of each of these institutions. How often and—more importantly—in which media outlets are these faculty engaging with broader publics through op-eds or by being quoted and cited as experts? We also draw comparisons along both these dimensions with institutions representative of the rejected *supplemental* (Blackstone) and *infiltration* (Notre Dame and Baylor) approaches.

Social Capital—Connectedness with the Christian Right

In terms of Support Structure Theory (SST), the ability to create *and* successfully transfer resources within the Christian Right movement is one important function of these Level 1 support structure institutions. As we discussed in Chapter 1, the transfer of capital and resources can be facilitated by networks that connect various levels of the Support Structure Pyramid. In this section we examine how well networked these law schools are with identifiable Christian Right movement institutions and actors. Our research revealed that this is, in fact, a fairly insular and tightly connected world, and each of these law schools offers multiple entry points into it.

It should be noted explicitly that, for all its drawbacks, this is one very big ad-vantage of the *parallel alternative* approach to institution building in our case study. Movement patrons have been able to handcraft a campus culture that promotes conservative Christian values, encourages anti-abortion activism and speakers, and curates internship and clinical opportunities geared toward Christian Right political and legal causes. For all of the benefits of the *infiltration* and *supplemental* approaches in terms of cost and credentialing, these approaches cannot replicate the scale of exposure and relationship building within the Christian Right that these mission-oriented institutions have managed to create.

Building a Pipeline into Public Interest Law and Culture Wars Litigation

As we reviewed in Chapter 3, each of the founding patrons of these new mission law schools used their relationships with prominent Christian Right Public Interest Law Organizations (PILOs) to broker partnerships between these litigation-based firms and their law schools. These partnerships, which have been formalized to varying degrees over the years, create a direct pipeline for litigation- or policy-interested students to plug into this world to gain experience and make connections for post–law school opportunities. From the perspective of the Support Structure Pyramid, which focuses on litigation-based change, access to some of the premier litigating firms on the Christian Right is one of the critical comparative advantages these law schools have (or had) over their competitors. As we show, Regent Law has managed to sustain the most productive and mutually beneficial partnership with its PILO, the American Center for Law and Justice (ACLJ). Liberty Law had a strained though somewhat beneficial arranged marriage with Liberty Counsel (LC) that eventually ended in divorce. AMSL had the potential for a fruitful partnership with Monaghan's Ann Arbor, Michigan–based PILO, Thomas More Law Center (TMLC), but this was never formalized to the same degree as the others and was geographically severed once AMSL moved from Michigan to Florida.

Regent Law and the American Center for Law and Justice[1]

According to one administrator at Regent Law, "That is longstanding. They're on the 4th floor [of the law school]. Even more important to me, my wife works up there. She's a senior attorney with the ACLJ. We've had a very longstanding relationship with the ACLJ. They hire a lot of our students as externs and clerks . . . So we've had a very good relationship with the ACLJ . . . I have a very good relationship with Jay [Alan Sekulow]. The school and the ACLJ have a very good partnership" (Regent Administrator 1 2016).

As this Regent Law administrator emphasized many times over in our interview, Regent Law and the Pat Robertson–founded PILO, the American Center for Law and Justice, have a "very good relationship." In fact, as previous scholarship has detailed, when he founded the American Center for Law and Justice in 1990, Robertson's goal was to build a powerhouse Christian litigation organization that would work synergistically with and within Regent Law School (Hollis-Brusky & Wilson 2017, 124; Hacker 2005, 22). Robertson's sibling support structures have maintained a "close relationship" over time, with the ACLJ offering internship programs to Regent Law students and even lending its attorneys to teach classes on campus (Bennett 2017, 22). Given this close and synergistic relationship, it is no coincidence that many of the ACLJ's attorneys are also graduates of Regent Law (Bennett 2017, 22).

As a Regent Law administrator noted in our interview, the ACLJ still maintains an office inside of and structurally atop of Regent Law School ("they're on the fourth floor"). Imagining the Support Structure Pyramid, in addition to the conceptual connection between these two institutions, in this case we observe a physical and structural connection between Regent Law as a Level 1 institution and the ACLJ as a Level 2 institution. As this same administrator noted, this relationship has facilitated the transfer of Regent Law students to ACLJ as "externs[]" and "clerks," where they gain exposure to Christian Right litigation and, more importantly, where they can be connected with one of the most powerful, well-networked and influential figures on the Christian Right—Jay Sekulow (Regent Administrator 1 2016).

Despite being a Messianic Jew, the ACLJ's General Counsel, Jay Sekulow, has been described as "the mouthpiece of the New Christian Right" (Hacker 2005, 19) and arguably "the most visible Evangelical Christian attorney in America" (Bennett 2017, 22). These are probably not overstatements. Sekulow hosts his own radio show, *Jay Sekulow Live!*, and makes regular appearances on Fox News, CNN, NPR, *Crossfire*, and Pat Robertson's *700 Club* program (Bennett 2017, 22; Hollis-Brusky & Wilson 2017, 124; Hacker 2005, 21). More recently, Sekulow has garnered notoriety for his very visible media presence as President Trump's personal attorney, making the rounds almost weekly on Fox News to defend the president against allegations related to the Russia probe and to promote the president's political agenda (Berenson 2018; Smith 2018; Davis & Boburg 2017).

The ACLJ is a PILO with a fairly broad mission, changing, as some of our interviewees intimated, to respond to whatever Jay Sekulow deems politically important at the moment (Hollis-Brusky & Wilson 2017, 131). This is reflected in the ACLJ's evolving mission statements over time. For example, in December of 1998 the ACLJ's banner slogan read, "Defending the Rights of Believers." Its "Welcome" message from Jay Sekulow read as follows: "You're going to see that our interests at the ACLJ are pretty broad: we're concerned about Religious Liberty; we're concerned about the Unborn Child; and we want to protect Your Family and Your Family's Rights."[2] By September of 2002, the banner slogan of "Defending Rights of Believers" had been removed, and the "Welcome" message from Sekulow read as follows: "Here you will learn that we are: Protecting the US Constitution; Protecting Religious liberty; Fighting to protect life; and fighting to protect the religious rights of Americans."[3]

The focus on family had been dropped, and an emphasis on the U.S. Constitution more generally was added. Also, "fighting to protect life" replaced the rights of the "unborn child," and this is not insignificant. It encapsulates the ACLJ's post-9/11 emphasis on national security issues and its support for and involvement with the Bush Administration's policies concerning the War on Terror. After the attacks of September 11, 2001, Republicans in Congress and the Bush Administration sought out Sekulow for legal support in drafting the policies that would guide the War on Terror, including the Patriot Act. In response, "Sekulow began to reformulate the ACLJ's organizational emphases toward policy making," including national security (Hacker 2005, 29).

The ACLJ now boasts a team of twelve full-time senior attorneys litigating cases on various issues around the globe, a government affairs team, and a five-person litigation department. In terms of its financial resources, ACLJ brings in annual revenues of around $17 million, which is second only to the ADF in terms of financing on the Christian Right (Bennett 2017, 10; Hollis-Brusky & Wilson 2017, 125). Its revamped mission statement not only reflects this growth and expansion of scope but also signals a connection to the natural law jurisprudence that scaffolds the curriculum at Regent Law and the other mission schools: "ACLJ is committed to ensuring the ongoing viability of freedom and liberty in the United States and around the world. By focusing on US Constitutional Law, European Union Law and Human Rights Law, the ACLJ is dedicated to the concept that freedom and liberty are universal, God-given and inalienable rights that must be protected" (Department of the Treasury Internal Revenue Service, American Center for Law and Justice 2012).

Still, the organization remains synonymous with and tightly tethered to the leadership of Jay Sekulow. Regent Law's "very good relationship," to recall the Regent Law administrator's characterization, with Sekulow has created opportunities for law students to easily build inroads into an organization at the center of the culture wars litigation. Indeed, a review of the ACLJ website reveals that 5 of the 12 Senior Counsel attorneys, every single member of the five-lawyer litigation division, and the Chief of Staff are all Regent Law graduates.[4] Through our Web-based alumni search (see Appendix A), we were able to identify an additional ten Regent Law graduates who listed ACLJ in their employment history.[5]

Equally important, Sekulow's connections give Regent Law grads inroads into and *social capital* within Republican politics and administrations. As we teased earlier, Sekulow's ties to the Republican Party, like those of founding patron Pat Robertson, run deep. Not only did Sekulow serve as a policy and legal consultant for George W. Bush, he also helped to vet Bush's judicial nominees, worked as an adviser to Republican presidential candidate Mitt Romney in both 2008 and 2012, and has been referred to as "the last man standing" on President Trump's legal team (Smith 2018). As we reviewed in Chapter 4, Regent Law consistently sends a higher percentage of its graduates into government (on average around 20%) than either its mission school competitors or higher-ranked schools like Baylor and Notre Dame. Jay Sekulow cannot account for this number on his own, of course, but it is safe to say that the relationships he builds and maintains with Republican operatives can facilitate the transfer of Regent Law graduates into these administrations.[6]

Liberty Law and Liberty Counsel (LC)[7]

According to one Liberty Law administrator, "One of the great perks about it though is that Liberty Counsel helps us with our constitutional litigation clinic, and other things like that. We have students that are interested in specific areas and we network with Liberty Counsel to be able to place students, to learn about a specific area that they're interested in that Liberty Counsel might be dealing with" (Liberty Administrator 1 2015).

This quote is excerpted from our 2015 interview with a Liberty Law alumna who at that time was also working as an administrator at Liberty Law School. It is important to note that this administrator used the phrase "we network with" LC rather than the term "partnership," which is how Jerry Falwell and LC founder Mat Staver described the relationship between the two organizations in 2003. As we recounted in Chapter 3, the terms of the then-termed "partnership" included Staver opening up a branch of Liberty Counsel in Lynchburg, Virginia, and establishing the Center for Constitutional Litigation and Policy (later renamed the Liberty Center for Law and Policy) on Liberty Law's campus to "train law students in all aspects of constitutional litigation, with a particular emphasis on the defense of religious liberty, the sanctity of human life, and traditional family values."[8] Fast forward twelve years, and this same administrator insisted emphatically in a follow-up question that "Liberty Counsel is separate and distinct from the law school," "it is very much a separate and distinct [organization]," and there was "no formal [relationship] between the Liberty Counsel and the student population or the alumni population" (Liberty Administrator 1 2015). Fast forward two more years, and as of 2017, all remnants of the Falwell–Staver partnership at Liberty Law School had disappeared. The break-up or dissolution of this partnership is part of the collateral damage from Mathew Staver's departure from Liberty Law School in 2014 after his eight-year deanship.

Though one might characterize the arranged marriage between Liberty Law School and LC as strained or uncomfortable at times, having a culture wars–focused PILO connected to the law school seemed to align directly with Falwell's vision of training foot soldiers or "junkyard dog lawyers" for the Christian Right. For LC founder Mathew Staver, the opportunity to grow his small, self-funded culture wars litigation shop into a premier organization with the institutional and financial support of Falwell and Liberty University was undoubtedly appealing.

Founded in 1989 as a small regional operation out of Orlando, Florida, Staver started the LC with the goal of supporting pro-life efforts in the Southeast. The LC is unique in that it had no parent organization or foundation support. For the first decade of the LC's existence, Staver supported the firm almost entirely with profits from his own private practice, Staver and Associates (Bennett 2017, 26; Hacker 2005, 58). As Hacker writes, "in 1994 the Liberty Counsel took in just over $200,000 in donations. Staver's private practice made up the over $1 million per year extra required to conduct the litigation on the Liberty Counsel's agenda" (Hacker 2005, 58).

The organizational structure changed dramatically in 2000 when Staver decided to sell the private practice and enter into a partnership with Falwell and Liberty Law School (Hollis-Brusky & Wilson 2017, 123; Hacker 2005, 58). This partnership allowed Liberty Law to donate valuable services to LC and to offset a good portion of their operating costs. For example, during fiscal year 2006, LC reported having received "donated services valued at $600,000 from Liberty University for services provided by attorneys and administrative personnel employed by Liberty University." This also included the use of "office facilities, furniture and equipment," the estimated value of which totaled an additional $63,150 (Department of the Treasury Internal Revenue Service Liberty Counsel 2006, 1). This financial underwriting from Falwell and Liberty University represented more than half of LC's total reported expenses from that same year (1).

Roughly two decades later, thanks in large part to Staver and Falwell's partnership, LC was in a much stronger financial position. With total revenues of around $5 million (Department of the Treasury Internal Revenue Service. Liberty Counsel 2014), LC now boasts offices in Florida, Virginia, and Washington, D.C., and even does outreach in Israel.[9] LC's banner mission statement of "Restoring the Culture by Advancing Religious Freedom, the Sanctity of Human Life and the Family" reveals its overt culture wars focus and orientation.[10] LC pursues this mission through litigation and through various other educational, training, and policy initiatives. In 2012, for example, Liberty Counsel spent $1,449,520 on litigation efforts and had 138 cases in active litigation or pre-suit status (Department of the Treasury Internal Revenue Service 2012). Some of its more high-profile cases have included *Madsen v. Women's Health Center* (1994), which successfully challenged a city ordinance imposing a 300-foot buffer zone around abortion clinics at the Supreme Court, *McCreary County, Kentucky v. ACLU of Kentucky* (2005), in which the Supreme Court ruled against Liberty Counsel's position that the Ten Commandments could be displayed in front of Kentucky courthouses, and *Miller v. Davis* (2016), a Sixth Circuit decision defending Kentucky Clerk Kim Davis for her refusal to issue marriage certificates to same-sex couples on religious liberty grounds.

In some ways, merging Liberty Law School and Liberty Counsel under the leadership of one person seems ideal from the perspective of the Support Structure Pyramid. It signals commitment to litigation-based change under the banner of the culture wars and makes the law school attractive to students and faculty who share this goal, facilitating recruitment. Additionally, Staver personally directing two organizations that straddle two levels of the Support Structure Pyramid facilitates the transfer of resources directly from Liberty Law into LC. To illustrate, our Web-search for Liberty Law alumni (see Appendix A) identified thirty-two alumni from the graduating classes of 2010–15 who listed a clerkship, externship, or internship with Liberty Counsel or one of its affiliates as their past employment.[11] Additionally, we identified seven Liberty Law alumni who had gone to work full-time for Liberty Counsel or one of its affiliates after graduation.[12] Of course, this sample represents fewer than half of all Liberty Law graduates, so there are undoubtedly dozens of other alumni who have worked or had experience through Liberty Counsel and the Liberty Center for Law and Policy.

There are also potential hazards when a law school's mission becomes too closely tied to a legal movement's goals or to a single individual's goals. As the evidence we presented in Chapter 4 suggests, Staver's narrow focus on making Liberty Law a viable and successful support structure institution for the Christian Right resulted in neglect of other parts of the law school, putting accreditation and survival of the law school as a professional training organization at risk. Founding Dean of Regent Law Herb Titus referred to the Liberty Counsel–Liberty Law partnership as a case of "the tail wag[ging] the dog":

> Mat Staver [was] the Dean of the law school, he's the president of Liberty Counsel and you can't do it. You can't mix the two. We never had that here at Regent. Yes, Jay [Sekulow] had some influence in regard to the law school but not in the same way that Mat did. Mat basically changed the mission of the law school. (Titus 2016)

Liberty Law's experience and Titus's warning speaks, more broadly, of the dangers of Level 1 organizations being too singularly focused on producing resources for Level 2 organizations, like PILOs. Not only does this handicap a law school's productive capacities in terms of influencing the legal profession more broadly, but it also ignores the fact that support structure institutions like law schools, which exist within broader political and professional contexts, must attend to institutional maintenance and professional concerns or risk collapse.

After the divorce between Staver and Liberty Law in 2014 and the formal dissolution of the Liberty Center for Law and Policy soon thereafter, some vestiges of the old partnership still remained when we visited campus a year later. LC maintained a relationship with the student body through the Liberty Counsel Student Organization (LCSO), which served as an intermediary between LC and the student body. We interviewed a student active in the leadership of that organization at the time. In the student's words,

> [LCSO] basically just tells students about what [Liberty Counsel does] and provides opportunities for us to interact with their lawyers . . . We bribe [students] with pizza, to have students come and hear from the lawyers directly about current cases, past cases, and the import of what they do. Then after the lawyers get to speak, we get to engage one on one, just have conversation with them to talk to them more about it. Another thing that LCSO does is encourages students to get into internships with

Liberty Counsel, whether it's in their litigative office here in Lynchburg, or their one in Orlando, Florida, or they have a public policy office up in D.C. (Liberty Student 1 2015)

But it appears that shortly after we visited, this student organization ceased to exist. According to the Wayback Machine, LCSO vanished from Liberty Law's "Student Organization" webpage sometime between March and April of 2017 and has not returned.

While on campus, we also asked whether LC tapped into the Liberty Law alumni network for affiliate attorneys to work pro bono on its cases, as we were only able to identify one alumnus from our Web search who listed "Liberty Counsel Affiliate Attorney" on their resume or LinkedIn profile (Douglas Wilson ('10)). An administrator said there is no formal communication between the two and, in a revealing portion of the interview, intimated that Staver no longer needs Liberty Law as a source of *human capital*: "Mat Staver who runs Liberty Counsel, he's got enough people calling to fill his bank of issues . . . Liberty Counsel already has a huge base of affiliate attorneys that they work with all over the country" (Liberty Administrator 1 2015).

In sum, the relationship between LC and Liberty Law was not, as the Regent Law administrator characterized that between ACLJ and Regent, "very good." Faculty we spoke with after Staver's departure characterized the relationship as one-sided—his single-minded pursuit of making the law school useful for LC and a serious player in the culture wars battles resulted in neglect of the law school as a site of professional development and training. While there is some truth to this allegation (see Chapter 4), as Dean of Liberty Law Staver also leveraged his own connections and *social capital* to plug dozens of young Liberty Law students into the heart of culture wars litigation through LC. And, as our alumni Web search confirmed, some of these Liberty Law alumni have used their training and experience with LC as a springboard to work for other likeminded organizations on the Christian Right such as Concerned Women for America,[13] Life Issues Institute,[14] Family Research Council,[15] Personhood U.S.A.,[16] and Republican Party politics.[17] From the perspective of SST, that is a "very good" thing.

AMSL and Thomas More Law Center

The Ann Arbor, Michigan–based TMLC was co-founded by AMSL founding patron Tom Monaghan and Richard Thompson in 1988, a year prior to Monaghan's founding of AMSL. Like the PILOs we explored earlier, TMLC was founded to "restore and defend America's Judeo-Christian heritage" and to counter "the destructive impact of organizations like the ACLU."[18] TMLC's governing board is populated by well-known, credentialed culture warriors on the Christian Right such as Michelle Bachman, Alan Keyes, and Alan West in addition to Monaghan.[19] President and

Chief Counsel Richard Thompson, who "won the hearts and minds of the pro-life community" for prosecuting Dr. Jack Kevorkian for his role in assisting the deaths of more than 100 terminally ill patients, compared TMLC to a "lean," "mean," "military unit" in the culture wars battles (Bennett 2017, 29–30). With only three to four full-time attorneys on staff and $2 million in annual revenues, TMLC is significantly smaller than LC and the ACLJ. (Bennett 2017, 29, 20). However, TMLC claims to have cultivated an impressive network of over 700 "affiliate attorneys" across the country who assist in cases pro bono (Department of the Treasury Internal Revenue Service Thomas More Law Center 2015).

Recalling the relationship between the other mission schools and their affiliated PILOs, AMSL was built a mere stone's throw away from the TMLC in the same complex (Monaghan's "Dominos Farms"), making the ties between the two—and the transfer of resources—easy and easily identifiable. While in Ann Arbor, AMSL students could receive credit for participating in an externship with TMLC. Here is the language AMSL used to advertise their externship on their website in 2001:

> Students in the externship program may choose from a variety of opportunities including working as a law clerk for a judge, participating in legal aid programs for the poor, assisting a legislator at the Michigan Statehouse, or working as an aide in the local office of one of Michigan's United States representatives or senators. Additionally, students may gain litigation and appellate advocacy experience by interning at the Thomas More Center for Law & Justice, a public interest law firm in Ann Arbor established to advance religious liberty, the culture of life, and pro-family issues.[20]

We can see the intentionality of the design from a support structure perspective. AMSL trains students in conservative Christian, natural law jurisprudence and then plugs those interested in litigation and the culture wars ("religious liberty, the culture of life, and pro-family issues") directly into the Monaghan-funded, co-located TMLC. While we do not know exactly how many students took advantage of this opportunity, we did identify three students from the Michigan era through our Web search who listed TMLC as past or current employment. Coincidentally, they are all named Erin. Erin M. McCartney ('07) was an intern with TMLC and Erin Mersino ('07) and Erin Kuenzig ('09) became staff attorneys with TMLC.

According to TMLC media and press releases, these AMSL alumni have been actively involved in culture wars litigation. For example, Erin Kuenzig led the charge on an abortion clinic buffer zone case in Maine about protests in front of Planned Parenthood.[21] Erin Mersino ('07) was lead counsel on the TMLC challenge to the Affordable Care Act's contraception mandate and was awarded the "Defender of Faith" prize from Monaghan's Catholic business round table, *Legatus*.[22] In the award announcement, presented jointly by Monaghan and John Hunt, the executive director of *Legatus*, Hunt highlights how Mersino represents the fruits of Monaghan's decades-long vision for reclaiming the "culture" and "country" for conservative Catholics and calls attention to the connections between Monaghan's investment in education and *human capital* at AMSL and the payoffs at TMLC:

> The lead counsel in the Legatus lawsuit is Erin Mersino, a 2007 graduate of Ave Maria School of Law. In this legal battle to protect the sanctity of life and freedom of conscience, it's not surprising that an Ave Maria graduate is fighting on the front lines. Mersino's education prepared her to combat the unconscionable governmental imposition of the HHS mandate head-on and with clear resolve . . . Legatus, the Thomas More Law Center, and Ave Maria School of Law exist because Monaghan was willing to engage in a struggle for our culture and our country.[23]

By moving the law school away from Domino's Farms and into southwest Florida, Monaghan disconnected the previously co-located AMSL and TMLC. The move may have also contributed to the lower overall percentages of AMSL graduates going into public interest law straight out of law school. ABA employment data from before and after the move illustrates this point. Between 2005 and 2009, for example, AMSL had an average of 5.33% of graduates going into public interest law after graduation, with two years topping 7% (2008 at 7.4% and 2009 at 7.1%). Averaging ABA data for the following eight years (2010–17) shows that AMSL has since sent only 2.7% of graduates into public interest law. Two AMSL classes (2011 and 2014) reported sending 0% into public interest law.

That being said, the connection between AMSL and TMLC has not been severed entirely. Evidence suggests that Monaghan actively works to maintain a connection between his Michigan-based TMLC and his Florida-based AMSL. Because he sits on the boards of both institutions and because both are funded by Monaghan's Ave Maria Foundation, there is overlap between these two networks. To illustrate, the Ave Maria Foundation holds an annual "Fall Fest" on Domino's Farms. This particular event is focused on recruiting Michigan-based conservative Catholic students for Ave Maria University and Ave Maria School of Law. At least one AMSL alum from the Florida era that we could identify (Kate Oliveri, '15) managed to find her way to TMLC post-graduation. In her first year as counsel, Oliveri successfully sought an injunction against a Portland, Maine, ordinance that would have prevented abortion clinic protestors from engaging in loud, disruptive speech outside of clinics.[24]

It is an interesting counterfactual to consider whether AMSL would have the same kind of productive and mutually beneficial relationship with TMLC that Regent Law has managed to sustain with ACLJ had the law school stayed in Ann

Arbor, Michigan. Alternatively, with Monaghan actively and deeply involved with both institutions, AMSL might very well have succumbed to the "tail wagging the dog," as Liberty Law did under Mat Staver, and the two might have been forced to undergo a messy divorce. As things stand now, with TMLC sitting roughly 1,300 miles away from Naples, Florida, the pipeline Monaghan had between his two support structure institutions no longer easily facilitates the transfer of resources from one to the other. Given the distance it is perhaps not too surprising that none of the AMSL students or faculty we interviewed in Naples, Florida, mentioned the connection with TMLC as a plus or opportunity for students who were interested in conservative Christian litigation. On the other hand, as we explore in this chapter, our interviews revealed that AMSL has cultivated a relationship with the Chicago-based Thomas More Society (TMS), a different conservative Catholic PILO. Several students spoke at length about meeting the leadership of this organization and hoping to intern for them over the summer.

Other Ways of Connecting to the Culture Wars

In addition to these more or less formalized institutional relationships with litigation-based firms, these mission institutions are more broadly connected to Christian Right's political and legal causes through their patron's and their faculty's relationships and networks. As we established in Chapters 2 and 3, Pat Robertson, Jerry Falwell, and Tom Monaghan were well-established Christian Right movement actors prior to founding and funding their Christian Worldview law schools. This is one of the primary reasons, as we argue, that these law schools can rightfully be understood as part of and extensions of the broader political projects connected to these patrons. Interviews with students and faculty at these institutions reveal some of the ways these preexisting connections to the Christian Right have translated into opportunities for internships and networking with movement leaders and institutions.

AMSL might well have one of the strongest anti-abortion law school campuses in the United States. As we recount in Chapter 3, having a truly "pro-life" law school was part of Tom Monaghan's animating motivation for founding AMSL. Recall that a group of conservative Catholic faculty from Detroit Mercy law school approached Monaghan, disaffected by their Catholic law school's acquiescence in the culture wars and their permissiveness in allowing pro-choice speakers and groups on campus. The belief that all existing Catholic law schools were not truly Catholic because they allowed pro-choice or Democratic clubs or LGBTQ clubs and speakers on campus was expressed repeatedly in our interviews. AMSL, on the other hand, has never invited or allowed students to invite pro-choice speakers to campus, it does not have an LGBTQ club on campus, and while there was a short-lived attempt by three students from Ohio to form a Democratic club on campus, they were told they needed to be a "pro-life" Democratic club.

What stood out throughout our interviews with students and faculty was the so-called "culture of life" on the AMSL campus and how the institution actively worked to support students in anti-abortion activism, identifying key organizations for internship opportunities, and bringing leaders of the anti-abortion movement to campus for big events. As an Ave Maria administrator remarked in our interview, "I think the folks who are really big on the pro-life stuff really see that as something they want to continue working on, and there are real opportunities, and many of our graduates are involved in serious pro-life work. That network is growing" (Ave Maria Administrator 1 2015).

From attending the March for Life in Washington, D.C., to participating in AMSL's very active student anti-abortion group, *Lex Vitae*, nearly every student we spoke with was plugged in to anti-abortion activism and groups. One student, who was finishing up her 1L year (first year) at AMSL, spoke enthusiastically to us about all the big players she had met in the "pro-life movement":

> I'm meeting people who are in the pro-life movement. I got to meet Forty Days for Life guy, the St. Thomas More president, the Vitae Foundation president, so just being able to meet these people that, in a different organization or a different law school, I'd never get the opportunity to meet. I met the president of Students for Life . . . Yeah, so just in one year I've met all those people, so in the next two years I can keep building on those relationships and maybe at the end of it know exactly how, where I fit in that world. (Ave Maria Student 4 2015)

"Forty Days for Life" is the "largest internationally coordinated pro-life organization in history," and seeks to end abortion "through prayer, fasting, and community outreach."[25] Similarly, the "Vitae Foundation" invests in "Right Brain Research" to discover and appeal to the emotional drivers behind the decision to have an abortion. It engages in mass media campaigns that target women who might seek an abortion and attempts to "make abortion unthinkable."[26] Students for Life is a national college student activist organization with 1,200 chapters encouraging students to get involved in the anti-abortion movement. As their website states, activism on campuses is vital to raise "a pro-life generation" and to "end abortion in our lifetime."[27]

As we teased in the previous section, several of our student interviews mentioned the Thomas More Society (TMS) and noted its strong presence on campus. Despite being located in Chicago, Illinois, TMS—a conservative Catholic PILO in the same vein as the TMLC—sent its leaders to AMSL to network with and recruit students interested in anti-abortion litigation for summer internships. Part of the enthusiasm for the TMS likely had to do with the timing of our visit. As one student noted, the TMS "was just here two days [ago] . . . they just hosted the first big dinner cruise here (AMSL Student 1 2015). Another student who attended elaborated on the nature of the "pro-life" cruise:

> Yeah, actually, I was able to participate in a pro-life cruise that went on on Monday. It was a fundraiser for St. Thomas More Society, based out of Chicago. We get to hear a bunch of pro-life speakers and some of them were lawyers. I was able to talk to them as well. Then as a continuation of that, there was a meet and greet breakfast yesterday morning, where the same speakers were here on campus, to meet some of the students on a more personal basis, and stuff like that. There's an internship, I am kind of thinking about, up in Chicago with St. Thomas More Society. (AMSL Student 5 2015)

Having attended this cruise and networked with anti-abortion leaders and lawyers, this particular student was considering interning with the TMS "up in Chicago" for the summer. From our Web search of AMSL alumni, we were able to identify three alumni who had interned with the TMS and listed it on their resume. John DeJak ('04) interned with the TMS and went on to become headmaster at a private Catholic high school. Danielle White ('14), who had also interned with Alliance Defending Freedom in addition to TMS, went on to become both a state and a federal law clerk. And Benjamin Bentrup ('13) went on to work as an editor at the "Culture of Life" Foundation, which, according to its website, seeks to "strengthen the foundations of our Judeo-Christian culture by offering to the public simplified and informative educational materials on current complex moral issues related to human life and dignity."[28]

Students we spoke with identified faculty and alumni as two excellent resources for finding work in and connecting with organizations engaged in anti-abortion activism. "We have connections with different people and we have alumni working for those groups now. It's pretty easy to find . . . If you wanted to find work there. Professors personally have connections with these people too, so it's very easy to find work in that field" (AMSL Student 1 2015). One alumnus whose name we heard several times was Royce Hood, who graduated from AMSL in 2012 and who is in many ways at the epicenter of anti-abortion work and organizing. In 2011, while still at AMSL, Hood launched the "Law of Life Summit" a self-proclaimed "strategy session on steroids" that brings together anti-abortion "lawyers, media and activists" around the March for Life in Washington, D.C.[29] In a 2012 interview with Life Legal Defense Fund—an anti-abortion PILO—Royce Hood credits his unwavering commitment to the anti-abortion cause to his time at AMSL: "It was at AMSL that I truly became PRO LIFE—capital letters all the way." Hood describes spending his Saturdays in front of the Planned Parenthood close to campus with fellow student members of *Lex Vitae*, attending the March for Life with students and faculty, and founding MariaNews, a "pro-life news and entertainment network" during his second semester of law school (Life Legal 2012).

In that same interview AMSL alumnus Royce Hood explains that he first became connected with the Life Legal Defense Foundation because it had partnered with then–Attorney General of Kansas Phil Kline in his litigation against Planned Parenthood. Kline achieved national notoriety during his time as attorney general and later as a district attorney for repeatedly filing hundreds of misdemeanor and felony charges against Planned Parenthood of Kansas City (Swenson 2007; Sanger 2017). Highlighting the connections between these mission schools and the tight-knit world of anti-abortion activism, Kline is now a faculty member at Liberty Law. Kline's faculty bio at Liberty Law highlights his work in the anti-abortion movement while also painting him as a persecuted victim, "villif[ied]" by pro-choice leaders and groups:

> Aside from these accomplishments, almost all media attention regarding Kline has focused on abortion. His efforts have led the national abortion industry to pour millions of dollars into Kansas to attack and vilify him. Through it all, he continued to fight to enforce Kansas law and hold all accountable under the law. His leadership, as written by columnist Bob Novak, opened a new front on the abortion wars and placed Kansas in the epicenter of the current battle over the sanctity of human life.[30]

Kline, who has been on the faculty since 2009, is one of the many faculty-centered nodes of connection that Liberty Law has with the anti-abortion movement specifically, and the culture wars more generally.

The hiring of Phil Kline is emblematic of Liberty Law's faculty-centric approach for creating pathways for its students into Christian Right causes and activism. One of the students we interviewed said he chose Liberty Law over Regent Law in part because he wanted to have Phil Kline as a "mentor" and because Kline has "led in a lot of different areas that that [he] wanted to go into" (Liberty Student 1 2015). Faculty connections have become even more important in the post-Staver era when Liberty Law has dissolved the pipeline to Liberty Counsel and, through it, into the heart of culture wars litigation. When asked to list the ways Liberty Law as an institution facilitates career advancement and job opportunities, administrators and students almost exclusively spoke about their professors. As a Liberty Law administrator emphasized in our interview, "Our faculty are out speaking at conferences, well-engaged. [Take] Professor [Basyle] Tchividjian, for instance . . . [he] is Billy Graham's grandson, and so there's great opportunities . . . There are networking opportunities, not just in terms of specific firms, but in multiple areas within the body of Christendom" (Liberty Administrator 1 2015).

Other examples of faculty who offer entry points into culture wars litigation include Professor Joseph J. Martins, who runs the constitutional litigation clinic at Liberty Law. Prior to joining the Liberty Law faculty, Martins was a litigator for Christian Right public interest firms the ADF and the National

Legal Foundation where, according to his faculty bio, he worked on "cases related to religious liberty, the traditional family, and the sanctity of human life."[31]
Similarly, Professor Scott Thompson, who directs Liberty Law's Center for
Lawyering Skills, where he interacts with almost the entire student body, also
has connections to ADF and the National Legal Foundation.[32] On a similar
note, a Liberty Law faculty member whom we interviewed said when he started
law school he wanted to become "the next Jay Sekulow," the lead attorney for
the ACLJ, which we explored earlier in this chapter. While this faculty member
admits that he knows that won't happen, he takes pride in the fact that he is
"training a generation of lawyers, some of whom will [become the next Jay
Sekulow]" (Liberty Faculty 2 2015).

Faculty we spoke with seemed to agree, however, that Liberty Law as an institution could be doing much better with career placement and with student networking. For example, one faculty member said that the career development office
at Liberty Law had been rather ineffective and that Liberty's networking and career
placement "really needs work" (Liberty Faculty 3 2015). Another faculty member,
when we asked, could not point to any "institutional mechanism" for networking at
Liberty Law beyond the faculty and their professional connections (Liberty Faculty
2 2015). Still another faculty member, who described networking at Liberty Law
as "ad hoc" emphasized that the law school needed to "do better" at connecting its
students with opportunities outside of Lynchburg, VA:

> Well, we're within 3 1/2 hours of DC so as Christians engaged in public
> service or affecting government look across the landscape from where they
> might draw talent to engage in that effort, there are very few Christian law
> schools and we're close. Plus we have some experience. There's a strength
> there. I think regionally we are developing some strength in recogni-
> tion . . . [but] there's only so many lawyers Lynchburg can take and we
> graduate a class people start hanging up shingles then we hear from the
> local bar. (Liberty Faculty 1 2015)

This excerpt alludes to something that we heard from other Liberty Law students
and faculty about the reluctance to leave Lynchburg, Virginia, after graduation.
As this faculty member says, "[t]here's only so many lawyers Lynchburg can take."
More so, it seems, than with Regent Law and AMSL, students who come to Liberty
Law are disinclined to leave what one student referred to as "the Liberty Bubble"
after graduation (Liberty Student 3 2015).

Still, our alumni research that we presented in Chapter 4, confirms that many
graduates do, in fact, leave "the Liberty Bubble," and some even make their way to
Washington, D.C., to do hands-on law and policy work with organizations such as
Concerned Women for America, The Heritage Foundation, the Family Research
Council, the Life Institute, and other culture wars–focused organizations. Our

campus interviews suggest, however, that especially in the post-Staver, post-LC era, Liberty Law has work to do in this area.

Tellingly, when asked about networking at Liberty Law, two faculty members there pointed to Regent Law as a school that does a better job institutionally of networking and placing its students. While it seems like Regent Law has a reputation for more effectively tapping into Christian Right networks, we don't have any interview data from students or faculty to triangulate. Because Regent Law tightly controlled with whom we were able to speak while on campus—and, indeed, Regent's public relations firm told us that we were not allowed to come to campus and speak with anyone when we first made plans to do so—we were not able to ask students or faculty about networking opportunities on campus.

That being said, we talked at length with one administrator about Regent Law's pipeline to the ACLJ, which we explored earlier, and about its successful history of placing students in the Blackstone Legal Fellowship. This administrator also claimed that Regent Law was the top feeder school for the ADF, stating that "If you look at all of the attorneys with ADF, Regent is, I think, the most represented law school there" (Regent Administrator 1 2016). This statement finds support on ADF's "Attorneys" list on its website. Of the forty-one attorneys listed on the site, seven earned their JD from Regent Law School, which is, in fact, more than any of the other law schools listed.[33]

Working at ADF, the largest and most high-profile Christian Right PILO (Hollis-Brusky & Wilson 2017), Regent Law graduates have been involved in some of the most important culture wars cases of the last decade. For instance, ADF Senior Counsel and Regent Law graduate David Cortman successfully argued and secured victories in *Trinity Lutheran Church v. Comer* (2017), which forced the state to pay for the church's playground resurfacing even though it is a tax-exempt organization, *Reed v. Town of Gilbert* (2015), which successfully challenged a local sign ordinance because it discriminated against religious messaging, *Conestoga Wood Specialties v. Burwell* (2014), which was consolidated with the Hobby Lobby case in a successful challenge to the Affordable Care Act's contraception mandate, and *Town of Greece v. Galloway* (2014), an establishment clause case that upheld the practice of opening a town legislative session with a prayer. Regent Law alumnus and ADF attorney Gary McCaleb defended a funeral home owner for firing an employee after revealing that she is a transgender woman in *R.G. & G.R. Harris Funeral Homes v. EEOC & Aimee Stephens* (2018)—a case ADF lost in the Sixth Circuit Court of Appeals and has appealed to the Supreme Court. And in the most recent flashpoint in the culture wars, in the Supreme Court case of *Masterpiece Cakeshop v. Colorado Civil Rights Commission* (2018), Regent Law grad Jeremy Tedesco successfully argued that a Colorado baker did not need to make a cake for a same-sex couple because it violated his freedom of speech and religion.

In addition to sending graduates to Christian Right powerhouse PILOs Alliance Defending Freedom and the American Center for Law and Justice, Regent Law would appear to be well networked with other prominent organizations through its alumni placement across the conservative Christian spectrum. Reviewing the results of our alumni Web search, we see Regent Law alumni working at The Heritage Foundation,[34] the American Family Association,[35] Family Research Council,[36] the Texas Center for Defense of Life,[37] Home School Legal Defense Association,[38] the Christian Broadcasting Network,[39] the National Right to Life Committee,[40] the Bopp Law Firm,[41] the Eagle Forum,[42] Concerned Women for America,[43] the National Christian Foundation,[44] ProtectMarriage.com,[45] and the National Legal Foundation.[46] These placements speak both to the initial *social capital* Regent Law graduates cashed in on to earn these employment opportunities—capital no doubt linked to the founding patrons and faculty of Regent Law—and the future potential for current Regent Law students to network with alumni from these Christian Right organizations and to expand these pipelines into the front lines of the culture wars.

Social Capital—Connectedness with the Conservative Legal Movement

Clearly these *parallel alternative* schools have a significant amount of *social capital* within Christian Right law and politics. But how well integrated are they and their ideas into the mainstream conservative legal movement, a movement that has grown up with an identifiable libertarian pro-business bent (Teles 2008; Hollis-Brusky 2015)? As Ann Southworth demonstrated in her path-breaking 2008 study of conservative lawyers, religious and libertarian lawyers on the right "have little in common" and are divided by "social characteristics, educational background, values, geography and professional identity" (Southworth 2008, 3). As indicative of dozens of quotes from interviews she mobilizes in the book, one prominent libertarian lawyer said "the religious right . . . makes my skin crawl" while a self-identified Christian lawyer said he left a big law firm because they viewed him as a "wild-eyed evangelical" and charged his pro-business conservative colleagues with worshipping "two false gods—personal autonomy and wealth" (Southworth 2008, 59, 58).

Mutual distrust and skepticism aside, in order to achieve their broad, transformative ambitions to rebuild the foundations of law from the bottom up, Christian Worldview adherents must first be taken seriously within the mainstream conservative legal movement. In this section we present findings from our analysis of faculty participation in Federalist Society conferences and events as a proxy for integration into the mainstream conservative legal movement. The Federalist Society for Law and Public Policy Studies has been described as a "mediator organization" at the "cross-roads of the conservative movement" (Southworth 2008, 124, 148) and a gatekeeper for conservative legal ideas and the conservative legal agenda (Teles 2008, 35–180; Hollis-Brusky 2015, 159–64). The Federalist Society has also become the de facto gatekeeper for appointments in Republican administrations, especially for nominations to the federal judiciary (Brand 2018; Kelly 2018; Toobin 2017; Hollis-Brusky 2015, 152–55). As such, Hollis-Brusky has shown how the Federalist Society operates as a political epistemic network (PEN), circulating ideas and *intellectual capital* through its members and transmitting them to judges and policymakers, who have used these ideas to radically change and restructure law and constitutional meaning (Hollis-Brusky 2015, 10–27). In sum, if any right-of-center movement hopes to have its ideas have consequences for law and politics, then having *social capital* within the Federalist Society network is very valuable.

To capture appearances, we searched for faculty names on the Federalist Society's very detailed archived events web page from 2000 to the present and recorded only those appearances that coincided with their active appointment to the faculty of our three mission schools as well as, for purposes of comparison, Blackstone Legal Fellowship, Notre Dame Law School, and Baylor Law School.[47] While we do find some evidence of faculty participation in Federalist Society events, our analysis confirms Southworth's findings from 2008 that there remains a good amount of professional, social, and intellectual distance between the Christian Right and the libertarian-leaning conservative legal movement as it has become operationalized by the Federalist Society. Specifically, while we find that the Federalist Society dedicates some agenda space to religious liberties and natural law jurisprudence, there are a small group of repeat players—primarily from Notre Dame Law School and Blackstone Legal Fellowship—who are invited repeatedly to represent these views at Federalist Society conferences. Faculty from the mission-based schools— Regent Law, AMSL, and Liberty Law—participate infrequently and, when they do, almost never discuss religious liberties or espouse Christian Worldview or biblical perspectives on law or jurisprudence.

The Blackstone Legal Fellowship, representing the *supplemental approach* in our study, has had far more faculty appearances at Federalist Society conferences than the *parallel alternative* and rejected *infiltration* schools. As illustrated in Figure 5.1, since 2000, Blackstone-affiliated faculty have made 355 appearances at Federalist Society events. Next, in order, come the faculties of Notre Dame Law School (117), Regent Law School (44), AMSL (21), and Liberty Law School (6). Because Baylor Law School only had three total Federalist Society faculty appearances, it was left off the graph.

Percentage-wise, the majority of each faculty have never appeared at a Federalist Society event archived on the website. For Blackstone, the percentage of faculty with no recorded Federalist Society event appearances was 53%, followed by Notre Dame Law School (64%), Regent Law School (71%), AMSL (75%), Liberty Law School (82.5%), and Baylor Law School (93%). The low rates of participation of Christian Worldview faculty in Federalist Society events is, on the one hand, surprising because, as our interviews confirmed, these institutions are populated almost exclusively with faculty who identify as conservative. On the other hand, as we noted before, the Christian Worldview perspective is still understood as being

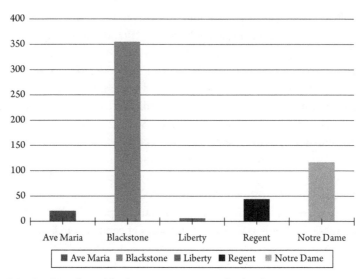

Figure 5.1. Total number of faculty appearances at Federalist Society Events, 2000–2018. *Source*: Results from search of Federalist Society events archive (https://fedsoc.org/) between June 2018 and October 2018.

outside the bounds of accepted mainstream legal discourse, perhaps accounting for the lack of integration of these schools' faculty within the Federalist Society network.

The Blackstone Fellowship also outperformed the law schools in terms of the number of appearances at National Student Conferences or National Lawyers Conventions, the two most high-profile and well-attended events that the Federalist Society hosts each year (Hollis-Brusky 2015, 24–25). This finding aligns with what we have previously described about Blackstone Legal Fellowship's strategic approach to networking, its desire to have its membership and ideas taken seriously by the mainstream legal and political elite, and its leadership's emphasis on (we paraphrase) playing the game where the game is played. And recall that it was an administrator at Blackstone who first introduced us to the phrase "credibility capital" (Blackstone Administrator 2 2015).

Upon closer inspection, however, we see that a small number of faculty account for the vast majority of Blackstone's total Federalist Society event appearances. Seven of the forty-three total Blackstone faculty members—William Saunders, Teresa Collett, John Baker, Kyle Duncan, John C. Eastman, Francis Beckwith, and Hadley Arkes—account for 280 of Blackstone's 355 appearances at Federalist Society events (79%). We refer to this group as "The Blackstone Seven."[48] This phenomenon was even more pronounced in national conferences, the highest profile Federalist Society events. "The Blackstone Seven," whom we profile in Table 5.1, made 41 of Blackstone Fellowship's 46 (89%) total appearances at national conferences.

Table 5.1. **Professional Profiles of "The Blackstone Seven"**

Name	Institutional Affiliations	Conservative Credentials	No. of Fed. Society Events
Hadley Arkes	Amherst College	James Wilson Institute on Natural Rights & the American Founding *First Things*, Advisory Board	19
John Baker	Georgetown Law School (visiting) Louisiana State Law School (emeritus)	Fellow, Heritage Foundation	106
Francis Beckwith	Baylor University (Philosophy Dept.) Co-Director, Institute for Studies of Religion	Fellow, Discovery Institute (proponent of Intelligent Design) Fellow, Center for Bioethics and Dignity	21
Teresa Collett	Univ. of St. Thomas School of Law	Publishes on marriage, religion and bioethics	28
Kyle Duncan	Judge, Fifth Circuit Court of Appeals (appointed by Trump)	General Counsel, Becket Fund for Religious Liberty Argued Hobby Lobby case before the Supreme Court	17
John Eastman	Chapman University Claremont Institute	Former law clerk to Clarence Thomas Reagan Administration Commission on Civil Rights	73
William Saunders	Americans United for Life, VP Legal Affairs Catholic University of America	Oversees all of Americans United for Life's legal work Senior Fellow at Family Research Council	16

Source: Number of Federalist Society events returned from search of Federalist Society events archive at https://fedsoc.org/ between June 2018 and October 2018. Profiles and professional associations of Blackstone affiliated faculty identified from name-based Web search.

Similarly, 57% of Ave Maria's total Federalist Society event appearances were done by two professors—Clifford Taylor and John Raudabaugh. Four faculty members—James Duane, Bradley Jacob, John Ashcroft, and Tessa Dysart—account for 62% of Regent Law's total Federalist Society appearances, and Liberty Law professor Jeffrey Tuomala's two appearances account for one-third of his institution's total archived Federalist Society event participation.

Perhaps our most interesting finding from this analysis of Federalist Society event participation involved the topics or issues Christian Worldview faculty were invited to discuss. One might think that, when invited to participate, given their expertise and grounding in the natural law and Christian jurisprudence, faculty from AMSL, Regent Law, and Liberty Law would be speaking either directly about religious liberty or natural law jurisprudence or about implicitly religious, culture wars–focused topics such as abortion, LGBTQ rights, or marriage equality. This was not the case. Conference appearances about explicitly religious issues—identified by a title that included a direct mention of religion or natural law—were extremely rare. Ave Maria Law faculty had zero archived appearances at Federalist Society events on explicitly religious topics. Regent Law and Liberty Law had only five and three appearances on explicitly religious topics, respectively. For example, in 2016 Regent Law faculty member Bradley Jacob spoke to the Chicago-Kent Student Chapter of the Federalist Society on "Religious Liberty: Under Attack from the Left and the Right." And Liberty Law faculty Jeffrey Tuomala presented in 2004 at the Liberty Law Student Chapter of the Federalist Society on "Law and Religion." His Liberty Law colleague Barbara Mouly moderated a 2017 Federalist Society Faculty Division panel on the "Effects of Recognition of Islamic Law in United States Courts."

When we factor in implicitly religious or culture wars–related topics (abortion, contraception, LGBTQ rights, marriage, religiously grounded freedom of association, homeschooling, or bioethics), AMSL's count jumps to one, Regent Law's total increases by six and Liberty Law by one. To illustrate, in 2011 AMSL faculty member Patrick Gillen gave a talk to the AMSL Student Chapter of the Federalist Society on "What Every Law Student Should Know about Bioethics," a talk we coded as implicitly religious or culture wars because of the connection between bioethics and "pro-life" beliefs on the Christian Right. Regent Law professor David M. Wagner has presented at two Federalist Society events on the constitutional right to homeschool—an issue at the heart of the culture wars.[49] And Liberty Law Professor Jeffrey Tuomala participated on a 2010 Liberty Law Student Chapter panel titled "A Discussion of Abortion and the Laws of the Nation." All three Christian Worldview schools had zero explicitly or implicitly religious archived appearances at National Student Conferences or National Lawyers Conventions—the biggest platforms the Federalist Society provides. On the other hand, as we see illustrated in Figure 5.2, the Blackstone Fellowship and Notre Dame Law School had significant numbers of faculty appearances on explicitly religious and implicitly religious topics—or more broadly, culture wars issues as we have defined them.

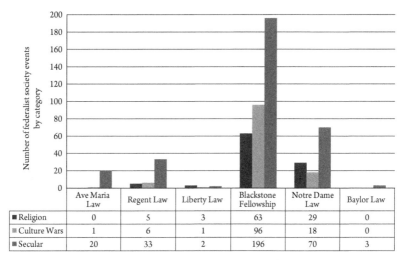

	Ave Maria Law	Regent Law	Liberty Law	Blackstone Fellowship	Notre Dame Law	Baylor Law
■ Religion	0	5	3	63	29	0
■ Culture Wars	1	6	1	96	18	0
■ Secular	20	33	2	196	70	3

Figure 5.2. Breakdown of topics at Federalist Society events (religion, culture wars, secular). *Source*: Results from search of Federalist Society events archive (https://fedsoc.org/) between June 2018 and October 2018. Event titles or talks were then coded for topic using scheme consistently employed throughout the book as "secular," "religious," or "culture wars" more generally.

So, if not religious liberties and culture wars issues, what are these Christian Worldview faculty speaking about on the rare occasion that they are invited to participate in Federalist Society events? Principally, faculty spoke on topics related to their particular areas of legal expertise and specialization. John Raudabaugh, AMSL faculty member and former Bush Administration National Labor Relations Board member, had six Federalist Society event appearances, all of which were on labor and employment law.[50] Fellow AMSL faculty member and former Dean of AMSL Bernard Dobranski moderated two Federalist Society panels, one titled "Competition Law and the Free Market—The Antitrust Paradox: A Policy at War with Itself"[51] and another titled "Manufacturers' Immunity: The FDA Compliance Defense."[52] In 2013, Liberty Law professor Rodney Chrisman spoke to Liberty law's student chapter of the Federalist Society on "Exploring the Intersection of Investment Banking, Entrepreneurship and the Law." Regent Law Professor James Duane has spoken at twelve Federalist Society events logged in the archive, and all of his talks have been on criminal process, the Fifth Amendment, and the right against self-incrimination.[53]

That is not to say that these Christian Worldview faculty members are not drawing, broadly speaking, on biblical ideas and natural law jurisprudence when presenting their arguments at Federalist Society events. Most of these events do not have audio recordings, but from the small percentage that did, we were able to identify only one instance where a Christian Worldview faculty member worked the natural law into a secular-sounding talk. In "Federalism v. Anti-Federalism in the American Founding," a rare local AMSL Federalist Society event containing audio, Ave Maria professor Patrick Gillen spoke about the Framers' protection against excess government: "The check is in the natural law, which was understood at the time to check all exercise of government authority, and the Constitution."[54] Again, we cannot say for sure whether or not other Christian Worldview faculty are disseminating ideas about the natural law in their secular-sounding talks. What we can say for sure is that from reviewing the archives they are not participating widely in Federalist Society events and, when they do, are not asked to speak on explicitly or even implicitly religious topics with any frequency.

This evidence demonstrates that the faculty of Notre Dame Law School and Blackstone Legal Fellowship, along with being better credentialed overall (see Chapter 4), are also better integrated into the conservative legal mainstream and recognized by the Federalist Society network and leadership as experts on issues of religious liberty and the natural law. For example, William Saunders (one of "The Blackstone Seven") chairs the Religious Liberties Practice Group for the Federalist Society and, in that capacity, organizes panels and acts as a gatekeeper for invitations to speak on the "Religious Liberties" panel organized annually at the National Lawyers Convention. This panel constitutes the premier religious liberties event and the only official panel the Federalist Society organizes on the topic throughout the year.

Table 5.2 identifies all participants who have participated on at least two of the Federalist Society's Religious Liberties panels at the National Lawyers Convention since the year 2000, with those from Blackstone and Notre Dame in bold. Of these ten Religious Liberties repeat players, we see two participants from Blackstone, one of whom is also on the faculty of Notre Dame Law School (Richard Garnett). Strikingly, we do not see a single faculty member of the Christian Worldview law schools presenting even once on this marquee Federalist Society religious liberties panel over the past eighteen years.

We also found that Federalist Society Religious Liberties panelists, even those with just a single appearance, are more likely to have participated in other Federalist Society events, indicating that they are not just religious liberties specialists or pinch hitters. We found that Religious Liberties panelists have appeared at an average of 14.9 total Federalist Society events. For reference, this number is higher than the average for a Blackstone faculty member (8.3), and far higher than the average for a faculty member at Notre Dame Law School (1.4), Regent Law (0.9), Ave Maria Law (0.4), and Liberty Law (0.15). This finding illustrates that the people discussing religious issues on the Federalist Society's highest stage are already well integrated into its mainstream.

In sum, reviewing all the evidence available, our analysis of the *social capital* of Christian Worldview institutions within the mainstream conservative legal movement confirms what Ann Southworth found in 2008: that is, that the Federalist Society for Law and Public Policy Studies is not the place where "Christian lawyers . . . get together. It's gonna be something else, it's gonna be Alliance

Table 5.2. **Participants in Multiple Federalist Society National Lawyers Convention Religious Liberties Panels 2000–2018**

Name	Institutional Affiliation	No. of Religious Liberties Panels
William P. Marshall	UNC School of Law	4
Michael W. McConnell	Stanford Law School & Hoover Institute	3
Walter Dellinger	Duke University School of Law	3
Kevin Hasson	Becket Fund for Religious Liberty	3
Richard W. Garnett	Notre Dame Law School & Blackstone Legal Fellowship	3
Robert George	Princeton University	2
Kent Greenwalt	Columbia Law School	2
Stanley W. Carlson-Thies	Institutional Religious Freedom Alliance	2
Melissa Rogers	Brookings Institute	2
John S. Baker Jr.	Georgetown Law & Blackstone Legal Fellowship	2

Source: Results from search of Federalist Society events archive at https://fedsoc.org/ between June 2018 and October 2018. Professional affiliations of Federalist Society participants identified through name-based Web search.

[Defending Freedom] probably or informally" (Southworth 2008, 146). This finding reinforces the perception within these Christian Worldview institutions of being outsiders, even within conservative circles. It also reinforces the importance of building *supplemental* and *parallel alternative* sites of intellectual development and networking, which is what the Christian Right has done since the mid-1980s.

Cultural Capital—Overcoming the Credibility Deficit

Establishing a brand-new law school is an uphill battle. In a professional market-place that places a premium on reputation, alumni, and job placement data, start-up law schools have a difficult time recruiting faculty and attracting students, who take a big risk by attending a school with no proven track record of post-graduation employment and bar passage. When we layer on top of this baseline challenge the fact that these Christian Worldview law schools were built with the purpose of teaching law from a biblical perspective—with a unique curriculum, mission, and focus— Regent Law, AMSL, and Liberty Law face even more significant reputational and cultural hurdles both within the legal community and with the public more broadly. We refer to these reputational and cultural hurdles collectively as the "credibility deficit."

The media coverage of these Christian Worldview institutions, some of which we reviewed in Chapter 3, mostly reinforces the dominant cultural assumptions about biblically grounded legal education and does little to help these schools overcome the credibility deficit. Recall that after the Monica Goodling scandal put the spotlight on Regent Law School, some high-profile media personalities such as *The Daily Show's* Jon Stewart portrayed Regent Law as a hack "Jiffy Law" drive-through law school on account of its low bar passage numbers, and comedian Bill Maher called Regent Law graduates "Jesus freaks" graduating from "a televangelist's diploma mill" (Vegh 2007). Similarly, The *Associated Press* reported on the founding of AMSL with the sensational headline, "Ex Pizza Magnate Builds Law School for God," and proceeded to describe AMSL as the pet political project of a very conservative Catholic pizza mogul (Hyde 1999). A 2004 issue of *Legal Affairs* covering the opening of Liberty Law School begins with the lede "Our reporter gets kicked out of Jerry Falwell's new law school." The article proceeds to describe the campus décor as "Best-Western-meets-dentist's-office" and notes that its setting in a former cell phone manufacturing plant is an appropriate fit for its mission of "manufacturing 'junkyard dog lawyers who believe in God and the Bible'" (Gagnon 2004).

These media characterizations have a similar effect, that is, to portray these Christian Worldview law schools as academically non-rigorous, secretive, and politically motivated institutions deeply tied to the Christian Right through their high-profile patrons. In other words, they feed into the broader cultural narrative that these Christian Worldview institutions, their students, and their faculty, are the stereotypical Bible-thumping wild-eyed evangelicals or (to quote an administrator at ADF), "Bayou Bob Bill shouting 'God's law over man's law!'" (Blackstone Administrator 2 2015).

Leadership, faculty, and students at these Christian Worldview institutions lament that this is the image the media chooses to portray of their law school. A 2007 article in the *Virginian-Pilot* titled "What Is the Real Face of Regent's Law School?" quoted two Regent Law students who had won a national competition hosted by the ABA, beating out competitors from Harvard Law, Yale Law, and other top-ranked schools, describing them as "irked" by the "ridicule and suspicion" they face on account of attending Regent Law. "'It's not just some weird religious school,'" one student said of Regent Law, "'We are a good—great—law school'" (Vegh 2007). Similarly, a student with whom we spoke at Liberty Law dismissed the crazy Christian stigma surrounding his law school as an unfair and inaccurate stereotype:

> If you go to Harvard, there's people that aren't going to want to hire you because you went to Harvard and you think you're better than everybody. That's just a stereotype. Same goes with Liberty. People are or aren't going to want to hire from Liberty because they think you're ultra conservative or you know, all you're going to do all day is read the Bible. Again, just a stereotype. (Liberty Student 3 2015)

Jeffrey Brauch, who served as the Dean of Regent Law, had the following to say about this kind of stereotype of Christian Worldview institutions: "My reaction has been, I wish they could see the real law school" (Vegh 2007).

Seeing "the real law school," as it turns out, is not always easy. A *Legal Affairs* reporter describes his attempt to interview faculty and visit with students on the campus of Liberty Law in 2004: "The dean's office declined my appeals for an interview or an informal visit, telling me that a look around would be 'disruptive to the start of classes.'" The reporter came anyway, and, in his words, "was reduced to skulking around" the campus (Gagnon 2004). Similarly, in the course of gathering data for this project, we had set up dozens of interviews via email with Regent Law faculty and student leaders in preparation for a planned campus visit on April 15–16, 2015. When Regent Law's communications department caught wind of our visit two weeks prior to our scheduled travel to campus on March 31, 2015, we received a phone call from Chris Roslin, a representative of Regent Law's public relations firm in New York City, telling us in no uncertain terms that we were prohibited from visiting campus and speaking with faculty, staff, or students. Jeffrey Brauch, the dean quoted as wishing people could "see the real law school," wrote us a follow-up email saying we could speak with select faculty and students via phone but reinforced the orders from the communications department.[55]

This commitment to keeping the wider world away or at arm's length feeds into the cultural narrative of Christian Worldview institutions as being self-segregated and secretive. One way to begin to combat this narrative, to begin to overcome the credibility deficit, is for the faculty members as the faces of these Christian Worldview institutions to put themselves out there into the wider world. In the previous section we showed that, on the whole, faculty members at these institutions have not integrated themselves with mainstream conservative legal organizations like the Federalist Society for Law and Public Policy Studies, thereby failing to use this venue to improve their *cultural capital*. Another way of building *cultural capital* is for faculty to engage the wider world through media as credible experts on the law, a potential avenue to which we will now turn.

Faculty Experts in the Media: What Are They Preaching and Who Is Listening?

To measure faculty *cultural capital*—that is, the extent to which faculty members are sought after as legal experts or simply mentioned by the media—we searched active faculty names at Regent Law, Liberty Law, and AMSL for print media appearances on LexisNexis Academic, downloading and counting all mentions in newspapers, industry trade presses, newswires, and press releases, legal news, and news transcripts.[56] We then coded and ranked newspaper appearances for reach and prestige using the newspaper's total 2015 circulation ranking as reported by Alliance for Audited Media. These circulation rankings matter in terms of the size of the audience being reached. One well-placed quote or opinion piece in a major outlet can carry more cultural weight and convey more authority than twenty or thirty mentions in a very small, niche newspaper. Finally, using the same coding scheme as we did for Federalist Society conference appearance topics (see Hollis-Brusky & Wilson 2017), we categorized the topic or issue being discussed in the article as "Religious," "Culture Wars," and "Secular." See Appendix A for more details.

Table 5.3 shows the total number of faculty print media mentions returned from our LexisNexis search for the three Christian Worldview law schools as well as the average number of media appearances per faculty member and the issue or topic of the article. We see that the more well-established and older Regent Law is actually at the bottom of its peer group in total number of media mentions. However, if we add in all media mentions found for Jay Sekulow, President of the ACLJ and affiliated Regent Law faculty member, Regent's total jumps to 1,130 mentions. As we noted earlier in this chapter, Sekulow's consistent media engagement has made him one of the most visible talking heads on the Christian Right. While almost all of Sekulow's media mentions, with the exception of ten, list his institutional affiliation only as ACLJ and do not mention Regent Law School at all; because both

Table 5.3. **Print Media Mentions by Active Christian Worldview Faculty Over Lifespan of Institution**

	Total Media Mentions	Average Mentions per Faculty Member	% Religious	% Culture Wars	% Secular
Regent Law School	140	~3	~22	~10	~68
Ave Maria School of Law	268	~6	~26	~11	~64
Liberty Law School	900	~23	~33	~30	~37

Source: LexisNexis Academic; data collected between November 2017 and August 2018.

Robertson-affiliated enterprises are so deeply intertwined, Sekulow's media work undoubtedly conveys *cultural capital* more broadly to Regent Law School even if the school is not mentioned directly.

Similar in kind but not in magnitude, former Liberty Law Dean and President of LC Mathew Staver accounts for more than one-third (39%) of Liberty Law's 900 total media mentions. However, unlike with Jay Sekulow, Mathew Staver's media appearances often (though not always) mention Liberty Law School, where he served as the dean from 2006 to 2014. Staver's inclusion in the counts does inflate Liberty Law's mentions per faculty member slightly.[57] Removing Staver from the analysis still leaves Liberty Law at the top of its peer group in terms of total mentions, but it drops the average mentions per faculty member from 22.5 to 14.

For both Regent Law and Liberty Law, these numbers illustrate yet another dimension of the value of being connected to a high-profile public interest law firm with a media arm—it facilitates the transfer of *cultural capital* to the wider world. AMSL, a school with loose to no institutional ties to a media savvy public interest law firm, lags behind its peers Regent Law (with Sekulow included) and Liberty Law (even with Staver excluded) in total faculty media mentions and in mentions per faculty member.

AMSL did earn some *cultural capital* and media attention in the beginning by bringing infamous failed Supreme Court nominee and renowned conservative scholar Robert Bork as a founding faculty member. However, when Bork's media search was restricted to mentions that include "Ave Maria," the search only returned seven results (all announcing that Bork had signed on as a founding faculty member at the new law school). A similar dynamic is at play with Regent Law bringing in former Bush Administration Attorney General John Ashcroft to the faculty in 2005. Aschroft is a well-respected, well-connected Republican player whose appointment confers with it instant credibility within conservative and GOP circles. However, when we restricted Ashcroft's media mentions to "Regent" and filtered for false hits, he only added twelve mentions to Regent Law's overall count. To be sure, this table does not reflect the kind of *cultural capital* and credibility institutions gain by bringing in high-profile personalities who convey a certain amount of legitimacy on the institution simply with their presence.

When we analyze faculty media mentions by issue type, we see a similar pattern to our Federalist Society participation analysis from earlier in this chapter. Again, surprisingly, only a minority of these Christian Worldview faculty's media mentions and appearances involve explicitly religious issues. For Regent Law, that percentage is ~22; for Ave Maria, ~26; and for Liberty Law, ~33. When we combine explicitly religious and other culture wars issues into a broader "mission" category, these categories still only account for ~32% and ~37% of Regent Law School and AMSL's faculty media mentions, respectively. Combining these categories for Liberty Law School reflects a slightly more mission-focused faculty media presence, accounting for ~63% of total mentions.

Liberty Law's more notable public-facing faculty presence on culture wars issues makes sense given the centrality of these issues to Mathew Staver and his influence on the culture wars during his deanship. Staver's media presence further illustrates his preoccupation with the culture wars—an astounding 91% of his 351 media mentions were categorized as religious or culture wars focused. Picking up the mantle from Staver, faculty member and interim dean appointed after Staver's departure, Rena Lindevaldsen, is frequently cited in media articles discussing (or more accurately denouncing) LGBTQ rights, same-sex marriage, and same-sex adoption in outlets as diverse as *The Washington Post*, the *Contra Costa Times* (California), the *New York Post*, and the *Daily Republic* (South Dakota). Of the 40 media mentions we identified for Lindevaldsen, only 2 were coded as secular. Both articles had to do with Liberty Law's bar passage rates during her time as interim dean.

With Liberty Law faculty as the exception, we found that Christian Worldview faculty are predominantly being cited and quoted in the media about secular or what we would call "non-mission" legal issues. For example, AMSL Professor John Raudabaugh had forty returned results from our media search (15% of AMSL's total number of faculty mentions). Several of these mentions were in top national media outlets such as *The Wall Street Journal* and *The Washington Post*. Every single article mentioned Raudabaugh in connection with his expertise in labor law. Similarly, Regent Law professor James Duane, referred to in one article as a "Harvard Law Graduate" and a "Fifth Amendment expert" is repeatedly cited or quoted in connection with his expertise in criminal procedure.

On the one hand, the fact that most of these faculty media mentions involve secular legal issues helps establish these institutions as more mainstream law schools and pushes back against the media-facilitated crazy Christian stigma that these schools and their students face. Showcasing the broad expertise of one's faculty can help to chip away at the credibility deficit these law schools face within the legal community as legitimate sites of legal expertise and professional training. On the other hand, if part of the reason for founding these Christian Worldview law schools was, as we established earlier in the book, to help change the culture and the conversation around law, and to bring God and the Bible back into the equation with American jurisprudence, then we see little evidence of that happening through faculty media engagement.

In addition to the content of these Christian Worldview faculty's media mentions, we were also interested in the size or scope of their potential audience. Using newspaper mentions, which comprise the majority of our returned search results on LexisNexis Academic, we broke down and ranked faculty mentions by the total published circulation of the newspaper outlet. There is a big difference in magnitude of potential cultural impact between being mentioned in or quoted by the *The New York Times* (circulation ~2 million) and the *Sarasota Herald-Tribune* (circulation ~47,000). As we see from Table 5.4, the majority of faculty newspaper mentions for all three of these Christian Worldview institutions appear in outlets

Table 5.4. **Percent of Christian Worldview Faculty Newspaper Mentions by Ranking of Outlet Based on Total Circulation**

Institution	% Top 10	% 11–25	% 26–50	% 51–100	% 100+	% Outside US
Regent Law School (*n* = 128)	~33	~2	< 1	< 1	~57	~7
Ave Maria School of Law (*n* = 228)	~14	~2	~2	~17	~57	~9
Liberty Law School (*n* = 844)	~12	~5	~4	~3	~62	~14

Source: Circulation rankings based on analysis by Alliance for Audited Media 2015.

with rankings of 100+, which means that each of these articles is reaching an audience of ~40,000 or fewer readers.[58] When we look at mentions in the top-50 newspaper outlets (indicating a circulation of ~100,000 or more),[59] 36% of Regent Law faculty mentions hit this mark, whereas only 17% of AMSL's faculty mentions and 21% of Liberty Law's faculty mentions reach this kind of audience. That being said, Liberty Law, padded by the media-active Mathew Staver, has the most overall newspaper mentions and the most in top-10 outlets by raw numbers (101).

We recognize that there is a qualitative difference between being simply mentioned in a top-10 newspaper article, being cited or quoted as an authoritative source or expert, and getting an opinion piece or letter accepted for publication with such an outlet. Moreover, newspaper mentions can be positive (chipping away at the credibility deficit), negative (adding to the credibility deficit), or neutral, depending on the context and perspective of the article. In recognition of this, we present a more granular analysis of articles appearing in top-10 newspaper outlets in Table 5.5, indicating what percentage of each institution's returned results in this category constituted opinion pieces, expert quotations, or mentions. We classified mentions as positive, negative, or neutral.

When it comes to top-10 newspaper coverage, faculty mentions reflect mostly positively on these Christian Worldview institutions, doing some work to chip away at the credibility deficit. For Liberty Law, 72% of their top-10 mentions portray their faculty as experts on a point of law. For AMSL, this number is just under half (48%), but if we include the 6% of mentions that were opinion pieces or published letters to the newspaper, that total is 54%. For Regent Law, 33% of mentions involved faculty citations on matters of law, 7% were faculty opinion pieces or published letters, and

Table 5.5. **Breakdown of Type and Tenor of Christian Worldview Faculty Mentions in Top-10 Newspapers**

Institution	% Opinion or Letter	% Quoted as Expert	% Mention (Positive)	% Mention (Negative)	% Mention (Neutral)
Regent Law School (*n* = 42)	~7	~33	~5	~24	~31
Ave Maria School of Law (*n* = 31)	~6	~48	0	~16	~29
Liberty Law School (*n* = 101)	0	~72	0	~16	~12

Source: Circulation rankings based on analysis by Alliance for Audited Media 2015. Articles where faculty were mentioned in Top-10 newspapers were read and coded for type (op-ed, quoted as expert) and tenor (positive, negative, neutral) of mention.

another 5% were positive mentions (which involved a mention of a Regent Law faculty member being appointed to a prestigious position in government).

Because each of these Christian Worldview institutions started out with a credibility deficit, it is important to examine where and in what context faculty are mentioned negatively in top media outlets. Regent Law had the greatest percentage of negative mentions in top-10 outlets (24%). Three scandals drove this negative coverage: Pat Robertson's controversial firing of founding Dean Herb Titus and Titus-loyal faculty in 1994, which resulted in multiple lawsuits, including a libel lawsuit against Robertson (see Chapter 3); the Monica Goodling scandal in the Justice Department (see Chapter 4), covered extensively by the national media in 2007; and coverage of the conviction of a former assistant Dean of Regent Law, Stephen McPherson, who was convicted of sexually abusing children in 2009.

With regard to the lawsuits against Robertson, for example, a *Washington Post* article published excerpts from a letter Robertson wrote in which he accused the fired faculty "of trying to cripple or shut down the law school. He wrote that the professors were 'second-rate legal minds,' 'inept as lawyers' and 'extremist fanatics.' "[60] For AMSL, nearly all the negative coverage (16% of all top-10 mentions) was driven by the controversy and firings resulting from Tom Monaghan's decision to relocate the law school from Ann Arbor, Michigan, to Naples, Florida. For Liberty Law, the 16% of negative mentions were almost exclusively about professor Judith Reisman—a culture wars crusader and pornography opponent often written about dismissively for her lack of credentials and described repeatedly as a "former songwriter for the Captain Kangaroo television show."[61]

It is difficult to assess whether the net benefits from having significantly more positive faculty mentions and showcasing of legal bona fides in top-10 media outlets outweighs the impact from the fewer scandalous or negatively framed media stories that reinforce some of the dominant cultural stereotypes about these Christian Worldview institutions—that they are populated with lightly credentialed culture warriors who (to quote Pat Robertson himself) are "second-rate legal minds," "inept as lawyers," and "extremist fanatics." Given this, the schools' media appearances present an ambiguous, at best, means to increasing their collective and individual *cultural capital*.

The Difficulty of Overcoming the Credibility Deficit through Faculty Media Engagement

To be sure, the production of *cultural capital* by law schools is a peripheral rather than a central institutional output. Training *human capital* and producing *intellectual capital*, or scholarship, are at the core of what law schools do as institutions. *Social* and *cultural capital* production is a byproduct of these core responsibilities, and certainly law schools facilitate the building and maintaining of networks as well as engagement with the media as experts and authorities. However, faculty members cannot be full-time media personalities while still accomplishing their primary responsibilities of teaching and research. It is, therefore, challenging for these Christian Worldview law schools to be real, sustained, and serious players in the media, thereby shaping the dialogue more broadly.

On the other hand, ADF's Blackstone Legal Fellowship—representing the *supplemental* model of support structure building in our study—can devote significant resources to building credibility capital. Blackstone-affiliated faculty commit only to participating in a two-week summer seminar with students rather than having to teach full-time. Blackstone affiliates without institutional ties to law schools are able to devote significant time and energy to shaping the cultural landscape through media engagement. Hugh Hewitt and David French, for example, had thousands of returned results from our media search on LexisNexis Academic. Hewitt is a contributing columnist for the *The Washington Post* and hosts his own radio program, *The Hugh Hewitt Show*. David French is a senior fellow and writer for the conservative magazine *The National Review*.

Even excluding these heavy hitters from our analysis, Blackstone-affiliated faculty are significantly more active in the media than their Christian Worldview counterparts, returning 1,616 results from our media search. Even limiting our media search to "The Blackstone Seven" (William Saunders, Teresa Collett, John Baker, Kyle Duncan, John C. Eastman, Francis Beckwith, and Hadley Arkes), who we established earlier in this chapter as the most active participants in Federalist Society events, returns 1,429 results. This constitutes 88% of Blackstone-affiliated faculty's hits. So here, again, we find evidence that those central figures active in the Federalist Society network—those with the most *social capital* within the conservative legal movement—are also engaging heavily with the media and the culture writ large.

Bringing the Support Structure Pyramid Back In

We began this chapter by introducing the term *credibility capital*—an umbrella term that captures the importance of two kinds of capital successful Level 1 support structure institutions generate for movements: *social capital* and *cultural capital*. *Social capital* refers to the extent to which law schools build and maintain networks and connections to actors and organizations with access to power, influence, and decision-making. *Social capital* can facilitate the transfer of *intellectual capital* or ideas from movement actors housed in these law schools to the movement writ large. Ultimately, the goal of litigation-based change is for actors outside of these Christian Worldview institutions to help these ideas have consequences by implementing or translating them into legal and judicial policy. Being connected with powerful actors through networks—having *social capital*—facilitates this transmission process up the pyramid to those at the top with access to the levers of power.

We present ample evidence to suggest that these Christian Worldview law schools are well connected with and well networked with Christian Right legal and political organizations but that they are not yet integrated into the conservative legal mainstream as measured by participation and involvement in the Federalist Society for Law and Public Policy Studies. This matters not only in terms of *social capital* and networking with one of the most important gatekeepers for judicial and legal positions with Republican administrations, but also in terms of the audience the Federalist Society provides for the vetting and legitimating of what is and what is not acceptable conservative legal and judicial ideology. If these Christian Worldview institutions hope to have their ideas migrate from the legal fringe into the mainstream, having the Federalist Society network's stamp of approval and endorsement is very important. On the other hand, we showed how faculty associated with the Blackstone Legal Fellowship (in particular "The Blackstone Seven") have become mainstays at Federalist Society conferences and events, suggesting that this organization representing the *supplemental* model in our study is far more well connected than its *parallel alternative* counterparts.

Relatedly, *cultural capital* refers to the broader acceptability and weight audiences give to a movement's actors and ideas. *Cultural capital* can prime an audience to find a movement's ideas legitimate and persuasive instead of dismissing them. We showed how these Christian Worldview institutions have a significant credibility deficit to overcome with elite and popular audiences. This deficit exists because these institutions are new, because they are doing something radical with their curriculum and training of law students, and because there is a broader cultural stereotype of the Bible-thumping crazy Christian that they need to actively overcome in order to be taken seriously as legal experts and authorities with viable ideas.

We suggest that one means of chipping away at this credibility deficit is for the faculty of these Christian Worldview institutions to present themselves as serious, credible experts and authorities on law in the media. Our analysis of faculty engagement with media suggests that while faculty members at each of the three Christian Worldview institutions are being sought after and cited as experts, the credibility benefits of these appearances may, in fact, be outweighed by the smaller portion of negatively framed stories and coverage of various scandals that reinforce the dominant cultural assumptions about crazy Christians. From the perspective of *cultural capital*, it is important to note that faculty engagement with the media is not the only way to overcome the credibility deficit. Faculty can also earn legitimacy and respect—at least from other elites—through their scholarship and the production of *intellectual capital*, which we examine in the next chapter.

Intellectual Capital: Preaching to Convert, or to the Converted?

> What an academic institution provides is the ability to think, to read, to talk, to write comprehensively . . . You can lay out things and really develop a different approach and a way of understanding the law and apply it. There's precious few schools like that . . . I only know a very small handful of people in the whole world that are trying to reform the law in terms of a comprehensive Christian worldview. That's where I want to get my focus and that's what I would like to see the law school doing.—Liberty Faculty 3 2015
>
> Notre Dame is trying to be excellent and Catholic. Regent and Liberty, for whatever it's worth, they're not going to get to excellent anytime soon . . . at least in any time in my lifetime.—Notre Dame Faculty 2 2016

As noted in the previous chapter, Christian Worldview law schools start off at a deficit when it comes to cultural credibility in the academic, legal professional, political, and popular spheres. One of the ways that these institutions can address these deficits is to produce scholarship that earns respect in the academic sphere—that is, to show that they are serious legal academies, and not "Jiffy Law" diploma mills populated by "Jesus Freaks" (Vegh 2007). Faculty attempt to prove themselves and the legitimacy of their home institutions by producing scholarship that is well placed (i.e., published in journals with high impact factors) and actively cited by others (as evidence of being read, discussed, and presumably validated).[1]

Law schools are unique as "support structures" in that they can serve as hothouses for new ideas, and the intent is that those ideas will have beneficial consequences for movements. As the Liberty Law professor insightfully states in the excerpt at the beginning of this chapter, "What an academic institution provides is the ability to think, to read, to talk, to write comprehensively . . . You can lay out things and really develop a different approach and a way of understanding the law and apply it" (Liberty Faculty 3 2015). It is through engaging in reflective scholarship and vigorously entering the marketplace of ideas through publishing that the faculty can uniquely help their institutions achieve the mission of changing law, culture, and policy.

Separate But Faithful. Amanda Hollis-Brusky and Joshua C. Wilson, Oxford University Press (2020). © Oxford University Press. DOI: 10.1093/oso/9780190637262.001.0001

In order to revolutionize the conversation and rebuild the foundations of law, Christian Worldview faculty scholarship needs to advance "a *different* approach and a way of understanding law" (Liberty Faculty 3 2015). While stressing this difference is absolutely necessary to this end, the prophet proclaiming his truth is often banished to the wilderness, facing marginalization and persecution (e.g., Acts 7:52; Isaiah 40:3; Matthew 23:34–37; Matthew 5:10–12; John 15:18–20; Luke 11:49; 1 Kings 18:17; 2 Timothy 3:12; 1 Peter 4:12–14; etc.). Transformative *intellectual capital* intended to change ongoing legal discussions, legal culture, and the law more broadly thus runs the risk of reinforcing the stereotypes that already marginalize these schools and their missions (Wilson and Hollis-Brusky 2018). In this way, mission-driven scholarly production can actually help undermine, rather than advance, both the credibility and *intellectual capital* gains sought by the movement.

Accepting the inherent but unavoidable risks of seeking to disrupt the dominant legal paradigm, there is still a question of what types of *intellectual capital* will best serve the movement. Is it better to seek incremental change that introduces new ideas but in a way that minimizes their difference, or is it better to launch an all-out assault on the status quo in hopes of sparking a more vigorous discussion? In other words, is it better to pursue *intellectual capital* that will supply a "short game" with the aim of winning discrete legal cases and building precedent within the legal system, or is it better to produce scholarship that aims at the "long game" of radically and fundamentally changing that same system?

We have seen shades of this pragmatic-versus-principled struggle throughout the book. We saw this struggle manifested in the tensions between Regent's founding patron Pat Robertson, the founding dean, Herb Titus, and the faculty loyal to Titus's vision for the Christian legal movement. We also saw examples of this tension in the questions regarding Liberty Law's faculty hiring practices and the discomfort of some faculty with the school's closeness to the Liberty Counsel under the former dean, Mat Staver. At Ave Maria School of Law (AMSL), this struggle reared its head in fights between the original faculty and Thomas Monaghan over his decision to relocate the campus from Michigan to Florida.

Within the scope of scholarship specifically, this short-game pragmatism versus long-game principle tension was most clearly articulated in our interview with one Liberty Law faculty member:

> Well this gets at the heart of what the real issue is in Christian legal education . . . [We] need a perspective from which to evaluate, not just evaluate in the sense of picking out things that are right or wrong . . . The only real foundation for that is a Christian worldview that makes a real clear distinction between Creator and creature . . . That's what I would like to see [as Christian legal education's] mission . . . That's aspirational for me . . . I wouldn't say it's aspirational for others because I don't think they've got a picture of it. Part of the problem is, it takes that vision from

the leadership and if you don't have that at the leadership, then the focus is on culture wars and particular issues, you're going to miss it. I think that's very problematic. I think that was a problem at Regent and it's a problem here [at Liberty]. You've got a lot of very good, bright, well-educated Christian lawyers, but . . . unless you've got leadership that has a bigger view of things, it's not going to change [the world in the ways sought]. (Liberty Faculty 3 2015)

While this faculty member has a clear vision of what Christian Worldview institutions should be pursuing, and what his role is in that pursuit—"I've known for the last thirty-three years what my duty is" (Liberty Faculty 3 2015)—he does not think that his long-view orientation is the dominant one within Christian law schools. Rather, the schools and the greater Christian conservative legal movement's (CCLM's) focus have turned to working within the existing system to pursue specific culture war policy victories.[2] His hope, though, is that by educating students who, in his words, "get it," the Christian legal academy can eventually get to where he wants it to be in "ten or fifteen years" (Liberty Faculty 3 2015).

As these Christian Worldview institutions' histories show, future faculty makeup is dependent on what the institutions value. Leadership—both within the schools and in the profession more broadly—determines these values and, thus, the course of the academy on both the campus and national levels. If scholarship directed toward short-game strategies or furthering ongoing discussions within the secular legal mainstream are prized, then faculty candidates seeking to contribute to the long game of grounding law and policy in a Christian biblical worldview have a harder time joining the academy.

The same is true for publishing. If the field does not value "long-game" contributions, or religiously grounded scholarship more generally, it is harder to publish such pieces. This raises one final consideration when thinking about these institutions' abilities to use scholarship to forward *cultural* and *intellectual capital* ends. Given that these schools were founded with the oppositional mission to change the law and the belief that they were actively discriminated against in the existing legal academy, the prospects of being able to publish Christian Worldview scholarship are presumably bleak. Studies of the academic publication process—from acceptance rates, to placement prestige, to citations—have been shown to be influenced by social and professional networks (Colussi 2017) and by perceptions of author prestige (Chilton et al. 2019; Tomkins et al. 2017), both of which work against upstart or *parallel alternative* institutions and faculty.

Considering the potential of being locked out by the mainstream, it is natural that the schools would create their own legal publications. University-based law reviews are the primary vehicles through which law faculty publish and, thus, the primary means by which the scholarly conversation takes place (Chilton et al. 2019).[3] Law reviews are also a traditional means by which schools train, credential, and network their top students. Law reviews thus serve multiple purposes, but from the perspective of Support Structure Theory they provide two specific services.

First, with regard to *intellectual capital*, in-house law reviews facilitate a conversation regarding grounding law and policy in a Christian Worldview. What's more, they do so in a way that invites others from beyond the host school to become involved in such a conversation.[4] The journals do this by providing a vehicle for scholars at Christian Worldview law schools to build a collective movement through intellectual exchange via their journals—publishing in one another's journals, and citing one another's work. In-house law reviews also broaden this conversation and build the movement beyond these schools by publishing the work of sympathetic faculty at other institutions. If they are successful in doing the latter, and in having articles published in the in-house law reviews cited elsewhere, the schools' journals can help raise the institution's profile and the movement's credibility capital.

The in-house law reviews' promise is coupled with possible challenges. While in-house journals provide an outlet for the schools' faculty, as well as a means by which to ensure that the ideas the schools were founded to develop and spread are put into circulation, they also stand to create what one interviewee derisively referred to as a "holy huddle" (Blackstone Administrator 2 2015). That is, the journals can turn into echo chambers of the likeminded. Even more problematic, they can turn into venues exclusively used by faculty at the other Christian Worldview law schools, or, in the worst-case scenario, publications dominated by those from the home institutions themselves.

With the goals, benefits, risks, and barriers set up in this way, the remainder of this chapter is dedicated to assessing if, how, and how well the schools as "support structures" have been able to use scholarship to advance the transformative ends of the Christian Right. The first section will pursue the question of using scholarship to help close the "credibility deficit." To do so we examine where faculty are publishing, how often their scholarship is cited and, relatedly, where their scholarship is being cited. As Chilton et al. note,

> There are three primary objective measures of a scholar's research record . . . : number of articles published, the journals those articles are placed in, and the citations to those articles. The number of articles an academic writes . . . is a measure of their productivity; the journals an academic publishes in might serve as measure of the quality of their research; and citations are the revealed preferences of peers, and therefore serve as a proxy for the quality and influence of the research. (2019, 11)

In order to give these descriptive statistics greater context, we will compare our three newly created Christian conservative law schools with a sample of eight other law schools—both religious and secular in nature—that cover a range of positions in the overall *U.S. News & World Report* law school rankings.[5]

Since, as we have established, the law schools' in-house law reviews are also a vehicle to address the credibility deficit and build *cultural* and *intellectual capital* for the
movement, we look at who is publishing in these journals, the rates at which articles
in these journals are cited, and where they are cited. In-house journals examined
include *Regent Journal of Law & Public Policy, Regent University Law Review, Ave
Maria Law Review, Liberty Law Review,* and *Liberty, Life, and Family.* The chapter's
final sections will employ data from the in-house law reviews to see whether they
are being used to disseminate mission-relevant scholarship, whether such mission
scholarship is being cited, and if so, at what rates and where is it being cited. We
also look for evidence that the faculty at these Christian Worldview institutions are
working together—whether intentionally or serendipitously—to create an intellectual movement, or whether they are working more as isolated actors within the
greater scholarly legal world.

A detailed discussion of the data collection and analysis methods used in this
chapter is available in Appendix A. Briefly, we searched each law school's websites to
collect faculty names.[6] We used the Internet Archive "Wayback Machine" (https://
archive.org/web/) to identify and catalogue former faculty. Once collected, we
used R and the legal scholarship database HeinOnline to collect bibliographic information (e.g., article name, publication venue, publication year, etc.) for all of the
works listed as authored by these faculty, and then all of the works that cite these
originally published works. The same process was applied to collecting the universe
of works published in the various schools' in-house law reviews. We then used a
2018 Wiley/Clarivate Analytics–produced, rank-ordered impact factor list of 147
law journals to assess the prestige of both the journal within which articles were
originally published, and the journals that published any citing articles.[7] While we
recognize that some data may have been missed, the same processes were applied
to all of the schools. What's more, as Tables 6.1 and 6.2 show, the data sample size
is large enough that we are confident that the aggregated finding trends are both reliable and informative.

Table 6.1. **Observable Lifetime Faculty and Their Publication Activity**

	Ave Maria	Liberty	Regent
Authors	42	33	40
Percent of Faculty Publishing	82%	83%	85%
Works per School	330	176	429
Mean Works per Faculty Member	6.5	4.4	9.1

Source. Faculty data for Regent extending from Fall 1986, Ave Maria from Fall 1999, and Liberty
from Fall 2004 up to the 2017–18 school year. Faculty lists collected using the Internet Archive
Wayback Machine, https://web.archive.org

Table 6.2. **Active Faculty and Their Lifetime Publication Activity with Comparisons**

	AMSL	Liberty	Regent	Baylor	ND	GMU	Pepp.	St. Thomas	Campbell	Quinn.	U. Wyo.
Authors	13	21	24	22	45	39	39	15	17	17	20
% Faculty Publishing	81%	91%	89%	100%	96%	87%	93%	75%	100%	100%	100%
Total Works per School	61	76	241	181	1103	912	738	612	121	266	253
Mean Works per Faculty Member	3.8	3.3	8.9	8.2	23.5	20.3	17.6	30.6	7.1	15.7	12.7

Source. Faculty lists collected using the Internet Archive Wayback Machine, https://web.archive.org. Active faculty included faculty listed for 2016–2017 and 2017–2018 academic years.

Scholarship, *Cultural Capital*, and the Credibility Deficit

The investigation of scholarship as a resource for the newly created Christian Worldview law schools and the greater CCLM starts with the most basic question of whether or not the faculty are publishing, what venues are they publishing in, and where and how often those publications are getting cited by other scholars. We then examine how these descriptive statistics compare with other law schools in our sample.

Entering the Marketplace of Ideas—A Threshold Measure of Quantity

As Tables 6.1 and 6.2 illustrate, there is meaningful variation in terms of the rates at which faculty at Ave Maria, Liberty, and Regent are producing *intellectual* and *cultural capital* through their scholarship. As we can see from Table 6.1, when it comes to the percentage of faculty[8] publishing at each institution, the three Christian Worldview law schools are within a few percentage points of one another—ranging from 82% to 85%. Differences begin to emerge when we consider the volume of scholarship faculty members have produced over their careers. In a pattern that will be repeated over the course of this chapter, Regent stands out as the most productive of the three Christian Worldview law schools, while Liberty is the least productive. Given the differences in the times that the schools have been in operation, the *mean* number of scholarly works produced is the most comparable figure. The previous order holds, placing Regent at the top, Liberty at the bottom, and Ave Maria in between.

We have also taken a more recent sample of faculty of record from the 2016–17 and 2017–18 academic years in order to compare them with the faculty from a range of law schools collected for the same time period. To differentiate this subset of faculty from the "lifetime" faculty sample seen in Table 6.1, we will refer to this 2016–18 sample as the "active" faculty. Finally, like Table 6.1, the data presented in Table 6.2 includes the lifetime of work published by these faculty members since it represents one measure of the faculty's collective *cultural capital*.[9]

Beginning within the three primary case study schools, the most immediate difference seen with the active faculty versus the larger lifetime faculty sample is the reordering of the percentage of faculty publishing. The focus on active faculty leads Ave Maria to slip by one percentage point, while Liberty jumps from 83% to 91% of faculty publishing, and Regent grows by a more modest amount from 85% to 89%. The mean number of works produced by faculty drops across all of the schools but the original ordering of Regent, followed by Ave Maria, followed by Liberty, remained constant. Most interestingly, while the mean number of works per faculty member slips across all of the schools, Ave Maria's precipitously declines from 6.5 to 3.8 when comparing the lifetime and the active faculty. This point once again reinforces the argument that Ave Maria experienced an overall drop in quality when it moved from Michigan to Florida.

In fact, when isolating and comparing the lifetime of scholarship produced by faculty from the first two years of faculty data versus the current active faculty, the degree to which Ave Maria has changed is magnified. While the percent of faculty publishing is relatively stable for Liberty and Regent, Ave's drops dramatically from 100% of the early faculty, to just 81% of the current active faculty publishing. Furthermore, while the number of Ave Maria faculty authors actually increases from 7 to 13, the total works produced drops from 102 to 61, and the mean works per faculty correspondingly drops from 14.6 to 4.7.[10] Ave Maria's active faculty is, thus, far less productive than its early faculty by all measures.[11]

Looking at the three schools in comparison with a range of others—both religious and secular—we begin to get a better idea of where these schools' active faculties exist within the greater legal academic landscape. Starting with the percentage of faculty publishing, four of the surveyed schools had 100% of their faculty publishing. Out of the collective eleven schools, Liberty, Regent, and Ave Maria occupied the seventh, eighth, and tenth spots, respectively. While they clearly reside at the lower end of the spectrum, with the exception of Ave Maria, the distance behind the rest of the field is not too great.

The gaps between the schools are more dramatic in terms of the mean number of publications per faculty member. St. Thomas, a Catholic law school in Minnesota started in 1999, ranked by the *U.S. News & World Report* (2017) at the 120th spot, stands out with a remarkable 30.6 articles per faculty member. They are followed by the more established and prestigious Notre Dame Law School (ranked 20th) with 23.5 publications per faculty member, and the ascendant George Mason Antonin Scalia Law School (ranked 41st) at 20.3 publications per faculty member. The mean articles stay in the teens through the top six of the sampled schools until it drops to Regent's 8.9 publications per faculty member at the number 7 spot. Ave Maria and Liberty constitute the pool's floor with means below 4. This is approximately three works less per faculty member than the next lowest school, the similarly unranked and religious Campbell University School of Law, which averaged 7.1 publications per faculty member.

To summarize, the Regent faculty is publishing at a rate comparable to the more prestigious 51-ranked, and Baptist affiliated, Baylor Law School, but below University of Wyoming's (112th) and Quinnipiac University's (127th) law schools—the secular regional schools in the sample. As an additional level of comparison, Chilton et al. (2019, 17) note that law professors who secured tenure averaged five pre-tenure publications in the 1980s and '90s, and six such articles in the 2000s. Given all of this, one can see Regent as being within the lower ranks of recognizable school performance, while Ave Maria and Liberty fall far short of the scholarly publication volume mark within the sample, as well as in comparison with successful pre-tenure law faculty nationwide for the past few decades.

Looking at schools with comparable faculty sizes to the three primary case study institutions, part of the importance of the differences in the mean number of works produced becomes apparent. Notre Dame, George Mason University (GMU), and Pepperdine—all with sizeable law school faculties (ranging in the forties) and all with *U.S. News* rankings consistently in the top 100—understandably produce far more scholarship than the rest of the field. Looked at alone, these three schools' faculty samples have produced more than 2,700 publications, with Notre Dame alone accounting for over 1,000. The remaining schools sampled, however, have smaller faculties, in the teens to the mid-twenties, and produce more modest, but still significant, numbers of publications.

Within this reduced set of smaller faculty institutions, Regent, with 241 publications, sits comfortably alongside Wyoming (253) and Quinnipiac (266), and above Baylor (181), which is far more highly ranked in the *U.S. News* than all of the schools with smaller faculty sizes. Liberty, with a comparable faculty size to all of these schools, trails all of these schools with just 76 publications. The two schools closest to Liberty in terms of sheer volume of publications are Campbell, whose much smaller 17 faculty members account for a far more 121 articles, and Ave Maria, whose total 16 faculty account for 61 total publications. Worse for Liberty, they have larger faculty sizes than Campbell and Ave Maria. They, in fact, have the third largest faculty of the eight smaller schools. Thus, while Liberty has improved the percentage of its faculty that is publishing, those faculty are not publishing very much.

To summarize, Liberty and Ave Maria are underproducing in terms of scholarship. This can possibly be explained by the change in faculty brought by Ave Maria's move from Michigan to Florida (see Chapter 3), and by the internal criticisms that Liberty has historically been too invested in hiring martyrs and champions from the culture wars over hiring faculty with a more traditional legal pedigree (see Chapter 5). Regent, on the other hand, has more successfully fostered faculty publications, though they are still at the lower end of the broader legal scholarly market. By these numbers alone, the three Christian Worldview law schools appear to be variably invested in faculty publications, but collectively underutilizing scholarship as a means to raising their *cultural capital* and, presumably by extension, altering the larger scholarly conversation to incorporate and reflect their interests.

Being Recognized within the Marketplace of Ideas— Measures of Quality

As any scholar knows, it is one thing to publish a lot. It is another thing to have those publications featured in prestigious venues, and yet another to have that scholarship cited by others. Academic careers—and by extension, faculty and institutional reputations—are evaluated using all of these markers, but the measures of quality are what really make a career and one's capital (Chilton et al. 2019; Heckman & Moktan, 2018; Liner & Sewell 2009; Mingers & Xu 2010). They are also variables that can begin the chapter's pivot from scholarship as *cultural capital*, to thinking more about scholarship as *intellectual capital* that can feed a legal movement.

As with the previous analysis, this section provides a mix of longer-view, and more current, comparative perspectives of how well the faculty at these schools are placing their works, and how frequently they are being cited by others. There are three basic themes that emerge from the placement data. The first, echoing the previous section, is a precipitous decline in Ave Maria's scholarly activity after their move from Michigan to Florida. The second, defying the previous section, is a flattening out of differences between the three primary case study schools in terms of the quality of the work they produce. Finally, and related to their collective quality, is the widening of the gap between the three Christian Worldview law schools and the rest of the comparative institutions.

In brief, then, this section illustrates that while the Christian Worldview law schools vary in terms of their efforts to enter the scholarly marketplace of ideas, by the measures used here, none of them have been particularly effective in successfully becoming recognized as major players within this marketplace. Given this and the relative performance of other religious law schools in our comparative sample, it again raises questions about the decision to create wholly new *parallel alternative* law schools as opposed to investing in existing institutions. It also lends quantitative support for the opening quote from the Notre Dame faculty member that Christian Worldview schools were "not going to get to excellent anytime soon" (Notre Dame Faculty 2 2016), thus limiting their *cultural capital*, and by possible extension, the recognized transferable value of their *intellectual capital*.

Starting with publication placement, Ave Maria, Liberty, and Regent have an abysmal record of placing faculty scholarship in top tier journals. When looking at lifetime faculty publications, Ave Maria accounts for 29 articles in the top 100 law journals, while Regent has 5 and Liberty has 1 such placement. Extending the count to all ranked journals, Christian Worldview faculty members as a collective have produced a total of 53 articles (6% of their combined scholarly production) in ranked law journals, in comparison with 844 (94%) in unranked journals.

When turning to the active faculty sample, Regent and Ave Maria's faculties have placed a total of 8 publications in ranked law journals and Liberty Law has placed zero (see Table 6.3). That means that of the 378 articles that Christian Worldview law schools' combined active faculties have published, only 2% have been in ranked journals, and less than 1% have been in top-100 journals. Standing on their own, 4.9% of Ave Maria's 61, 1.7% of Regent's 241, and 1.3% of Liberty's 76 active faculty publications are in ranked law journals. Put simply, all three of these schools are seriously struggling to place scholarship in ranked, let alone top-100, law journals.[12] These placement patterns matter not only in terms of a means of evaluating and

Table 6.3. **Active Faculty Publication Placement**

	AMSL	Liberty	Regent	Baylor	ND	GMU	Pepp.	St. Thomas	Campbell	Quinn.	U. Wyo.
Total Works	61	76	241	181	1103	912	738	612	121	266	253
Top-25	0	0	0	0	104	46	24	40	1	15	6
	—	—	—	—	9.4%	5.0%	3.3%	6.5%	0.8%	5.6%	2.4%
Top-50	0	0	1	1	151	119	46	64	2	21	18
	—	—	0.4%	0.6%	13.7%	13.0%	6.2%	10.5%	1.7%	7.9%	7.1%
Top-100	1	0	2	3	237	185	82	85	3	40	24
	1.6%	—	0.8%	1.7%	21.5%	20.3%	11.1%	13.9%	2.5%	15.0%	9.5%
All Ranked Journals	3	1	4	5	263	206	94	93	7	45	30
	4.9%	1.3%	1.7%	2.8%	23.8%	22.6%	12.7%	15.2%	5.8%	16.9%	11.9%
Not Ranked	58	75	237	176	840	706	644	519	114	221	223
	95.1%	98.7%	98.3%	97.2%	76.2%	77.4%	87.3%	84.8%	94.2%	83.1%	88.1%

Source. Faculty lists collected using the Internet Archive Wayback Machine, https://web.archive.org. Active faculty included faculty listed for 2016–17 and 2017–18 academic years.

increasing prestige, but also in terms of reaching an audience. As Chilton et al. note, "higher-ranked journals have higher circulation. An article is simply more likely to be seen and subsequently cited because it is in a higher-ranked journal" (2019, 12). By placing what relatively low volume of scholarship they do produce in lower-ranked journals, the Christian Worldview schools are further undermining their ability to utilize scholarship as a means to elevate their prestige and disseminate their ideas.

As we also see from Table 6.3, the evaluation of the schools' performances does not improve when held up against the spectrum of eight comparative law schools. At first glance, there is only one other school, Baylor, that fails to have at least one active faculty publication placed in a top-25 legal journal. Notre Dame and George Mason occupy the top story when one looks at the percentage of placements in ranked, top-100, and top-50 legal journals. Both schools, in fact, have over 20% of their faculty's publications in top-100 legal journals and over 13% in top-50 journals. St. Thomas, Quinnipiac, Pepperdine, and Wyoming round out the next level of publication placements with roughly 12%–17% of their publications appearing in ranked journals, 9.5%–15% in top-100 journals, and 6%–10% in top-50 journals. Campbell and Baylor are the only two schools close to the Christian Worldview law schools in terms of their scant representation in ranked, top-100, and top-50 journals.

The vast gap between the Christian Worldview law schools and the overwhelming majority of comparative cases returns us to the question of whether the founders of these schools would have done better to have invested in existing law schools—the *infiltration* strategy—instead of creating wholly new *parallel alternative* institutions. It appears that patrons and the movement would have made negligible gains in scholarly production investing in Baylor, but that they could have gained much more from investing in institutions such as the Protestant Pepperdine or Catholic Notre Dame.

The final and arguably more pertinent measures of quality are citation rate and citation placement. While one might not place an article in a top-tier journal, a publication can go on to gain prestige and value by being read and discussed by others—though, as noted above, prestigious placement is the first step in garnering substantial citations (Chilton et al. 2019, 12). Starting again with the lifetime faculty, familiar patterns return. As illustrated in Table 6.4, over the lifetime of the schools, Regent (73%) and Ave Maria (72%) are a close one and two in terms of the percentage of publications that are cited, and Liberty lags behind with 51% of their publications garnering citations.

At first glance it appears that Ave Maria has produced the highest number of citations with a mean number of cites at 11.7 versus Regent's 9.5 and Liberty's 5.9, but this is due to the inclusion of a handful of Robert Bork's earlier articles garnering overwhelming citation rates.[13] The numbers become far more comparable when

Table 6.4. **Citation Rates for Christian Worldview Lifetime Faculty**

	Ave Maria	*Liberty*	*Regent*
Works per School	330	176	429
Cited Articles	239	90	315
Number of Cites	2786	530	2994
% of Articles Cited	72%	51%	73%
Mean Cites per Article	11.7	5.9	9.5
Median Cites per Article	5	4	5

Source. Citation data collected using Web-scraping algorithm in R, which scraped and collected data from the legal database HeinOnline (see Appendix A for details).

one turns to the median number of cites, Ave Maria and Regent have median cites of 5 and Liberty with 4.

Pivoting to the active faculty, Ave Maria's numbers drop significantly, while the other schools remain rather steady. Median citations sit at 4 and 5, with Ave Maria slipping to join Liberty, and the mean citations sitting at a more comparable 7.73 for Regent, 6.85 for Ave Maria, and 5.54 for Liberty. While notably seen in Ave Maria's mean number of cites, their more meaningful drop is seen in the decline in the percentage of articles cited.[14] Ave Maria's percentage of publications cited for their lifetime versus active faculty drops from 72% to 56%.

The story changes when looking at the citing audiences. When looking at the prestige of the journals citing the various school's faculty scholarship, Ave Maria far outperforms the other two schools. In terms of lifetime faculty, Ave Maria has an impressive 64% of cites in ranked journals, 61% in top-100 journals, and 22% in top-50 journals. Regent and Liberty lag behind with 9–10% in ranked journals, roughly 7% in top-100 journals, and roughly 5% in top-50 journals. Removing Bork and other more established faculty from Ave Maria's earlier years helps to significantly reduce this gap, but Ave Maria faculty still have a higher percentage of their work garner conversation in more elite journals than the active faculty at Regent and Liberty.

As Table 6.5 shows, comparing across schools, Regent is the only school with the percentage of articles cited that is on par with the rest of the field in multiple categories. Regent, however, joins Ave Maria and Liberty in the drop off when turning to the rest of the descriptive statistics. The mean number of citations earned is the in the double digits for all of the comparative schools except for Campbell and Wyoming which are both still higher than any of the Christian Worldview law schools. Campbell joins Regent with the median cites earned, and Baylor and Wyoming sit just above Regent, but the rest of the field begins to pull away from the Christian Worldview law schools. St. Thomas and George Mason set the high bar

Table 6.5. **Active Faculty Citation Rates and Placement**

	AMSL	Liberty	Regent	Baylor	ND	GMU	Pepp.	St. Thomas	Campbell	Quinn.	U. Wyo.
Articles Cited	56%	49%	74%	69%	71%	77%	71%	70%	74%	81%	79%
Mean Cites	6.9	5.5	7.7	10.5	16.9	17.7	15.7	21.8	8.7	14.3	9.4
Median Cites	4	4	5	6	8.5	10	8	10	5	7	6
In Top-50	9%	1%	5%	8%	30%	19%	11%	16%	7%	18%	12%
In Top-100	11%	4%	8%	11%	44%	25%	17%	22%	10%	23%	16%
In Ranked	16%	8%	10%	14%	50%	28%	19%	24%	13%	26%	19%
In Unranked	84%	92%	90%	86%	50%	72%	81%	76%	88%	74%	81%

Source. Faculty lists collected using the Internet Archive Wayback Machine, https://web.archive.org. Active faculty included faculty listed for 2016–17 and 2017–18 academic years. Citation data collected using Web-scraping algorithm in R, which scraped and collected data from the legal database HeinOnline (see Appendix A for details). A 2018 Wiley/Clarivate Analytics–produced, rank-ordered impact factor list of 147 law journals was used to assess the prestige of both the journal within which articles were originally published, and the journals that published any citing articles.

with median citations that are two or more times as high as those of Regent, Ave Maria, and Liberty.

It is not just that the comparative law schools are being cited more frequently, but that they are being cited far more frequently in the more prestigious legal journals that set the tone for the larger academic conversation. It is again worth noting that these journals are ranked according to their impact factors, and that impact factors are statistics representing the frequency with which articles published in those journals are cited by others. In other words, an impact factor is a measure of a journal's weight within the contemporary legal academic conversation. Thus, having one's work published in such a journal is a promising sign of it eventually being cited, and having one's work cited in such a journal is another way of being included within and understanding its importance to the most discussed conversations in the legal academic marketplace.

Notre Dame proves its prestige by having half of its citations come in ranked journals, 44% from top-100 journals, and still 30% in top-50 journals. Excluding Baylor and Campbell, the rest of the field has percentage ranges for scholarship cited in ranked journals between 19%–28%, in top-100 journals at 16%–24%, and in top-50 journals it is still in the double digits with 11%–19%. The low end of each of these ranges is still greater than the high end for the three primary case study schools which are 8%–16% for ranked journal citations, 4%–11% of top-100 cites, and 1%–9% for top-50 cites. Not only, then, are publications from faculty at the comparative schools earning more citations, but these citations are appearing in the journals that set the agenda for and carry weight within the legal academy.[15]

As Chilton et al. (2019) point out, prestige in legal faculty law review publication is predictably self-reinforcing. That is, faculty in prestigious schools have two built-in advantages by virtue of their institutional placement. First, because law reviews are student run versus peer reviewed and double blind as in the rest of academia, faculty at prestigious schools are better able to garner acceptances from more highly regarded law reviews by virtue of their credentials versus the quality of their work alone. Second, the publications from such scholars in such journals are similarly more likely to garner citations given their perceived prestige, the increased circulation of such journals, and the desire of subsequent faculty authors "in part to signal to student editors that their article under review is of similar significance" (Chilton et al. 2019, 12).

Looking at this section as a whole, it is not only that the Christian Worldview law schools are collectively struggling to enter the academic marketplace of ideas, but also that when they do enter it they are doing so more at the academic margins than at the center and are falling behind most of the regional, as well as the national, schools in the sample. What's more, they are also being eclipsed by St. Thomas— another newly created Christian law school. St. Thomas's success suggests that age, overt religious orientation, U.S. News ranking, and the self-reinforcing cycle of publication prestige cannot on their own account for Ave Maria's, Liberty's, and Regent's struggles.

In sum, the data presented in this section demonstrates that Ave Maria, Regent, and Liberty are collectively failing to effectively mobilize scholarship as a means to address what we have referred to as their credibility deficit. It is fair to say that Liberty is having the most trouble in terms of effectively mobilizing scholarship, and that Regent and Ave Maria are doing better by comparison, but that they are still significantly underperforming in relation to the spectrum of other schools that have been examined. It remains to be seen, however, whether these schools are having any more success in mobilizing scholarship as a form of *intellectual capital* to realize the vision of altering legal culture and policy to better reflect their Christian Worldview approach to the law.

Scholarship as Movement Capital for the Christian Right

As stated in this chapter's introduction, it is one thing for the faculty to be producing secular legal scholarship, and another for them to also or exclusively be producing mission-driven scholarship. Our faculty interviews and the institutions' founding histories suggest that they should, in fact, be producing mission-driven work since it is so central to the reasons the schools were created, and faculty cited the ability to give voice to their religious readings of law as among their reasons for coming to these schools.

For example, the desire to bring his Christian faith to bear on his teaching and scholarship is central to founding Regent Dean Herbert Titus's story of his decision to leave a tenured position at the more prestigious and stable University of Oregon for the uncertainty of Oral Roberts and then Regent Law School. The valuing of a Christian variation of academic freedom discussed in Chapter 4—a freedom inclusive of both the classroom and scholarly production—is also seen in one Regent faculty member's effusive extolling of one of Regent's unique virtues as a law school: "So that love of Christ combined with the commitment to a first-rate academic excellence really equals academic freedom . . . So we have just so much academic freedom here . . . Just tons of freedom, academic freedom" (Regent Faculty 1, 2016).

While this impulse is clearly present, there are at least three interrelated reasons that Christian Worldview faculty might be hesitant to produce—or at least produce exclusively—mission-driven scholarship. First, authoring such work is risky in terms of reinforcing existing prejudices. Second, given the legal academy's presumptive marginalization of Christian legal scholarship, there are reasons to doubt the ability to publish such work outside of the schools' own law reviews. Finally, a third reason to question the rates of mission-driven scholarly production and publication comes from the schools' own histories in the classroom. That is, as Chapters 3 and 4 discuss, while the schools were started with the desire to teach a religiously informed curriculum, the need to make sure that students could pass the bar exam and be "practice ready" became apparent and resulted in modifications to the schools' curricula. One can thus imagine that as the schools shifted their focus toward crafting practice-ready students, the faculty makeup and scholarship might similarly shift in focus.

The look into scholarship as movement capital will proceed here in two parts. First, we will look to the schools' in-house journals. As noted earlier, such journals not only serve to train students, but they can also serve as vehicles to raise the schools' profiles, disseminate mission-driven scholarship, broaden the range and numbers of those interested in the legal issues most central to these schools, and affect the larger scholarly conversation. Second, the chapter will return to the scholarship produced by the schools' faculties in order to ask whether and how frequently they are using their research and writing to address mission-related issues or not, and how such scholarship travels in the academic marketplace of ideas.

In-House Journals, *Cultural Capital*, and *Intellectual Capital*

The data for this section is comprised of the five still active journals housed at the three schools—one from Ave Maria School of Law, one from Liberty Law, and three from Regent Law School.[16] All of these journals contain references to having a distinctly religious focus in their descriptions.

The *Ave Maria Law Review*'s (*AMLR*'s) self-description combines its positioning as Catholic and, therefore, interested in "affirming the Catholic legal tradition," with the practical benefits that it provides for its students and a stated desire to engage with "the whole legal community in thoughtful dialogue on the entire spectrum of legal issues" (*ALMR*, "Ave Maria Law Review"). As such, *AMLR* can be seen as a vehicle meant to promote the school's larger religious mission, but it is also not limited to this interest:

As a Catholic legal journal, the *Ave Maria Law Review* is dedicated to:

- Promoting excellence in the presentation of legal scholarship in all areas of the law in order to be an authoritative and reliable source for the research needs of lawyers, judges, professors, and students.
- Developing the scholarly writing and technical skills of its members through active involvement in the writing, editing, and production of an excellent legal journal.
- Engaging the whole legal community in thoughtful dialogue on the entire spectrum of legal issues, while affirming the Catholic legal tradition, built upon the foundation of faith and reason.[17]

It should be noted that the journal has the stated aspiration of pursuing its ends in the way that Notre Dame faculty saw themselves as realizing, but that they questioned for the three newly created Christian Worldview law schools. That is, they aim to engage with the entire legal community, and not just those who share their religious orientation. The other law schools' journals echo this point to varying degrees, but they are more direct in their announced interest in Christian legal scholarship and controlling the conversations they seek to host, possibly feeding into the Notre Dame faculty's conceptions of them as insular and unwilling to engage with the wider world.

The *Liberty University Law Review* (*LULR*) web page is clearly directed at students interested in serving on the school's one formal academic journal, but it ends with an external invitation to potential authors to submit "well-written articles, essays, and book reviews that promote the Christian intellectual tradition by drawing upon legal, historical, philosophical, and theological sources."[18] Its narrowed invitation raises questions about the audience and the possibility of speaking within the "holy huddle" echo chamber and, thus, not beyond it.

The Regent journals similarly advertise their focus on Christian legal scholarship, but they couple this with promoting their pioneering position within the Christian legal academic sphere, as well as their desired audience. The *Regent Journal of International Law* (*RJIL*) proudly states that, "RJIL is the first Christian academic forum dedicated to scholarly publications on issues of international law . . . [and] features articles, notes, case comments, reviews, and bibliographies submitted by prominent scholars, practitioners, and students."[19] With this language, the *RJIL* seems to narrow its audience to the Christian legal world and states that its authors are limited to the elite within this group. Regent's second specialty journal, the *Regent Journal of Law & Public Policy* (*RJLPP*), announces that it "exists to provide a premier forum for articulating the vital intersection of law and public policy, while integrating Christian perspectives, developing professional relationships, and incorporating intellectual scholarship to better understand the American legal and policy landscape . . . RJLPP is one of the first Christian academic journals dedicated to scholarly publications on issues of law and public policy."[20]

Finally, the school's flagship publication, the *Regent University Law Review* (*RULR*), announces its aspirations, its religious focus, and a highly moderated openness in the dialogue that it is seeking to promote:

> Regent University Law Review seeks to present academically excellent scholarship on relevant issues facing the legal community today from the perspective of a historic Christian worldview. It is committed to a jurisprudence based upon a Higher Law; that is, law based upon the Law of God, yet remains open to publishing opposing viewpoints *in certain contexts*. It is the goal of the Law Review to provide a forum for scholarship that applies this perspective to our current legal system and that edifies the

practicing bar ... Past contributors include United States Supreme Court Justice Clarence Thomas, Attorney General John D. Ashcroft, Judge Edith H. Jones, Attorney General Edwin Meese III, Robert P. George, George Allen, Charles W. Colson, Charles E. Rice, Phillip E. Johnson, David Barton, Nancy R. Pearcey, Professor Lyman Johnson, and James Bopp.
Soli Deo Gloria. (emphasis added)[21]

This framing is particularly interesting in that it is simultaneously clear and ambiguous. The *RULR* is the most forceful and detailed in the language used to announce its Christian focus—going so far as to define what it means by this concentration, and then ending its entire opening statement with the phrase "glory to God alone" in Latin. At the same time, though, it leaves open the possibility to gain permission to challenging some undefined elements of the worldview that both it and its home institution seek to promote. The statement's moderated openness to "opposing viewpoints in *certain contexts*" is also compelling given the Regent Law faculty's exultation of the school's exceptional levels of academic freedom. Whatever the substantive scope of contributors, the explicit desire is that they will publish "academically excellent scholarship on relevant issues" with the aim of edifying a broad, practical audience in "the practicing bar." What's more, the *RULR* aims to support their track record in doing so by listing various prominent figures from the broader conservative legal movement as being among its authors.

The question remains as to what these data tell us about the various journals' successes or failures in these areas. To better understand the journals within the legal landscape, we will look at the professional positioning of authors publishing in these journals, the rates at which articles the journals publish are cited, and the citing journals' rankings. Beyond this, we will also look at the unique opportunities the schools' journals offer in terms of building a movement. That is, since the schools and their publications are collectively interested in advancing Christian legal scholarship, the journals provide a potential place wherein the faculty from these schools can interact and collectively build a scholarly movement. The rates at which they publish in and cite works from one another's journals can give us an idea about whether they are collectively working to build movement capital or not.

Starting with the professional positioning of the journals' authors as a measure of the ability to attract the legal profession's top scholars, these numbers tell a different story from the journals' self-descriptions (see Table 6.6).[22] Collectively, only 3.6% of the schools' combined 1035 authors were from law schools listed in the top-50, and that percentage only grows to 5.5% when it is extended to include authors from schools in the top-100. These percentages are eclipsed by the near 92% of authors who are affiliated with unranked law schools or who are from outside the legal academy. Looked at individually, *AMLR* outpaced the other schools with 7.6% of its publications coming from those affiliated with top-50 institutions, most of which were from top-25 schools. That said, 86% of its overall authors were still from

Table 6.6. **Christian Worldview In-House Law Journal Author Statistics**

	Ave Maria Law Review	Liberty University Law Review	Regent Journal of Int'l Law	Regent Journal of Law & Public Policy	Regent University Law Review	Combined Statistics
Top-50	19	3	3	0	12	37
	7.6%	1.4%	3.0%	—	2.9%	3.6%
Top-100	24	5	5	0	23	57
	9.6%	2.4%	5.0%	—	5.5%	5.5%
100+	10	2	1	0	10	23
	4.0%	1.0%	1.0%	—	2.4%	2.2%
Unranked, Unaffiliated	215 86.3%	202 96.7%	95 94.1%	61 100%	382 92.0%	955 92.3%
Total Authors	249	209	101	61	415	1035

Source. Citation and author data collected using Web-scraping algorithm in R, which scraped and collected data from the legal database HeinOnline (see Appendix A for details). Author affiliated institution ranked using *U.S. News & World Report* law school rankings.

unranked law schools or from outside of legal higher education. The rest of the field, though, pulled anywhere from 92% (*RULR*) to 100% (*RJLPP*) from authors from unranked law schools or beyond the legal academy. As a whole, then, by this measure the in-house journals at these Christian Worldview law schools are collectively failing to significantly engage the prestigious authors they aspire to attract.

The audience appears relatively constant when turning attention to who is citing works from these Christian Worldview law schools' in-house journals (see Table 6.7). Starting with simple citation rates, the journals represent a broad spectrum of how frequently articles they publish are garnering citations. *RULR* establishes the high end of the spectrum with 80% of its articles earning citations, and a median number of cites standing at 4. Ave Maria's law review is second with the same median number of cites per article, but only 67% of its published pieces earning cites. The *RJIL* rounds out the top tier with 60% of its works cited, but it earns a median number of 2 cites per piece. Liberty's law review stands on its own in the rankings, but it represents a steep decline with only 43% of its articles earning a median 3 cites per article. Regent's *RJLPP* comprises the spectrum's floor, with only 16% of its articles earning cites, and of those, the median number of cites is 2.

Given these numbers, it is hard to see these journals as having much pull within legal academia more generally. This impression is reinforced when looking at where

Table 6.7. **Citation Data for Christian Worldview In-House Law Journals**

	Ave Maria Law Review	Liberty University Law Review	Regent Journal of Int'l Law	Regent Journal of Law & Public Policy	Regent University Law Review
Articles Cited	67%	43%	60%	16%	80%
Mean Cites	6.3	3.5	3.0	2.7	5.8
Median Cites	4	3	2	2	4
Cites in Top-50	50 4.8%	7 2.3%	1 0.6%	1 3.7%	111 5.8%
Cites in Top-100	92 8.8%	14 4.5%	4 2.2%	2 7.4%	177 9.2%
Cites in 100+	39 3.7%	4 1.3%	11 6.1%	1 3.7%	52 2.7%
Cites in Unranked	914 87.5%	293 94.2%	166 91.7%	24 88.9%	1698 88.1%

Source: Citation data collected using Web-scraping algorithm in R, which scraped and collected data from the legal database HeinOnline (see Appendix A for details). A 2018 Wiley/Clarivate Analytics–produced, rank-ordered impact factor list of 147 law journals was used to assess the prestige of both the journal within which articles were originally published, and the journals that published any citing articles.

these citations are being made. Just as these journals' authors disproportionately come from those affiliated with unranked law schools or from outside of the legal academy, the same is overwhelmingly true for the rankings of the journals that are citing these works. Of all of the citations to works from these journals, only 4.9% are from top-50 journals, and the percentage only improves to 8.3% when the count is extended to the top 100. As a whole, 89% of the citations to these journal's articles come from similarly unranked publications. What's more, these collective numbers are disproportionately rooted in citations to just two of the five journals—the flagship law reviews from Regent and Ave Maria. Without them, the citation rates are far weaker.

These data speak to the marginal position the schools' journals occupy in the legal academy. The in-house journals do not appear to be very useful vehicles for either raising the schools' *cultural capital*, or for shepherding their particularly Christian *intellectual capital* into the ranks of the more elite legal academic conversation. They can, however, still serve as useful movement capital for the Christian Right if they serve as a means to bring the various schools together in scholarly dialogue. That is, if the journals provide a way for the similarly interested Christian authors at these three schools to have a conversation, they can create a means for building a combined intellectual movement. Again, though, the story here is one of such an opportunity being lost.

As illustrated in Table 6.8, of the 321 times that faculty affiliated with the three Christian Worldview law schools published in one of these in-house journals, all but 11 of these instances represents a time when the authors were publishing in one of their *own* institution's journals. As a collective, then, only 3.4% of these publications were featured in another one of these institutions' journals, in comparison with 96.27% of them being in one's home journals. Ave Maria and Liberty, in fact, only have one instance each of publishing in another Christian Worldview institution's journals, while they have 83 and 123 instances of publishing in their own. Regent has the most instances (9) of faculty publishing in either an Ave Maria or Liberty journal, but that is similarly eclipsed by the 104 instances of their publishing in Regent's own journals. Evidence of interaction and collectively building an intellectual movement only slightly improves when looking at citations between the schools' faculty members and the respective in-house journals. As a whole, only 10% (70) of these cites to articles published in these journals are from an author housed at a different institution, versus 90% (609) cites to one's own home publications.

The collective portrait these numbers draw of the in-house journals is one of a hyper-insulated version of the "holy huddle." Instead of forming a bridge to the greater legal world or building a collective intellectual movement between these schools, these journals are evidence of the Christian Worldview schools' combined and individual isolation. In fact, while Liberty appears to be the

Table 6.8. **Christian Worldview Cross-Campus Citation and Interaction through In-House Law Journals**

	Own Christian Worldview In-House Journals	*Other Christian Worldview In-House Journals*
Ave Maria Author in	83	1
Liberty Author in	123	1
Regent Author in	104	9
Ave Maria Cites to	240	14
Liberty Cites to	128	36
Regent Cites to	241	20

Source: Citation and author data collected using Web-scraping algorithm in R, which scraped and collected data from the legal database HeinOnline (see Appendix A for details).

most aggressive in terms of citing works published by Regent and Ave Maria, it comprises almost the majority of its *own citing audience*. Of the total 311 cites to publications featured in the *LULR*, 128 (41%) are from Liberty-housed authors. Such behavior does not serve as an effective way to build *cultural capital*—in fact, if recognized, it would have the opposite effect—nor does it serve as a means to send one's ideas into circulation. Broadening out, the description this section's statistics convey is one of isolation to a degree that goes beyond that assumed by the Notre Dame faculty cited at this chapter's outset. It is not only that these schools appear to be cut off from the legal mainstream, but they also appear to be cut off from one another.

The Schools as Effective Engines of Mission-Driven Intellectual Capital?

In this final section we examine a recent snapshot of the schools' faculties, as well as the in-house journal publications, as possible engines of *intellectual capital* for the Christian Right—or, more specifically, as movement capital. In order to both make the inquiry manageable and to try to isolate the effect of the conditions set up by these schools, this section's analysis has moved from the broader investigation of faculty scholarship that opened this chapter's examination to a more targeted one. Specifically, we will primarily be looking at scholarship produced by the active faculty from the times that each faculty member joined their respective institution. To start, though, as part of the overall examination of these schools as producers of mission-driven *intellectual capital*, we will begin by looking at the types of articles published in the various schools' in-house journals, and how they circulate within the marketplace of ideas.

While all of the in-house journals noted their religious orientations in their self-descriptions, a closer examination of the articles that they have published shows that their output is not limited to what we term *mission-driven* work. Ave Maria's law review had the highest percentage of mission-driven work (72%) versus the rest of the field, ranging from the *RJIL*'s 42%, to the *RULR*'s 55%. Thus, while the journal's descriptions would lead one to expect mission-driven work such as "The Corporation as a Community of Work: Understanding the Firm within the Catholic Social Tradition" (Naughton, 2006), "America's Two First Freedoms: A Biblical Christian Perspective on How the Second Amendment Secures First Amendment Rights" (Blackwell, 2015), and "Child Molestation and the Homosexual Movement" (Baldwin 2001–2002), such pieces sit alongside a substantial collection of more standard legal scholarship such as "Patents, Trolls, and Personal Property: Will eBay Auction Away a Patent Holder's Right to Exclude" (Mersino, 2007), "Making Sense of the New Financial Deal" (Skeel, 2011), and "Nontestimonial Hearsay after *Crawford, Davis* and *Bockting*" (Kirkpatrick 2007).

While noting that they are not dominated by mission-driven scholarship, these journals are still collectively dedicating over half (56%) of their publication space to such work. As such, they are clearly serving as a means to disseminate mission-driven scholarship. What's more, these journals are not only collectively publishing the type of scholarship that the schools were founded to promote, but they are also managing to get such works cited. When looking at the mission-driven articles across the publications, a collective 69% of these works are earning citations. These two descriptive statistics seem promising in terms of the in-house journals working to disseminate the mission-driven *intellectual capital* that the schools were arguably created to produce. The story, however, is not as positive as it appears through these collective numbers.

As Table 6.9 illustrates, Regent's and Ave Maria's flagship law reviews are doing a disproportionate amount of the scholarly work for the movement. While their mission-driven median citation rates are comparable to the other journals, their mean cites are double those of the other journals, and their combined raw mission-driven cites outnumber the remaining journals 2,005 to 246. As the most dramatic contrast, *Regent University Law Review* has 198 mission-driven articles cited 1,248 times, while the *Regent Journal of Law & Public Policy* has only 5 that account for a total of 15 cites.

The evidence of mission-driven work's small citing audience is joined by the evidence of this audience's marginality in legal academia. In terms of percentages, between 0% and 4.3% of the citations garnered by mission-driven publications in these journals were in top-50 publications. As a collective, only 7% of the citations to mission-driven articles from these journals appeared in top-100 publications. On the flip side, 90% of the cited mission-driven *intellectual capital* appeared in unranked journals. This does not bode well for the journals, individually or collectively, reaching audiences that hold power within the legal academy.

Going back to the desire to place mission-driven *intellectual capital* into circulation in meaningful ways, these data show a range from failure to modest-at-best success in reaching these ends through the in-house journals. While their citation rates are uneven, the top earners are still only garnering a mean of just over 6 cites, and a median of 4. What's more, the citations earned across these journals are overwhelmingly in other unranked journals. Such *intellectual capital* published in these venues, then, is rarely being discussed, and when it is, it is overwhelmingly taking place on the margins of the academic legal marketplace of ideas.

Turning from the scholarship published in these journals back to scholarship produced by the schools' faculty members, we get to this chapter's final question regarding the schools functioning as producers of *intellectual capital* via faculty-produced scholarship. In comparing an older two-year sample of faculty with the most recent two-year active faculty sample, we see that Regent's faculty members have maintained an impressive 58%–60% of their lifetime scholarship being mission driven, with a slight decline between the older and newer samples. Ave Maria,

Table 6.9. **Journals and Citation Information**

	Ave Maria Law Review		Liberty University Law Review		Regent Journal of Int'l Law		Regent Journal of Law & Public Policy		Regent University Law Review	
	Mission	Other	Mission	Other	Mission	Other	Mission	Other	Mission	Other
Total Articles	180	69	104	105	42	59	27	34	226	189
	72%	26%	50%	50%	42%	58%	44%	56%	55%	45%
Cited Articles	119	48	51	39	24	37	5	5	198	132
	66%	70%	49%	37%	57%	63%	19%	15%	88%	70%
Total Cites	757	288	157	154	74	107	15	12	1248	684
Mean Cites	6.4	6	3.1	3.9	3.1	2.9	3	2.4	6.3	5.2
Median Cites	4	4	3	3	2.5	2	2	2	4	4
Cites in Top-100	47	45	8	6	2	2	2	0	99	78
	6%	16%	5%	4%	3%	2%	13%	0%	8%	11%
Cites in Unranked	679	235	149	144	69	97	12	12	1108	590
	90%	82%	95%	94%	93%	91%	80%	100%	89%	86%

Source: Citation data collected using Web-scraping algorithm in R, which scraped and collected data from the legal database HeinOnline (see Appendix A for details). A 2018 Wiley/Clarivate Analytics–produced, rank-ordered impact factor list of 147 law journals was used to assess the prestige of both the journal within which articles were originally published, and the journals that published any citing articles. Articles were coded using scheme employed throughout, with "Religious" and "Culture Wars" collapsed here into the category "Mission" and "Secular" coded as "Other."

on the other hand, has significantly increased its mission-driven scholarly output, going from just 28% of the older faculty's scholarly output to 46% of the active faculty's scholarly production. Finally, Liberty comes in below the other schools with its older faculty dedicating 34% of its scholarship to mission-driven work, while the current faculty dedicates only 37% of its efforts to producing such intellectual scholarship. As such, Liberty's current faculty is underperforming in comparison with the other two schools, as well as in relation to the percentage of scholarship dedicated to mission-driven work across the in-house journals. Regent's and Ave Maria's faculties, on the other hand, stick within the percentage range of mission-versus non-mission-driven scholarship established by the schools' journals.[23]

Not surprisingly, the active faculty at these Christian Worldview law schools have had a difficult time placing their mission-driven work in prestigious journals. While the same is true for their non-mission scholarship, of the 196 pieces of mission-driven scholarship that we collected from the active faculty since their arrival at these schools, only 1 article (.5%) was published in a ranked journal, and it was published in a journal placing in the 100+ category. The rest (99.5%) of the mission-driven work produced by active faculty while at these schools has appeared in unranked journals like their own in-house publication venues.[24] Again, though, while pieces may not be published in the more prestigious venues, they can still go on to circulate in the academic marketplace, possibly garnering attention in more prestigious publications via citations.

The data on the continued life of faculty scholarship produces mixed results. As with the in-house journal statistics, at first glance there is reason to think that the school's recent faculty members have been dedicating significant efforts to authoring mission-driven texts since arriving at their respective institutions and that those texts have been garnering citations. In fact, in a trend that is consistent across the three schools, a higher percentage of their mission-driven scholarship has earned citations than their non-mission scholarship. As with the in-house journals, though, the positive-appearing trends are tempered by subsequent descriptive statistics.

While the mean number of cites per mission-driven article ranges from 5.1 to 7.6 and the median number of cites is from 3 to 4, these numbers are slightly outpaced by the mean (5.8–8.6) and median (4–5) number of cites earned by their non-mission publications. What's more, the numbers for these mission-driven works is dwarfed by the earlier citation data presented in Table 6.3, where publications from faculty from comparative schools had earned a mean number of cites of 19.5–73.3 and a median of 18–49 cites per publication. Considering this, the faculties' mission-driven work is faring far less well than the presumably more mainstream work produced by faculty at the comparative schools, and slightly less well than their own mainstream legal scholarship.

The places where these cites to mission-driven work are coming from is similarly mixed. On the positive side, there are far more cites coming from ranked journals than there were ranked journals that published the faculties' original articles.

Again, just one, or .5%, of the original mission-driven articles was published in a ranked journal, while 10.4% of the citations to these works are coming from ranked journals. Within this, 5% are from top-50 journals, and 7% are from top-100 journals. Looking individually, as Table 6.10 shows, well-established patterns reemerge. Ave Maria faculty have the best numbers in terms of earning ranked citations to their mission-driven work, with Regent trailing just slightly, while Liberty again lags far behind. While these collective and individual numbers represent a significant increase from where the authors' works started, the reality is that as a whole they are barely cracking into the academic conversation taking place in the top-tier journals, 90% of the citations to mission-driven *intellectual capital* produced by recent faculty are coming from unranked journals, and, individually, Ave Maria's faculty is the only school to pull slightly away from that 90% anchor.[25]

While the continued life of these publications shows some growth, the discussion of mission-driven ideas is still relatively small and overwhelmingly limited to

Table 6.10. **Active Faculty Scholarship Citation Data Broken Out by "Mission" and "Other" Type of Articles**

	Ave Maria		*Liberty*		*Regent*	
	Mission	*Other*	*Mission*	*Other*	*Mission*	*Other*
Articles	28	33	28	48	140	100
Published	46%	54%	37%	63%	58%	42%
Cited Articles	20	14	14	23	109	71
	71%	42%	50%	48%	78%	71%
Mean Cites	5.7	8.6	5.1	5.8	7.6	8
Median Cites	3.5	4.5	3	4	4	5
Cites in Top-50	7	13	1	2	40	36
	6%	11%	1%	2%	5%	6%
Cites in Top-100	11	15	2	6	59	49
	10%	13%	3%	5%	7%	9%
Unranked Cites	97	99	64	125	741	498
	85.8%	82.5%	90.1%	93.3%	90.0%	88.9%

Source: Faculty lists collected using the Internet Archive Wayback Machine, https://web.archive. org. Active faculty included faculty listed for 2016–17 and 2017–18 academic years. Citation data collected using Web-scraping algorithm in R, which scraped and collected data from the legal database HeinOnline (see Appendix A for details). A 2018 Wiley/Clarivate Analytics–produced, rank-ordered impact factor list of 147 law journals was used to assess the prestige of both the journal within which articles were originally published, and the journals that published any citing articles. Articles were coded using scheme employed throughout, with "Religious" and "Culture Wars" collapsed here into the category "Mission" and "Secular" coded as "Other."

the fringes of the legal academic marketplace.[26] What's more, we see this not only in the faculty-produced scholarship most recently examined, but also in the mission-driven work published in the schools' journals. Considered together, then, there is reason to doubt the ability of these schools to influence the legal academic conversation, the profession, and eventually policy via the *intellectual capital* that they produce.

Bringing the Support Structure Pyramid Back In

Christian Worldview law schools have established records of engaging in the academic marketplace of ideas—through faculty scholarship and by housing in-house law journals. Mission-driven *intellectual capital* is a significant portion of each of these mechanisms of scholarly production and dissemination. The data regarding publication venue, citation rates, and citation venue, however, shows that Christian Worldview law schools are collectively struggling to access the upper echelons of the legal academic conversation. Instead, these schools are laboring at the margins of the academic marketplace of ideas, attracting small audiences, and generating little in the way of evidence of their influencing the conversation. Put differently, their collective scholarship is not producing the sort of premium *cultural* and *intellectual capital* that the greater CCLM would want.

While it is useful to think of these Christian Worldview law schools as being part of a collective effort to bring the law closer to their religiously informed conceptions of what it ought to be, there are two fundamental problems with seeing them as part of a coordinated and effective intellectual movement. First, the three schools are producing scholarship—both mission-driven and non-mission driven—at substantially different rates. Regent Law and AMSL do the majority of this work for the movement, while Liberty Law lags substantially behind. Furthermore, there is evidence throughout this chapter that Ave Maria's role as a leading producer of *intellectual* and *cultural capital* via scholarship was harmed by the move from Michigan to Florida. Thus, while they are all contributing mission-driven scholarship to the conversation, the distribution is neither equitable nor consistent over time.

Moreover, our analysis of in-house journal citation data shows that there is little interaction between the three faculties and the various in-house journals. Just, then, as the founders of these schools and of the greater Christian Right have historically exhibited a tendency to labor on their own and to not coordinate and combine their efforts, intentional or not, the same appears to be the case with the faculties at these schools. In comparison, then, to the efforts of earlier conservative intellectual movements (see, generally, Teles 2008 and Hollis-Brusky 2015), the low levels of networking and interaction exhibited in Chapter 5, and the lack of intellectual coordination examined in this chapter do not bode well for the CCLM influencing the broader legal conversation.

The intellectual movement, therefore, is best seen as coincidental and not coordinated. In fact, one Liberty Law professor's description of gathering a small, dedicated group of students who "get it" off campus at his "house every other week in the evening" (Liberty Faculty 3 2015) appears to be a surprisingly fitting description of the current state of the intellectual movement he seeks to foster—isolated and removed from the legal academy, including the specific institutions ostensibly dedicated to fostering it.

While the schools are clearly struggling to translate academic scholarship into valued *cultural* and *intellectual capital* within the legal academy, the ultimate test rests with the top of the Support Structure Pyramid. While legal academics are giving little, if any, attention to the issues championed by these schools, the *human capital* produced by these schools can try to shepherd this work into the courts. As we have seen, though the numbers are small, individual articles have been able to find their way to more highly ranked journals and their more influential audiences. When thinking about the law, it takes only small numbers of similarly receptive judges to give such *intellectual capital* meaning within the legal policy sphere.

The Apex of the Support Structure Pyramid

> We are under a constitution. But the constitution is what the judges
> say it is.
>
> —Charles Evans Hughes, Speech before the
> Chamber of Commerce, Elmira, New York (1907)[1]

> Scarcely any political question arises in the United States that is not
> resolved, sooner or later, into a judicial question. Hence all parties are
> obliged to borrow, in their daily controversies, the ideas, and even the
> language, peculiar to judicial proceedings . . . the spirit of the law, which
> is produced in the schools and courts of justice, gradually penetrates
> beyond their walls into the bosom of society, where it descends to the
> lowest classes, so that at last the whole people contract the habits and the
> tastes of the judicial magistrate.
>
> —Tocqueville, Democracy in America, Book I,
> Chapter 16 (1831)

Judges and courts are essential—though not exclusive—gatekeepers in the battle
for control of the law and legal culture. Positioning judges at the apex of the Support
Structure Pyramid, as we have done in our model, draws attention to the formal
decision-making and policy powers of judges, that is, their powers to resolve legal
conflicts and to issue written opinions that shape, constrain, and influence the behavior of other political actors and citizens alike (Silverstein 2009; Hollis-Brusky
2015). The oft-deployed quote by Charles Evans Hughes cited at the beginning
of this chapter underscores one important part of this formal judicial power—the
ability for five Justices on the Supreme Court of the United States to have the final
say on constitutional meaning: the power to "say" what the constitution is and, by
extension, what it is not.

But there are many other ways in which judges—federal and state—help de-
termine the structure of political life in America. Federal judges play a critical role
in statutory interpretation by resolving ambiguities and filling in gaps in otherwise vague statutes (VanSickle-Ward 2014). They also weigh in on the rules and
regulations issued by the vast bureaucracy of administrative agencies, determining
whether or not they are consistent with the scope and meaning of the federal statutes that authorize them (Melnick 1994). While federal judges capture most of the

Separate But Faithful. Amanda Hollis-Brusky and Joshua C. Wilson, Oxford University Press (2020). © Oxford University
Press. DOI: 10.1093/oso/9780190637262.001.0001

public attention, state-level judges, numbering close to 30,000, hear and resolve the vast majority (95%) of all legal issues in the United States (Bannon 2016). The formal powers of judges are so expansive, in part, because, to quote Alexis de Tocqueville, "scarcely any political question arises in the United States that is not resolved, sooner or later, into a judicial question" (1835, I, 330).

Still, the role and influence of judges within the system of litigation-based change is not limited to their formal institutional powers. The second half of the cited Tocqueville quote begins to get at the cultural authority and influence judges have by virtue of their position at the top of the legal profession. Judges are guardians of "the spirit of the law," and, as such, the way they speak about the law, the legal authorities they draw on, their legal reasoning, and language have the power to trickle down and "penetrate[]" into the "bosom of society," shaping or reshaping the habits of other lawyers, politicians, and even citizens. In other words, judges have the ability to powerfully influence legal culture outside of the courts.

These trickle-down and radiating effects are captured in the Support Structure Pyramid, the model that animates and organizes our analysis. As we discussed in Chapter 1, there are several ways in which judges, who are primarily consumers of movement capital, also send valuable capital back down to the lower tiers of the pyramid and into the greater political and social contexts within which the pyramid is embedded. For example, judicial opinions, even dissenting opinions, can provide salience for a set of legal issues (*cultural capital*) that might result in attracting or securing additional patronage for Level 1 and Level 2 institutions, or just improving the perceived legitimacy of the institutions. Additionally, the reasoning deployed by judges and Justices in their written opinions can legitimate or delegitimize movement capital by drawing on it or rejecting it in their written opinions. In a similar vein, judicial opinions can also open up and encourage new avenues for the development of *intellectual capital* by Level 1 and Level 2 actors. Eventually, these benefits can flow back upstream in the form of better capital and more effective access to the pyramid's higher tiers.

Acknowledging the complex and cyclical dynamic between the apex, the lower tiers of the Support Structure Pyramid, and the surrounding contexts, our analysis in this chapter is not limited to counting wins in court or litigation victories by actors associated with these Christian Worldview institutions. To capture a fuller picture of this dynamic, we chart the general cartography of Christian Worldview faculty participation in state and federal litigation. Using named parties on legal briefs as our indicators of faculty participation in litigation, we identify Christian Worldview faculty activity as litigators, representing the parties in a case, and as *amici curiae*. Literally meaning "friends of the court" in Latin, *amici curiae* are groups or individuals who are not named parties in a case but who, nonetheless, have an interest in the outcome. Individuals or groups can petition the court for permission to submit an amicus curiae brief, with the goal of providing information to the judges in the hopes of influencing the decision in the case.

This map of Christian Worldview faculty participation in litigation helps identify potential "conduits" through which ideas or *intellectual capital* can be transmitted or diffused to judicial decision makers (Hollis-Brusky 2015, 151). Additionally, because we know that *intellectual capital* need not travel through a Christian Worldview conduit to be useful to judicial decision makers looking to scaffold or support a decision (Hollis-Brusky 2015, 147–52), in this same analysis we also examine court briefs and judicial opinions for citations to Christian Worldview faculty.

We find that with the exception of five "repeat players" (Galanter 1974) whom we discuss separately, the three Christian Worldview faculties are not well represented when it comes to direct litigation. This is consistent with what we would expect for legal academics whose primary job is not to litigate cases but to educate law students. That being the case, evidence of participation in litigation as *amici curiae,* or friends of the court, is more prevalent. Our evidence suggests that faculty at these Christian Worldview law schools participate in amicus curiae briefs above the national averages for general faculty amicus participation. That being said, a handful of faculty account for the vast majority of individual instances.

Christian Worldview faculty engagement in litigation is important because it presents opportunities for mission-driven *intellectual capital* to flow up to the top of the pyramid and for the specific institutions and the greater movement to benefit from the various feedback loops outlined earlier in this chapter. That is, this engagement opens up direct avenues for ideas about the natural law and the biblical foundations of law to be carried by these faculty from their law schools directly into litigation. That being said, we find that the numbers of Christian Worldview faculty who have been cited in either court briefs or judicial decisions for mission-related cases is quite small. When we combine this finding with the take-home findings from Chapter 6, we suggest that there is an inefficiency within the Support Structure Pyramid. While Christian Worldview faculty are producing mission-driven scholarship and individuals associated with these schools have a relatively high degree of interaction with the top of the pyramid, these individuals are not effectively transferring identifiable Christian Worldview scholarship and *intellectual capital* to judicial decision makers on the courts.

As in other chapters, we compare these Christian Worldview law schools with the Blackstone Legal Fellowship. We find that in mission-driven litigation— the litigation at the very core of the Christian conservative legal movement— Blackstone affiliates outperform the Christian Worldview faculties both in amicus curiae participation and, most importantly, in citations to their scholarship in court briefs and judicial decisions. Considering this, these data again bring into question the choice to invest in new stand-alone law schools (*parallel alternative* approach) as opposed to the *infiltration* or *supplemental* strategies represented by Blackstone.

The Cartography of Christian Worldview Faculty Participation in Litigation

As noted in the opening, interactions with the top of the pyramid stand to produce both general and specific value for both the individual schools as well as for the broader Christian conservative legal movement (CCLM). Faculty who have prior track records of litigation and engagement with actors at the apex bring a certain amount of "credibility capital"—that is, *cultural* and *social capital*—with them to these law schools. Restated, by having established litigation records, these faculty signal to the broader legal profession that they have engaged with the profession's most identifiable activity and are, thus, more mainstreamed legal insiders to some degree. As such, they provide a more general form of value to the schools and the movement.

The more specific benefits that accrue from litigation—wins, of course, but also moving the needle on the broader policy project to reframe law as having a biblical foundation—are derived principally from participation in mission-related litigation. Given this, litigation that explicitly or implicitly addresses an aspect of the Christian Right's core mission needs to be separated out from general litigation participation to better understand how faculty are contributing to this end.

We have identified three ways that faculty engaged in litigation can try to be part of and influence the broader legal discussion on behalf of their schools' missions— by directly litigating, by writing *amicus curiae* (friend of the court) briefs, and by having their scholarship and ideas picked up by legal counsel, other *amici curiae*, and judicial decision makers.

Representing a party in litigation as counsel of record in a case is a direct way of ferrying one's own and one's colleagues' scholarship to the pyramid's apex. However, since the majority of faculty at Christian Worldview law schools are primarily employed *as faculty* and not as litigators, we would expect evidence of faculty participating as attorneys of record on mission-related cases to be concentrated in times when these faculty were not full-time faculty and/or among those who are on faculty but in ways that minimize their classroom, service, and academic research obligations (Newton 2010, 128–29). What's more, the incentives of the tenure system push faculty to engage in scholarship over advocacy. Given this, authoring amicus curiae briefs is another means of directly shepherding one's own and one's colleagues' scholarship to the courts. Amicus curiae participation, which requires overall less time and investment than participating in litigation as counsel of record, fits more comfortably with the demands and career trajectory of a legal academic (147–48). Even still, participating in court cases as amicus curiae is still considered a rather uncommon activity for most law faculty.

Publishing legal scholarship and having those ideas carried by others who are more directly connected to litigation is, therefore, the most likely way in which faculty can influence courts and judicial decision-making. As discussed in Chapter 6, publishing is an essential part of a legal academic's regular duties, and a substantial number of these faculty meet this expectation by publishing mission-driven scholarship (see Table 6.10). While the previous chapter showed that these publications are variably successful in circulating among parts of the legal academy, the critical question from a support structure perspective is whether or not these ideas are able to make it outside academia's ivory tower and inside the courthouse's marble columns.

In order to pursue these questions, we rely on the same faculty lists in this chapter as we have in past chapters.[2] As a result, adjunct and other faculty with modified professorial duties, whom we would expect to be most involved with litigation efforts, have been largely excluded from our data.[3] With these qualifications explained, we will briefly look at lifetime litigation rates for the faculty but spend more time and attention analyzing forms of engaging with the top of the pyramid, where regular full-time faculty are more likely to be found—amicus curiae participation and citations to scholarship in lawyer briefs and judicial decisions/opinions.

The instances of case participation as attorney of record or amicus curiae and identifiable citations to scholarship in a legal brief or judicial opinion data were collected between May 2018 and January 2019 using Bloomberg Law.[4] Once records were gathered, all the litigation participation data was recorded and coded by type of participation (counsel of record or amicus curiae), level of court participation (state/federal, trial/appellate/court of last resort), and by issue or legal question using the same coding scheme ("mission" and "non-mission") we employed with the scholarship analyzed in Chapter 6. We also searched for and coded citations to faculty scholarship in lawyers' briefs (counsel and amicus curiae) and in judicial decisions or opinions.

The goal of the search design was to be under-inclusive rather than over-inclusive, as it could have been easy to misattribute records.[5] However, because the same parameters were applied to all three Christian Worldview law schools and the Blackstone Legal Fellowship, we are still confident in claims involving relative rates of participation and citation captured by this search. Additionally, it should be noted that this kind of search does not fully capture the overall influence of a particular search target. Unlike in academic publishing, there are more opportunities in these materials for an individual to have been influential but not cited. Lawyers will often read documents and, particularly, law review articles to get an impression of an issue and to learn about key or obscure cases discussed to gain insight and understanding prior to making arguments in court. This search is incapable of capturing that influence.

Finally, as foreshadowed in the reference to "repeat players," it should be noted that with the exception of Table 7.1, most of the analysis in this section excludes five specific Christian Worldview faculty members who are included elsewhere in this book—Jay Sekulow and John Ashcroft from Regent Law, Phillip Kline and

Mathew Staver from Liberty Law, and Robert Bork from Ave Maria School of Law. The reasons for these exclusions are both practical and substantive. Each of these individuals has extensive case records that make the data too numerous to analyze and skew the more general perceptions of litigation activity related to the institutions studied here. Sekulow and Staver are at the helm of major Christian conservative public interest legal organizations (PILOs), Kline and Ashcroft have extensive public service litigation records as district attorneys and attorneys general, and Bork served as solicitor general and as a federal court judge.[6] Additionally, these last three largely ceased to engage in litigation once they arrived on the faculty of their respective Christian Worldview law schools.

While they have been excluded from the aggregated data, we do not want to, nor should we, wholly exclude these faculty from the discussion. Just as including them in the aggregated statistics would distort the perception of the schools' interactions with the apex of the pyramid, excluding them would likewise distort our analysis in at least two ways. First, the schools presumably pursued connections with these faculty members to benefit from their reputations as high-profile public figures and litigators. These "repeat players" (Galanter 1974) bring with them to the law schools the sort of *cultural capital* we discussed earlier and, further, can draw and attract *human capital* (faculty and students) to the school. Second, as seen with Sekulow and Staver and discussed in greater detail in Chapter 4, select faculty hires can also better connect the law schools to mission-related or culture wars litigation, creating the type of conduit or direct pipeline from the law schools to Level 2 of the Support Structure Pyramid that we are specifically interested in here. It is with these interests in mind that we now more directly turn to these select "repeat players" in starting our investigation of if and how these schools engage with judicial actors.

Identifying Direct Conduits—Faculty as Litigators and "Friends of the Court"

As noted in Table 7.1, the five identified repeat players account for over 2,800 cases. John Ashcroft and Phillip Kline, the two attorneys general, are associated with the highest numbers of cases, followed by fellow public servant Robert Bork. Jay Sekulow and Mathew Staver, the two lawyers who head Christian conservative PILOs, account for a combined caseload above 500.

The number of cases associated with these five men is more than double the instances (564) of the attorney of record returned results for the combined 135 regular faculty at these Christian Worldview law schools. That being said, 43% of the regular faculty in our sample returned results for participation as attorneys of record. The vast majority of these instances (87%) are in cases that were coded as secular, as opposed to mission-related, litigation. This kind of engagement with the apex of the pyramid does not necessarily advance the ends of the Christian conservative legal movement, but it might help overcome the "credibility deficit" we discussed in

Table 7.1. **"Repeat Players" at Christian Worldview Law Schools**

	Instances of Case Participation
Robert Bork Ave Maria School of Law	484
Mathew Staver Liberty Law	254
Phillip Kline Liberty Law	831
Jay Sekulow Regent Law	275
John Ashcroft Regent Law	1000+

Source: Bloomberg Law. Counts include U.S. courts, all opinions, unpublished opinions, court documents, pleadings, and amici filings. Max results returned for each query = 1000.

Chapter 5. In other words, faculty engagement with the apex signals to the broader legal profession that Christian Worldview schools can and do prepare students for the realities of mainstream litigation—a point emphasized in Chapters 3 and 4 with the turn away from polemic, mission-laden language and toward training "practice-ready" lawyers.

The pivot to mission-specific or movement capital derived from engaging with the apex of the pyramid tells a mixed story. As discussed in Chapters 3 and 5, each of these three schools has had connections to mission-focused PILOs. These formal relationships between the law schools and litigation organizations provided opportunities for faculty involvement with litigation (again, as counsel of record or amici), but such instances are more realistic for adjunct faculty and others who are jointly appointed at the schools and the respective PILOs. Sekulow and Staver provide the most obvious examples here but there are others. Regent Law faculty members Shaheryar Gill and Laura Hernandez worked with the American Center for Law and Justice (ACLJ). Liberty Law faculty member Rena Lindevaldsen served as a senior litigator with Mat Staver's Liberty Counsel prior to joining the faculty. According to her Liberty profile, "While at Liberty Counsel, she was a part of numerous cases representing Child Evangelism Fellowship" (Liberty University, 2019).

Whether through these specific PILOs or through other means, we found evidence that 12% of the faculty had directly litigated mission-related cases, and that such efforts accounted for 72 instances, or 13% of all faculty-associated litigation. These faculty and their associated cases, therefore, stand as evidence of full-time faculty potentially serving as direct conduits of mission-driven scholarship and ideas to the top of the pyramid. This potential is then multiplied by Sekulow and Staver's extensive engagement with the courts. Even limiting their records to cases that specifically mention their affiliated PILO yields a combined 282 cases.[7] Rephrased, it yields 282 potential conduits for idea diffusion from their affiliated Christian Worldview law schools, through their PILOs, to judges at the apex.

As discussed in this chapter, since law professors are expected to dedicate most of their time and energy to the classroom and not the courtroom, we would expect the majority of their participation in litigation to be in the form of amicus curiae or friend of the court briefs. And, indeed, it is. We could not find comprehensive data on how often across the whole professoriate law professors participate in litigation as *amici curiae*, though scholars agree that there has been an uptick in faculty involvement as a result of the increasingly formalized, coordinated, and professionalized "amicus machine" that now exists to lobby courts at all levels (Larsen and Devins 2016). Still, even with this increase in participation, two law school administrators and experts on the legal profession we consulted estimate that 10% or fewer of all legal academics engage the courts through amicus curiae briefs.[8] Considering these (albeit impressionistic) estimates, the percentage of faculty across Christian Worldview law schools engaging the courts as *amici curiae* actually appears quite high.[9]

As seen in Table 7.2, the rates of general faculty involvement with amicus briefs is two to three times greater than the estimated national averages, even if, as the total instances data confirms, the total number of times these faculty have engaged the courts as amicus curiae appears to be quite low. We found only 27 and 29 instances of faculty involvement as *amici curiae* for Ave Maria School of Law (AMSL) and Liberty, respectively. Regent Law looks high comparatively, with our search capturing 143 instances of faculty listed on amicus curiae briefs.

When pivoting to amicus curiae activity in mission-related cases as a percentage of that overall amicus curiae participation, we see that with the exception of Liberty (38%), well over half of Christian Worldview faculty amicus engagement is in mission cases. A small minority of faculty, however, appear to account for the vast majority of this mission case engagement. To illustrate, three faculty at Ave Maria account for 79% of their total instances of amicus curiae participation in mission cases (Bruce Frohnen, James A. Sonne, and Timothy Tracey). Similarly, Regent Law's Steven W. Fitschen is responsible for 70% of his institution's totals in this area. With Liberty Law, Rena Lindevaldsen alone accounts for 89% of mission-related amicus briefs. Unsurprisingly, the majority of these faculty also have affiliations with a PILO. To this end, Liberty's Lindevaldsen used to work for the Liberty Counsel, Regent's Fitschen is the president of the National Legal Foundation, and Ave Maria's Sonne went on to found Stanford Law School's Religious Liberty Clinic.

These observations lead to a few interim conclusions. First, these data underscore that while Christian Worldview faculty have likely higher than normal rates

Table 7.2. **Christian Worldview Faculty Participation in United States Court Cases as *Amici Curiae* ("Friends of the Court")**

	Ave Maria	*Liberty*	*Regent*	*Blackstone*
Total Faculty in Sample	50	39	46	44
Number of Faculty Listed on Amicus Briefs and as % of All Faculty	10 20%	8 21%	14 30%	26 59%
Number of Faculty Listed on Mission Amicus Briefs and as % of Total Amicus Participation	6 60%	3 38%	11 79%	26 100%
Total Instances of Faculty Listed on Amicus Briefs	27	29	143	64
Total Instances of Faculty Listed on Mission Amicus Briefs and as % of Total	14 52%	19 66%	132 92%	61 95%

Source: Bloomberg Law. Counts include U.S. courts, all amici filings. Max results returned for each query = 1000. Faculty data for Regent extending from Fall 1986, Ave Maria from Fall 1999, and Liberty from Fall 2004 up to the 2017–18 school year. Faculty lists collected using the Internet Archive Wayback Machine, https://web.archive.org. Cases were coded using scheme employed throughout, with "Religious" and "Culture Wars" collapsed here into the category "Mission."

of amicus participation overall, the uneven distribution of instances speaks to the persistent rarity of faculty involvement as amicus curiae. Second, the skewed distributions again raises the repeat player phenomenon and its importance to the schools. While participation might not be evenly distributed, and while it mostly occurs when faculty are not serving as full-time faculty, these repeat players stand as highly productive and, thus, highly likely conduits for conveying mission-driven scholarship and ideas to courts.

The importance of connections to PILOs in terms of the potential to find conduits for mission-driven scholarship and ideas returns us to the Blackstone Legal Fellowship and the importance of its institutional relationship with the Christian Right litigating behemoth Alliance Defending Freedom (ADF). Interestingly, our search of Blackstone faculty produced low rates of their being attorneys of record on cases while it unearthed significant percentages of amicus participation. Only five Blackstone-affiliated faculty (11%) had litigation backgrounds, and only three faculty had litigated a total of four mission-related cases. In terms of participation as amicus curiae, on the other hand, 59% had been involved in such work in both general/secular and mission-related cases. What's more, the Blackstone-affiliated faculty's collective efforts produced an impressive 61 instances of amicus participation in mission-related cases. This equates to 95% of their amicus brief activity being in mission-related cases.

Blackstone's collective productivity in mission-related cases puts them right alongside Regent Law as a leading likely venue for the transfer of mission-driven *intellectual capital* to judges at the apex of the Support Structure Pyramid. Unlike Regent Law, whose productivity was borne by a handful of faculty, Blackstone Legal Fellowship's productivity is more evenly distributed across the faculty as a whole. This point further illustrates one of the advantages of the *supplemental* model we have highlighted throughout the study. Unlike the Christian Worldview law schools, Blackstone does not need to hire across the legal curriculum. Rather, as an intensive summer supplemental education program, it is able to hire with the narrower interest of training legal culture warriors.

This fact is further underscored by our striking finding that, as Table 7.2 illustrates, 100% of the Blackstone affiliates we identified on amicus curiae briefs were participating in cases coded as mission related. Additionally, the discrepancy between Blackstone's attorney of record and amicus curiae rates illustrates their view that such training requires more than just lawyers. Rather, Blackstone hires faculty from a broad range of backgrounds—policy, media, and political influencers— across the conservative spectrum. As a result, few of them can litigate directly, but the majority of them still participate in litigation indirectly as *amici curiae*.

Having surveyed a legal landscape relatively ripe with—if highly concentrated— potential conduits for the movement's *intellectual capital*, the question becomes whether or not there is demonstrable evidence that lawyers and judges are citing these faculty, that is, picking their ideas up and incorporating them into their briefs and decisions. Given both the skewed distribution of litigation and amicus curiae participation among the law school faculty, as well as the limited number of overall instances of full-time faculty working directly as shepherds for *intellectual capital* to the courts, there is pressure on the faculty to produce other forms of capital that can increase the efficacy of their contributions to the movement.

Lawyer and Judicial Citations—Quantifying Faculty Idea Diffusion at the Apex

While Chapter 6 provides a detailed study of the rates of the Christian Worldview law schools' collective and individual *intellectual capital* production, as well as the placement and citations of this work within the academy, this chapter will look to see if their audience extends to the lawyers litigating and the judges and Justices deciding mission-related cases. By also including Blackstone in this discussion, these data also provide another means of evaluating both the overall efficiency of the CCLM's support structure as well as the comparable efficiencies of the *parallel alternative* and *supplemental* approaches to creating Level 1 support structure institutions.

As stated at this section's outset, there are structural reasons that lead to our expectation that limiting our search to citation rates undercounts the actual transfer of *intellectual capital* to the top of the pyramid. In spite of this, citations are quantifiable and, thus, valuable as a measure of supplying *intellectual capital* to both Level 2 (litigators and PILOs) and judicial actors at the apex of the Support Structure Pyramid. Getting lawyers and judges to cite Christian Worldview scholarship is especially important if these institutions hope to have a transformative influence on the law and the legal profession as a whole (Wilson and Hollis-Brusky 2018). This being the aspiration, the rate at which Christian Worldview *intellectual capital* is cited in state and federal legal briefs—both amicus briefs and counsel briefs—as well as state and federal legal rulings/opinions is not encouraging.[10]

Looking at Table 7.3[11] we can see clearly that the total numbers and percentages of Christian Worldview faculty cited in briefs and/or judicial opinions are quite low and consistently so across all three schools. So, unlike with faculty

Table 7.3. **Citations to Christian Worldview Faculty Scholarship in United States Court Decisions and Legal Briefs with Percent of Those Citations in "Mission" Cases**

	Ave Maria	*Liberty*	*Regent*	*Blackstone*
Total Faculty in Sample	50	39	46	44
Number of Faculty Cited and as % of Total Faculty Sample	9 18%	8 21%	12 26%	12 27%
Number of Faculty Cited in Mission Cases and as % of Faculty Cited	5 56%	2 25%	5 42%	12 100%
Total Instances of Citations to Faculty	33	14	41	66
Instances in Mission Cases and as % of Total Instances of Citation	7 21%	2 14%	10 24%	27 41%
Instances of Lawyer Citations to Faculty in Mission Cases	4	1	4	14
Instances of Judicial Citations to Faculty in Mission Cases	3	1	6	13

Source: Bloomberg Law. Counts include U.S. courts. Max results returned for each query = 1000. Faculty data for Regent extending from Fall 1986, Ave Maria from Fall 1999, and Liberty from Fall 2004 up to the 2017–18 school year. Faculty lists collected using the Internet Archive Wayback Machine, https://web.archive.org. Cases were coded using scheme employed throughout, with "Religious" and "Culture Wars" collapsed here into the category "Mission."

participation in litigation, we see little meaningful variation between the three Christian Worldview schools in terms of citation to faculty scholarship. The total number of citations across the board is also strikingly low. Our search yielded only eighty-eight total records of citation by lawyers and judges to Christian Worldview scholarship. Perhaps most surprisingly, citation to faculty scholarship in mission cases constituted less than one-quarter of this total. While the absolute number is small—only nine lawyer cites and ten judicial cites were found in our search—the venues citing their work are encouraging for the prospect of overall influence and impact.

All nine of the lawyers brief citations we identified were found in amicus curiae briefs submitted to the United States Supreme Court. Not surprisingly, these briefs cover a range of traditional Christian conservative legal issues, with some leading Christian conservative cases included, such as *Zubick v. Burwell* (2015) disputing the Affordable Care Act's birth control mandate, *Obergefell v. Hodges* (2015) disputing marriage equality, and *Masterpiece Cakeshop v. Colorado Civil Rights Commission* (2018) defending the CCLM's construction of religious liberty. For example, an article by Ave Maria School of Law faculty member Nora O'Callaghan ("Lessons from Pharaoh and the Hebrew Midwives: Conscientious Objection to State Mandates as a Free Exercise Right") was cited in the amicus curiae brief submitted to the Supreme Court by the Justice and Freedom Fund in *Zubick v. Burwell* (2015).[12] This same article was also cited in two amicus curiae briefs submitted to the Supreme Court three years later in *Masterpiece Cakeshop v. Colorado Civil Rights Commission* (2018)—one by the Family Research Council[13] and one by the Foundation for Moral Law.[14]

Regent Law professor Lynne Marie Kohm, who teaches courses in family law, had three separate articles cited in three distinct *amicus curiae* briefs submitted to the Supreme Court in *Obergefell v. Hodges* (2015)—each of which argued against same-sex marriage. Her *Regent University Law Review* article "Cohabitation and the Future of Marriage" was cited in an amicus curiae brief, which she co-authored with John C. Eastman and submitted on behalf of "Scholars of the Welfare of Women, Children and Underprivileged Populations."[15] Another titled "The Homosexual 'Union'—Should Gay and Lesbian Partnerships Be Granted the Same Status as Marriage?" was cited in the amicus curiae brief submitted on behalf of Agudath Israel of America.[16] Finally, a third amicus curiae brief authored by Gene Schaerr and submitted on behalf of "100 Scholars on Marriage" cited Kohm's co-authored piece from the *Regent University Law Review*, titled "A Fifty State Survey of the Cost of Family Fragmentation."[17]

While none of the aforementioned scholarship was successfully picked up by the Justices at the nation's highest court and incorporated into their opinions—arguably the ultimate goal of movements looking to influence the pinnacle of law and the legal system—other courts and judges have found Christian Worldview *intellectual capital* useful in their opinions. As we mentioned earlier, our search yielded a total of ten citations to Christian Worldview faculty in judicial opinions (see Table 7.4). While the total number is admittedly small, it is important that all ten judicial citations to Christian Worldview scholarship appear in opinions dealing with issues at the core of the Christian Right mission. Three of these judicial citations come in cases dealing with religious liberty, and the other seven cover a variety of culture wars issues—assisted suicide, same sex marriage, sex trafficking/ abuse, and abortion.

Encouragingly for these Christian Worldview law schools, 8 of the 10 judicial citations to faculty scholarship appear in the majority or concurring opinion, that is, on the winning side of the legal issue. The two that appear in dissent are both cited in the case *Czekala-Chatham v. State* (2015)—a Mississippi State Supreme Court case in which a lesbian couple was seeking and ultimately granted a divorce. The dissenting Justice refused to recognize their marriage as legal even after the Supreme Court's ruling in *Obergefell v. Hodges*, which legalized same-sex marriage nationwide. Two Regent Law professors—Bradley Jacob and James Davids—are cited among a group of thirty-one law professors who signed a public statement encouraging constitutional resistance against the Supreme Court's ruling in *Obergefell*:

> As stated above, numerous noted legal publications and scholars have advanced arguments that the *Obergefell* decision crossed the line of legitimate constitutional interpretation, and that state courts should not follow it. For instance, the following legal scholars have gone on record as suggesting that "state officeholders" should "refuse to accept *Obergefell* as binding precedent."[18]

The referenced public statement—formally titled *Statement Calling for Constitutional Resistance to Obergefell v. Hodges*—was issued by The American Principles Project a few months after the Supreme Court's ruling and articulated an argument for constitutional resistance against the decision, referring to it at various points as illegitimate. In particularly polemic language, the statement calls on "all federal and state officeholders" to "pledge full and mutual legal and political assistance to anyone who refuses to follow Obergefell for constitutionally protected reasons."[19]

Returning to Table 7.4, we see familiar patterns in terms of who is being cited from each of these Christian Worldview law schools. Six of the ten citations to Christian Worldview faculty in judicial opinions are claimed by Regent Law faculty—Scott Pryor, Lynne Kohm (who has two citations), Tessa Dysart, Bradley Jacob, and James Davids. Three of these citations are to AMSL faculty scholarship, though it is important to note that two of these three scholars—Stephen Safranek and Lee Strang—were from the Michigan-era of the school and did not follow AMSL to Florida in 2009. The lone judicial citation to Liberty Law faculty that we

Table 7.4. **Judicial Citations to Christian Worldview Scholars and Scholarship with Citing Judge, Judicial Venue, and Case Issue**

Name	School	Case	Original Work Cited	Judges Citing Work	What Type of Decision	Issue	Court	Full Citation of Case
Eugene Millhizer	Ave Maria	*State v. Gutierrez-Perez* (2014)	So Help Me Allah: An Historical and Prudential Analysis of Oaths as Applied to the Current Controversy of the Bible and Quran in Oath Practices in America	Matthew Durrant	Majority	Religious Oath	Supreme Court of Utah	2014 UT 11
Lee J. Strang	Ave Maria	*Zhang Jingrong v. Chinese Anti-Cult World All.* (2018)	The Meaning of "Religion" in the First Amendment, 40 Duq. L. Rev. 181, 182 (2002)	Jack B. Weinstein	Majority	Religious Liberty	United States District Court for the Eastern District of New York	311 F. Supp. 3d 514 (E.D.N.Y. 2018)
Stephen J. Safranek	Ave Maria	*Myers v. Schneiderman* (2017)	Can the Right to Autonomy Be Resuscitated after Glucksberg?, 69 U Colo L Rev 731, 733-742 [*18] [1998]	Judges Rivera, Stein, Fahey, Garcia and Wilson	Concurring	Assisted Suicide	Court of Appeals of New York	*Myers v. Schneiderman*, 30 N.Y.3d 1, 62 N.Y.S.3d 838, 85 N.E.3d 57 (2017)

C. Scott Pryor	Regent	*Barber v. Bryant* (2016)	Puritan Revolution and the Law of Contracts	Judge Carlton W. Reeves	Majority	Establishment Clause	United States District Court, Southern District of Mississippi	193 F. Supp. 3d 677
Lynne Kohm	Regent	*Goodridge v. Dep't of Pub. Health* (2003)	The Homosexual "Union": Should Gay and Lesbian Partnerships be Granted the Same Status as Marriage?	Justice Robert J. Cordy	Concurring	Same Sex Marriage	Supreme Judicial Court of Massachusetts	440 Mass. 309
Lynne Kohm	Regent	*State v. Rodriguez* (2008)	Sex at Six: The Victimization of Innocence and Other Concerns over Children's "Rights"	Judge William C. Koch	Majority	Sexual Abuse	Supreme Court of Tennessee	254 S.W.3d 361
Tessa Dysart	Regent	*People v. Cardenas* (2014)	The Protected Innocence Initiative: Building State Protective Law Regimes for America's Sex-Trafficked Children	Judge Steve Bernard	Majority	Sex Trafficking	Colorado Court of Appeals	2014 COA 35

(continued)

Table 7.4. Continued

Name	School	Case	Original Work Cited	Judges Citing Work	What Type of Decision	Issue	Court	Full Citation of Case
James Davids	Regent	Czekala-Chatham v. State (2015)	Statement Calling for Constitutional Resistance to Obergefell v. Hodges, The American Principles Project (October 8, 2015),	Jess H. Dickinson	Dissent	Same Sex Marriage	Supreme Court of Mississippi	195 So. 3d 187
Bradley Jacob	Regent	Czekala-Chatham v. State (2015)	Statement Calling for Constitutional Resistance to Obergefell v. Hodges, The American Principles Project (October 8, 2015),	Jess H. Dickinson	Dissent	Same Sex Marriage	Supreme Court of Mississippi	195 So. 3d 187
Jeffrey Tuomala	Liberty	Hicks v. State (2014)	Nuremberg and the Crime of Abortion	Judge Roy Moore	Concurring	Child Care	Supreme Court of Alabama	153 So. 3d 53

Source: Bloomberg Law. Counts include U.S. courts. Max results returned for each query = 1000. Faculty data for Regent extending from Fall 1986, Ave Maria from Fall 1999, and Liberty from Fall 2004 up to the 2017–18 school year. Faculty lists collected using the Internet Archive Wayback Machine, https://web.archive.org

could identify belongs to Jeffrey Tuomala. That being said, this one case provides a textbook example of how the Support Structure Pyramid can and ideally would function for movements.

In this single example from the Alabama Supreme Court in *Hicks v. State* (2014), we see the fruitful transmission of *intellectual capital* in the form of a citation to Liberty Professor Jeffrey Tuomala's article *Nuremberg and the Crime of Abortion* (2011). According to an article published by Liberty, this capital was shepherded from the classroom into the courtroom by *human capital* in the form of Liberty Law graduates serving as judicial clerks in the court. What's more, in between graduating and accepting clerkships in the Alabama Supreme Court, these alumni also cycled through the then-affiliated Liberty Counsel:

> Three graduates of Liberty University School of Law have the privilege of serving as law clerks for Alabama Supreme Court Chief Justice Roy Moore, who issued a landmark ruling on April 18 that the word "child" in Alabama's chemical-endangerment statute applies both to the born and unborn . . . Clark, Wishnatsky, and Boyd became the first Liberty alumni to land full-time positions in a state supreme court in 2012 after completing internships with Liberty Counsel. "These grads love the law school and are making a huge impact," said Mat Staver, dean of Liberty University School of Law. "As the law school ages, we will see more of this as our graduates move up in the ranks." (Liberty University News Service, 2014)

As the article continues, this ruling did not just include a reference to a faculty member's scholarship. In a citation that our data collection process would not pick up, the article notes that the successful functioning of the Support Structure Pyramid extended to other *intellectual capital* produced by Liberty:

> This is also the first case in which the *Liberty University Law Review*, published three times a year by Liberty Law students, has been cited in any court opinion. Alabama Justice Tom Parker referred to Wishnatsky's article, "The Supreme Court's Use of the Term 'Potential Life': Verbal Engineering and the Abortion Holocaust," written when he was still in law school and published in the winter of 2012 after he had completed his internship with Liberty Counsel." (Liberty University News Service, 2014)

In this one example, then, we can see the law school successfully training students, placing them in a Level 2 organization, and from there helping them access the apex of the Support Structure Pyramid. Once there, the graduates successfully worked as conduits for *intellectual capital* to the top of the pyramid, contributing to a successful mission-driven legal outcome. Finally, Liberty Law's publicity of this multi-layered success story goes on to show how such attention cycles back down to the law school, allowing it to announce its effectiveness to elites and the public, as well as potential students, faculty, and donors. What's more, Staver's statements clearly illustrate how leaders within the law school and the greater movement hope that this type of success will accelerate, propelling a cycle of legal and political change the Christian Right has long sought. While clearly a remarkable instance of the CCLM's support structure functioning as intended, the data presented in Table 7.3 suggests that this is much more the exception than the rule.

Moving from the Christian Worldview law schools to the Blackstone Legal Fellowship, the schools' collective success rate is contextualized. While Blackstone faculty are cited in court materials in all types of cases at a comparable rate to the schools, their individual success in having 12 faculty cited in mission-related cases is equal to the three schools' collective 12 faculty cited in such cases. Even more impressive, Blackstone's 12 faculty produce 27 citing instances in comparison with the law schools' collective 19.

Blackstone's higher numbers, however, reflect similar patterns to the Christian Worldview law schools. Like the three law schools, Blackstone basically evenly splits its cites between lawyers and judges, its amicus brief citations are all at the U.S. Supreme Court, its judicial cites favorably skew toward Southern state courts of last instance, and its lawyers' cites—with one exception—are all in amicus briefs. Blackstone's sole faculty cite in a counsel brief, however, is at the U.S. Supreme Court in the case of *Southern Nazarene University v. Burwell* 136 S. Ct. 445 (2015), which disputed birth control mandates in the Affordable Care Act. Like the Blackstone Legal Fellowship itself, this case is linked to ADF.

Seen as a collective movement, while we do see instances of these Level 1 law schools successfully having their *intellectual capital* transmitted to the nation's high courts, including the United States Supreme Court in the form of *amicus curiae* briefs, there are a few important caveats to note. First, this scholarship is exclusively being transmitted by indirect parties to these cases—that is, *amici curiae*—as opposed to the lawyers making the in-court arguments. Judges and Justices are free to ignore the arguments and briefs of *amici curiae* but are required to read and consider the briefs representing the parties in the case. Liberty Law's example of judicial attention in *Hicks v. State* (2014) is impressive but with just twelve instances of judicial citations to their faculties over the collective lifetimes of the Christian Worldview schools, we see that such examples of judicial attention are few and far between. That said, as the former dean Mat Staver noted, as these institutions age they hope to "see more of this as our graduates move up in the ranks" (Liberty University News Service, 2014).

Second, the one time we found an instance of a lawyer of record's brief citing Christian Worldview scholarship was an ADF attorney citing a Blackstone-affiliated scholar. The link between ADF and Blackstone might have helped facilitate this transmission of *intellectual capital* from Blackstone to the apex. Considering, as we detail in Chapter 4, the fact that each of the Christian Worldview law schools has or has had connections to such PILOs, this one instance highlights the apparent failure of the conduit between Level 1 and Level 2 institutions in transferring *intellectual capital* in all of the other cases. That is, while we have identified multiple litigators linked to the Christian Worldview law schools participating in litigation, our inability to find a counsel brief citing Christian Worldview faculty scholarship illustrates a leaky pipeline.

This imbalance between amicus briefs and counsel briefs might also highlight a discrepancy between the issues that the faculty take up in their scholarship, and the arguments that litigators believe will work in court. Steven Brown's book *Trumping Religion* (2002) outlines the turn in Christian conservative PILOs from principle-based arguments to more legal pragmatic approaches. This turn in strategy looks to argue for ends sought by the CCLM, but not necessarily through the means created by those invested in fundamentally reorienting law. This divide was, in fact, raised in an interview with Regent's founding Dean Herbert Titus. With reference to the work that he is still engaged with, Titus stated:

> we do friend of the court briefs. Why? Because in today's legal atmosphere we can't, in many instances, represent a client consistent with our Christian foundations. We can do that, however, for Christian organizations in our friend of the court brief because we don't have to be concerned about our responsibility to a client to win their case ... We have a different mission, it's what you might call the Watchman's mission, if you've ever read Ezekiel, Chapter 3, you'll see there's a Watchman's ministry which means that you speak the truth to power, that's a modern way of putting it, and that's what these briefs are designed to do. For example, if you look at the *Zubick* brief, that's the Little Sisters case. We address the Little Sisters issue very differently than anybody else. (April 12, 2016)

While this is Titus's particular approach, it does not speak to all of the scholarly works cited in amicus briefs. For example, Lynn Marie Kohm's *The Homosexual "Union": Should Gay and Lesbian Partnerships be Granted the Same Status as Marriage?* was used to bolster a "rational basis test" argument meant to insulate legislative choices to ban same sex marriage from constitutional challenge in *Obergefell v. Hodges* (2015) (Agudath Israel of America, 2015). That said, Titus's statement posits one way of understanding the exclusive citations to Christian Worldview scholars and scholarship in *amicus curiae* briefs as opposed to counsel briefs.

Finally, the total number of instances of citations by lawyers and judges is arguably small. When one thinks about all the potential mechanisms by which these law schools could transmit *intellectual capital* to lawyers and judges in litigation—faculty connections to PILOs, faculty involvement with litigation as lawyers of record or amici, and alumni participation in litigation—an inefficiency in the Support Structure Pyramid is clearly present.

Here, again, the question is raised as to whether creating wholly new law schools was a defensible strategic choice. Yes, some of the alumni go on to staff PILOs like ADF, but such graduates are apparently not seeing their alma maters' faculty as good sources of directly applicable *intellectual capital* in court. While one can reference the citing norms in legal briefs and decisions as a reason for undercounting the schools' faculty contributions, the imbalance between Blackstone and the schools' citation rates works against this defense. For law schools, then, that were ostensibly created to help fight the culture wars, and that are able to exercise the most control over their faculty composition and scholarly productivity, it is hard to see these faculty as directly contributing to this mission where it matters most—in litigation.

At the Apex: The Christian Worldview Scorecard and Prospects for Victory

As we wrote in the introduction to this chapter, courts and judges—whom we have located at the apex of the Support Structure Pyramid—are important (though not exclusive) gatekeepers in the battle for control of the law. This is first and foremost on account of their formal decision-making authority: their ability to "say what the law is," to return to the Charles Evans Hughes quote. And this power should not be underestimated for groups and movements looking to transform the law. With just five votes, for example, the Supreme Court in the near future could overturn *Roe v. Wade* (1973)—the landmark precedent protecting a woman's right to choose an abortion—and deliver an unequivocal victory for the Christian Right and the CCLM. But the influence of judges on law extends beyond these formal powers, "penetrat[ing] . . . into the bosom of society," to paraphrase Tocqueville, shaping or reshaping legal culture by influencing the habits and strategies of lawyers, politicians, and even citizens.

In the Support Structure Pyramid, we have identified these dynamic trickle-down effects of engagement with the apex in the form of *cultural capital* (e.g., judicial decisions and opinions legitimating or delegitimizing movements and their reasoning) and *intellectual capital* (e.g., judicial opinions opening up and encouraging new avenues for the development of *intellectual capital* by Level 1 and Level 2 actors). With repeated interactions and under favorable conditions, eventually these benefits can flow back up the Support Structure Pyramid in the form of better, more valuable, and more effective capital for judicial decision-makers to consume. These benefits also radiate outward—to the broader contexts in which the pyramid is embedded. In order to capture the actual and potential results of these cyclical and radiating dynamics that result from interactions with the apex, we mapped the cartography of Christian Worldview faculty participation in litigation. This allowed us to identify key "repeat players" (Galanter 1974) whose histories and/or continued engagement with the apex open up potential pathways for the ideas and alumni of these Christian Worldview institutions to influence judges and judicial decisions.

In addition to these repeat players, our analysis revealed that faculty at Christian Worldview institutions are participating as *amici curiae* (friends of the court) at significantly higher rates than scholars estimate the average law faculty participates in this form of engagement with litigation. If we believe the estimates that 10% or fewer of full-time faculty members at law schools participate in litigation as *amici curiae*, then even Ave Maria School of Law and Liberty Law participate at twice that rate, while Regent faculty members do so at three times the rate. Moreover, in coding the legal questions for cases Christian Worldview faculty are participating in as *amici curiae*, we find that well over half (83%) of this participation for all schools is what we would code as mission related, that is, as involving religious and culture wars cases. Strikingly, for Regent Law School, 92% of their faculty participation as *amici curiae* over time have been in mission cases. In fact, the lowest percentage of mission-related *amici curiae* participation, 52% at Ave Maria, is still remarkable.

While these percentages are impressive—and consistent with the founding missions of these schools to be an outward-oriented Christian hub of transformative influence on the law and legal profession as a whole—faculty associated with the Blackstone Legal Fellowship, representing the *supplemental* model in our study, participated at higher rates (59%) than their Christian Worldview law school counterparts. Moreover, we find that 95% of this Blackstone faculty participation as *amicus curiae* was in mission cases. As we have noted throughout the book, the *supplemental* model of support structure building is free of some of the *parallel alternative* model's constraints, at least in the context of legal education. Furthermore, as we discuss in Chapter 5, Blackstone-affiliated faculty are not all full-time faculty at law schools, and so they do not need to divide their attentions between the classroom and the courtroom. Faculty at the Christian Worldview law schools, on the other hand, are first and foremost expected to train and credential law students (*human capital*) and, secondarily, publish scholarship or produce *intellectual capital*. Engagement with courts and litigation outside of the classroom is a secondary expectation and must of necessity take a backseat to their primary duties.

These constraints noted, it speaks to the dedication and commitment to the broader goals and visions of the founding patrons that full-time faculty at these Christian Worldview institutions seem to be participating in litigation as *amici curiae* at higher—indeed, significantly higher—rates than their counterparts at other law schools. Furthermore, unlike in other areas examined in this book, the distance between Blackstone and the three mission law schools is not as pronounced as it first appears in the aggregate. With the exception of the number and percentage of faculty involved in mission-related amicus briefs, Blackstone and Regent are similarly situated. Indeed, Regent actually outperforms Blackstone in terms of the overall instances of mission amicus brief participation. Considering this, we can understand the case study field as divided into two discernible tiers. Regent Law and Blackstone Legal Fellowship are the clear leaders in submitting mission-related amicus briefs, while AMSL and Liberty Law form the second tier. Noting this internal differentiation, we would again emphasize that all of the Christian Worldview schools appear to be outpacing national law school averages.

Given this high level of participation, we would also expect to see these *amicus curiae* briefs functioning as conduits for the diffusion of Christian Worldview *intellectual capital* from the law schools, through these faculty, and into briefs and ideally judicial decisions. Our search for citations to Christian Worldview faculty scholarship in briefs (amicus and counsel-of-record) and judicial opinions did not return huge numbers, but it did reveal two interesting findings: the majority (78%) of citations to Christian Worldview faculty scholarship are happening in non-mission cases, and in the few instances where judges are citing their scholarship, 67% of these citations have been in opinions issued by state courts of last resort (state supreme courts).

Having presented all of our empirical findings, the concluding chapter of the book aggregates insights from the preceding chapters. It asks, in sum, what does the CCLM as a case study tell us about (1) the strategic options available to patrons looking to bolster the support structures for their movement and (2) the consequences of those choices? In addition to summarizing our findings, this chapter revisits Support Structure Theory and the Support Structure Pyramid we introduce in Chapter 1 and brings it into conversation with social movement theory, scholarship on legal mobilization and the legal profession, and contemporary works on religion and politics in order to suggest areas for future development, integration, and inquiry based on the insights generated from our case study.

Conclusion

The Polonius Standard and Other Measures of Success

Led by men of God . . . spiritually energized colonial Americans began to reclaim their God-given rights. The Church became a clarion of civic thought and a regiment of black-robed ministers became messengers of freedom. Spreading the idea of the rule of law under God and equality before God.

. . . Universities such as Princeton, Columbia, Brown, Rutgers, and Dartmouth were formed to train ministers and further spread the Gospel. The rule of law was again understood to ultimately come from the King of kings, not an earthly king.

. . . By the latter part of the twentieth century, cracks began to form in America's republican form of government. As the formerly influential Church stood quietly by, America's courts began to deconstruct the rule of law embodied in natural law and revealed law.

. . . As courts began to remove God from the public square, the rule of law, which emanates from God, was likewise discounted in favor of the whim of the ruling class.

. . . At the epicenter of the deconstruction of law and the upheaval of moral values is the United States Supreme Court.

. . . The mission of the law school is to restore the rule of law. When rooted in the proper foundation, law advances life over death, liberty over tyranny, and order over chaos.

—Liberty University School of Law,
"Foundations Hall, History of the Rule of Law"

This concluding chapter is primarily interested in measures of success. We use these closing pages to consider the generalizability and utility of the models that structured our inquiry, as well as to consider the success, failure, or something in between, of the specific moves made here to build legal support structures for the Christian Right.

The questions posed at the book's start were:

Separate But Faithful. Amanda Hollis-Brusky and Joshua C. Wilson, Oxford University Press (2020). © Oxford University Press. DOI: 10.1093/oso/9780190637262.001.0001

1. Why did New Christian Right patrons reject the lower-cost, lower-risk, *infiltration* approach to support structure building in favor of a mix of *parallel alternative* and *supplemental* approaches?
2. What are the consequences of these strategic choices in terms of support structure efficacy and viability?
3. What does the Christian Conservative Legal Movement (CCLM) as a case study tell us about how we can conceive of and think about the strategic options available to those who, regardless of a movement's ideological orientation, are looking to build or bolster the "support structures" for their movement?

In approaching the case study specific questions, one can simply ask whether it was worth it to build these wholly new schools and the Blackstone Legal Fellowship training program. Should they be considered as successes in part or in whole, collectively or individually? While this question appears straight forward, it is deceptively complex. The reason for this is the openness of what we can and should consider as success.

Starting with a look back at the Support Structure Pyramid, success would appear to be defined as the ability to influence the apex of the pyramid—to win court cases and, by doing so, change law and policy. While that end is important, as we have repeatedly emphasized in the book, the Support Structure Pyramid, in fact, represents a series of cyclical, dynamic, and interrelated processes. The ultimate goal of engaging in support structure building is not only to win in court, but also to build a movement capable of affecting the legal, political, and broader culture. Success is, therefore, not all or nothing. Moreover, success cannot be ultimately assessed and known at a specific point in time like a race. The multiple steps in the process, and the multiple larger goals sought, allow for a range of ways to ask whether a movement is persisting and, better yet, progressing in a desirable direction. That is, are they building robust movement organizations? Are they entering the conversations in social, political, and legal venues? And finally, are they being noticed and exerting some influence in these venues? These types of questions allow us to assess whether a movement is engaging in the long game of change, whether they are playing a short game, or whether they are being thought of—by insiders and/or outsiders— in an overly myopic way.

Let us return to Charles Epp's definition of support structure success as the ability to create the conditions for "sustained judicial attention," that is, the ability to consistently raise issues in court (2011, 406–7). This measure rejects the temptation to measure success exclusively in terms of court victories. Instead, Epp embraces the idea that movements can still benefit even when they lose in court. As we discuss in Chapter 7, repeated engagement with the apex can raise an organization's status or profile, increase the publicity of valued issues, develop and test advantageous frames and narratives, etc. What really matters is that movements are continuing to "play the game," and by persisting, they can keep their issues and organizations alive, make incremental advances, learn, and hope to improve their future prospects for influencing policy (Albiston 2011; McCann 1994; NeJaime 2011).

It is important to recognize the maybe-too-obvious fact that movements are not always able to persist and find ways to benefit from litigation, as is well noted by Catherine Albiston (2011). That is, time and courts are not always friendly. Both can help a movement to develop, but they can also erode and bury a movement. Whether time and courts are positive or negative is tied up with factors that are both immediately in and beyond a movement's control. Movements cannot immediately change political conditions like the absence of an existing law or precedent in one's favor, or the domination of state institutions by one's political opponents. They can, however, try to change both in the longer term. They can also strive in the present to control how developments are publicly and more privately framed, effectively assess and respond to political conditions, and creatively use the various venues that are made available by the United States' fractured and decentralized legal and political systems (see, e.g., Kagan 2003). Doing so allows them to work with conditions as they are, to strive to change future conditions, and to be well positioned to take advantage of whatever the future may hold. To do any and all of this, though, they must first persist as viable institutions.

It is here that we begin to see how the tiers of the Support Structure Pyramid provide multiple points of evaluation of movement efficacy and success. Starting with the base of the pyramid, we can ask whether movement organizations and institutions are attracting and sustaining patronage that allows them to pursue their own self-defined ends? Are Level 1 institutions (law schools and training programs) creating a supply of *human, social, cultural*, and *intellectual capital* in both quantity and quality relevant to the movement? That is, can they reasonably control their internal standards and curricula in order to stay true to their missions? Are their graduates able to find their way into legal, political, educational, and/or cultural institutions? Are their scholars able to raise the movement's interests and develop innovative new frames consumed in legal, political, and/or public spheres? Are these institutions able to access or create networks that allow for collective action and influence? In sum and reduced to the core, *can they persist as functioning institutions while staying true to their founding visions, standing as beachheads and beacons for the movement?* One might call this the "Polonius standard," after the Shakespearean character's advice to his son Laertes: "This above all: to thine own self be true" (*Hamlet*, Act I, Scene III, 82).

Moving to Level 2 institutions, Epp's (2011) standard exposes the more traditional concern at this tier—whether movement lawyers are able to bring "sustained judicial attention" to the issues that matter to them. Given the more expansive view of change and success, however, one should also assess their engagement with broader cultural and political audiences. Movement lawyers' abilities to do all of these things are tied to whether or not they can successfully secure stable funding, pull on Level 1's various resources, and possibly even generate their own *human, social, cultural,* and *intellectual capital.* It also depends on their abilities to assess and exploit political conditions and opportunities. If they are able to do all or most of these things, evidence of their success might be seen in their ability to attract more funding, as well as their abilities to contribute issue frames for broader political, cultural, and legal audiences. As with the previous level, however, one can return to persistence, fidelity, and continued engagement as the base standards and then add degrees of detail to get a more complete assessment of a movement's efforts and degrees of success or failure.

It is only after assessing the functioning of the pyramid's lower tiers that we finally arrive at the apex. Even here, though, success is not limited to courtroom victories. As argued by NeJaime (2011), McCann (1994), and others, savvy movements can produce benefits from the top of the pyramid even when they lose in court. Again, returning to Epp's (2011) assessment, "sustained judicial attention" is the common denominator or necessary condition of success at this level. That said, we also need to look for how movements mobilize their sustained attention to further attract and develop resources, and to engage their various audiences and publics (i.e., movement members and supporters, the greater voting public, legal scholars, the practicing Bar, policymakers, the media, etc.).

As noted in previous chapters, resources and benefits run up and down the model, and their effectiveness is enabled and facilitated by the greater political and social contexts within which they play out. Those greater contexts are also part of what the actors at the different levels of the support structure are trying to influence. These diverse but interrelated ends, as well as the importance of staying true to one's founding vision, are captured in the lengthy description, excerpted at the beginning of this concluding chapter, that accompanies Liberty Law School's Foundations Hall paintings (for more on the paintings, see Chapter 3). In that excerpt, we see that while the Supreme Court is portrayed as the "epicenter" of the destruction wrought by the abandonment of religion and the natural law, there are many accomplices, and the effects on culture and "morality" more generally have been wide ranging.

The fundamental importance of fidelity to a founding religious mission and persistence is noted in an administrator's assessment of what differentiates Liberty Law, in this case, from older schools that had religious missions: "I think one of the distinctions between . . . a newer school and an older school like Notre Dame or some of the other ones like Cornell . . . that started out with a mission focus [is] that their shifting has changed in all areas, not just in the legal community. Whereas here at Liberty nothing is shifting in terms of the Christian Worldview [as] still the important thing" (Liberty Administrator 1 2015). Those other schools may have found popularly recognized power and prestige, but in this assessment, they achieved those things by sacrificing their mission. In fact, in doing so, they are viewed as having contributed to the conditions that spawned the need for the

Christian Right, the CCLM, and, now, a new set of support structures for law, policy, and cultural change.

As we have seen throughout this book, Liberty, Regent, Ave Maria, and Blackstone are invested in creating a new wave of "spiritually energized . . . Americans . . . to reclaim their God-given rights," to once again quote from the opening excerpt from Liberty's Foundations Hall. Joining the Church, and reasserting its lost place, these collective institutions strive to become, "a clarion of civic thought and . . . messengers of freedom. Spreading the idea of the rule of law under God." Considering this, the movement's own measures of success seem to align with ours in this book. Preserving their missions and engaging not just with the judiciary, which sits at "the epicenter of the deconstruction of law and the upheaval of moral values," but with broader publics and cultures, matters both for courtroom success and the broader diagnosed problem. They are all part of a long-term strategy of change, or as conceived of by this movement, reformation and revival. The questions then become: are they succeeding in these ends, and what can we take from their experiences more broadly?

The abilities to persist, stay true to one's vision, and to otherwise be seen as effective are differently situated depending on the strategy selected for accessing Level 1—*infiltration, parallel alternative,* or *supplemental.* To recall, opting for the *infiltration strategy* lowers financial costs and may increase access to standing avenues to power and prestige, but it can come at the cost of realizing one's core vision if that vision is deemed too radical. That is, it is difficult to infiltrate existing law schools— especially those with more broadly recognized capital—if one's vision is perceived as potentially detrimental to an existing institution's reputation.

To this point, as we discussed vis-à-vis Baylor in Chapter 2, the university was self-consciously dedicated to the conviction "that the world needs a preeminent research university that is unambiguously Christian," and that Baylor was striving to occupy that space (Noll et al. 2012, 4–5). At the same time, they also recognized that "Christian intellectual life . . . requires an exercise in tightrope walking," and that extreme visions of the place of faith in public life stood to knock institutions off of that tightrope. "[Z]ealous adherents to Scripture simply toss the baby of well-grounded learning with the bathwater of learning abused for God-denying purposes. These examples include manic single-issue public advocacy that claims to represent 'biblical politics; runaway Americanism that depicts our nation's early history as the land of the converted and the true-blue evangelical . . .'" (96–97). With the assumption that this view was not limited to Baylor—an assumption supported by this book's interviews with Notre Dame faculty, a survey of the broader tumult within Protestant higher education in the late twentieth century, and Ann Southworth's (2008) discussion of the divisions within the conservative legal community—it is hard to see how patrons like Pat Robertson, Jerry Falwell, and Thomas Monaghan would be able to meaningfully gain access to existing schools. What's more, even if they did, it is a clear question of how much control they would be given if admitted.

Considering these things, this study cannot deeply speak to the efficacy of the *infiltration strategy*. Rather, it stands as evidence of how this relatively lower-cost strategy is not as open as one might initially think. Substantial sums of patron money cannot buy whatever is wanted. That being said, our brief comparative analysis of Notre Dame Law School can be instructive. As told to us by Notre Dame Law School faculty, and as further supported in Chapters 5 and 6, the law school serves as an example of a form of *infiltration*—or at least the substantial substantive reform of an existing institution—and its latent potential as a means to effectively generate multiple forms of valued capital, successfully placing it into circulation within the Support Structure Pyramid.

At the turn of the twenty-first century, Notre Dame's law school underwent a substantial rebuilding—both physically and intellectually. Under the guidance of a new dean, the law school reformed itself as a conservative legal hub, and the faculty and leadership "recruited to the school were very invested in that idea" (Notre Dame Faculty 1, 2016). Fueled by ample funding and a clear mission, the law school has become not only the place where conservative judges and Justice "go for your clerks" and where you regularly run into current Supreme Court Justice, but it has also become the source of at least one conservative judicial appointee—Judge Amy Coney Barrett—for the Trump administration who was also considered for the U.S. Supreme Court (Notre Dame Faculty 3, 2016). Not surprisingly, it has also coupled this link to the top of the Support Structure Pyramid with a strong reputation within both the legal academy and the profession. Chapter 6's data stands as evidence of the faculty's impressive *intellectual capital* production and placement, and its rankings within the *U.S. News & World Report* speak to its overall reputation.

While our exploration of Notre Dame could be greatly expanded in order to better understand its specific history, what initiated the particular reform, and how the school came to work so effectively within the Support Structure Pyramid model, it clearly suggests the *infiltration* strategy's value and thus the value of continuing to explore it through other case studies. George Mason's Antonin Scalia Law School, for example, is another ripe case study for furthering our understanding of the *infiltration* model. Steven Teles's (2008) discussion of the school introduces the value of the case study and the strategy, but there is more work to do here. For example, the controversy surrounding the law school's renaming that reflects its longer-standing intellectual and ideological reorientation suggests that it might be illustrative in considering not only the benefits but some additional risks and limits of the *infiltration* model.

George Mason's law school was renamed in 2016 after the then-recently departed conservative Supreme Court Justice, founding faculty adviser of the Federalist Society, and overall conservative icon, Antonin Scalia. What's more, the name change was prompted by a sizable donation from, in part, an equally recognizable and politically divisive conservative patron, Charles Koch (Jackman 2016).[1] As a testament to the strength of patrons to influence institutions, as well as the law school and the university both being thought of as an infiltration target, George Mason University (GMU) has received "some $50 million worth [of donations from the Koch brothers], as of 2016" (Flaherty 2018). At least $10 million of that money has gone directly to the law school in conjunction with an additional $20 million from an anonymous donor whose investment in the law school is represented by Federalist Society Executive President Leonard Leo (Flaherty 2018).

Although the name change occurred in 2016, and the associated boost in patron support enhanced its capacities to serve as a support structure for the conservative legal movement, the school's affiliation with this movement extends back far earlier (Teles 2008). Scalia Law's dean, Henry N. Butler, is a compelling starting point for understanding the name change, its reflection of deeper changes within the school, and the risks and benefits of the *infiltration* model. Dean Butler served as an Olin Fellow in Law and Economics at the University of Chicago—another, though more elite, epicenter of the law and economics movement—and joined GMU with law and economics patron Henry Manne, helping lead and then head the center that Manne created. Butler left George Mason for a period in the 1990s to take Koch-funded law and economics faculty positions at the University of Kansas (Teles 2008). Finally, returning to GMU to head the Law & Economics Center and then as dean, Butler help further the school's status as a conservative movement support structure with the help of Koch and other conservative patron money (George Mason University 2018; Flaherty 2016, 2018; Larimer 2018).

As a public institution, however, Scalia Law is not totally independent from the state, the rest of GMU, and the associated regulations and diverse interests in the university. Like Notre Dame, it is a comprehensive example of the *infiltration* strategy—so comprehensive, in fact, that one can wonder whether it is better thought of as a *parallel alternative* institution. The school, however, was not created whole cloth by Manne, and its reformation does not afford the level of control associated with the *parallel alternative* archetype.[2] Rather, it was targeted by Manne and then comprehensively rebuilt. Noting the preexisting elements of the institution, Scalia Law has recently been subject to significant internal and external criticism for the terms of the donation that changed the law school's name and increased its positioning as an *infiltration* strategy support structure (Flaherty 2016, 2018; Larimer 2018; Patrice 2018).[3]

The fact that Scalia Law strains and maybe straddles the typologies we develop helps spur discussion of what enabled the degree of investment and ensuing change that is so dramatically seen in GMU's law school. For example, the nationwide trend of decreasing state funding for public institutions has pushed them to seek out donor investment, making them open to donor influence and the *infiltration* strategy. In the language of the models offered here, the connection between Level 1 and the base has been destabilized, and the greater context within which this has happened enables—if not outright encourages—external donor investment, inviting the *infiltration* strategy. However, as institutions with established histories, missions to serve the greater public, regulations calling for transparency, etc., they are also subject to backlash for accepting such investment. Again, this draws attention to the importance of attending to the greater context within which the institutions are situated. Such questions extend past public institutions, too. Preexisting private institutions also actively seek donors, and while they may be more insulated from the public, elements within such established institutions can still resist and fight infiltration investment.

Given the above, there is potentially interesting research to be done regarding *infiltration* strategies, both successful and unsuccessful, and the greater contexts that create or limit opportunities. What's more, while the examples of Notre Dame and George Mason given here present arguably the most robust versions of the *infiltration* strategy, work should also be done to better understand the costs and benefits of smaller scale *infiltration* strategies, such as endowing one or more chairs in an academic department. Doing so will add to better understanding a more complete range of support structure development and efficacy.

Considering the limitations of the *infiltration* strategy, the *supplemental* approach offers the means to pursue more radical ends as a result of its increased distance from existing institutions and its freedom from accreditation standards. This freedom, however, comes most obviously at the potential cost of limited control over the desired audience. While *supplemental* institutions can free-ride off of the credentialing and networking power of existing schools while adding their own additions to students' curriculum and networks, participants are not wholly insulated from the problems that led to the *supplemental* institutions' founding. As a result, while the *supplemental* model's costs are moderate to inexpensive, and the immediate control over the students and the mission are increased in comparison with the *infiltration* model, efforts can be eroded or undermined by the home law school's greater controls and time with the students.

What's more, while the *supplemental* model provides for the creation of *human* and *social capital*, the means of independently producing *intellectual* and *cultural capital* for the movement are less obvious. The faculty brought together temporarily or permanently to staff the *supplemental* institution might produce *intellectual* and *cultural capital*, and the *supplemental* institution presumably recruits them as a result of these qualities, but the *supplemental* institution itself does not directly produce or even strongly incentivize the creation of these forms of capital.[4] *Supplemental* institutions' more indirect contributions to this end can, however, be predicted through connections made through participant involvement. That is, shared involvement in the program can spur networking that results in future collaboration that can subsequently produce *intellectual capital*, as is seen with the Federalist Society (Hollis-Brusky 2015).

While we do not see evidence of such networking and collaboration resulting in *intellectual capital* in Alliance Defending Freedom's (ADF's) Blackstone Legal Fellowship, our analysis of Blackstone does allow us to say something about the virtues and limitations of this strategy. Before getting to consolidating and considering our findings across this book regarding the *supplemental* approach, though, the final means to form Level 1 institutions needs to be briefly reintroduced.

The primary benefit offered by pursuing the *parallel alternative* model to Level 1 institutions is maximizing control with regards to the founding mission and vision. Since patrons and other visionaries are coming together to create a wholly new and comprehensive institution, they can exercise maximal control in doing so. Preexisting interests don't stand in the way of pursuing more radical ends as obviously or as directly. As the home institution, the *supplemental* institution problem of having limited time with and control over students is also eliminated. Finally, as an academic institution, there are clear traditions and norms that suggest how the schools can work as engines of the full range of capital and resources. This increased control and range, however, come with the greatest financial cost, by far, of all of the approaches. What's more, as the case studies have also shown, these institutions are not built in a legal and professional landscape free of constraints.

While the schools themselves are new, legal academia is definitely not. It is not only an occupied terrain but also a governed one. There are preexisting rules, regulations, and economies, and if a new institution wants to be seen as a viable one by faculty, staff, students, and the broader legal, political, and general populations, it will need to interact with that established world to varying degrees. New or reformed institutions can wage wars against these constraints, but such resistance comes with significant risks. Bending to these preexisting structures, however, also poses substantial risks. Again, as Polonius entreated his son, "This above all: to thine own self be true." If one undertakes massively investing in a new institution, preserving and realizing the reasons for that investment are paramount. Considering this, the *parallel alternative* model's claim to freedom and control is fundamentally brought into question, and our starting point for their evaluation via our case studies is now fully charted.

It should be noted, though, that while the case studies pursued here allow for a more detailed exploration of these strategies via their costs and benefits as well as their efficacy within the Support Structure Pyramid, we fully understand that they are just initial forays into our understanding of support structures along the lines proposed in this book. Considering this, we hope that others will continue to apply and modify the models as they continue to add to our collective understanding of support structures and the processes of litigation-driven legal, policy, and social change.

Evaluating and Comparing CCLM Support Structure Success

As stated at this book's outset, the Blackstone Legal Fellowship, as well as Regent, Liberty, and Ave Maria's law schools, are all dedicated to realizing a "Christian Worldview," defined as legal education that is aligned "with godly standards" in order to produce lawyers equipped and motivated to "restore American law to its original Biblical foundation" (Titus & Thompson 1985). To recall, adherents of this Christian Worldview believe that the nation was founded with a specific Judeo-Christian biblical vision in mind that structured law, the state, and social relations, but that this foundation of all things had been dangerously eroded and supplanted in the last century. The worldview that motivated the creation of the schools, then, underscores the reasons why the primary standard for evaluating support structure success must give primacy to each institution's ability to stay true to this mission.

Internally, fidelity is seen as necessary both because it is central to the movement's means and ends, and because it is seen as foundational. Emphasizing this latter point, the motivating worldview is deeply existential, and thus staying true to it is a requirement. To fail in doing so would be to fail in a profound way. Beyond this, since the institutions were founded to represent an alternative and competing conception of law, their continued fidelity and existence allow them to—if nothing more—stand as a reminder of their opposition to the prevailing culture, politics, and law. That is, their persistence in and of itself is a statement of defiance. To that end, Oral Roberts University's successful fight against the American Bar Association's (ABA's) accreditation standards and the surviving three Christian Worldview law schools securing of and maintaining of their ABA accreditation are evidence of the struggle to survive, the statement made through persistence, and the substantive changes that can derive from both. As more of the book has shown, though, the existential concerns do not end with ABA accreditation.

The remaining measures of success are all derived from the practical elements of persisting and engaging in a thick conception of litigation-driven change. In order to enumerate specific elements while avoiding earlier levels of detail, we have holistically summarized the primary findings from Chapters 4–7. The first collection of factors is roughly seen as internal to the institutions, though they also relate to the production of *human, social,* and *cultural capital.*

In relation to these internal factors, we first look at the "base" by asking if the various institutions have ample, stable, and deferential funding that allows them to pursue their ends as they see fit. Next, we look at the institutions' abilities to recruit prestigiously credentialed faculty, a part of the ability to create *human, social, cultural,* and *intellectual capital.* Finally, turning to the "Polonius standard," we then compare the extent to which each institution has been able to effectively institutionalize and preserve their Christian Worldview mission. Indicators of this measure include curricula, institutional rules, norms expressed in the various interviews, and signs of securing a significant number of quality, mission-driven students (i.e., number of students from religious undergraduate institutions versus regional students, GPA and LSAT scores, overall admissions selectivity, and assessments of students and institutional culture).

As we have previously discussed, earlier-established religious schools sacrificed adherence to a Christian Worldview in favor of acceptance and prestige brought by pursuing, for example, highly credentialed faculty and students who may not have been devoted to the religious mission and ends of the school. Considering the limited pool of highly credentialed faculty and students who also share the institutions' worldview, there is a possible tension between the goals of quality *human capital* and commitment to Christian Worldview. That said, we do not expect there to be an inverse relationship between the traditional markers of prestige and the evidence of worldview adherence. Rather, we recognize that there is a possible tension between the two, and so there is a need for institutions to work to maintain a balance in their pursuit of both ends.

The Polonius Standard

Looking across the internal measures of whether these institutions are staying true to their founding Christian Worldview missions while still attending to student and faculty quality, there is evidence to suggest that they are, on the whole, managing well. The data presented, however, shows that the ability to strike the balance between traditional credentialing and prestige on one hand and realizing the founding mission on the other is uneven across the institutions.

This book's early chapters show that these new law schools faced substantial challenges in the forms of ABA accreditation and the previous nearly two decades' substantial contractions of the legal marketplace (Hartman 2019). In spite of these challenges, we conclude that, at least up to this point, they have stayed faithful to their founding visions. Yes, larger constraints have forced them to adapt, but in adapting they have made sure to preserve multiple forms of their demonstrable Christian Worldview—from keeping required worldview courses in the curriculum, to the regularity of including prayer and other forms of religious expression in the classroom, etc.

While an achievement by their own standards, the institutions' rigid adherence to their particular constructions of a Christian Worldview have impacted their abilities to recruit from a complete range of potential students and faculty. Quantitative data presented in Chapter 4 show that while the strength of their students has varied over time, these schools have generally attracted B-range students as their incoming class averages. Interviews and some supporting quantitative data also suggests that the schools have used their missions and honors tracks to successfully recruit a smaller number of more highly qualified students who could have gone to better-ranked schools. Interviews with those connected to Blackstone also suggest that that program has moved from relying on fellows who come from schools such as Regent and Ave Maria, to more highly regarded schools such as Notre Dame and University of Pennsylvania Carey Law School (Penn Law). Collectively, then, student quality is not an overall strength, but these institutions have found the means of securing a smaller, select number of more qualified students that can be exposed to their Christian Worldview and potentially brought into the CCLM.

Similarly, with the exception of Liberty, which entered a more constrained marketplace for faculty who would be attracted to such an institution, the remaining
institutions have been able to recruit a fair number of more highly credentialed faculty. On the other hand, Regent, like Liberty, still has a disproportionate number
of faculty from low-ranking or unranked institutions. Notably, Blackstone has been
demonstrably able to avoid this problem, recruiting more highly credentialed and
connected faculty for the less encompassing commitment of their summer program.

Collectively, then, like with the ability to recruit and secure top students, these
institutions have had some success in recruiting traditionally highly credentialed faculty, but there is much more variation across the institutions. This variation suggests
both the limited marketplace of such faculty and the *supplemental* approach's apparent advantages in this area. The enduring and generalizable strengths of this
latter point, however, are still open questions.

The *supplemental* approach presents the same attractive offer to faculty and
students. They are able to reap the benefits of belonging to more broadly prestigious
institutions while still being connected to a community and movement that they ostensibly value. A question remains, however, as to whether the limited marketplace
problem can still impact *supplemental* institutions. As of now, Blackstone represents
the primary option for such *supplemental* legal training. It is unclear whether the
market could support more related *supplemental* institutions and, thus, when such
institutions would start forming tiers, diluting resources, and/or experiencing other
potential inefficiencies as seen with the newly created Christian Worldview law
schools. Given that, while Blackstone appears universally stronger than the three
schools in the measures examined here, and these strengths are linked to its position
as a *supplemental* institution, it is not evident that *supplemental* institutions always
hold these advantages.

Turning to other lessons coming from the individual variations between the case
studies, the Ave Maria School of Law (AMSL) stands in a precarious place in relation to the others when it comes to pursuing quality while preserving its mission. In
terms of faculty with traditional credentials, Ave Maria sits alongside Regent with
just over 40% of its faculty coming from top 20–ranked schools. As such, this does
not stand as a problem for AMSL. Its student recruitment, however, does.

As noted in the earlier chapters, Ave Maria's relocation from Michigan to Florida
and the uncertainty of Thomas Monaghan's continued financial support have
combined to shake the institution's foundation. That instability in the base of the
Support Structure Pyramid has impacted the ability to recruit and retain academically strong students just as it has hindered the ability to secure a critical mass of
mission students. It should be remembered that it was through our interviews at
Ave Maria that we first encountered the terms *mission* and *non-mission* student—
the naming of types as a sign of the awareness of the problem and, possibly, a recognition of its significance. While the exact percentage and where AMSL stands
in relation to it is unclear, the case study suggests that there is a tipping point in

terms of the minimum number of mission students needed to preserve and re-alize the institution's Christian Worldview nature. If one falls below this line, the non-mission influence of the students can overwhelm and undermine the mission-driven institutional elements.

Relatedly, AMSL faces another more institution-specific challenge. As one of many Catholic law schools, it faces a relatively competitive marketplace for strong, mission-driven students. The number of existing Catholic law schools can create a larger pool of potential faculty for AMSL, but it also poses a problem for student recruitment. As this book has shown, while AMSL positions itself as a uniquely orthodox and conservative Catholic law school, high-achieving conservative Catholics have good reason to still see Notre Dame as a preferable option. What's more, while the range of other Catholic law schools may not be seen as conservative and Catholic enough for Ave Maria's founders, they still may be seen as Catholic enough for the range of high-achieving aspiring conservative Catholic students.

By contrast, Regent and Liberty are better positioned as a result of the lack of strong alternatives for devout conservative Protestant evangelicals. The likes of Baylor, Pepperdine, and others may compete for these students, but the internal history of conservative Protestant higher education and the construction of the Christian Right arguably do more to limit the competition coming from these schools. What's more, Blackstone's *supplemental* institution status, as well as its distance from a specific Christian tradition, enables it to avoid this competition problem altogether. Again, though, it is not clear how many more *supplemental* institutions could enter the marketplace before it would become oversaturated.

Thus, while all of the schools have faced and variously responded to the re-cent stresses of the changing legal market and the constraints of accreditation, Ave Maria's internal instabilities appear to have affected the school in a way unseen in the others. What's more, Blackstone's insulation from these stresses and from real marketplace competition have shown the value in it specifically, and for the *supplemental* approach more generally. Even with such variations, though, the four institutions are all, as of now, properly recognized as symbols of defiance.

They have heretofore survived, they have preserved their Christian Worldview missions in demonstrable ways, and they have persistently made this worldview part of their outward-facing brand. Regent still recruits students by noting its "rig-orous and Christ-centered education" (Regent University School of Law, n.d.). Liberty still calls students to "Be among the next generation of Christian lawyers who will make a difference in the courtroom, the political arena, and the world" (Liberty University School of Law, n.d.). AMSL takes pride in being "named 'Most Conservative' and 'Most Devout' law school by *PreLaw* magazine" (Ave Maria School of Law, n.d.). Blackstone opens its online pitch by offering to prepare, "Christian law students for careers marked by integrity, excellence, and leadership" (Blackstone Legal Fellowship, n.d.).

Through preserving their missions, then, while variably adapting to preexisting constraints, the four case studies have been successful in the most basic and fundamental way. While rightfully noted, however, these internal measures have also begun to introduce the significant variations in how well they translate their dedication to a Christian Worldview into specific resources and capital for the greater CCLM.

Success as Valued Capital Suppliers

An evaluation of this movement's success also requires us to look at institutional outputs.[5] In measuring *human capital* production, the question is how the institutions compare in terms of bar passage, employment rates, and employment placement. In assessing the institutions tapping into professional networks for *social capital*, we compared the connections with CCLM public interest law firms, the quality of those connections, links to broader Christian Right political organizations, and connections to the Federalist Society, as arguably the most important conservative legal organization.

Turning to *cultural capital*, we compared the number and quality of citations in popular print media as well as the faculties' overall scholarly productivity. The institutions' varying levels of connection to the Federalist Society also tells us about their latent *cultural capital* since faculty involvement can increase an institution's perceived standing in the conservative legal and policy communities.

The final comparative measure of output is in terms of *intellectual capital*. The detailed presentation and consideration of these data span two chapters in this book. Distilled here, we compare the law schools' faculty publication rates, publication venues, citation rates, and citation venues—including both academic and judicial venues. These data again tell us about their supplying raw materials for the CCLM, the movement's use of those materials, and the schools' attempts to engage with broader contexts.[6]

When evaluating the range of resources produced by these institutions and their value, the results are uneven. This unevenness reveals itself both in terms of the Christian Worldview law schools' collective outputs, as well as in differences between each institution.

Starting with their collective strengths, in terms of *human capital*, all three schools are placing significantly more alumni in government positions, educational institutions, and public interest law than the national averages. While, as we note, the raw numbers of graduates entering these support structure–critical positions are small, they are evidence of success nonetheless. Realistically, because these institutions are and must be full-service law schools, one cannot expect all, or even a majority of graduates to pursue careers in these traditional spheres of policy and cultural influence. With this constraint in mind, the placement of roughly 19% of graduates in government, 4% in education, and—excepting AMSL's near 4%—7% in public interest law, is impressive and should be considered a success.

Another strength in terms of considering support structure efficacy, and one that likely contributes to the placement of graduates in the aforementioned positions, is the Christian Worldview institutions' connections to Christian Right organizations. All three of the schools as well as Blackstone have identifiable links to Christian conservative public interest legal organizations (PILOs). Regent and Blackstone benefit from their still-present formal connections to the two most prominent CCLM PILOs—American Center for Law and Justice and ADF, respectively. Liberty and Ave Maria have less formalized connections to similar, but not as prominent, PILOs as well.

Beyond these connections, each institution generates varying degrees of *social* and *cultural capital* as a result of its founding patron's connections to the broader Christian Right, in addition to individual faculty members' connections. In fact, students repeatedly referred to their faculty as the means by which they would seek to get connected to movement organizations and other avenues to influence. As in the previous section, though, this strength for the schools is tempered by the comparison with Blackstone. While the Blackstone Legal Fellowship formalizes the networking process, interviewees at the law schools either could not identify formally institutionalized means of networking students or cited this as a weakness. Problems and relative strengths accepted, the formal and informal links between the four case study organizations and actors and institutions elsewhere in the pyramid are evidence of being well positioned as support structures for the CCLM.

Finally, the four case study institutions all provide evidence of actively engaging with the apex of the Support Structure Pyramid (courts and litigation). Although the comparative benchmark in Chapter 7 is an estimated one, a higher percentage of faculty at these institutions are engaged in litigation than law faculty across the nation, especially as *amici curiae* (friends of the court). Furthermore, mission-related litigation occupies a substantial portion of this engagement. Again, the raw totals of faculty, instances of mission-related litigation involvement, and citations to faculty in court materials here may not appear overwhelming—roughly fifty faculty participating, just over 225 instances of participation, and just over thirty cites to faculty—and the distribution heavily favors Blackstone and Regent over Ave Maria and especially Liberty. That said, the collective signs of engagement with the apex of the pyramid are evidence of their work to mobilize capital and resources in service of the CCLM.

Whether these signs of success are worth the financial cost of starting these law schools, though, is an open question. Specific data from Blackstone was not available in terms of *human capital*, but given the fellowship's ability to try to benefit from established law schools' credentialing and networks, as well as the program's overt efforts to network its fellows with institutions and actors who wield influence within law, policy, and cultural spheres, the question of costs and benefits is raised here. Cost–benefit questions become all the stronger when looking at the schools' limited abilities to produce other forms of valued capital that they, versus Blackstone, are uniquely positioned to produce.

As discussed in Chapter 5, by virtue of their newness and their Christian Worldview missions, the schools all start with a "credibility capital" deficit. The book's data regarding the ability to mobilize media as a means to fight this deficit is ambiguous at best. In fact, as Chapter 5 showed, there are plenty of examples where media helped to create or reinforce their credibility shortfalls. Additionally, we show that Blackstone in general (and "The Blackstone Seven" in particular) has an overwhelming advantage in terms of its integration into the Federalist Society as measured by conference invitations, venues that perform a gate-keeping function for right-of-center ideas and individuals to be taken seriously within the conservative legal movement specifically, and within the Republican Party more generally.

Related data on *human capital* shows that the schools, as a whole, are uneven in their abilities to prepare their graduates for the bar exam and finding employment within nine months of graduating—traditional measures of law school quality. Regent is better positioned than its peers with respect to these markers, and Liberty is uneven but improving, but Ave Maria is clearly struggling. Numeric differences aside, as signs of their collective problems in being seen as properly preparing students, they all now tout their abilities to create "practice-ready" law students via their various lawyering skills programs, and, when possible, they foreground their moot court victories as evidence of their success in this area.

Finally, the production of *intellectual capital*—the resource that law schools are best positioned to produce—is an area wanting significant improvement. The data examined in Chapters 6 and 7 shows that significant numbers of the faculty engage in scholarly publication, but that in comparison with the range of schools we mobilize to give context, their individual productivity is lower, their rates of being cited are low, and their articles tend to be placed in marginal venues. As a result, their scholarly production is not serving to significantly battle their credibility deficit.

In turning to data on their mission-related scholarly productivity, the issues persist. While the rates of publishing mission-related scholarship dramatically vary across the schools, the shared problem that undermines their collective impact are marginal placement, limited citation rates, and, when cited, being cited in marginal publications. As we explored, the same problems plague their in-house academic journals. Furthermore, there isn't evidence of the Christian Worldview law schools using scholarship as a means to create a collective movement. Not only are the faculties not producing at equitable rates, there are remarkably few examples of faculty collaborating or citing works between the institutions. Thus, as concluded in Chapter 6, anything identified in these data as evidence of an intellectual movement is largely coincidental and not coordinated.

While these data on scholarship can be characterized as problematic in terms of addressing the credibility deficit and supplying influential and potentially transformative *intellectual capital*, they can also be read in a more positive light. The fact that between 42% and 72% of the in-house journal articles are mission related, and that between 37% and 58% of the active faculty's scholarship is similarly mission related, is additional evidence of how the institutions are staying true to and realizing their Christian Worldview missions. The strength of the law schools' standing as an alternative voice and a point of significant resistance against the legal establishment, however, is diminished by their marginal placement and citation rates. Considering all of these factors, it is, therefore, not surprising that these law school faculty are not viewed as leading experts on mission-related issues within the legal academy, the Federalist Society, and the courts. In sum, there is evidence of their giving voice to a Christian Worldview, but little evidence of it reaching and shaping their desired audiences within the broader context of the Support Structure Pyramid.

The Overall Question of Value

Considering the collective difficulties in entering and influencing conversations in the full range of publics or audiences targeted by movements and the schools themselves, we are again returned to questions about whether it was worth creating new law schools. The *infiltration* model, for example, could serve as a means of producing *intellectual capital*, and the infiltrated institution's prestige could reasonably help with such work garnering more traction with scholarly, legal, and policy audiences. The rates of Blackstone faculty—faculty borrowed from other, more well-established institutions—being invited to Federalist Society events and being cited in or participating in litigation, and their engagement with media, suggest as much. The data from the range of comparative law schools further suggests that infiltration could be a means to both produce desired scholarship and more effectively circulate that scholarship. *Supplemental* institutions could also be used to try to facilitate connections between faculties and faculty members, fermenting *intellectual capital* for the movement along the lines of what the Federalist Society has done for secular conservatives.

All of these options could be lower-cost and higher-impact means to produce *intellectual capital*. Yet, in spite of this, the high financial costs, and the relative predictability of the struggles the schools would face starting up and in accruing credibility, a select group of Christian conservative patrons still opted to pursue the highest cost plan of creating *parallel alternative* institutions. Why?

Considering political history and the data from this book, two justifications stand out. First, the history of the most well-known and thoroughly studied litigation-driven movement—the Civil Rights Movement—suggested the value of the *parallel alternative* approach. Second, the Christian Right's self-perception further suggested the felt need of pursuing this strategy.

To the former point, Howard University School of Law's multiple connections to the Civil Rights Movement and that movement's litigation success present a strong prima facie case for creating new institutions (see Epp 1998; Johnson 2010; Kluger 2004; Tushnet 1987). The conceptualization of Howard University School of Law as an explicitly created movement support structure is clear from the start. Congress has written that the law school "opened in an effort to address the great need to train lawyers who would have a strong commitment to helping African-Americans secure and protect their newly established rights granted by the 13th and 14th amendments to the Constitution" (Congress 2009). John Mercer Langston, the law school's founder, repeatedly emphasized to the school's first students that their education endowed them with the responsibility to "lead the freedmen out from under laws, rules, regulations, and human conduct that denied, negated, or restrained the virtue of Liberty" (Smith 1999, 43).

Starting in the late 1920s and early 1930s, with the arrival of Charles Hamilton Houston, the school adopted an even more explicit support structure orientation. In Houston's words, "A lawyer's either a social engineer or . . . a parasite on society . . . A social engineer [is] a highly skilled, perceptive, sensitive lawyer who [understands] the Constitution of the United States and [knows] how to explore its uses in the solving of problems of local communities and in bettering conditions of the underprivileged citizens" (Jamar, n.d.). Houston went on to state that, "If a Negro law [school] is to make its full contribution to the social system it must train its students and send them [into situations to apply pressure] . . . [This requires] a difference in emphasis with more concentration on the subjects having direct application to the economics, political and social problems of the Negro" (Smith 1999, 50).

By the mid-1930s, Howard professor James Madison Nabrit, Jr., had developed the first civil rights law school course in the United States. This course was intended "to discover what the law was in respect to minorities in this area of civil rights; second, to develop techniques for raising constitutional questions in respect to disabilities affecting minorities . . . and third, to separate those disabilities for which legislative action would be required for their elimination" (Smith 1999, 51). Nabrit's language here crystalizes Howard's status as a *parallel alternative* institution self-consciously serving as a support structure for the burgeoning Civil Rights Movement roughly sixty years after its creation.

That is, Howard was creating and sending resources into circulation in the pyramid, fueling Level 2 lawyers and, later, PILOs—primarily the NAACP's Legal Defense Fund—as they worked to bring cases to the nation's high court. The clear and deliberate interaction between Howard's law faculty, Level 2 actors, and the courts extends beyond Nabrit's class, as well. Dean William Henry Hastie, beginning in 1939, focused on enriching academic research occurring at the law school, "[helping] to establish a 'methodology by which a large volume of civil rights litigation was conducted out of the nexus of the Howard Law School [by] key black [faculty] ... [which] joined ranks to mold legal arguments which would have lasting effect on American law" (Smith 1999, 52–53). One year later, Howard Law graduate Thurgood Marshall helped established the NAACP's Legal Defense Fund and went on to lead the PILO for the next twenty-one years. Relatedly, Dean Hamilton Houston was "the mastermind behind the brilliant strategy that attacked the 'separate but equal doctrine,' which led to the destruction of legal segregation" (Howard University, n.d.).

In sum, then, Howard's role as an essential support structure for the Civil Rights Movement is clear and multifaceted. The Civil Rights Movement's success is as well. Linking the two, the *parallel alternative* approach to movement support structures seems like a promising one. This quick progression to a high-cost conclusion, however, ignores details that might suggest otherwise.

First, it must be noted that Howard University's law school was created and served as a movement support structure because other options did not exist. It is important—though somewhat obvious—to note that racism functionally eliminated the *infiltration* and *supplemental* strategies for obtaining such institutions. That is, racial exclusion from other law schools made it impossible to meaningfully infiltrate such institutions or to provide supplemental education for students already enrolled in them. Howard, therefore, served as a *parallel alternative* support structure for the Civil Rights Movement out of absolute necessity.

Over time, however, as access to other law schools became available, the number of strategic options for the Civil Rights Movement expanded. As this change in the greater political and cultural context altered the support structure options, it also affected Howard's efficacy as well as the greater movement's abilities to put meaningful capital into circulation in the Support Structure Pyramid. This leads to the second point that pushes against the allure of the high-cost *parallel alternative* strategy.

Starting in the 1960s, Howard began to face increased competition from other, and in some cases more broadly prestigious, law schools that were admitting increasing numbers of black students. In the language of the Support Structure Pyramid model, Howard's efficacy was destabilized by events in the wider political and social context. Somewhat ironically, but also as suggested in the previous discussion of the offered models, Howard was starting to lose ground as a support structure as a result of the advances fueled by their successful service for the Civil Rights Movement. As an example, Harvard Law School admitted 15 African American students in 1965, 22 in 1967, 40 in 1969, and 65 in 1971 (Kidder 2003, 10).

Increasingly, then, top-tier students could choose to attend more traditionally elite law schools over historically black law schools like Howard. Seen in terms of producing *human capital*, analyzing black judges who graduated from the 1970s until the 1990s revealed that only 4.8% graduated from historically black law schools. Exhibiting a similar decline is the fact that only 10% of black attorneys listed in the *Who's Who Among Black Americans* who graduated during this period gained their degree from a historically black law school. For the top 1,000 black attorneys ranked in the same study, only 20% graduated from historically black law schools—a significant number, but one dwarfed by black lawyers graduating from other institutions (Ehrenberg 1996, 118).

Coupled with this increased competition, Howard's government funding has significantly declined over time, destabilizing its financial base (Hunter-Gault 2014). To remain viable and competitive amid these challenges, Howard continues to advertise and define itself via its unique and historic social change mission and tangible accomplishments. It has arguably, however, never been able to reclaim the efficacy it experienced as a support structure in the 1930s through the 1960s.

A closer attention to the rise and subsidence of Howard as a support structure should lead to the conclusion that it may not be the best way to produce legal movement capital. In sum, Howard rose as a support structure out of necessity born from rigid racist exclusion, but its centrality subsided as other options opened up and presented their own advantages. This suggests that movements can be well served by those other options if they are available to them.

Returning to the Christian Right, this book's early chapters show how Christian conservatives have felt themselves barred from entry into traditional law schools, and thus patrons may have felt that their only option was to create new institutions. While this adversity lens is commonly found in Christian conservative circles and forwarded by these very patrons, the perceived exclusion certainly does not rise to the formal and violent levels of exclusion that spurred Howard's creation and ascent as a support structure.

Christian conservative patrons may have found it challenging to infiltrate some existing law schools, but they likely could have found avenues into others. What's more, Christian conservative students could definitely formally access existing law schools, and so a *supplemental* strategy that was unavailable to African Americans could have been pursued. As suggested by Teles's (2008) work on the law and economics movement and the Federalist Society, a robust Christian conservative *supplemental* approach could reasonably lead to increased future infiltration options. Regardless, these options were not initially pursued.

Two additional related features also arguably added to the desire to create separate institutions. Along with the feeling of exclusion, Christian conservatives clearly see existing institutions as being part of the deeply problematic changes that they are seeking to reverse. Given that, the earlier discussed fears of dilution and the lack of control presented by the *infiltration* and *supplemental* approaches are warranted. As a reminder, Ave Maria's law school was created because of just such perceived insurmountable flaws in existing institutions.

Second, as Chapters 2 and 3 show, Christian Right patrons have a well-established history of creating their own institutions regardless of what already exists. That is, there is a history of creating institutions that are the extension of a strong central leader who seeks to maximize control. Such leaders, and by extension their institutions, are naturally wary of collaborating with others or ceding control. This repeated apprehension, then, works against seeing *infiltration* and *supplemental* strategies as viable options. What's more, at Regent and Liberty, the law schools could be seen as logical expansions of the already existing University, further helping to obscure alternative means to developing support structures.

Whatever the exact combination of factors that led to intense investment in *parallel alternative* institutions over other options may be in each instance, the book's case studies have shown that while the strategy affords relative control, it is constrained and hindered in a multitude of ways. As each means to a support structure has shown, at every turn there are tensions. Increased control is often in tension with means to credibility capital and influence, and credibility and influence can be in tension with fidelity to one's motivating values.

Movement actors, thus, need to ask what they seek most from the institutions they create. Do they see more value in being the prophet proclaiming truth, but facing the likelihood of speaking from the margins, or do they want to seek change from the inside where they may have to temper their expectations, language, and actions in various ways that may be uncomfortable or otherwise problematic? Finally, do they have enough elemental resources to try to pursue both simultaneously, and if so, can they do so harmoniously, or will more tensions arise with the proliferation of different institutions?

Looked at as a whole, creating new *parallel alternative* institutions was and is likely only the best option in extreme circumstances. The specific histories and perspectives of the Christian Right as a movement, therefore, go far in explaining why the highest-cost option was pursued at the outset even when lower-cost and effective alternatives existed. As a more generalizable point, then, answering why the CCLM pursued the routes it did pushes researchers to pay close attention to movement histories and actors in order to understand the choices they make, and the consequences that follow. Just as this book argues for a thick understanding of support structures, then, it also argues for deeply contextual understandings of movements.

In service of the desire for depth, complexity, and contextual embeddedness, we will end by considering one more way to respond to questions of success with these case studies. Looking beyond the legal audience and toward the other audiences and publics that the CCLM is speaking to, we must also consider how these CCLM institutions fit within the Christian Right and the greater conservative movement. In other words, while the four case studies have had variable success in the terms measured so far, can they be seen as valuable within conservatism and the Christian Right?

CCLM Support Structure Success within the Christian Right

The Christian Right started as a politically naïve outsider movement in the late 1970s and early 1980s that was not initially welcomed by the whole Republican Party, but it rapidly rose to prominence and power within conservatism and the GOP. It is not an exaggeration to claim that in doing so, it is one of the greatest political success stories in modern American politics. To this point, as Christopher Baylor (2017) argues, "Republican politicians and party officials before 1980 showed little or no interest in changing party positions to win the votes of cultural conservatives" (143). Since then, though, the Christian Right has successfully worked to increase their power within the party. Thus, Republican political candidates now treat "cultural conservatives as if they were a necessary constituency . . . no longer viewed . . . as optional" (174).

The Christian Right's precipitous rise from marginalization to centrality came as a result of a savvy understanding of political opportunities and access points to power within traditional electoral politics. Fueled by grassroots staffing and state-level activism, and guided by the expertise of groups like Pat Robertson and Ralph Reed's Christian Coalition, Christian conservatives organized and infiltrated the GOP. Again citing Baylor's work, in the 1990s, "cultural conservatives were well-organized . . . Furthermore, they were poised to provide the campaign with the specialists and unpaid volunteers necessary to any presidential campaign" (185). As a result, at the national level, "by 1993, religious conservatives controlled 38 of 58 Republican central committees" (Grossman & Hopkins 2016, 89). At the state level, "measures of Christian Right influence in the states shows an increase over time, with twenty-two states reporting strong influence of the Christian Right in Republican state politics by 2008" (Conger 2018, 96). What, then, was once a loose collection of political novices has since resulted in Christian conservatives being "ingrained into all levels of the party apparatus" (Lewis 2019).

As a sign of their continued investment in activism as a successful means to influence and power, "in 2016, white evangelicals were the religious group with the greatest number of party activists," and their priorities are reflected in GOP platforms and policy pursuits (Lewis 2019). The group's centrality to the GOP is further underscored by their support for candidate and President Trump and the administration's subsequent catering to their interests (Lewis 2019; WVLT 2019). While Trump's relationship with evangelicals is not monolithic (Galli 2019), " . . . evangelical Republican activists are still the 'life of the party'" (Layman & Brockway 2018, 43).

Given this, the Christian Right's path to political power is clearly and primarily understood as running through traditional electoral politics. The path to influence and power in the judicial sphere, however, is significantly different. While the former runs off of popular mobilization, the latter is exclusive and deeply elitist. The legal sphere is one of complex rules, formality, mediated involvement, and limited access points. As a result, it requires highly specialized elites with specialized training—lawyers—to gain access and to effectively function within this sphere (Kagan 2003). The emphasis on required specialization, training, and skill primes it to be a forum that recognizes and rewards traditional signs of prestige. What's more, while popular support is an asset, it is not a requirement in the "juridical field" (Bourdieu 1987).

The judicial realm's institutional features have motivated this book's forms of assessment, and, thus, the case studies have appeared variably effective in accruing influence and power. Blackstone, by adhering most closely to the traditional requirements of the "juridical field," appears most successful. The law schools, on the other hand, face far more challenges and experienced mixed—at best—success as new arrivals that more overtly reject or otherwise challenge a broader range of the "body of internal protocols and assumptions, characteristic behaviors and self-sustaining values" collectively recognized as the *internal politics of the profession* (Bourdieu, 1987, 806).[7]

Compared as a whole alongside the Christian Right's traditional political institutions and measures of success, we might come to the dual conclusions that the case study institutions are variably—at best—effective within the legal sphere and are far less successful when compared with the Christian Right's traditional political institutions and efforts. While these conclusions are supported and justified in many ways over the course of this book, ending there overlooks other roles that the case study institutions play within the Christian Right's internal, popularly driven, political and cultural ecosystem. As within the legal academy more generally, but with far more potency, these institutions stand as symbols of resistance. Relatedly, they also help to fuel the "culture war" issues that help motivate and educate the Christian Right's rank-and-file voters.

As we have repeatedly noted, the idea of being under attack by the broader culture is a prominent part of the conservative white evangelical political identity—and, similarly, the larger GOP political identity (Delehanty et al. 2019; Grossman & Hopkins 2016; Whitehead et al. 2018). In Kevin Den Dulk's assessment, "over the past two decades, the GOP could have advanced an inclusive strategy . . . But the Republican Party took a different path . . . It doubled-down on an exclusivist approach that highlights the threats that new social forces represent to a Judeo-Christian America" (2018, 64–65). For an audience primed to see the country's defining identity as Christian, and that identity as being under attack, these schools are evidence of fighting back. If, then, the Christian Right's activists and rank-and-file voters are centered as the case study institutions' audience, these Christian Worldview institutions are more clearly understood as successes.

The traditional legal world may not see much value in the schools, the scholarship, and the other products produced by these support structures, but the popular Christian Right audience can. In the words of Grossman and Hopkins,

> Republican perceptions of widespread bias in the mainstream media and academic community encourage party members to view themselves as engaged in an ideological battle with a hostile liberal establishment, turning even their choice of news sources into a conscious act of conservative self-assertion. Consumers of conservative media are exposed to a steady flow of content that further promotes this view, even warning that the Republican Party leadership is itself prone to intellectual corruption by this establishment and therefore requires vigilant ideological policing. (2016, 132)

Regent and Liberty occupy a significant space in the Christian conservative community as fortresses in this "ideological battle with a hostile liberal establishment" (Grossman & Hopkins 2016, 132). Regent has been called the "Harvard of the Religious Right," and Liberty has touted itself as the largest Christian university in the world (Cox 1995; Jenkins 2018). Liberty University's hosting speeches from both candidate and President Trump, Jerry Falwell Jr.'s closeness to Trump, as well as his Trump-style of attacking of critics have only helped raise the University's and, by extension, the law school's profile for this constituency (McDonald 2019; Ambrosino 2019). The popular awareness of these universities, their law schools, and related Christian PILOs can serve as an assurance that Christian conservatives are not alone in this fight. While these rank-and-file conservative Christians need to police Republican leaders, they are joined in doing so by these institutions.

More overtly, the "explicitly conservative media ecosystem" also provides forums in which the law school faculty, alumni, and other affiliates of the case study institutions can serve as experts since, as further noted by Grossman and Hopkins (2016), "we also find differences in the content . . . of information sources on each side, which reinforce appeals to ideology among Republicans" (132). In understanding the extent of the opportunities open to those affiliated with these support structure institutions, it is important to note that conservative media is not limited to Fox News. Rather, Fox was preceded by decades of Christian conservative media (Dochuk 2012). One need only recall where many of the founding patrons in the Christian Right and the CCLM accrued their substantial financial resources.

As a result, while figures such as Jay Sekulow make regular appearances on Fox News, he also has his own radio show with "Jay Sekulow Live!," regular access to Pat Robertson's Christian Broadcasting Network and the popular 700 Club. Beyond this prominent example, there are a variety of others. As Den Dulk (2008) has elsewhere argued, the major legal organizations within the CCLM are best referred to as "advocacy conglomerates" since their work extends beyond the courtroom and into politics and the public via media and other resources that target the broader

Christian conservative community. Therefore, while the case study affiliates may not stand to have many opportunities to access mainstream media (see Chapter 5), the vast network of Christian and secular conservative media outlets provide ample opportunity for them to serve as experts for this public.

By serving as symbols of ideological defiance and by directly and indirectly speaking to Christian conservatives, as well as the more generally conservative community, these support structures can also help keep the core of the Christian Right's real political power mobilized. That is, while the evidence of traditional influence within courts and the narrower legal community is mixed, the schools' and Blackstone's continued existence stands to support the Christian Right and the GOP's continued investment in the "culture wars."

Political scientists interested in religion and politics have wondered if the Christian Right's ascent within the GOP, its increased institutionalization, and the accompanying "involvement with views that deviate from those held by members of the Christian Right . . . may in turn precipitate attitudinal changes among rank-and-file members of conservative Christian (and other) organizations as the natural course of social influence processes" (Djupe et al. 2018, 188). Instead of realizing the "inclusion moderation thesis," however, evidence has mounted that the Christian Right's elites, institutions, and popular membership have stayed true to their motivating visions (Lewis 2019). Rather than Christian conservatives being pulled to the GOP's center, the Christian Right has been able to draw the GOP closer to it. Citing the work of Stratos Patrikios (2013) and Michele Margolis (2018), Lewis (2019) further notes that, "in political life, evidence suggests that evangelical and Republican identities have become 'fused.' This finding has only enhanced the research that suggests that partisanship might also shape one's evangelical affiliation, with Republicans being more likely to attach to conservative religious life."

Whether from a classroom lectern, an interview desk, or the courtroom, these support structures now stand alongside the proliferation of Christian Right and other conservative political and cultural institutions that help form a comprehensive separate partisan universe. In creating this comprehensive parallel institutional world, the Christian Right has succeeded in fighting its way into the Republican Party establishment, educating white evangelicals as to why they should care about a broader range of traditional conservative policy issues, and, simultaneously, bringing the GOP closer to those same white evangelical elites and voters (Deckman et al. 2017; Grossman & Hopkins 2016; Layman 2001; Lewis 2017).

Christian Worldview law schools and training programs are then possibly best understood as the most recent addition to this longer process. They are new institutions built to train and house new types of ideological experts who offer new expertise to first feed the Christian conservative community, and then maybe later conservatives and the more general political and legal publics. As of now, their greatest contributions are in serving as symbols of the Christian Right's earnest and increasingly comprehensive investment in completely entering the political and cultural fight. Thus, by staying true to their Christian Worldview vision, CCLM support structures present themselves as another resource to help Christian conservative elites and voters to stay true to the same. Removed from the wider legal political world, and seen in their more insular one, there is little space to question the value and worth of these institutions regardless of their form or costs.

Appendix A

DATA COLLECTION AND METHODS

Interviews and Participant Observation

Between April 2015 and April 2016, we conducted forty-two semi-structured interviews with faculty, staff, and students and engaged in participant observation at each of the three primary institutions (Regent Law, Ave Maria School of Law [AMSL], Liberty Law School) and at two of our secondary sites, Blackstone Legal Fellowship and Notre Dame Law School. These interviews helped us better understand each organization's history and mission; better understand how their histories potentially relate to divisions between the Christian and secular conservative legal movements; and to gauge what draws students and faculty to these schools and programs, with particular interest in understanding how these actors see (or do not see) these institutions and their own actions as relating to the Christian conservative legal movement. With the exception of one interviewee who wanted to be on record (Herbert Titus), all interviewees were anonymized. Our interview protocols, which were approved by the Institutional Review Boards of Pomona College and University of Denver (IRB Protocol #638536-2), are in Appendix B. All interviewees signed consent forms and agreed to participate in this research (consent forms are on file with authors).

Document and Artifact Collection (Chapters 3–5)

We constructed a database of over 800 primary institutional documents housed, coded, and analyzed using Atlas.ti qualitative data management software. In addition to founding documents, mission statements, and all publicly available promotional and Web material over time, and media articles about each institution over the life span of its existence, this database includes curricular data (required classes, electives, concentrations offered, syllabi for courses, readings and textbooks assigned, clinical opportunities, internship opportunities, detailed course outlines purchased through OutlineDepot), student life data (lists of student groups and their leadership, events sponsored by student groups, publications), faculty biographies (demographic information on faculty, degrees and law schools attended, professional activity and memberships), 990 forms filed with the IRS, reports from the American Bar Association and *U.S. News & World Report*, and ethnographic artifacts collected at each site (photographs of campus, syllabi, required reading, and booklists for courses).

Human Capital—Alumni Employment Data (Chapters 4 and 5)

Because we were only able to distribute our alumni survey to AMSL despite initial agreement from all three schools, we had to get creative in tracking down alumni to see where they were employed. Using graduation lists obtained from our visits to campus and cross-referencing these with the annual graduation programs from AMSL, Liberty Law, and Regent Law, we searched for alumni employment between June 2015 to August 2015 on the Web using a combination of Linked-In Recruiter, Facebook alumni groups, Martindale, and name-based Google searches. This search returned results for 1,580 Regent Law alumni (~48%), 649 AMSL alumni (~43%), and 490 Liberty Law alumni (~52%). Percentages of Regent Law alumni were calculated based on the Regent Law website self-report available at https://www.regent.edu/school-of-law/admissions-aid/ (accessed October 2, 2018). AMSL alumni percentages were calculated based on email correspondence with Amy Howarth, director of alumni relations at AMSL on October 4, 2018 ("we have 1,515 alumni"). Liberty Law alumni percentages are based on Liberty Law's "Class Profiles" from 2007 to 2017 available at https://www.liberty.edu/law/class-profiles/ (accessed October 2, 2018).

After identifying alumni and their occupation, we coded for the type of legal job or sector using the following code list:

- Clerk—working as a clerk for a judge
- Government Federal—working for the federal government/a federal agency
- Government State—working for the state government
- Government Local—working for local government
- Higher Education—professors, administrators, etc., working for colleges, universities, law schools
- In-House Counsel—working as a lawyer for a corporation

- Judge—judges and magistrates at any level
- Private practice—Working in a law firm or solo private practice
- Military Legal—in military in some sort of legal capacity (JAG, etc.)
- Public Interest Law—working in a public interest law firm
- State Attorney—an attorney for a state
- Policy—working for an organization that targets government policy advocacy/ lobbying
- Non-JD Legal—a job that does not require a JD but is in the legal field, like a paralegal
- Non-JD Non-Legal—job that does not require a JD and is not directly related to law/politics
- Unemployed—not currently working but looking for a job.

We also coded the location of their place of employment at the time of search by region using U.S. Census categories (North/South/Midwest/Mountain/Pacific/ International). Additionally, we collected available information about where each alumnus obtained their undergraduate degrees and coded for type of undergraduate institution ("Christian" or "Secular" and "Public" or "Private") as well as the regional location of their undergraduate institution (using the same U.S. Census categories).

Survey Data from Alumni Survey (Chapters 4 and 5)

With the help of our project consultant Dr. David Glick (Boston University, Political Science), we conducted a Web-based survey of alumni of Ave Maria School of Law, which was in the field from January 29, 2018, to February 25, 2018. See Appendix C for the survey instrument. While we initially had agreement at all three primary institutions to conduct the survey, Ave Maria was the only one that followed through on our agreement in the end. The survey was conducted using Qualtrics and distributed by the Alumni Affairs department at Ave Maria School of Law via their Constant Contact service. Ave Maria maintained the email list and communication with their alumni. We did not recruit participants directly. The Alumni office at Ave Maria sent an invitation (including the Qualtrics link) on Monday, January 29. They then sent a reminder on February 13. Ave Maria opted not to send any additional reminders. One hundred and twenty-three alumni completed the survey (there were a few other partials). According to our contact at Ave Maria, approximately 1,400 people were on the email list in January 2018. They currently have 1,515 alumni. Moreover, according to Constant Contact, 23% opened the email with the survey request. Thus, our survey represents about 9% of those in the alumni network at the time the survey was implemented and 38% of those who opened the email invitation.

Intellectual Capital—Works and Works Cited
(Chapter 6)

For the three primary case study institutions, we used the Internet Archive Wayback Machine to collect past faculty names. The earliest available lists of faculty profiles via this method are 1997 for Regent, 2000 for Ave Maria, and 2005 for Liberty. The final year for faculty name collection was for the spring of 2018. These names were collected from the schools' active web pages. In terms of the comparative schools, we limited our faculty name collection to the faculty in the 2016–17 and 2017–18 school years. In order to accurately compare our three primary case study law schools with the eight selected case law schools, we similarly used a sample of the 2016–17 and 2017–18 faculty from Regent, Ave Maria, and Liberty's law schools. Finally, all of these faculty lists exclude Lecturers, Distinguished, Visiting, Library, and Clinic Professors.

Bibliographic information for all of the works listed as authored by these faculty, and then all of the works that cite these originally published works, were collected using a Web-scraping algorithm developed by our project consultant Dr. Jason Renn (Messiah College, Politics and International Relations). Dr. Renn created a script in R using functionality from the "rvest" software package. This script helped automate most of the data collection for authorship and citations. The main corpus for this automated collection process was HeinOnline. After research assistants helped identify author profile pages on HeinOnline, the script scraped metadata from these pages and parsed author name, article titles, journals, publication years, and the URL to the main works as well as pieces that cite this work. Human coders also examined the output of the machine-coded data for reliability. The most notable exclusion from this collection process are books (which are unlisted in HeinOnline but do appear in Google Scholar) as well as the soft limit of 100 to the number of search results that HeinOnline returns with some searches. Given this count, the limit was rarely, if ever, a factor in limiting results collected.

The same automated collection process was applied to collecting the universe of works published in the various schools' in-house law reviews. These law reviews consist of *Regent Journal of Law & Policy, Regent University Law Review, Ave Maria Law Review, Liberty Law Review,* and *Liberty, Life, and Family.* The data collection started at the first available issue on HeinOnline up to the collection date in June 2018. The collected articles were then coded for content. Articles were coded for content by reading titles, abstracts, and when needed, introductions. These materials were then coded as "explicitly religious" (i.e., with the work's question or subject dealing directly with the religion clauses or religious liberty statutes such as the Religious Freedom Restoration Act and the Religious Land Use and Institutionalized Persons Act), "implicitly religious" (i.e., with the work's question or subject concerning a non-religious issue such as free speech or employment law but still having clear ties to religious or traditionally Christian Right issues such as abortion or religious discrimination), or "secular" (i.e., with the work's question or subject being non-religious and having no clear or immediate ties to religious issues or the Christian Right). This coding process had the added benefit of allowing for verifying the attribution accuracy of the collected articles and cases. In the analysis, explicitly and implicitly religious categories were collapsed into one category labeled as "mission" publications. Beyond this substantive coding, all relevant faculty publications, in-house law review publications, and citing of academic works were coded for prestige using a 2018 Wiley/Clarivate Analytics-produced rank-ordered impact factor list of 147 law journals.

Analysis of the coded data for scholarly works/works cited and in-house law journals was performed by our project consultant Dr. Seth Masket (University of Denver, Political Science). Dr. Masket used Excel and Stata to produce the basic descriptive statistics employed in Chapter 6.

Case Participation and Litigation Activity (Chapter 7)

Faculty name lists for the three primary schools (see previous descriptions for how these lists were collected and curated) were also used in searches for case participation and citation in state and federal litigation via Bloomberg Law. Project consultant Roger Huddle (J.D., Berkeley Law) searched faculty names as keywords (e.g., as John w/2 Smith or "John C. Smith") in "U.S. Courts Only" (options selected: Combined Courts, Court Opinions, Court Briefs, Other Pleadings, & Court Publications) in the Bloomberg Law database. The data was collected between May 2018 and January 2019. Once records were gathered, all the litigation participation data was recorded in an Excel spreadsheet. The case participation type was coded as "counsel of record," "amicus curiae," or as a "citation" in a brief or opinion. The level of court deciding the case was also coded ("state" or "federal") as was the year of the case. The issue being litigated was recorded (e.g., "tax," "marriage," "free speech") and coded using the same coding scheme as we employed with the scholarship ("explicitly religious," "implicitly religious," or "secular"). This data was then aggregated to produce the descriptive statistics of faculty participation in litigation in Chapter 7.

INTERVIEW PROTOCOLS

Faculty and Administrator Protocol

1. What made you decide to pursue a career in law?
   a. Did you consider any alternative careers or career paths?
   b. How did your family and other members of your social circle respond to your decision to attend law school and potentially pursue a career in law?
2. Why did you choose the law school that you did?
3. What was your experience like in law school?
   a. Did you find the curriculum, faculty, and/or student body welcoming, neutral, or hostile to your beliefs as a Christian?
   b. Were you a member of any clubs or associations?
      i. If so, why those clubs/organizations?
      ii. Did your experience with them influence your career path?
4. How important do you consider your religious faith to be?
   a. How, if at all, would you describe your faith as influencing your life?
   b. How, if at all, would you describe your faith as influencing your career choices?
5. How did you end up here [at Christian law school]? Did you consider any other schools or opportunities? What factors influenced your decision to come work here?
6. How would you describe the experience of teaching and working here?
7. How do you think that your life would be different if you were at a secular law school?
   a. Do you think it would be difficult for Christian Lawyers to teach and thrive in a mainstream or non-Christian law school?
   b. Do you think mainstream law schools have become more or less welcoming/accepting of the distinctly Christian view of law and lawyering over time?
      i. What, from your perspective, is driving that?

8. From your experience, what draws *other* faculty members to [this school]?
9. Why do you think [insert Christian law school] was founded when it was?
    a. Why weren't many of these kinds of schools established earlier, during the big law school boom?
    b. Why has it been just in the last thirty years?
10. What are the main components—curricular, clinical, cultural, etc.—that make your institution distinctly Christian?
    a. Which of these, do you think, has been most successful in both attracting and preparing lawyers to practice law in a distinctly Christian or faith-based way?
    b. How do you understand your role in terms of preparing students as lawyers and/or as distinctly Christian lawyers?
11. From your experience, what draws the majority of students to [this school]?
    a. Are there many students who are not drawn by the religious mission? That is, do you have students, like at Georgetown or Notre Dame, who see it as a law school only, and not as a Christian law school?
12. From your experience, what is your sense of what the majority of students hope to do after they graduate?
    a. Do many of the students you come across express an interest in public service and/or public policy?
    b. If so, what opportunities does your institution/law school provide for them to train to use their skills in that way?
13. Do many of your students join the Federalist Society Student Chapter here?
    a. Do you see that as a way for them to become more plugged in to mainstream networks or, alternatively, do you think that Chapter is bringing the distinctly Christian viewpoint to a mostly libertarian-oriented organization?
    b. How often, if ever, do you interact with that network, either formally or informally?
    c. Are there other faculty here that do so with any frequency?
    d. Are there any other student organizations that you see as being particularly well suited to or adept at helping your student plug into a greater Christian legal practice and/or political network?
14. How would you describe the relationship between your institution/law school and [insert clinical training program here]?
    a. Is it a pretty good pipeline for careers in policy, public interest law, etc.?
    b. Are there any other good pipelines for careers in policy, public interest law, etc.?
15. Finally, where do you see the biggest impact of your law school or of Christian law schools more generally? In other words, if these kinds of schools did not exist, how might the legal profession, legal culture or the law be any different today? How might it be different thirty years from now?

Student Protocol

1. What made you decide to attend law school?
2. Do you plan on pursuing a career in law?
   a. Did you consider any alternative careers or career paths?
   b. What do your family and other members of your social circle think about your decision to attend law school and potentially pursue a career in law?
3. How did you end up here at [Ave Maria/Regent/Liberty]?
   a. Did you consider any other schools?
   b. What factors influenced your decision to come here?
4. How important do you consider your religious faith to be?
   a. How, if at all, would you describe your faith as influencing your life?
   b. How, if at all, would you describe your faith as influencing your career choices?
5. In what ways do you think it would have been different for you to pursue your education in a non-Christian law school?
6. What are the main components—curricular, clinical, cultural, etc.—that make [Ave Maria/Regent/Liberty] particularly attractive for aspiring Christian lawyers?
   a. Which of these, do you think, has been most successful in both attracting and preparing aspiring Christian lawyers like yourself?
7. What is your sense of what the majority of students hope to do after they graduate?
   a. Do many of the students you come across express an interest in public service and/or public policy?
   b. If so, what opportunities does your institution/law school provide for them to train to use their skills in that way?
8. What is or are the most desired internships or clinical experiences here on campus?
9. What would you say is the most popular student organization on campus?
   a. What kinds of events do they hold/activities do they engage in?
   b. Why do you think that they are the most popular?
10. Do many students join the Federalist Society Student Chapter here?
    a. What kinds of events do they hold?
    b. How often, if ever, do you interact with that network, either formally or informally?
11. How would you describe the relationship between your law school and [insert clinical training program here]?
    a. Is it a pretty good pipeline for careers in policy, public interest law, etc.?
    b. Are there any other good pipelines for careers in policy, public interest law, etc.?

12. If you could describe your ideal post–law school job or career, what would it be?
    a. In what ways has your law school prepared you well for that job—in terms of coursework, clinical programs, internships, alumni connections, or otherwise?
    b. If you do not plan on a career in public service or public interest law, do you intend to serve a cause in any other capacity (e.g., dedicating pro bono hours, etc.)?
13. Finally, if you had to name two or three real strengths of your law school, what would they be?
    a. Any weaknesses or areas for improvement?

Appendix C

ALUMNI SURVEY INSTRUMENT

Q1 Describe your current employment status by checking the appropriate box below.

☐ Full time
☐ Part time
☐ Not employed

Q2 What type of organization are you employed by? (select one option only)

○ Solo practice
○ Private law firm
○ Federal government (including judiciary)
○ State or local government (including judiciary)
○ Legal services or public defender
○ Public interest organization
○ Other non-profit organization
○ Educational institution
○ Professional service firm (e.g., accounting, investment banking, consulting)
○ Other Fortune 1000 industry/service
○ Other business/industry
○ Labor union, trade association
○ Other (Please Specify:) _____

Q3 What is the name of your current primary employer?

Q4 If you are practicing law, how many hours of pro bono work did you perform during the last 12 months?

Q5 Do you approach any organization in order to find pro bono cases? Select all that apply.

☐ ADF (Alliance Defending Freedom)
☐ ACLU (American Civil Liberties Union)
☐ ACLJ (American Center for Law and Justice)
☐ Federalist Society
☐ I find pro bono cases in other ways: (Please explain:) _____
☐ Not applicable

Q6 From where did you receive your undergraduate degree?

Q7 When did you receive your law degree?

Month
Year

Q8 From which law school did you receive your law degree?

Q9 What was your law school class rank?

○ Top 10%
○ Top 11–25%
○ Second quarter of class (Top 26–50%)
○ Third quarter of class (Top 51–75%)
○ Fourth quarter of class (Top 76–100%)
○ Don't know

Q10 Did you participate in an honors program or track in law school?

○ Yes
○ No
○ NA / Law school did not have one

Q11 What were the three most important goals behind your decision to attend law school? Please check the top three.

☐ Intellectual challenge of the law
☐ Desire to help individuals
☐ Desire to develop a satisfying career
☐ Desire to defer entry into the job market
☐ Desire for financial security
☐ Becoming influential in a powerful profession
☐ Desire to build a set of transferable skills
☐ Desire to effect political or social change
☐ Other (Please specify:) _____

Q12 What primarily drew you to your law school? Select the top three reasons.

☐ Prestige
☐ Location
☐ Perceived ideological orientation
☐ Fit with the mission
☐ Specific program offered (Please specify) _____
☐ Specific clinical or other practical offerings (Please specify) _____
☐ Other (Please specify) _____

Q13 To what extent did your law school experience match your expectations?

○ Exceeded my expectations
○ Met my expectations
○ Failed to meet my expectations

Q14 Which of the following activities did you participate in during law school? Please check all that apply.

☐ General law review
☐ Other law review
☐ Moot court
☐ School government
☐ Political advocacy group
☐ The Federalist Society, Student Division
☐ The American Constitution Society, Student Division
☐ Public interest law group
☐ Political party
☐ Other (Please specify:) _____

Q15 Did you ever apply to the Blackstone Legal Fellowship while in law school?

○ Yes
○ No

Q16–Q17 are only displayed to those who said they <u>applied</u> to the Blackstone Legal Fellowship

Q16 What were you hoping to gain from your experience? Please select all that apply in rank order by putting a number next to each that applies. Put "1" next to the most important. Leave all that you do not think are pertinent blank.

_____ Exposure to curriculum that was not provided at my home law school
_____ Networking connections for my career
_____ Social connections with likeminded religious law students and lawyers
_____ Practical professional skills training
_____ Other (please briefly specify):

Q17 Did you participate in the Blackstone Legal Fellowship program while in law school?

O Yes
O No

Q18–Q24 are only displayed for those who said they <u>participated</u> in the Blackstone Legal Fellowship

Q18 How did your Blackstone curricular experience measure against your expectations?

O Exceeded expectations
O Met my expectations
O Failed to meet my expectations
O Other (please briefly specify) _____

Q19 How did your Blackstone networking experience measure against your expectations?

O Exceeded expectations
O Met my expectations
O Failed to meet my expectations
O Other (please briefly specify) _____

Q20 How did your Blackstone social connections experience measure against your expectations?

O Exceeded expectations
O Met my expectations
O Failed to meet my expectations
O Other (please briefly specify) _____

Q21 How did your Blackstone practical professional skills experience measure against your expectations?

O Exceeded expectations
O Met my expectations
O Failed to meet my expectations
O Other (please briefly specify) _____

Q22 Would you recommend Blackstone to current law students?

O Yes
O No

Q23 Are you in continued contact with Alliance Defending Freedom (ADF) through any of the following means? Please select all that apply:

☐ I receive emails from ADF
☐ Legal Education classes
☐ Pro Bono work
☐ I am an ADF Volunteer
☐ I am an ADF Allied Attorney
☐ I am an ADF Alumni Attorney
☐ I am an ADF Honor Corps member
☐ I am an ADF staff legal counsel
☐ I work in another capacity for ADF (please specify): _____

Q24 Do you list your Blackstone Legal Fellowship on your resume?

○ Yes
○ No

The following questions are displayed to everyone

Q25 Have you ever been admitted to the bar?

○ Yes
○ No

Q26 In which states have you been admitted to the Bar? Please use two-letter state abbreviations.

State 1
State 2
State 3
State 4
State 5

Q27 Have you had a judicial clerkship since law school?

○ Yes
○ No

This question is only displayed to those who indicated they have had a clerkship

Q28 Specify the type of court in which you served one or more judicial clerkship(s). Check all that apply.

☐ State trial
☐ State appellate
☐ Federal district

☐ Federal appellate
☐ United States Supreme Court
☐ Specialized court, e.g., patent, bankruptcy (Please specify) _____

Q29 Which three of the following do you believe were most helpful for you in obtaining your first job after law school? Check all that apply.

☐ Family and/or friends
☐ Law school classmates / Alumni network
☐ Response to an advertisement
☐ Law school's placement office
☐ On-campus interview process
☐ Hired following a summer position
☐ Hired following a part-time position held during law school
☐ Unpaid internship with first employer
☐ Recommendation of a law professor
☐ Experience in a judicial clerkship
☐ My law school's lawyering skills program
☐ The reputation of the law school I attended
☐ The reputation of the undergrad school I attended
☐ My participation in law journal or moot court
☐ Prior work experience
☐ Other (Please specify:)

Q30 We hear a lot of talk these days about liberals and conservatives. On most political issues, do you think of yourself as liberal, moderate, or conservative?

○ Liberal
○ Moderate
○ Conservative

Follow up for those that select "liberal" in Q30

Q31 Is that extremely liberal or somewhat liberal?

○ Extremely liberal
○ Somewhat liberal

Follow up for those that select "conservative" in Q30

Q32 Is that extremely conservative or somewhat conservative?

○ Extremely conservative
○ Somewhat conservative

Follow up for those that select "moderate" in Q30

Q33 Would you say that you are more on the liberal side or the conservative side?

○ Liberal side
○ Conservative side
○ Neither

Q34 Generally speaking, do you usually think of yourself as a Republican, Democrat, an Independent, or what?

○ Republican
○ Democrat
○ Independent
○ Other

Follow up for those that select "Republican" in Q35

Q35 Do you think of yourself as a strong Republican or a not very strong Republican?

○ Strong
○ Not very strong

Follow up for those that select "Democrat" in Q35

Q36 Do you think of yourself as a strong Democrat or a not very strong Democrat?

○ Strong
○ Not very strong

Follow up for those that select "Independent" or "Other" in Q35

Q37 Do you think of yourself as closer to the Republican Party or to the Democratic Party?

○ Closer to Republican
○ Neither
○ Closer to Democratic

Q38 Do you like President Donald Trump, dislike him, or neither like nor dislike him?

○ Like
○ Dislike
○ Neither like nor dislike

Follow up for those that select "Like" in Q38

Q39 Do you like him a great deal, a moderate amount, or a little?

○ Like him a great deal
○ Like him moderate amount
○ Like him a little

Follow up for those that select "Disike" in Q38

Q40 Do you dislike him a great deal, a moderate amount, or a little?

○ Dislike him a great deal
○ Dislike him moderate amount
○ Dislike him a little

Q41 Indicate whether you have participated in each of the following organizations. Check all in which you have participated.

☐ Political advocacy groups (Specify:) _____
☐ Law school alumni/ae associations
☐ American Bar Association
☐ State or local bar associations
☐ Substantive sections of bar associations (Specify:) _____
☐ The Federalist Society
☐ The American Constitution Society
☐ Other (Specify:) _____

Q42 Please name your top three means of professionally networking (responses may include, for example, organizational memberships, conferences, training, on-line social networking groups)

Networking method one
Networking method two
Networking method three

Q43 What is your racial/ethnic group? Check all that apply

☐ Black/African American
☐ Hispanic/Latino
☐ Native American/American Indian
☐ Asian/Pacific islander
☐ White/Caucasian
☐ Other (Specify:) _____
☐ Other (Specify:) _____

Q44 In what year were you born?

Year

Q45 Are you male or female?

○ Male
○ Female

Q46 What is your religious preference or affiliation?

○ Roman Catholic
○ Protestant—Denomination: _____
○ Jewish—Denomination: _____
○ Muslim—Denomination: _____
○ Other—Specify: _____
○ None

Q47 OPTIONAL Because of the importance of this study, we may be contacting you again for brief follow-up questions. Please provide your email address so that we can keep in touch with you, and keep you updated about the project. Your email address will only be used for correspondence directly related to our study.

○ My email address is: _____
○ I prefer not to be contacted

NOTES

Chapter 1

1. Letter from Felix Frankfurter, Professor, Harvard Law School, to Mr. Rosenwald (May 13, 1927) (Felix Frankfurter papers, Harvard Law School library), quoted in Jack and Jack (1989, 156).
2. Furthermore, the schools and training program used here each advertise their global ambitions and reaches. One can look to, for example, Regent's Center for Global Justice; Liberty's International Law Concentration; Ave Maria's "Links to International Catholic Entities involving AMSL Professors"; and ADF International's promotion of, and testimonials from, international students. The conservative Christian PILOs associated with Regent, Liberty, and Blackstone also have offices and active cases beyond the United States. Finally, Cichowski's (2016) study of "theoretically significant institutional factors that help us understand change in interest and advocacy group participation" in the European Court of Human Rights includes the Regent-connected PILO European Center for Law and Justice.
3. "Conscience and Religious Freedom Division | The Federalist Society." Accessed February 14, 2018. https://fedsoc.org/events/conscience-and-religious-freedom-division

Chapter 2

1. While many people may conflate fundamentalist and evangelical Christians, and many conservative Christians have adopted the evangelical moniker, they can be seen as distinct groups. This is especially true in the early to mid-twentieth century. A simple way of summarizing the division as used in this book is between evangelicals who were more open to collaboration and engagement with the wider world, and fundamentalists who were far less open to such prospects.
2. Also see Dochuk (2012) and Moreton (2010) regarding the importance of Christian colleges and universities for the creation of the Christian Right and the modern conservative coalition.
3. For more on the Christian Coalition's cultivation of the persecuted minority frame, see Williams (2010), pp. 227–35. For more on its power, see Klemp, Nathaniel, & Stephen Macedo, "The Christian Right, Public Reason, and American Democracy." In *Evangelicals and Democracy in America, Vol. 2: Religion and Politics*, edited by Steven Brint and Jean Reith Schroedel, 249–79. New York: Russell Sage Foundation, 2009; Ingersoll, Julie. "Mobilizing Evangelicals: Christian Reconstructionism and the Roots of the Religious Right." In *Evangelicals and Democracy in America, Vol. 2: Religion and Politics*, edited by Steven Brint and Jean Reith Schroedel, 179–208. Russell Sage Foundation, 2009; and Lewis, Andrew R.

The Rights Turn in Conservative Christian Politics: How Abortion Transformed the Culture Wars. Cambridge; New York: Cambridge University Press, 2017.

4. Emphasis in original. For more on this regarding conservatives as a whole, see Batchis, Wayne. *The Right's First Amendment: The Politics of Free Speech & the Return of Conservative Libertarianism.* 1st ed. Stanford, CA: Stanford Law Books, 2016.

5. For more on CCLOs pursuing litigation beyond their more narrowly conceived missions, see Hollis-Brusky, Amanda, and Joshua C. Wilson. "Playing for the Rules: How and Why New Christian Right Public Interest Law Firms Invest in Secular Litigation." *Law & Policy* 39, no. 2 (April 1, 2017): 121–41.

6. For a discussion of the Alliance Defending Freedom's openness to Judeo-Christian faiths, see Wilson (2016), Part II.

7. "NLF Staff." Accessed March 9, 2018. http://www.nlf.net/About/Staff.html; Alliance Defending Freedom. "Allies." Accessed March 9, 2018. http://www.adflegal.org/about-us/allies

8. For example, in 2007 they only had one attorney on staff. Alliance Defending Freedom. "NLF Staff," September 13, 2007. https://web.archive.org/web/20070913083031/http://www.nlf.net:80/About/Staff.html

9. For a more detailed description and analysis of the early Christian Right's legal resources, see Part II of Wilson, Joshua C. *The New States of Abortion Politics.* 1st ed. Stanford, CA: Stanford Briefs, 2016.

10. Alliance Defending Freedom. "Frequently Asked Questions—Alliance Defending Freedom." Accessed November 1, 2013. http://www.alliancedefendingfreedom.org/about/faq

11. Alliance Defending Freedom. "Our New Name—and The Reasons Why." Accessed March 13, 2018. http://www.adflegal.org/detailspages/blog-details/allianceedge/2017/10/18/our-new-name-and-the-reasons-why

12. However, it is important to note that ADF does still fund and supply other needed resources to litigation efforts pursued by lawyers who are not on staff at the organization.

13. This is a theme repeated in various venues in conservative Christianity. Conservative American Protestantism is, in part, defined by the continual process of new churches being founded as leaders and congregants break off from existing ones with which they find some point of conflict. New schools and colleges are founded for the same reasons, as are political organizations. Jerry Falwell and Pat Robertson's personal empires can be seen as interesting examples of this trend. Jerry Falwell's organizations offer Sunday school, parochial school, various social services, and higher education via Falwell's Liberty University. In the political sphere Falwell helped found and run the Moral Majority. As such, Falwell's empire illustrates the desire for strong central control and a lack of cooperation or burden sharing with others.

14. One can see the Rutherford Institute as a cautionary tale of a CCLM PILO that similarly refused to join forces with would-be allies, but that subsequently paid a heavy price at the hands of other Christian Right organizations. (Brown 2002, 36; Rosin 1998)

15. Teles's (2008, Chapters 4 and 6) discussion of Henry Manne's infiltrations of the University of Miami, Emory University, and ultimately George Mason University's law schools is a particularly good example of this strategy being employed to creating support structure institutions.

16. Given the number of existing Catholic law schools, infiltration would seem an especially attractive option for Tom Monaghan, even if Notre Dame specifically may not have been. As recounted in this book's introduction, however, Ave Maria School of Law's origin story is explicitly tied to the rejection of an existing Catholic law school.

17. "Critical mass" institutions are defined as those that have "a critical mass of adherents to inhabit all the main constituencies of the university to define, shape, and maintain its religious identity. This is often a minority of staff, but a strong minority." When considered on a four-point typology scale from most religious to least religious, they are below "Orthodox" institutions, which are "trying to assure a Christian account of life by requiring all its members to subscribe to a statement of belief so that there is a common commitment to the Christian

faith," but above "Intentionally Pluralist" and "Accidentally Pluralist" institutions. In order, Intentionally Pluralist institutions are defined as "respecting the relationship to the sponsoring tradition, ensuring that some members of this religious tradition are sprinkled around the institution, and ensuring that the main motivation of the institution is academic excellence and being inclusive of all," while Accidentally Pluralist ones have undergone full-scale secularization, and their religious history may be wholly unidentifiable (Arthur 2006, 31).

18. For more on the takeover of national Baptist organizations, see Lewis (2017).

19. Emphasis added.

20. For a discussion of the Christian Right's increasing embrace of Catholics, with mixed results, see First Things. "Evangelicals & Catholics Together: The Christian Mission in the Third Millennium | Various." Accessed June 26, 2018. https://www.firstthings.com/article/1994/05/evangelicals-catholics-together-the-christian-mission-in-the-third-millennium; Wilcox, Clyde, Mark J. Rozell, and Roland Gunn. "Religious Coalitions in the New Christian Right." *Social Science Quarterly* 77, no. 3 (1996): 543–58; and Bendyna, Mary, John C. Green, Mark J. Rozell, and Clyde Wilcox. "Catholics and the Christian Right: A View from Four States." *Journal for the Scientific Study of Religion* 39, no. 3 (n.d.): 321–32.

21. University of Notre Dame. "Patricia O'Hara // The Law School // University of Notre Dame." The Law School. Accessed May 3, 2018. https://law.nd.edu/directory/patricia-ohara/

22. Not surprisingly, like Baylor, there are also no religious requirements for law students. Undergraduates, however, are required to take two courses in theology, as well as two philosophy courses, one of which can be satisfied by a "Catholicism and the Disciplines" course (University of Notre Dame. "FAQ // Core Curriculum // University of Notre Dame." Core Curriculum. Accessed June 28, 2018. https://corecurriculum.nd.edu/starting-fall-2018/faq/).

23. It is unclear to what degree the lack of investment was also due to traditional divisions between conservative Protestants and Catholics. That said, in the case of Ave Maria, it is readily apparent that the rejection of Notre Dame was rooted in a belief that, in spite of its demonstrable conservatism and religious commitment, Monaghan and others viewed Notre Dame as not being truly Catholic.

24. Beyond this, some Notre Dame faculty, controversially, helped with the creation of Ave Maria.

25. However, one Notre Dame Blackstone alum interviewee spoke disparagingly of the program.

Chapter 3

1. Plaque outside of Regent University Administration Building. Virginia Beach, VA. Photo taken on April 12, 2016. On file with authors.

2. Plaque, "The Cape Henry Cross." Virginia Beach, VA. Photo taken on April 12, 2016. On file with authors.

3. Plaque, "Eternal Gospel Flame." Virginia Beach, VA. Photo taken on April 12, 2016. On file with authors.

4. Regent University School of Law. "About Us." Accessed June 20, 2018. https://www.regent.edu/school-of-law/about/

5. Ibid.

6. Ibid.

7. "Founding Dean of Ave Maria Law School Has Died." *News-Press*. March 26, 2016. Accessed July 11, 2018. https://www.news-press.com/story/news/2016/03/26/founding-dean-ave-maria-law-school-has-died/82309464/

8. "Ave Maria School of Law to Relocate to Southwest Florida." *Catholic News Agency*. February 21, 2007. Accessed July 11, 2018. https://www.catholicnewsagency.com/news/ave_maria_school_of_law_to_relocate_to_southwest_florida

9. See, generally, Internet Archive Wayback Machine. https://archive.org/web/

10. Ave Maria School of Law. "Mission Statement." February 15, 2001. Retrieved from Internet Archive Wayback Machine. http://web.archive.org/web/20010215170025/http://www.avemarialaw.edu/philosophy/mission.html (accessed July 28, 2018)

11. Ave Maria School of Law. "Mission Statement." Accessed June 28, 2018. https://www.avemarialaw.edu/campus-life/catholic-law-schools/

12. Thomas More Law Center. "History of the Law Center." Accessed July 11, 2018. https://www.thomasmore.org/history-of-the-law-center-1/

13. Ave Maria School of Law. Home web page. Accessed June 28, 2018. https://www.avemarialaw.edu/

14. Blackstone Legal Fellowship. "FAQ's." Accessed July 28, 2018. http://www.blackstonelegalfellowship.org/?page_id=1993

15. Alliance Defending Freedom. Form 990. "Program Service Accomplishments." Part III, Line 4C, p. 55. Accessed July 27, 2018. https://adflegal.blob.core.windows.net/mainsite-new/docs/default-source/documents/resources/support-resources/financials/990-public-adf-june-2017.pdf?sfvrsn=b97bba78_4

16. Blackstone Legal Fellowship. "Intern Overview." Accessed May 11, 2020. https://www.adflegal.org/training/blackstone

17. Alliance Defense Fund. Form 990, 2001. Page Two, Part III.' Accessed July 17, 2018. http://990s.foundationcenter.org/990_pdf_archive/541/541660459/541660459_200206_990.pdf#page=25

18. Helen V. Alvare, who is also on the Board of Governors for Ave Maria School of Law.

19. Dr. Francis Beckwith.

20. Dr. J. Budziszewski.

21. Alliance Defense Fund, Form 990, 2001. Page Two, Part III. .

22. Liberty University. "We the Champions." Accessed July 24, 2018. https://www.liberty.edu/champions/

23. Ibid.

24. Liberty University School of Law Foundations Hall. "History of the Rule of Law." Pamphlet on file with authors.

25. Liberty University School of Law. "LU School of Law Welcomes Its Inaugural Class." August 13, 2004. Accessed May 11, 2020. https://www.liberty.edu/law/uncategorized/lu-school-of-law-welcomes-its-inaugural-class/

26. Liberty University School of Law. "About Us." December 5, 2003. Retrieved from the Internet Archive Wayback Machine. Accessed July 28, 2018. http://web.archive.org/web/20031205185848/http://www.liberty.edu/Academics/Law/index.cfm?PID=4932

27. Liberty University School of Law. "About Us." Accessed July 25, 2018. http://www.liberty.edu/law/about-liberty-law-school/: "at Liberty Law, our uniquely tailored legal program taught with sound biblical principles will equip you in your pursuit of justice in your community and in the world. Choose from our 11 areas of specialization, Liberty University's 8 dual-degree programs, and our expansive experiential learning opportunities to add even more to your Liberty legal education."

28. Liberty University School of Law. "About Us"

29. "Liberty law school, Liberty Counsel launch religious liberty center." Baptist Press. October 24, 2003. Accessed May 11, 2020. http://www.bpnews.net/16933/liberty-law-school-liberty-counsel-launch-religious-liberty-center

30. For a detailed list of ABA rules and regulations for compliance, see ABA. Standards. Accessed July 26, 2018. https://www.americanbar.org/groups/legal_education/resources/standards.html

31. See, for example, the recent revocation of accreditation for Arizona Summit Law School. "27 March Public Notice of Arizona Summit on Probation." Accessed July 26, 2018. https://www.americanbar.org/content/dam/aba/administrative/legal_education_and_admissions_to_the_bar/council_reports_and_resolutions/March2017CouncilOpenSessionMaterials/

2017_march_public_notice_re_arizona_summit_probation.authcheckdam.pdf. See also Ward, Stephanie Francis. "Arizona Summit Loses Accreditation Approval, Which May Be a First for an Operating Law School." *ABA Journal*. June 11, 2018. Accessed July 26, 2018. http://www.abajournal.com/news/article/arizona_summit_loses_accreditation_approval_which_may_be_a_first_for_operat/ ("Arizona Summit, an InfiLaw school, was placed on probation in March 2017. According to the decision, the for-profit school was out of compliance with academic standards and admissions.")

32. *Holy Bible*, New International Version®, NIV® Copyright ©1973, 1978, 1984, 2011 by Biblica, Inc.® Used by permission. All rights reserved worldwide.

33. American Bar Association. Section of Legal Education and Admission to the Bar. "Council Decision Public Notice of Specific Remedial Action. Ave Maria School of Law." August 2016. Accessed July 26, 2018. https://www.americanbar.org/content/dam/aba/administrative/legal_education_and_admissions_to_the_bar/governancedocuments/2016_august_ave_maria_public_notice_of_specific_remedial_action.authcheckdam.pdf

34. Liberty University School of Law. "Honor Code." Section 8, Administrative Policies and Procedures. Accessed July 26, 2018. http://www.liberty.edu/media/1191/Law-School-Honor-Code.pdf

35. *Holy Bible*, New International Version. Accessed July 26, 2018. https://www.biblestudytools.com/luke/14-28.html

36. Moody's. "Moody's Downgrades Regent University to Baa3 Outlook Negative." Accessed July 27, 2018. https://www.moodys.com/credit-ratings/Regent-University-VA-credit-rating-804304580

37. Moody's. "Moody's Upgrades Liberty University to Aa3 Outlook Stable." Accessed July 27, 2018. https://www.moodys.com/credit-ratings/Liberty-University-VA-credit-rating-822321921

38. Federal Student Aid. An Office of the U.S. Department of Education. "Heightened Cash Monitoring." Accessed July 27, 2018. https://studentaid.ed.gov/sa/about/data-center/school/hcm

39. Alliance Defending Freedom, Form 990. Part III, Line 4C, p. 55.

40. Ave Maria School of Law. Form 990. Accessed July 27, 2018. https://projects.propublica.org/nonprofits/organizations/383519708

41. Alliance Defending Freedom, Form 990 Part III, Line 4C, p. 55.

42. Blackstone Legal Fellowship. "Frequently Asked Questions." Accessed July 27, 2018 http://www.blackstonelegalfellowship.org/?page_id=1993

Chapter 4

1. Jerry Falwell, Founder Liberty University and Liberty Law School as quoted in Anderson (2007): "The 10 Commandments cannot be posted in public places. Children cannot say grace over their meals in public schools. No prayers at football games and on the list goes, virtually driving God from the public square. And then, of course, Roe vs. Wade in the middle of all that . . . Now, the redefining of the family or the attempt to. So, all of this reinforced our belief that we needed to produce a generation of Christian attorneys who could, in fact, infiltrate the legal profession with a strong commitment to the Judeo-Christian ethic."

2. American Bar Association. "ABA Standards and Rules of Procedure for Approval of Law Schools 2017–2018. Chapter 2." Law School Governance. Accessed July 30, 2018. https://www.americanbar.org/content/dam/aba/publications/misc/legal_education/Standards/2017-2018ABAStandardsforApprovalofLawSchools/2017_2018_standards_chapter2.authcheckdam.pdf ("Consistent with sound educational policy and the Standards, a law school shall demonstrate by concrete action a commitment to diversity and inclusion by having a faculty and staff that are diverse with respect to gender, race, and ethnicity.")

3. Liberty University. "Doctrinal Statement, Statement of Professional Ethics, & Harassment and Discrimination Avoidance Policy." Accessed July 29, 2018. https://www.liberty.edu/

media/1312/hr_formsmanager_forms/Signoff%20for%20Doctrine,%20Ethics,%20&%20
Harassment-full%20version%20(01-2015).pdf

4. Regent University. "About Regent | Statement of Faith." Accessed July 29, 2018. https://www.
regent.edu/about-regent/vision-mission/

5. See American Association of University Professors. "1940 Statement of Principles on
Academic Freedom and Tenure." Accessed July 31, 2018. https://www.aaup.org/report/
1940-statement-principles-academic-freedom-and-tenure#B5

6. American Bar Association. "ABA Standards and Rules of Procedure for Approval of Law
Schools 2017–2018. Chapter 4. The Faculty, Standard 405(b)." Accessed July 30, 2018.
https://www.americanbar.org/content/dam/aba/publications/misc/legal_education/
Standards/2017-2018ABAStandardsforApprovalofLawSchools/2017_2018_standards_
chapter4.authcheckdam.pdf

7. American Bar Association. ABA Standards and Rules of Procedure for Approval of Law
Schools 2017–2018. Appendix. Accessed July 31, 2018. https://www.americanbar.
org/content/dam/aba/publications/misc/legal_education/Standards/2017-
2018ABAStandardsforApprovalofLawSchools/2017_2018_standards_appendices.
authcheckdam.pdf See also American Association of University Professors. "1940 Statement
of Principles on Academic Freedom and Tenure". Accessed July 31, 2018. https://www.aaup.
org/report/1940-statement-principles-academic-freedom-and-tenure#B5

8. Ibid, Footnote 5 ("Third 1970 comment: Most church-related institutions no longer need or
desire the departure from the principle of academic freedom implied in the 1940 "Statement,"
and we do not now endorse such a departure").

9. Regent University. Faculty Application. Accessed July 31, 2018. https://www.aaup.org/re-
port/1940-statement-principles-academic-freedom-and-tenure#B5; and https://www.re-
gent.edu/admin/hr/forms/faculty_application.pdf

10. Liberty University. Faculty Handbook 2018–2019. 3.3.2 "Statement on Principles of Academic
Freedom." At 20. Accessed May 11, 2020. https://www.liberty.edu/human-resources/wp-
content/uploads/sites/112/2019/11/2018-2019__Faculty_Handbook.pdf

11. Based on publicly available list of faculty posted on each institution's websites. These counts
excludes Lecturers, Distinguished, Visiting, Library, and Clinic Professors. The rankings of
JD-granting institutions taken from U.S. News & World Report, 2016.

12. These counts excludes Lecturers, Distinguished, Visiting, Library, and Clinic Professors. The
rankings were taken from U.S. News & World Report, 2016.

13. U.S. News & World Report. "Methodology: 2019 Best Law Schools Rankings." Accessed
July 31, 2018. https://www.usnews.com/education/best-graduate-schools/articles/
law-schools-methodology

14. Percentages based on a list of forty-four total Blackstone faculty accessed from Blackstone's list
of "Past Faculty" (retrieved Dec 1, 2015).

15. See Department of Education, Office of Civil Rights. "Nondiscrimination in Federally
Assisted Programs." Accessed August 2, 2018. https://www2.ed.gov/about/offices/list/ocr/
docs/racefa.html ("Title VI of the Civil Rights Act of 1964 [Title VI], which states that no
person in the United States shall, on the ground of race, color, or national origin, be excluded
from participation in, be denied the benefits of, or be subjected to discrimination under any
program or activity receiving Federal financial assistance.").

16. Regent University. Juris Doctor—Honors Program. Accessed August 2, 2018. https://www.
regent.edu/program/juris-doctor-jd-honors-program/

17. Liberty University School of Law. "Liberty Law Announces Honors Program to Reward
Academic Excellence." Accessed August 2, 2018. https://www.liberty.edu/law/news-and-
events/?artid=262745

18. Liberty University School of Law. "Liberty University School of Law Honors Program."
Accessed September 14, 2008. https://www.liberty.edu/law/index.cfm?PID=39723

19. Based on graduation date. Subset of alumni identified through LinkedIn, Facebook, Martindale, and name-based Google searches for lists of graduating classes). The "South" was determined by the U.S. Census categories and included undergraduate institutions in the following states: Delaware, Maryland, West Virginia, D.C., Virginia, Kentucky, Tennessee, Arkansas, Oklahoma, Texas, Louisiana, Mississippi, Alabama, Georgia, South Carolina, North Carolina, and Florida.

20. Law School Admissions Council. "June 2014–February 2017 LSAT Score Distributions." Accessed September 24, 2018. https://www.lsac.org/sites/default/files/legacy/docs/default-source/data-%28lsac-resources%29-docs/lsat-score-distribution.pdf

21. See U.S. News & World Report. "Methodology." Accessed September 24, 2018. https://www.usnews.com/education/best-graduate-schools/articles/law-schools-methodology

22. Ibid.

23. Regent University. Course Descriptions. Juris Doctor. Law 511. Accessed August 3, 2018. https://www.regent.edu/acad/schlaw/student_life/docs/coursedescriptions.pdf

24. Course notes. Regent Law School. Christian Foundations. Dean J. Brauch. Purchased from OutlineDepot.com (on file with authors).

25. Liberty University. Graduate Catalog. Law 501—Foundations of Law I. Accessed August 3, 2018. http://www.liberty.edu/index.cfm?PID=19959&action=courseDetail&CatID=14&CourseID=24

26. Liberty University. Graduate Catalog. Law 502—Foundations of Law II. Accessed August 3, 2018. http://www.liberty.edu/index.cfm?PID=19959&action=courseDetail&CatID=14&CourseID=25

27. Course notes. Liberty Law. Foundations of Law I. Professor Bruce Green. Fall 2005. Purchased from OutlineDepot.com (on file with authors).

28. Course notes. Liberty Law School. Foundations of Law II. Professor Rena Lindevaldsen. Spring 2011. Purchased from OutlineDepot.com (on file with authors).

29. Ave Maria School of Law. Course Schedule. Fall 2006, 3–520 (on file with authors).

30. Course notes. Criminal Law. Purchased from OutlineDepot.com (on file with authors).

31. Course Syllabus. Law 531. Constitutional Law I. Fall 2014. Professor Jeffrey C. Tuomala (on file with authors).

32. Course notes. Liberty Law School. Constitutional Law I. Fall 2007. Professor Jeffrey C. Tuomala. Purchased from OutlineDepot.com (on file with authors).

33. Course notes. Regent Law School. Family Law. Professor Lynne Marie Kohm. Purchased from OutlineDepot.com (on file with authors).

34. Course notes. Regent Law School. Property II. Professor Eric DeGroff. Spring 2004. Purchased from OutlineDepot.com (on file with authors).

35. Course Outline, Regent Law School. Contracts. Professor C. Scot Pryor. Purchased from OutlineDepot.com (on file with authors).

36. Ave Maria School of Law. "Curriculum." Retrieved from the Internet Archive Wayback Machine. Accessed September 14, 2008. http://web.archive.org/web/20011225202410/http://www.avemarialaw.edu/curriculum/religion.html

37. Course outline, Ave Maria School of Law. Criminal Law. Professor Eugene Millhizer. Purchased from OutlineDepot.com (on file with authors).

38. Liberty University School of Law. "Practical Skills – Center for Lawyering Skills." Accessed May 22, 2020. https://www.liberty.edu/law/academics/practical-skills-lawyering-skills/

39. The American Bar Association voted to change its reporting requirements for law school employment in 2015. See, e.g., https://www.insidehighered.com/quicktakes/2015/08/04/aba-tightens-rules-employment-reporting ("The ABA affirmed a decision from earlier this year that requires law schools, starting next year, to count school-funded positions and fellowships separately from other employment. Critics of this process claimed that schools with large fellowship programs had inaccurately inflated employment figures.")

40. Percentages calculated based on Regent Law website self-report available at https://www.regent.edu/school-of-law/admissions-aid/ (accessed October 2, 2018).
41. Percentages calculated based on email correspondence with Amy Howarth, director of alumni relations at Ave Maria Law School on October 4, 2018 ("we have 1,515 alumni")
42. Percentages calculated based on Liberty Law's "Class Profiles" from 2007 to 2017 available at https://www.liberty.edu/law/class-profiles/ (accessed October 2, 2018).
43. See, e.g., Regent University. School of Law News and Events. Accessed October 4, 2018. http://regentlawnews.blogspot.com/2010/09/regent-law-alumnus-faculty-in-news.html ("Virginia Governor Robert F. McDonnell appointed [Regent Law alumnus J. Neal] Insley the Virginia Department of alcoholic Beverage Control [ABC] chairman in May 2010"; http://regentlawnews.blogspot.com/2010/01/regent-alums-in-news.html ("Law alumnus '99 J. Jasen Eige has been appointed as counselor and senior advisor to Governor-elect Bob McDonnell").
44. See Texas House of Representatives. "Biography." Accessed October 4, 2018. https://www.house.texas.gov/members/member-page/?district=93
45. See Drew Menard. "Alumnus poised ot take seat in Texas House." Liberty News Service. June 7, 2012. Accessed May 12, 2020. http://www.liberty.edu/news/index.cfm?PID=18495&mid=56797

Chapter 5

1. Parts of this section first appeared in Hollis-Brusky and Wilson (2017).
2. See https://web.archive.org/web/19981206192657/http://www.aclj.org/ (accessed November 7, 2015)
3. See https://web.archive.org/web/20020913173813/http://aclj.org/about/welcome.asp (accessed November 7, 2014).
4. American Center for Law and Justice. "Our Staff." Retrieved from https://aclj.org/our-mission/staff (accessed October 15, 2018). Regent Law alumni listed include Robert "Skip" Ash, Matthew Clark, Cece Heil, Miles Terry, Benjamin Sisney, Olivia Summers, Shahsyor Gill, Marshall Goldman, Abigail Southerland, Michelle Terry, and Erik Zimmeran.
5. Jordan Sekulow ('09), Kim Shaftner ('09), Carly Gammill ('07), Kris Wenberg ('01), Patricia Bast Lyman ('97), David Cortman ('96), Shannon Woodruff ('95), Shawn Voyles ('98), Tiffany Barrans ('09), and Allison Murray Fick ('14).
6. For one high-profile example of Regent Law's placement success under Republican administrations, see discussion in Chapter 4 of Regent Law graduate Monica Goodling and her colleagues in the George W. Bush Justice Department who came under fire for partisan- and politically motivated firings of U.S. Attorneys in 2006.
7. Parts of this section first appeared in Hollis-Brusky and Wilson (2017).
8. Baptist Press. "Liberty law school, Liberty Counsel launch religious liberty center." October 24, 2003. Retrieved from http://www.bpnews.net/16933/liberty-law-school-liberty-counsel-launch-religious-liberty-center (accessed May 12, 2020).
9. https://www.lc.org/about (accessed October 16, 2018).
10. https://lc.org/about-liberty-counsel (accessed October 16, 2018).
11. Adam Birr ('10); Antonio Cerevantes ('10); David Mitchell Graham ('10); Jeremy Morris ('10); Chuck Sharkey ('11); Hannah Tomlinson ('11); Kerry Tilley ('11); Mary Enstrom ('11); Reagan Starner ('11) Anna Walker Higgins ('12); Kristal Dahlager (12); Philip Marbury ('12); Ethan Hargraves ('12); Rachel Brenke ('12) Hilary Leitch ('13); James Edward Eugene Kimmey ('13); Meghan Lynn Chapman ('13); Jeffrey Brown ('13); Kate Trammell ('13); Kevin Fritz ('13) Susan Alkire ('13) Amanda Horne ('14); Justin Goins ('14); Lucy Brado ('14); Michael Johnson ('14); Stephen Reese ('14); Thomas Vick ('14); John Scott ('15); Joshua Hetzler ('15); Lindsay Utsman ('15); Luke Douglas ('15).

12. Matthew Krause ('07) opened LC Texas office in Dec 2007; Susan Seitz ('07), Legal Director Liberty Center for Law and Policy; Kristin Kilgore ('09), Liberty Center for Law and Policy; Mandi Ancalle ('09), Director of LC Action and attorney; Mandi Campbell ('13), Legal Director Liberty Center for Law and Policy; Mark Trammell ('12), Legal Director Liberty Center Law and Policy; Douglas Wilson ('10), LC affiliate attorney.

13. Anna Walker Higgins ('12); Lindsay Utsman ('15).

14. Kerry Tilley ('11).

15. Paul Broderson ('12); Lucy Brado ('14).

16. Paul Broderson ('12).

17. Matthew Krause ('07); John Scott ('15).

18. Thomas More Law Center. "History of the Law Center." Retrieved from https://www.thomasmore.org/history-of-the-law-center-1/ (accessed July 11, 2018).

19. See https://www.thomasmore.org/governing-boards/ (accessed October 19, 2018).

20. See, e.g., Ave Maria School of Law. "Learning Beyond the Classroom, Externships." December 25, 2001. Retrieved from the Internet Archive WayBack Machine at http://web.archive.org/web/20011225205817/http://www.avemarialaw.edu/curriculum/beyond.html (accessed October 17, 2018).

21. See https://www.thomasmore.org/news/maine-pro-lifers-must-wait-a-little-longer-to-learn-the-fate-of-their-sidewalk-ministry/ (accessed October 17, 2018).

22. https://www.thomasmore.org/news/defender-the-faith-award-presented-tmlc-attorney-erin-mersino/ (accessed October 17, 2018).

23. https://legatus.org/tag/thomas-more-law-center/ (accessed October 17, 2018).

24. Thomas More Law Center. "Thomas More Law Center Wins Huge Victory for Free Speech and Unborn Babies against Planned Parenthood." Retrieved from https://www.thomasmore.org/news/thomas-law-center-wins-huge-victory-free-speech-unborn-babies-planned-parenthood/ (accessed October 30, 2018).

25. See http://www.smcrcc.org/40-days-for-life (accessed October 22, 2018).

26. See https://vitaefoundation.org/ (accessed October 22, 2018).

27. See https://studentsforlife.org/ (accessed October 22, 2018).

28. See https://www.cultureoflife.org/mission-and-vision/ (accessed October 2, 2018).

29. See http://lawlife.org/ (accessed October 2, 2018).

30. Liberty University School of Law. "Faculty. Phillip Kline." Retrieved from http://www.liberty.edu/law/faculty/phillip-kline/ (accessed October 22, 2018).

31. Liberty University School of Law. "Faculty. Joseph J. Martins." Retrieved from http://www.liberty.edu/law/faculty/joseph-martins/ (accessed October 22, 2018).

32. Liberty University School of Law. "Faculty. Scott Thompson." Retrieved from http://www.liberty.edu/law/faculty/scott-thompson/ (accessed October 22, 2018).

33. See Alliance Defending Freedom. "About Us. Attorneys." Retrieved from https://www.adflegal.org/about-us/attorneys (accessed October 23, 2018). ADF attorneys who listed Regent Law as their alma mater include Caleb Dalton, David Cortman, Gary McCaleb, Jake Warner, Jeremy Tedesco, Ray Kaselonis, and Tyson Langhofer.

34. Brian Walsh ('00).

35. Brian Fahling ('89.)

36. Travis Suren Weber ('10).

37. Greg Terra ('01), Michael Casaretto ('10), Stephen Casey ('07).

38. Jim Mason ('96).

39. Carl Jens Stevens ('92).

40. Dorothy Yeung ('04).

41. Jeffrey Gallant ('01).

42. Colleen Holmes ('99).

43. Erin Elizabeth Kube ('06); Matt Barber ('99).

44. Mick Cummins ('92).

45. Brian Raum ('94).
46. Steven Fitschen ('99) is the President of the National Legal Foundation.
47. Searches were conducted in June 2018 and October 2018. Faculty names were entered within parentheses into the search bar of the Federalist Society website (https://fedsoc.org/). If the faculty member had a profile on the Federalist Society website, it would appear in the search, and the "events" appearing on the profile were analyzed first. In order to verify that the faculty member's name had actually appeared on each "event" program, each individual program was clicked on, and control-F was used to search for the faculty member's last name. Then, if the name appeared, the full name and accompanying institution were checked as well to ensure it was, indeed, the same faculty member. To encompass all faculty who had changed institutions (such as Lee Strang, who moved from Ave Maria to Toledo Law School), if the name on the Federalist Society event program was the same but the corresponding institution was not the one expected (the Christian law school being studied), the faculty member was Googled. Their CV was also used to verify that they were, indeed, employed by the law school appearing on the event program at the same time the event occurred.
48. Gratitude to Pomona College student research assistant Hutchinson Fann., who helped gather data for this section and also coined the term "The Blackstone Seven."
49. "Grounding a Constitutional Right to Homeschool," 2014 Annual Faculty Conference; "Meyer and Pierce: From a Right to Earn a Living to a Right to Homeschool?" 2013 Arkansas-Fayetteville Student Chapter.
50. See, e.g., "NLRB Trumps Five Obama Board Precedents," 2018 Labor and Employment Law Practice Group; "Government Unions: An Update from the Battle Fronts," 2015 Minnesota Lawyers Chapter; "Labor & Employment: 80th Anniversary of the National Labor Relations Act & Congressional Action," 2015 National Lawyers Convention; "The New NLRB Representation Case Rule," 2015 Labor and Employment Law Practice Group; "Labor & Employment: Recess Appointments: Implications of Noel Canning," 2013 National Lawyers Convention; "Labor: Organized Labor and the Obama Administration," 2011 National Lawyers Convention.
51. 2007, Washington, D.C., Lawyers Chapter event.
52. 2006, Administrative Law and Regulation Practice Group event.
53. "Police Tactics and the Fifth Amendment," 2018 Pace Student Chapter; "The Perils of Talking to the Police," 2018 Southern Arizona Lawyers Chapter; "Silence is Golden: Why You Should Never Talk to the Police," 2018 Arizona Student Chapter; "Don't Talk to the Police? Right Against Self Incrimination," Arizona State Student Chapter; "The Right to Remain Silent," 2018 Arizona State Student Chapter; "Why You Should Never Talk to Police," 2016 Georgetown Student Chapter; "Why Should You Never Talk to the Police?," 2015 Pittsburgh Student Chapter; "In Praise of the Fifth Amendment: Why No Criminal Suspect Should Ever Talk to the Police," 2013 Vanderbilt Student Chapter; "Why Even Innocent People Shouldn't Talk to the Police," 2013 Maryland Student Chapter; "Know Your Rights," 2013 Duke Student Chapter; "The Fifth Amendment," 2012 Northeastern Student Chapter; "The 5th Amendment," 2008 Washington & Lee Student Chapter.
54. AMSL Student Chapter. "Federalism v. Anti-Federalism in the American Founding." 2009. Retrieved from https://fedsoc.org/commentary/videos/federalism-v-anti-federalism-in-the-american-founding-event-audio-video (accessed November 6, 2018).
55. We did eventually visit Regent Law campus a year later in 2016 after we planned a visit to Virginia Beach specifically to speak with Herb Titus, founding Dean of Regent Law who had been controversially ousted by Pat Robertson. We were only permitted to speak with the communications department, two administrators, and one former student who was now teaching at Regent Law. We were escorted around campus by Regent Law representatives and were allowed to sit in on one class.
56. Faculty members with special circumstances include Robert Bork (AMSL), John Ashcroft (Regent), and Jay Alan Sekulow (Regent). Because each of these very public figures returned

thousands of hits on LexisNexis Academic, we limited our search to only those articles that included their affiliation with the institution under study (John Ashcroft + Regent; Jay Alan Sekulow + Regent; Robert Bork + Ave Maria). This allowed us to include them in the analysis as valuable cultural assets for each institution without artificially inflating either the total media counts per institution or the average media mentions per faculty.

57. Unlike Sekulow, Bork, and Ashcroft, Staver could not be restricted by searching Staver + Liberty. Because both "Liberty Counsel" and "Liberty Law" contain the phrase "Liberty" and because "law" and "counsel" often appeared in articles under both search terms, limiting Staver's counts for Liberty was trickier. Staver also served simultaneously as Dean of Liberty Law and President of Liberty Counsel for eight years, so we could not limit by time period.

58. Clearly, this figure does not account for the potential number of online shares of articles in lower-ranked newspaper outlets.

59. Rankings were drawn from an article on 24/7 Wall Street, which drew its data from the Alliance for Audited Media. As 24/7 describes: "Below are the 100 largest newspapers in the United States based on combined print and digital paid subscriptions. Circulation data was provided by the Alliance for Audited Media and is for the third quarter of 2015. Circulation is the five-day average for publications that are published Monday through Friday. The list only compares newspapers that report this five-day average. To be included in total circulation figures, digital subscriptions must be restricted access and comply with AAM standards. Circulation figures also include affiliate publications as grouped by the AAM." See https://247wallst.com/media/2017/01/24/americas-100-largest-newspapers/ (accessed 12/4/18).

60. "Robertson Libel Suit"; "Around the Region." *The Washington Post*. August 31, 1997, METRO B03.

61. See, e.g., Howard Kurtz, "$734,371 Later . . . 1,600 page study of portrayal of children in leading sex magazines inconclusive." *The Washington Post*. September 21, 1986, A21.

Chapter 6

1. An impact factor is a measure of the average number of citations that articles in a journal have received, and it is commonly used as a quantifiable measure of a journal's significance and prestige. Also, we acknowledge that having one's work cited is not necessarily evidence of its acceptance—one can cite a work in order to criticize it—but it is still evidence of one's work having been read, considered, and deemed important enough to be referenced. Given that, citation rates are a good quantifiable marker of one's ability to enter the intellectual marketplace of ideas.

2. As Brown describes in *Trumping Religion* (2002), similar conflict took place within the Christian public interest litigation sphere. In brief, there was a conflict in the 1990s between those who wanted to litigate cases arguing on behalf of religion's primacy and importance (principle), and those who wanted to use existing precedent within free speech jurisprudence on behalf of their client's interests (pragmatism). The conflict arose since the latter avoided discussing religious speech's content, deeming it irrelevant and, thus, on the same level as past cases regarding pornography and other forms of "offensive speech"—a move deemed offensive to many within the Christian conservative community. As Brown and the decades since have illustrated, though, these pragmatic, "content neutral" approaches won out since they produced victories in court. That said, Herb Titus made a point of noting in our interview with him that he is still involved in submitting amicus briefs that introduce the older, more principled argument regarding religious exceptionalism.

3. See, also, published law school tenure expectations; for example, the University of Iowa's College of Law tenure standards states that "The normal expectation is that a candidate's scholarly work will be published in law reviews, other scholarly journals (interdisciplinary or from another discipline), or as a book or book chapter." University of Iowa. "College of Law Tenure

Standards and Procedures," March 13, 2008. https://uiowa.edu/conflictmanagement/sites/
uiowa.edu.conflictmanagement/files/Law.pdf

4. This spreading of ideas and growing of the desired intellectual conversation is one way of understanding the importance of "intellectual entrepreneurs" in Teles's (2008) alternative governing coalition model.

5. The comparative schools, in order of the *U.S. News & World Report* 2017 rankings, are Notre
Dame (20, Private-Catholic), George Mason University (41, State), Baylor (51, Private-
Protestant), Pepperdine (72, Private-Protestant), University of Wyoming (112, State), and
University of St. Thomas (Minnesota, 120, Private-Catholic), Quinnipiac University (127,
Private-Secular), and Campbell University (Ranking Not Published, Private-Protestant).

6. The earliest available lists of faculty profiles are 1997 for Regent, 2000 for Ave Maria, and 2005
for Liberty. The final year for faculty name collection was for the Spring 2018. In terms of the
comparative schools, we limited our faculty name collection to the faculty in the 2016–17
and 2017–18 school years. In order to accurately compare our three primary case study law
schools with the eight selected comparative case law schools, we similarly used a sample of
the 2016–17 and 2017–18 school years from Regent, Ave Maria, and Liberty's law schools.
Finally, all of these faculty lists exclude Lecturers, Distinguished, Visiting, Library, and Clinic
Professors.

7. Similar methods have been used by others who have investigated law school publications and
prestige (Chilton et al. 2019).

8. By "observable lifetime of the institutions," we mean the earliest faculty lists that we could find
using the Internet Archive Wayback Machine, https://web.archive.org. Through this means
we have faculty data for Regent extending from Fall 1986, Ave Maria from Fall 1999, and
Liberty from Fall 2004 up to the 2017–18 school year. Furthermore, it should be noted that
the data in Table 6.1 includes any publications produced before or after faculty members may
have been associated with the respective school studied here. While this is arguably overly inclusive, this was done for two reasons—one practical, the other substantive. First, the volume
of data and the difficulty in determining when exactly each faculty member joined and possibly left each institution was too labor intensive to be done in an efficient manner. Second,
as described previously, these descriptive statistics relate to scholarly production and *cultural
capital*. One's publication record is a likely significant motivating reason in hiring potential
faculty members—especially those who already have appointments elsewhere. That is, they
are hired, in part, to bring their *cultural capital* to their new school. What's more, if a faculty
member leaves an institution, their future publications can still indirectly reflect well upon a
school's reputation. While the former is stronger than the latter, the point remains that *cultural
capital* extends to scholarship and experience that extends beyond a given school's borders.
Finally, this chapter does examine samples of the data to look at scholarship produced while
faculty are specifically at our primary case study institutions.

9. Since the faculties at the eleven observed schools were quite stable, and because of the proximity of the faculty name collection to the collection of the publication data, Table 6.2's and
other comparative data in the chapter's remainder are not arguably overly inclusive in the way
that Table 6.1's data might be.

10. By way of comparison, Liberty and Regent also have drops in the mean number of works
produced by their current, as opposed to their earlier, faculty, but they are far less dramatic.
Liberty's mean number of works produced goes from 7.2 to 4, and Regent's moves from 17.2
to 11.5. Unlike Ave Maria, though, while all three schools have nearly doubled the sizes of
their faculty over this time, Liberty and Regent have seen increases in the numbers of works
produced, with Liberty moving from 65 to 76 works, and Regent moving from 189 to 241
publications for its faculty. Given these comparisons, Ave Maria's decline over time is all the
more evident.

11. While publication prestige as measured by the publishing journal's impact factor will be
discussed later, it is worth noting here that not only is Ave Maria's active faculty less prolific, but

it is also far less successful in placing its fewer publications than were their faculty predecessors. While the earlier faculty placed 13.7% of its publications in top-50 journals, 18.6% in top-100 journals, and 78.4% in unranked journals, the active faculty have 0 top-50 placements, 1.6% (or 1 publication) in a top-100 journal, and 95.1% of its work published in unranked journals. While this shows a massive decline in prestigious placements between earlier and more recent Ave Maria faculty, the new rates are far more comparable, and even marginally better, than any faculty sample from Liberty or Regent. As such, we can see that while Ave Maria has changed significantly, the field of newly created Christian conservative law schools consistently fares poorly when it comes to publication prestige. Finally, as with the previous paragraph, while citation rates and prestige will be discussed in detail later, we again see evidence of Ave Maria's decline over time in this area. The earlier faculty sample had 83% of its lifetime publications cited with a mean of 20.25 and a median of 8 cites per article. What's more, 31% of these cites came from top-50 journals, and 40% came from top-100 journals. Ave Maria's active faculty sample only has 56% of their works cited with a mean of 6.85 and a median of 4 cites per article. That represents a drop of 27% in cited articles, an almost two-thirds drop in the mean number of cites, and a halving of median cites earned. Turning to the prestige of the citing journals, only 8.6% of the active faculty cites are found in top-50 journals, and 11% are found in top-100 journals. While those rates are drastically below the earlier faculty, underscoring the degree of their decline, Ave Maria is still outperforming active faculty at Liberty (1.5% and 3.9%, respectively) and Regent (5.5% and 7.8%, respectively) in citation prestige, while their citation rates marginally outpace Liberty (51%) and fall significantly below Regent (77%).

12. For more on patterns regarding publication placement and prestige, see note 11.

13. According to HeinOnline's author data, Robert H. Bork has been cited 4,606 times in scholarly articles, making him HeinOnline's 59th topmost-cited scholar in articles. HeinOnline's metric of the average number of citations for Bork's articles comes to 112.34. "Bork, Robert H." n.d. HeinOnline. Accessed January 30, 2019. https://heinonline-org.du.idm.oclc.org/HOL/AuthorProfile?action=edit&search_name=Bork%2C%20Robert%20H.&collection=journals

    While this clearly speaks to Bork's prestige within the legal academy, it is worth noting that he only published three articles while he was affiliated with Ave Maria, and of these three he only listed his faculty affiliation in one—which was published in the *Ave Maria Law Review*—and his faculty affiliation came after noting three other titles (Bork, 2003). That said, this one article was cited twenty-six times.

14. The shift in mean is largely due to the exclusion of Bork from the count of active faculty.

15. That said, as Chilton et al. (2019) argue, prestige in legal faculty law review publication is predictably self-reinforcing. That is, faculty in prestigious schools are likely better able to garner acceptances from more highly regarded law reviews by virtue of their credentials (versus the quality of their work) given that law reviews are student run (versus peer reviewed and double blind), and publications from such scholars in such journals are similarly more likely to garner citations given their perceived prestige, the increased circulation of such journals, and the desire of subsequent faculty authors "in part to signal to student editors that their article under review is of similar significance" (12).

16. Data collection for these journals was performed in June of 2018 using HeinOnline. Given that, HeinOnline provided access to journal issues running from 2006–16 for the *Ave Maria Law Review*, 2006–18 for *Liberty Law Review*, 2003–14 for *Regent Journal of International Law*, 2009–14 *Regent Journal of Law & Policy*, and 1991–2018 for *Regent University Law Review*. Interestingly, Liberty University housed a journal akin to a law review, titled *Liberty, Life, & Family* before it started its law school. Since it predates the school and stopped publishing in 2000, we have excluded it from this study.

17. Ave Maria School of Law. "Ave Maria Law Review." Accessed January 23, 2019. https://avemarialaw-law-review.avemarialaw.edu/

18. Liberty University School of Law. "Law Review." Accessed January 23, 2019. https://www.liberty.edu/law/law-review/

19. Regent University School of Law. "Regent Journal of International Law | HeinOnline." Accessed January 23, 2019. https://home.heinonline.org/titles/Law-Journal-Library/Regent-Journal-of-International-Law/?letter=R<

20. Regent University School of Law. "Regent Journal of Law & Public Policy | HeinOnline." Accessed January 23, 2019. https://www.regent.edu/acad/schlaw/student_life/studentorgs/rjlpp/home.cfm<

21. Emphasis added. Regent University School of Law. "Regent Law Review." Accessed January 23, 2019. https://www.regent.edu/school-of-law/about/regent-law-student-organizations/law-review/

22. We recognize that this is a rough measure of quality at best since many fine scholars exist across the spectrum of law schools. That said, the most highly ranked law schools tend to compete for the most well-regarded legal scholars. What's more, if one is looking to either increase their institutional prestige and/or influence the legal profession, the ability to attract the attention of scholars from the nation's most prestigious institutions is clearly a help.

23. These patterns might be explained by the school's fostering of such scholarship. In terms of the older faculty samples, we were able to collect data for what can roughly be called the original faculty for both Ave Maria and Liberty by virtue of their later founding dates. Regent, however, posed a problem since it was founded in 1986, and, thus, the earliest faculty profiles were not available via the Internet Archive Wayback Machine. As a result, our older faculty sample for Regent consists of the faculty from the 1997–98 and 1998–99 school years, after Regent had been in existence for over a decade. This can explain its apparent consistency over time. That is, by this point in time Regent was able to hire faculty earlier in their careers, thus having an influence over more of their scholarly life, which is reflected in the consistent percentages of mission-driven scholarship. Ave Maria's early faculty, on the other hand, established the school after having spent lengthy careers at established institutions that likely did not encourage such mission-driven scholarship given the faculty's desire to found a new school that would reflect their values and interests. Once established, though, Ave Maria, like Regent, could hire faculty attracted to its mission, and they could, subsequently, encourage such mission-driven scholarship, accounting for the increase in the share of their scholarship that can be seen as *intellectual capital* for the CCLM.

    Liberty's consistent lower percentages of mission-driven scholarly production, however, are not easily explained in this manner. Instead, one might look to two elements from this story for insight. First, according to his experience and observations, Liberty's leadership has been less interested in fostering scholarship and more interested in hiring from, and producing other forms of capital for, the CCLM. Such a criticism seems to be supported in the data presented throughout this chapter, with Liberty's consistently lower rates of publishing, prestigious placement, etc. This diminished or diverted interest away from scholarship and *intellectual capital*, as well as its hiring practices, however, go further in explaining their overall low levels of scholarly production than they do in the nature of what scholarship they do produce.

    A second hypothesis stems from, as recounted elsewhere in this book, Liberty Faculty 3 noting Liberty's struggles with bar passage rates and related professional placement, and both his and the institution's turn toward making sure that its graduates are practice ready. If Liberty's hiring reflected this concern, and not just finding culture warriors, one might expect the publications produced to reflect those interests. Still, given Liberty's aggressive self-presentation as a hub of the culture wars and its clear desire to reform American law and politics—one must only look back to their painting series on the history of law to see an at least surface-level interest in scholarship and its relevance for law, policy, and culture—their low levels of mission-driven scholarship are somewhat difficult to account for.

24. Again, these faculty members have been similarly unsuccessful in placing their non-mission work in ranked journals as well, but they have been marginally more successful with 7 of 181 publications (4%).

25. In terms of comparison, these numbers are very close to those for the faculties' non-mission work, which has 11% of cites in ranked journals, and 89% coming from unranked journals.

26. Table 6.3, again, while somewhat different, provides another means of putting these numbers in context and showing the gap that exists between the prestige of citing venues for such faculty-produced, mission-driven *intellectual capital*, and the venues that are citing the work produced by faculty at the comparative schools.

Chapter 7

1. See "Charles Evans Hughes." C250 Celebrates Columnians Ahead of Their Time. Columia 250. Retrieved May 22, 2020 from http://c250.columbia.edu/c250_celebrates/remarkable_columbians/charles_hughes.html

2. As in Chapter 6, we used the Internet Archive Wayback Machine to collect past faculty names. Again, all of these faculty lists exclude Lecturers, Distinguished, Visiting, Library, and Clinic Professors.

3. However, by virtue of their positions within the faculty and the associated incentives, we would also expect these faculty to publish less than full-time tenure track faculty would, and possibly to not publish at all.

4. The "U.S. Courts Only" (options selected: Combined Courts, Court Opinions, Court Briefs, Other Pleadings, and Court Publications) in the Bloomberg Law database was used to search faculty names as keywords (e.g., as John w/2 Smith or "John C. Smith").

5. The search function often did collect records not associated with the search target, but context clues in the document were used to ensure that a particular record was accurate. This included indicators like middle initial, time frame (i.e., if the professor graduated from law school in 2000 and the record was from 1994, it could not have been the search target), and geography. Outside of Supreme Court and some circuit court amici filings, there was little consistency across the formatting of documents. This means that some records may not have been captured or may have been overlooked. This is particularly true for decision or brief citations and may have been why this record, in general, had fewer entries, as inconsistent formatting made collection more difficult. Formatting varies depending on the court's local rules, record collection by Bloomberg, and formatting decisions made by attorneys or judges in drafting opinions. Some records that were particularly difficult to collect were of those individuals who were cited extensively, or were extremely active in litigation, with amici participation being a particular area of issue. For those extensively cited, it was difficult to capture every record without double-capturing a record. Conversely, it was also difficult to ensure that there wasn't double collection when a person may have been cited in multiple amici briefs for the same case. While the goal was to capture as extensive records as possible, for the very prolific this collection was not perfect given that the collection method involved a broad search and hand collection of each document, rather than automated collection and categorization.

6. It should also be noted that Mathew Staver would also have been excluded from the count since his position at Liberty University School of Law was administrative (dean) as opposed to being a regular full-time faculty member.

7. When their name searches are combined with their affiliated PILO—Sekulow's ACLJ filings total 87 results (78 federal, 9 state) and Staver's Liberty Counsel numbers total 195 (151 federal, 44 state).

8. Email correspondence with Bryant Garth, Associate Dean of Irvine Law School on May 17, 2019. Email correspondence with Ann Southworth, Professor of Law and Head of the Center for the Study of the Legal Profession at Irvine Law School, on May 17, 2019.

9. Again, the five "repeat player" faculty have been excluded from these data. Furthermore, these data are for the lifetime of the faculty. That is, the amicus participation is not limited to when each faculty member was affiliated with a given law school. Rather, it can include amicus authorship before, after, or while appointed as full-time faculty.

10. In this section we again used our faculty name lists—this time including the four faculty excluded in the previous section—and Bloomberg Law to search for instances where the faculty from our three case study schools and Blackstone were cited in all state and federal counsel briefs, amicus briefs, judicial rulings, and judicial opinions. Also as before, we used the same mission/non-mission coding scheme for the found cases. The summary of the findings are available in Table 7.3.

11. Lynn Marie Kohm, who is both a Regent faculty member and who has served on Blackstone's faculty, has her citations individually counted in the Regent, Blackstone, and the Total School tallies. The Total with the Blackstone tally, however, only counts her citations one time. This accounts for what might appear to be a counting error in that row.

12. "Brief of Justice and Freedom Fund AS Amicus Curiae in Support of Petitioners" at 7, 11, 20, 26 (citing Nora O'Callaghan, *Lessons from Pharaoh and the Hebrew Midwives: Conscientious Objection to State Mandates as a Free Exercise Right*, 39 Creighton L. Rev. 561 [2006]).

13. Brief of North Carolina Values Coalition and the Family Research Council as Amici Curiae in Support of Petitioners, at 16, 19 (citing Nora O'Callaghan, *Lessons from Pharaoh and the Hebrew Midwives: Conscientious Objection to State Mandates as a Free Exercise Right*, 39 Creighton L. Rev. 561 [2006]).

14. Brief Amicus Curiae of the Foundation For Moral Law In Support of Petitioners, at 27 (citing Nora O'Callaghan, *Lessons from Pharaoh and the Hebrew Midwives: Conscientious Objection to State Mandates as a Free Exercise Right*, 39 Creighton L. Rev. 561 [2006]).

15. See "Brief of Amici Curiae Scholars of the Welfare of Women, Children and Underprivileged Populations in Support of Respondents," at 29 (citing Kohm, Lynne Maire, and Groen, Karen M. *Cohabitation and the Future of Marriage*, 17 Regent U. Law Rev. 261 [2005]).

16. See "Brief of Amicus Curiae Agudath Israel of American in Support of Respondents," at 11 (citing Lynne Marie Kohm, *The Homosexual Union: Should Gay and Lesbian Partnerships Be Granted the Same Status as Marriage?* 22 J. Contemp. L. 51 [1996]).

17. See "Brief of Amici Curiae 100 Scholars of Marriage in Support of Respondents," at 17 (citing Kohm, Lynne Marie & Rachel K. Toberty, *A Fifty-State Survey of the Cost of Family Fragmentation*, 25 Regent U. L. Rev. 25 [2012]).

18. *Czekala-Chatham v. State* (2015), No. 2014–CA–00008–SCT. MS Supreme Court.

19. American Principles Project. "Statement Calling for Constitutional Resistance to Obergefell v Hodges." October 8, 2015. Retrieved October 1, 2019, from https://contemporaryprofes sionalresponsibility.com/2015/10/18/catholic-lawyers-call-for-constitutional-resistance-to-obergefell-v-hodges%E2%80%AF-american-principles-project/

Conclusion

1. The Charles Koch Foundation supplied $10 million to the school, while another $20 million was donated by an anonymous donor.

2. However, as we show in our work on newly created Christian conservative law schools, even *parallel alternative* institutions are variously constrained.

3. As the cited articles show, though, the criticism extends past the law school and includes donations to various entities across the GMU campus.

4. Though one can imagine that connections made via involvement with the *supplemental* institution might result in future collaborations that can produce *intellectual capital* as is seen with the Federalist Society, *supplemental* institutions targeting Level 1 as imagined here are less disposed to do so.

5. Due to the limits on available data, the comparisons between the three case study law schools and Blackstone become problematic. Continuing the comparisons across the ranges of interests also frequently devolves into comparing quantified with impressionistic data. The assessment of Blackstone's contributions to *human* and *cultural capital*, then, is unable to be as rigorous as desired. As discussed previously, Blackstone's nature as a *supplemental*

institution also eliminates it from a comparison in terms of contributing to *intellectual capital*. Acknowledging these limitations while still wanting to provide a baseline for comparison, this book has used data from a range of law schools in order to assess Regent, Liberty, and Ave Maria's more concrete support structure contributions to the Christian conservative legal movement. It has also included Blackstone where possible.

6. While this, as well as some of the earlier elements, gives glimpses of the various institutions' connections to the top of the Support Structure Pyramid, the focus of the book was not on this step of litigation-driven change. Engaging in process tracing (see, e.g., Hollis-Brusky 2015) and more closely mapping any connections between cases and these institutions via *human* and *intellectual capital*, however, is an obvious next step in extending the groundwork laid here.

7. Emphasis in original.

REFERENCES

1 Kings 18:17, *Holy Bible: King James Version*.
Acts 7:52, *Holy Bible: King James Version*.

Agudath Israel of America. "Brief of Amicus Curiae in Support of the Respondents." *Obergefell v. Hodges*, 576 U.S.__(2015).

Albiston, Catherine. "The Dark Side of Litigation as a Movement Strategy." *Iowa Law Review* 96 (2011): 61–77.

Alliance Defending Freedom. "Frequently Asked Questions—Alliance Defending Freedom." Accessed November 1, 2013. http://www.alliancedefendingfreedom.org/about/faq

———. "NLF Staff." Accessed March 9, 2018. http://www.nlf.net/About/Staff.html; "Allies." Alliance Defending Freedom. Accessed March 9, 2018. http://www.adflegal.org/about-us/allies

———. "Our New Name—And The Reasons Why." Accessed March 13, 2018. http://www.adflegal.org/detailspages/blog-details/allianceedge/2017/10/18/our-new-name-and-the-reasons-why

Ambrosino, Brandon. "'Someone's Gotta Tell the Freakin' Truth': Jerry Falwell's Aides Break Their Silence." *POLITICO Magazine*, September 9, 2019. https://politi.co/2A4gYpy

American Bar Association. 2013. "Lawyer Demographics." Retrieved from https://www.americanbar.org/content/dam/aba/migrated/marketresearch/PublicDocuments/lawyer_demographics_2013.authcheckdam.pdf (accessed October 3, 2018).

———. 2018. "Section of Legal Education Bar Passage Report." Retrieved from http://abarequireddisclosures.org/BarPassageOutcomes.aspx (accessed September 19, 2018).

Americans United. 2004. "Jerry Falwell Opens Law School to Train 'Radical' Attorneys. *Church and State Magazine*. October 2004. Retrieved from https://www.au.org/church-state/october-2004-church-state/people-events/jerry-falwell-opens-law-school-to-train-radical (accessed July 28, 2018).

Anderson, Lisa. 2007. "Falwell Saw Law School as Tool to Alter Society." *Chicago Tribune*, May 21, 2007, sec. E.

Arthur, James. 2006. *Faith and Secularisation in Religious Colleges and Universities*. London; New York: Routledge.

Ave Maria School of Law. "Our Story." https://www.avemarialaw.edu/law-schools/our-story/ (accessed December 16, 2019).

Baker, Thomas E., and Timothy W. Floyd, eds. 1997. *Can a Good Christian Be a Good Lawyer?: Homilies, Witnesses, and Reflections*. 1st ed. London: University of Notre Dame Press.

Baldwin, Steve. "Child Molestation and the Homosexual Movement: Truth Be Told." *Regent University Law Review* 14 (2002): 267–82.

Balkin, Jack M. 2001. "Bush v Gore and the Boundary between Law and Politics." *The Yale Law Journal* 110, no. 8 (2001): 1407–58.

Balmer, Randall. 2014. "The Real Origins of the Religious Right." *Politico Magazine*. May 27, 2014. Retrieved from https://www.politico.com/magazine/story/2014/05/religious-right-real-origins-107133 (accessed July 28, 2018).

Bannon, Alicia. 2016. "Rethinking Judicial Selection in State Courts." *Brennan Center for Justice*. Retrieved from https://www.brennancenter.org/sites/default/files/publications/Rethinking_Judicial_Selection_State_Courts.pdf (accessed February 15, 2019).

Barbash, Fred. 1981. "ABA Revokes Ban on Religious Bias at Private Law Schools." *The Washington Post*, August 13, 1981. Retrieved from https://www.washingtonpost.com/archive/politics/1981/08/13/aba-revokes-ban-on-religious-bias-at-private-law-schools/c3de5ff4-394c-41b5-8943-0d59dada9202/.

Barton, Benjamin H. 2015. *Glass Half Full: The Decline and Rebirth of the Legal Profession.* New York: Oxford University Press.

Batchis, Wayne. 2016. *The Right's First Amendment: The Politics of Free Speech & the Return of Conservative Libertarianism.* 1st ed. Stanford, CA: Stanford Law Books.

Baum, Lawrence. 2006. *Judges and Their Audiences.* Princeton, NJ: Princeton University Press.

Baylor, Christopher. 2017. *First to the Party: The Group Origins of Political Transformation.* Philadelphia: University of Pennsylvania Press.

Becker, Gary S. "Investment in Human Capital: A Theoretical Analysis." *Journal of Political Economy* 70, no. 5 (1962): 9–49.

———. 1994. *Human Capital: A Theoretical and Empirical Analysis with Special Reference to Education.* 3rd ed. Chicago: University of Chicago Press.

Bendyna, Mary, John C. Green, Mark J. Rozell, and Clyde Wilcox. "Catholics and the Christian Right: A View from Four States." *Journal for the Scientific Study of Religion* 39, no. 3 (n.d.): 321–32. https://doi.org/10.1111/0021-8294.00027

Bennett, Daniel. 2017. *Defending Faith: The Politics of the Christian Conservative Legal Movement.* Lawrence: University Press of Kansas.

Berenson, Tessa. 2018. "How Jay Sekulow Became Trump's Top Lawyer in the Mueller Investigation." *Time Magazine*, March 28, 2018. Retrieved from http://time.com/5219245/jay-sekulow-donald-trump-russia-lawyer/ (accessed October 15, 2018).

Blackstone Legal Fellowship. "Preparing Christian Law Students for Careers Marked by Integrity, Excellence, and Leadership." Accessed December 16, 2019. http://www.blackstonelegalfellowship.org/

Blackwell, J. Kenneth. "America's Two First Freedoms: A Biblical Christian Perspective on How the Second Amendment Secures First Amendment Rights." *Liberty University Law Review* 9 (2015): 215–64.

Bork, Robert H. "The Judge's Role in Law and Culture Symposium: Law and Culture." *Ave Maria Law Review* 1 (2003): 19–30.

"Bork, Robert H." n.d. HeinOnline. Retrieved from https://heinonline-org.du.idm.oclc.org/HOL/AuthorProfile?action=edit&search_name=Bork%2C%20Robert%20H.&collection=journals (accessed January 30, 2019).

Bourdieu, Pierre. "The Force of Law: Toward a Sociology of the Juridical Field Essay." *Hastings Law Journal*, 38, no. 5 (1987): 805–13.

Bowen, John. 2005. "Zones of Methodological Convergence in Qualitative Social Science Research." In *Workshop on Interdisciplinary Standards for Systematic Qualitative Research*, edited by Michele Lamont and Patricia White, 64–65. Washington, DC: National Science Foundation.

Brand, Madeline. 2018. "How the Federalist Society Shapes the Supreme Court." *Press Play with Madeline Brand on KCRW*. Retrieved from https://www.kcrw.com/news-culture/shows/press-play-with-madeleine-brand/how-the-federalist-society-shapes-the-supreme-court (accessed November 2, 2018).

Brauch, Jeffrey A. 1999. *Is Higher Law Common Law? Readings on the Influence of Christian Thought in Anglo-American Law*. Littleton, CO: Red B. Rothman & Co.

———. 2008. *A Higher Law: Readings on the Influence of Christian Thought in Anglo-American Law*. 2nd ed. Buffalo, NY: William S. Hein & Co.

Brint, Steven, and Jean Reith Schroedel, eds. 2009. *Evangelicals and Democracy in America, Vol. 1: Religion and Society*. New York: Russell Sage Foundation.

Brown, Steven P. 2002. *Trumping Religion: The New Christian Right, the Free Speech Clause, and the Courts*. 1st ed. Tuscaloosa: University of Alabama Press.

Budlender, Steven, and Gilbert Marcus. 2008. "A Strategic Evaluation of Public Interest Litigation in South Africa." *Atlantic Philanthropies*, June 24, 2008.

Bullard, George. 2000. "Ave Maria Readies Its First Class: Opening Draws Plenty of Attention." *The Detroit News*, August 7, 2000, Metro, 01D.

Carosa, Alberto. 2014. "The Remnant Interviews CEO of Alliance Defending Freedom." *The Remnant: a National Catholic Newspaper Established 1967*. May 8, 2014. Retrieved from https://remnantnewspaper.com/web/index.php/articles/item/624-the-remnant-interviews-ceo-of-alliance-defending-freedomculum

Chilton, Adam S., Jonathan S. Masur, and Kyle Rozema. "Rethinking Law School Tenure Standards." SSRN Scholarly Paper. Rochester, NY: Social Science Research Network, January 30, 2019.

Cichowski, Rachel A. 2016. "The European Court of Human Rights, Amicus Curiae, and Violence against Women." *Law & Society Review* 50, no. 4: 890–919.

CNN. 2007. "God's Christian Warriors." *CNN Video*. Retrieved from *https://edition.cnn.com/videos/international/2012/08/23/amanpour-christian-warriors-a.cnn* (accessed July 28, 2015).

Colussi, Tommaso. "Social Ties in Academia: A Friend Is a Treasure." *The Review of Economics and Statistics* 100, no. 1 (April 10, 2017): 45–50.

Conger, Kimberly H. "A Matter of Context: Christian Right Influence in U.S. State Republican Politics." *State Politics & Policy Quarterly* 10, no. 3 (2010a): 248–69.

———. "Party Platforms and Party Coalitions: The Christian Right and State-Level Republicans." Party Politics 16, no. 5 (2010b): 651–68.

———. 2018. "Rethinking the State-Level Strategy: The Christian Right and Left in States." In *The Evangelical Crackup?: The Future of the Evangelical-Republican Coalition*, edited by P. Djupe and R.L. Claassen, 94–105. Philadelphia: Temple University Press.

Conger, Kimberly H., and Paul A. Djupe. 2016. "Culture War Counter-Mobilization: Gay Rights and Religious Right Groups in the States." *Interest Groups & Advocacy* 5 (3): 278–300.

Congress. "H. RES. 684 (Engrossed-in-House)," September 23, 2009. https://www.congress.gov/111/bills/hres684/BILLS-111hres684eh.xml

Cox, Harvey. "The Warring Visions of the Religious Right." *The Atlantic*, November 1, 1995.

Creswell, J. W., V. L. P. Clark, M. L. Gutmann, and W. E. Handson. 2003. "Advanced Mixed Methods Research Designs." In *Sage Handbook of Mixed Methods in Social & Behavioral Research*, edited by A. Tashakkori and C.B. Teddlie, pp. 209–40. Berkeley, CA: Sage.

Cross, Mai'a. "Rethinking Epistemic Communities Twenty Years Later." *Review of International Studies* 39, no.1 (2013): 137–60.

Cummings, Scott L., and Deborah Rhode. "Public Interest Litigation: Insights from Theory and Practice." *Fordham Urban Law Journal*, XXXVI (2009). Available at SSRN: https://ssrn.com/abstract=1425097

Davis, Aaron C., and Shawn Boburg. 2017. "Trump Attorney Jay Sekulow's Family Has Been Paid Millions from Charities They Control." *The Washington Post*, June 27, 2017. Retrieved from https://www.washingtonpost.com/investigations/trump-attorney-jay-sekulows-family-has-been-paid-millions-from-charities-they-control/2017/06/27/6428d988-5852-11e7-ba90-f5875b7d1876_story.html?noredirect=on&utm_term=.ef49030d0e6c

Davis, Marc. 1995. "Regent University's Struggle for Accreditation From the ABA." *The Virginian-Pilot*, June 19, 1995, A1.

———. 1996. "ABA Grants Accreditation to Regent Law School." *The Virginian-Pilot*. A1. Wednesday, August 7, 1996.

Deckman, Melissa, Dan Cox, Robert Jones, and Betsy Cooper. "Faith and the Free Market: Evangelicals, the Tea Party, and Economic Attitudes." *Politics and Religion* 10, no. 1 (March 2017): 82–110.

Delehanty, Jack, Penny Edgell, and Evan Stewart. "Christian America? Secularized Evangelical Discourse and the Boundaries of National Belonging." *Social Forces* 97, no. 3 (March 26, 2019): 1283–306.

Den Dulk, Kevin R. 2006. "In Legal Culture, but Not of It: The Role of Cause Lawyers in Evangelical Legal Mobilization." In *Cause Lawyers and Social Movements*, edited by Austin Sarat and Stuart Scheingold, 197–219. Stanford, CA: Stanford University Press.

———. 2008. "Purpose-Driven Lawyers: Evangelical Cause Lawyering and the Culture War." In *The Cultural Lives of Cause Lawyers*, edited by Austin Sarat and Stuart Scheingold, 56–78. New York: Cambridge University Press.

———. 2018. *"The GOP, Evangelical Elites, and the Challenge of Pluralism."* In *The Evangelical Crackup?: The Future of the Evangelical-Republican Coalition*, edited by P. Djupe and R. L. Claassen, 63–76. Philadelphia: Temple University Press.

Department of the Treasury Internal Revenue Service. American Center for Law and Justice. 2012. "Return of Organization Exempt From Income Tax." Form 990.

Department of the Treasury Internal Revenue Service. Liberty Counsel. 2006. Department of the Treasury Internal Revenue Service. "Return of Organization Exempt From Income Tax." Form 990.

Department of the Treasury Internal Revenue Service. Liberty Counsel. 2012. Department of the Treasury Internal Revenue Service. "Return of Organization Exempt From Income Tax." Form 990.

Department of the Treasury Internal Revenue Service. Liberty Counsel. 2014. Department of the Treasury Internal Revenue Service. "Return of Organization Exempt From Income Tax." Form 990.

Department of the Treasury Internal Revenue Service. Thomas More Law Center. 2015. "Return of Organization Exempt from Income Tax." Forom 990.

De Vogue, Ariane. 2014. "Hobby Lobby Wins Contraceptive Ruling in Supreme Court." *ABC News*. June 30, 2014. Retrieved from https://abcnews.go.com/Politics/hobby-lobby-wins-contraceptive-ruling-supreme-court/story?id=24364311.

Diamond, Sara. 1998. *Not by Politics Alone: The Enduring Influence of the Christian Right*. New York, NY: Guilford Press.

Djupe, Paul, Jacob Neiheisel, and Anand Sokhey. 2018. "The Political Networks of Evangelicals, 1992–2016." In *The Evangelical Crackup?: The Future of the Evangelical-Republican Coalition*, edited by P. Djupe and R. L. Claassen, 174–93. Philadelphia: Temple University Press.

Dochuk, Darren. 2007. "Evangelicalism Becomes Southern, Politics Becomes Evangelical: From FDR to Ronald Reagan." In *Religion and American Politics: From the Colonial Period to the Present*, edited by Mark Noll and Luke Harlow, 2nd ed., 297–325. New York: Oxford University Press.

———. 2012. *From Bible Belt to Sunbelt: Plain-Folk Religion, Grassroots Politics, and the Rise of Evangelical Conservatism*. New York: W. W. Norton & Company.

Dudas, Jeffrey R. *Raised Right: Fatherhood in Modern American Conservatism*. 1st ed. Stanford, CA: Stanford Law Books, 2017.

Edelman, Lauren B, Gwendolyn Leachman, and Doug McAdam. 2010. "On Law, Organizations, and Social Movements." *Annual Review of Law and Social Science*. 6, no. 1: 653–85.

Edwards, Bob and John D. McCarthy. 2007. "Resources and Social Movement Mobilization." In *The Blackwell Companion to Social Movements*, edited by David A. Snow, Sarah A. Soule, and Hanspeter Kriesi, 116–52. New York, NY: Blackwell Publising.

Ehrenberg, Ronald G. "Are Black Colleges Producing Today's African-American Lawyers?" *The Journal of Blacks in Higher Education* 14 (1996): 117–19.

Epp, Charles R. 1998. *The Rights Revolution: Lawyers, Activists, and Supreme Courts in Comparative Perspective.* 1st ed. Chicago: University of Chicago Press.

———. "The Support Structure as a Necessary Condition for Sustained Judicial Attention to Rights: A Response." *The Journal of Politics* 73, no. 2 (April 2011): 406–9.

Fitzgerald, John J. "Today's Catholic Law Schools in Theory and Practice: Are We Preserving Our Identity?" *Notre Dame Journal of Law, Ethics and Public Policy* 15, no. 9 (2014): 245–306.

Flaherty, Colleen. "George Mason Faculty Senate Asks University to Hold off on Koch-Funded Law School Renaming." *Insider Higher Ed*, May 5, 2016. https://www.insidehighered.com/news/2016/05/05/george-mason-faculty-senate-asks-university-hold-koch-funded-law-school-renaming

———. "Koch Agreements with George Mason Gave Foundation Role in Faculty Hiring and Oversight." *Insider Higher Ed*, May 1, 2018 https://www.insidehighered.com/news/2018/05/01/koch-agreements-george-mason-gave-foundation-role-faculty-hiring-and-oversight

Gagnon, Geoffrey. 2004. "Onward Christian Lawyers." *Legal Affairs*. November-December. http://www.legalaffairs.org/issues/November-December-2004/scene_gagnon_novdec04.msp

Galanter, Marc. "Why the Haves Come Out Ahead: Speculations on the Limits of Legal Change." *Law and Society Review* 9, no. 1 (1974): 95–160.

Galli, Mark. "Trump Should Be Removed from Office." *ChristianityToday*, December 19, 2019. https://www.christianitytoday.com/ct/2019/december-web-only/trump-should-be-removed-from-office.html.

Galligan, Brian, and F. L. Morton. 2013. "Protecting Rights Without a Bill of Rights: Institutional Performance and Reform in Australia." In *Protecting Rights Without a Bill of* Rights, edited by Tom Campbell, Jeffrey Goldsworthy, Adrienne Stone, 17–39. Burlington, VT: Ashgate Publishing.

Gallup. "Five Key Findings on Religion in the U.S." Gallup.com. Retrieved from http://news.gallup.com/poll/200186/five-key-findings-religion.aspx (accessed March 2, 2018).

Garth, Bryant, Robert L. Nelson, Ronit Dinovitzer, Gabriele Plickert, and Joyce Sterling. 2014. "After the JD: Third Results from a National Study of Legal Careers." *The American Bar Foundation and The NALP Foundation for Law Career Research and Education.* Retrieved from http://www.americanbarfoundation.org/uploads/cms/documents/ajd3report_final_for_distribution.pdf (accessed October 3, 2018).

Gauri, Varun and Daniel M. Brinks (eds). 2008. *Courting Social Justice.* 1st ed. New York, NY: Cambridge University Press.

George Mason University. "Butler, Henry N. | Scalia Law School." Retrieved from https://www.law.gmu.edu/faculty/directory/fulltime/butler_henry (accessed July 16, 2018).

Geroux, Bill. 1994. "Academic Freedom Issues Haunt Law School—Robertson's New Dean Redirects Quest for Accreditation." *Richmond Times Dispatch*, December 25, 199. City, A1.

Glendon, Mary Ann. 1993. *Rights Talk: The Impoverishment of Political Discourse.* New York: Free Press.

Glenn, Brian J., and Stephen Teles. 2009. *Conservatism and American Political Development.* Oxford; New York: Oxford University Press.

Goldwater, Barry Morris. 2007. *The Conscience of a Conservative.* Princeton, NJ: Princeton University Press.

Granfield, Robert, and Lynn Mather, eds. 2009. *Private Lawyers and the Public Interest: The Evolving Role of Pro Bono in the Legal Profession.* New York: Oxford University Press.

Grossmann, Matt, and David Hopkins. 2016. *Asymmetric Politics: Ideological Republicans and Group Interest Democrats.* Oxford; New York: Oxford University Press.

Guzman, Andrew. 2013. "International Organizations and the Frankenstein Problem." *European Journal of International Law* 24, no. 4: 999–1025.

Haas, Peter M. "Introduction: Epistemic Communities and International Policy Coordination." *International Organizations* 46, no. 1 (1992): 1–35.

Hacker, Hans. 2005. *The Culture of Conservative Christian Litigation*. New York: Roman & Littlefield.

Hall, Peter Dobkin. 2009. "The Decline, Transformation, and Revival of the Christian Right in the United States." In *Evangelicals and Democracy in America, Vol. 2: Religion and Politics*, edited by Steven Brint and Jean Reith Schroedel, 249–79. New York: Russell Sage Foundation.

Hammack, Laurence. 2012. "Litigating for the Lord." *The Roanoke Times*. May 6, 2012.

Hankins, Barry. 2008. *Francis Schaeffer and the Shaping of Evangelical America*. Library of Religious Biography. Grand Rapids, MI: William B. Eerdmans Pub.

Hartman, Mitchell. "Downsizing Hits Legal Education." *Marketplace*, February 21, 2019. https://www.marketplace.org/2019/02/21/downsizing-hits-legal-education/

Harvard Law Review. 2014. "Town of Greece v. Galloway." *Harvard Law Review*. Retrieved from https://harvardlawreview.org/2014/11/town-of-greece-v-galloway/ (accessed February 19, 2019).

Heckman, James J., and Sidharth Moktan. "Publishing and Promotion in Economics: The Tyranny of the Top Five." Working Paper. National Bureau of Economic Research, September 2018.

Hidalgo, Carolina. 2015. "Ave Maria School of Law on Federal Financial Watch List." *Naples Daily News*. April 17, 2015.

Hollis-Brusky, Amanda. "Support Structures and Constitutional Change: Teles, Southworth, and the Conservative Legal Movement." *Law and Social Inquiry* 36, 2 (2011): 516–36.

———. "'It's the Network:' The Federalist Society as a Supplier of Intellectual Capital for the Supreme Court. *Studies in Law, Politics, and Society* 61 (2013): 137–78.

———. 2015. *Ideas with Consequences: The Federalist Society and the Conservative Counterrevolution*. New York: Oxford University Press.

Hollis-Brusky, Amanda, and Joshua C. Wilson. "Playing for the Rules: How and Why New Christian Right Public Interest Law Firms Invest in Secular Litigation." *Law and Policy* 39, no. 2 (2017): 121–41.

Howard University. "Home, Charles Hamilton Houston National Moot Court Team." Retrieved from http://law.howard.edu/bryantmoore/home.html (accessed July 18, 2018).

Hunter-Gault, Charlayne. "Hard Times at Howard U." *New York Times*, February 4, 2014. Retrieved from https://www.nytimes.com/2014/02/09/education/edlife/a-historically-black-college-is-rocked-by-the-economy-infighting-and-a-changing-demographic.html.

Hyde, Justin. 1999. "Ex-Pizza Magnate Builds Law School for God." *Associated Press*, April 23, 1999. Business, C1.

Ingersoll, Julie. 2009. "Mobilizing Evangelicals: Christian Reconstructionism and the Roots of the Religious Right." In *Evangelicals and Democracy in America, Vol. 2: Religion and Politics*, edited by Steven Brint and Jean Reith Schroedel, 179–208. New York: Russell Sage Foundation.

Irons, Peter. 1993. *The New Deal Lawyers*. Princeton, NJ: Princeton Univeristy Press.

Isaiah 40:3, *Holy Bible: King James Version*.

Jack, Rand, and Dana Crowley Jack. 1989. *Moral Vision and Professional Decisions: The Changing Values of Women and Men Lawyers*. New York, NY: Cambridge University Press.

Jackman, Tom. "George Mason U. Changes Name of Scalia Law School to Avoid Embarrassing Acronyms." *The Washington Post*, April 5, 2016. Retrieved from https://www.washingtonpost.com/news/true-crime/wp/2016/04/05/george-mason-u-changes-name-of-scalia-law-school-to-avoid-embarrassing-acronyms/?utm_term=.a5a259408035.

Jamar, Steven D. "Charles Hamilton Houston." Retrieved from http://law.howard.edu/brownat50/BrownBios/BioCharlesHHouston.html (accessed July 18, 2018).

Jenkins, Jack. "Liberty University Is No Longer the Largest Christian University." *Religion News Service*, April 27, 2018. https://religionnews.com/2018/04/27/liberty-university-is-no-longer-the-largest-christian-university/

John 15:18–20, *Holy Bible: King James Version*.

Johnson, Emily. "A Theme Park, a Scandal, and the Faded Ruins of a Televangelism Empire." *Religion & Politics* (blog), October 28, 2014. http://religionandpolitics.org/2014/10/28/a-theme-park-a-scandal-and-the-faded-ruins-of-a-televangelism-empire/

Johnson, Kimberley. 2010. *Reforming Jim Crow: Southern Politics and State in the Age before Brown*. New York: Oxford University Press.

Kagan, Robert A. 2003. *Adversarial Legalism: The American Way of Law*. Cambridge, MA: Harvard University Press.

Kellner, Mark A. 2015. "Can America's Faith-Based Law Schools Restrict Sexual Activity to Heterosexual Marriage?" *Deseret News*. January 31, 2015. Retrieved from https://www.deseretnews.com/article/865620856/Are-US-religiously-affiliated-law-schools-under-threat-for-sexual-honor-codes.html (accessed July 28, 2018).

Kelly, Mary Louise. 2018. "What Is the Federalist Society and How Does It Affect Supreme Court Picks?" *All Things Considered on National Public Radio*. Retrieved from https://www.npr.org/2018/06/28/624416666/what-is-the-federalist-society-and-how-does-it-affect-supreme-court-picks (accessed November 2, 2018).

Kidder, William C. "The Struggle for Access from Sweatt to Grutter: A History of African American, Latino, and American Indian Law School Admissions, 1950–2000." *Harvard BlackLetter Law Journal* 19 (2003): 1–41.

Kirkpatrick, Laird C. "Nontestimonial Hearsay after *Crawford, Davis* and *Bockting*." *Regent University Law Review* 19 (2007): 367–86.

Klemp, Nathaniel, and Stephen Macedo. 2009. "The Christian Right, Public Reason, and American Democracy." In *Evangelicals and Democracy in America, Vol. 2: Religion and Politics*, edited by Steven Brint and Jean Reith Schroedel, 249–79. New York: Russell Sage Foundation.

Kluger, Richard. 2004. *Simple Justice: The History of Brown v. Board of Education and Black America's Struggle for Equality*. New York, NY: Knopf-Doubleday.

Krugman, Paul. 2007. "For God's Sake." *The New York Times*. April 13, 2007. A19. https://www.nytimes.com/2007/04/13/opinion/13krugman.html

Larimer, Sarah. "George Mason President: Some Donations 'Fall Short' of Academic Standards." *The Washington Post*, April 28, 2018, sec. Education. https://www.washingtonpost.com/local/education/george-mason-president-some-donations-fall-short-of-academic-standards/2018/04/28/bb927576-4af0-11e8-8b5a-3b1697adcc2a_story.html?utm_term=.5703a36af480

Larsen, Allison Orr, and Neil Devins. "The Amicus Machine." *Virginia Law Review* 102 (2016): 1901–68.

Layman, Geoffrey. 2001. *The Great Divide: Religious and Cultural Conflict in American Party Politics*. New York: Columbia University Press.

Layman, Geoffrey, and Brockway, Mark. 2018. "Evangelical Activists in the GOP: Still the Life of the Party?" In *The Evangelical Crackup?: The Future of the Evangelical-Republican Coalition*, edited by P. Djupe and R. L. Claassen, 32–48. Philadelphia: Temple University Press.

Levin, Yuval. "Partisans of Liberal Education." *National Review*, December 4, 2016. https://www.nationalreview.com/corner/partisans-liberal-education-yuval-levin/.

Levinthal, Dave. 2015. "Spreading the Free-Market Gospel." *The Atlantic*. October 30, 2015. Retrieved from https://www.theatlantic.com/education/archive/2015/10/spreading-the-free-market-gospel/413239/.

Lewis, Andrew R. 2017. *The Rights Turn in Conservative Christian Politics: How Abortion Transformed the Culture Wars*. Cambridge; New York: Cambridge University Press.

———. "The Inclusion Moderation Thesis: The U.S. Republican Party and the Christian Right." *Oxford Research Encyclopedia of Politics*, August 28, 2019. DOI: 10.1093/acrefore/9780190228637.013.665

Lewis, Nancy. "Pornography Panel Ordered to Rescind 'Blacklist' Letter." *The Washington Post*. July 4, 1986. Retrieved from https://www.washingtonpost.com/archive/politics/1986/07/04/pornography-panel-ordered-to-rescind-blacklist-letter/c338f75b-6bf2-473f-9fd1-8a86d80a7acd/.

Liberty University. 2019. "Biography: Lindevaldsen, Rena M. | Liberty University School of Law." Retrieved from https://www.liberty.edu/law/faculty/rena-indevaldsen/ (accessed May 15, 2020).

Liberty University News Service. "School of Law Grads Witness Alabama Supreme Court." April 29, 2014. http://www.liberty.edu/news/index.cfm?PID=18495&MID=118545

———. 2016. "Liberty Law Notches Second Highest Bar Exam Pass Rate in Virginia." October 26, 2016. Retrieved from http://www.liberty.edu/law/aba-accredited-law-school/ (accessed September 19, 2018).

Liberty University School of Law. "Official Page | Liberty University School of Law." Accessed December 16, 2019. https://www.liberty.edu/law/.

———."Liberty University School of Law Foundation Hall History of the Rule of Law." Liberty Law, April 2015. In Authors' Possession.

Life Legal. 2012. "An Interview with Royce Hood." August 29, 2012. *Life Legal Defense Foundation.* Retrieved from https://lifelegaldefensefoundation.org/2012/08/29/an-interview-with-royce-hood/ (accessed October 22, 2018).

Liner, Gaines H., and Ellen Sewell. "Research Requirements for Promotion and Tenure at PhD Granting Departments of Economics." *Applied Economics Letters* 16, no. 8 (May 14, 2009): 765–68.

Lithwick, Dahlia. 2007. "Justice's Holy Hires." *Washington Post.* April 8, 2007; at B2.

Los Angeles Times. Articles about Jimmy Swaggart—Latimes." Retrieved from http://articles.latimes.com/keyword/jimmy-swaggart (accessed March 7, 2018).

Lowndes, Joseph E. 2009. *From the New Deal to the New Right: Race and the Southern Origins of Modern Conservatism.* New Haven, CT; London: Yale University Press.

Luke 11:49, *Holy Bible: King James Version.*

MacGillis, Alec. 2018. "How Liberty University Built a Billion-Dollar Empire Online." *New York Times Magazine,* April 17, 2018. https://www.nytimes.com/2018/04/17/magazine/how-liberty-university-built-a-billion-dollar-empire-online.html

Margolick, David. 1993. "At the Bar; The Waters Roil in Virginia Beach, Home of Pat Robertson's Distinctive Law School." *The New York Times.* October 1, 1993.

Margolis, Michele F. 2018. *From Politics to the Pews: How Partisanship and the Political Environment Shape Religious Identity.* Chicago: University of Chicago Press.

Margolis, Wendy, Bonnie Gordon, and David Rosenlieb, eds. 2013. *ABA LSAC Official Guide to ABA-Approved Law Schools.* Chicago, IL: American Bar Association.

Margolis, Wendy, Bonnie Gordon, and David Rosenlieb, eds. 2012. *ABA LSAC Official Guide to ABA-Approved Law Schools.* Chicago, IL: American Bar Association.

Margolis, Wendy, Bonnie Gordon, and David Rosenlieb, eds. 2011. *ABA LSAC Official Guide to ABA-Approved Law Schools.* Chicago, IL: American Bar Association.

Margolis, Wendy, Bonnie Gordon, and David Rosenlieb, eds. 2010. *ABA LSAC Official Guide to ABA-Approved Law Schools.* Chicago, IL: American Bar Association.

Margolis, Wendy, Bonnie Gordon, and David Rosenlieb, eds. 2009. *ABA LSAC Official Guide to ABA-Approved Law Schools.* Chicago, IL: American Bar Association.

Margolis, Wendy, Bonnie Gordon, and David Rosenlieb, eds. 2008. *ABA LSAC Official Guide to ABA-Approved Law Schools.* Chicago, IL: American Bar Association.

Margolis, Wendy, Bonnie Gordon, and David Rosenlieb, eds. 2007. *ABA LSAC Official Guide to ABA-Approved Law Schools.* Chicago, IL: American Bar Association.

Margolis, Wendy, Bonnie Gordon, and David Rosenlieb, eds. 2006. *ABA LSAC Official Guide to ABA-Approved Law Schools.* Chicago, IL: American Bar Association.

Margolis, Wendy, Bonnie Gordon, and David Rosenlieb, eds. 2005. *ABA LSAC Official Guide to ABA-Approved Law Schools.* Chicago, IL: American Bar Association.

Matthew 5:10–12, *Holy Bible: King James Version.*

——— 23:34–37, *Holy Bible: King James Version.*

Mayer, Jane. 2016. *Dark Money: The Hidden History of the Billionaires Behind the Rise of the Radical Right.* New York, NY: Anchor Press.

McCann, Michael. 1994. *Rights at Work: Pay Equity Reform and the Politics of Legal Mobilization.* 1st ed. Chicago: University of Chicago Press.

McDonald, Jordan. "Trump Backer Jerry Falwell Jr. Says Ex-Liberty U. Board Members Engaged in 'Criminal Conspiracy' in Effort to Oust Him as School President." *CNBC* (blog), September 10, 2019. https://www.cnbc.com/2019/09/10/jerry-falwell-jr-accuses-ex--liberty-board-members-of-conspiracy.html

McGirr, Lisa. 2002. *Suburban Warriors: The Origins of the New American Right*. Princeton, NJ; Chichester, UK: Princeton University Press.

Mello, Joseph. 2016. *The Courts, the Ballot Box, and Gay Rights: How Our Governing Institutions Shape the Same-Sex Marriage Debate*. Lawrence: University Press of Kansas.

Melnick, R. Shep. 1994. *Between the Lines: Interpreting Welfare Rights*. Washington, DC: Brookings Institution Press.

Mersino, Paul M. "Patents, Trolls, and Personal Property: Will eBay Auction Away a Patent Holder's Right to Exclude? Pope John Paul II and the Law, Part II: Note." *Ave Maria Law Review* 6, no. 1 (2007): 307–40.

Meyer, David S. 2004. "Protest and Political Opportunities." *Annual Review of Sociology* 30, no. 1: 124–45.

Miller, John J. 2006. *A Gift of Freedom: How the John M. Olin Foundation Changed America*. San Francisco, CA: Encounter Books.

Mingers, John, and Fang Xu. "The Drivers of Citations in Management Science Journals." *European Journal of Operational Research* 205 (2010): 422–30.

Moreton, Bethany. 2010. *To Serve God and Wal-Mart: The Making of Christian Free Enterprise*. Cambridge, MA.: Harvard University Press.

Morton, F. L., and Avril Allen. 2001. "Feminists and the Courts: Measuring Success in Interest Group Litigation in Canada." *Canadian Journal of Political Science/Revue Canadienne de Science Politique* 34, no. 01: 55–84.

Naughton, Michael. "The Corporation as a Community of Work: Understanding the Firm within the Catholic Social Tradition Symposium: The Corporation and the Human Person." *Ave Maria Law Review* 4 (2006): 33–76.

Neil, Martha. "Goodling Scandal Spotlights Christian Law School." *ABA Journal*, April 9, 2007. Retrieved from https://www.abajournal.com/news/article/goodling-scandal-spotlights-christian-law-school (accessed May 15, 2020).

NeJaime, Douglas. "Winning through Losing." *Iowa Law Review* 96 (2011): 941–1012.

Newton, Brent. 2010. "Preaching What They Don't Practice: Why Law Faculties' Preoccupation with Impractical Scholarship and Devaluation of Practical Competencies Obstruct Reform in the Legal Academy." *South Carolina Law Review* 62: 105–781.

Newton, Chuck. 2008. "Ave Maria School of Law." *Chuck Newton Rides the Third Wave*. Retrieved from http://stayviolation.typepad.com/chucknewton/2008/03/ave-maria-schoo.html (accessed July 11, 2018).

Noll, Mark, Lee S. Shulman, and Kenneth Winston Starr. 2012. *A Higher Education: Baylor and the Vocation of a Christian University*. Waco, TX: Baylor University Press. http://ebookcentral.proquest.com/lib/du/detail.action?docID=1059703

Noll, Mark A., and Luke E. Harlow, eds. 2007. *Religion and American Politics: From the Colonial Period to the Present*. 2nd ed. Oxford; New York: Oxford University Press.

Ohlin, Jens David. "The Changing Market for Criminal Law Casebooks." *Michigan Law Review* 114, no. 6 (2016). https://scholarship.law.cornell.edu/cgi/viewcontent.cgi?referer=https://www.google.com/&httpsredir=1&article=2583&context=facpub

O'Keefe, Mark. 1994. "Ex-Regent Dean: His Views Got Him Fired. He Says Robertson Put Politics Ahead of Academic Freedom." *The Virginian-Pilot*, January 23, 1994. Local, B1.

Patrice, Joe. "ASSLaw Update: University President Finally Forced to Admit that Donation 'Falls Short' of Academic Standards." *ABOVE THE LAW* (blog), May 1, 2018. https://abovethelaw.com/2018/05/asslaw-update-university-president-finally-forced-to-admit-that-donation-falls-short-of-academic-standards/

Patrikios, Stratos. "Self-Stereotyping as 'Evangelical Republican': An Empirical Test | Politics and Religion | Cambridge Core." *Politics and Religion* 6, no. 4 (December 2013): 800–22.

Peppers, Todd. 2006. *Courtiers of the Marble Palace: The Rise and Influence of the Supreme Court Law Clerk*. Palo Alto, CA: Stanford University Press.

Peter 4:12–14, *Holy Bible: King James Version*.

Pew Research Center. "Evangelical Protestants—Religion in America: U.S. Religious Data, Demographics and Statistics." Pew Research Center's Religion & Public Life Project. Retrieved from https://www.pewforum.org/religious-landscape-study/ (accessed December 3, 2019).

Polletta, Francesca. 2000. "The Structural Context of Novel Rights Claims: Southern Civil Rights Organizing, 1961-1966." *Law & Society Review* 34: 367.

Pounds, Jessie. 2014. "Bar Exam Pass Rates a Priority as Liberty Searches for New Law School Dean." *The News and Advance*. October 26, 2014. http://www.newsadvance.com/news/local/bar-exam-pass-rates-a-priority-as-liberty-searches-for/article_7a306982-5d80-11e4-9dba-001a4bcf6878.html

Prud'Homme, Alex. 1999. "Taking the Gospel to the Rich." *The New York Times*. February 14, 1999.

Pryor, C. Scott. "Mission Possible: A Paradigm for Analysis of Contractual Impossibility at Regent University." *St John's Law Review* 74, no. 3 (2000): 691–730.

Regent University School of Law. "School of Law | Regent University." Retrieved from https://www.regent.edu/school-of-law/ (accessed December 16, 2019).

Ringenberg, William C. 2006. *The Christian College: A History of Protestant Higher Education in America*. 2nd ed. Grand Rapids, MI: Baker Academic.

Robichaux, Mark. 1996. "But Those Same Family Ties May Pose Obstacle to Success." *The Wall Street Journal*. August 29, 1996. Retrieved from https://www.wsj.com/articles/SB841267106346771500.

Rosenberg, Gerald N. 2008. *The Hollow Hope: Can Courts Bring About Social Change?* Second Edition. Chicago, IL: University of Chicago Press.

Sanchez Urribarri, Rual A., Susanne Schorpp, Kirk A. Randazzo, Donald R. Songer. 2011. "Explaining Change to Rights Litigation: Testing a Multivariate Model in a Comparative Framework." *Journal of Politics* 32, no. 2: 391–405.

Sanger, Carol. 2017. *About Abortion: Terminating Pregnancy in Twenty-First-Century America*. Cambridge, MA; London: Belknap Press: An Imprint of Harvard University Press.

Santos, Carlos, and Pamela Stallsmith. 2007. "Falwell's Legacy Seen at Liberty Graduation—Commencement Today Marks New Beginning for School He Founded." *Richmond Times-Dispatch*. May 19, 2007.

Sauder, Michael, and Wendy Espeland. "The Discipline of Rankings: Tight Coupling and Organizational Change." *American Sociological Review* 74 (2009): 63–82.

Savage, David G. 2014. "Prayer Case Divides Supreme Court Justices along Religious Lines." *Los Angeles Times*. May 5, 2014. https://www.latimes.com/nation/nationnow/la-na-nn-supreme-court-religion-catholics-jews-20140505-story.html.

———. 2007. "Scandal Puts Spotlight on Christian Law School Grads Influential in Justice Dept." *The Boston Globe*, April 8, 2007, A1.

Scarnecchia, D. Brian. 2010. *Bioethics, Law, and Human Life Issues*. Plymouth, UK: The Scarecrow Press, Inc.

Schaeffer, Pamela. 1999. "Wanted: Different Kind of lawyer." *National Catholic Reporter*. August 13, 1999. http://natcath.org/NCR_Online/archives2/1999c/081399/081399d.htm

Scheingold, Stuart A. 2004. *The Politics of Rights: Lawyers, Public Policy, and Political Change*. 2nd ed. Ann Arbor: University of Michigan Press.

Scheingold, Stuart A., and Austin Sarat. 2004. *Something to Believe in: Politics, Professionalism, and Cause Lawyering*. Stanford, CA: Stanford Law and Politics.

Schickler, Eric. 2016. *Racial Realignment: The Transformation of American Liberalism, 1932–1965*. Princeton, NJ: Princeton University Press.

Schulman, Bruce J., and Julian E. Zelizer. 2008. *Rightward Bound: Making America Conservative in the 1970s*. Cambridge, MA: Harvard University Press.

Schultz, Marisa. 2007. "Ave Maria Law School to Leave Ann Arbor." *The Detroit News*, February 21, 2007, Metro.

Schuman, Samuel. 2010. *Seeing the Light: Religious Colleges in Twenty-First-Century America.* Baltimore: Johns Hopkins University Press.

Schwartz, Emma. 2004. "Falwell's School Joins Others in Teaching Law to their Flocks." *Los Angeles Times*, November 21, 2004. Retrieved from https://www.latimes.com/archives/la-xpm-2004-nov-21-na-lawschool21-story.html.

Sebenius, James. "Challenging Conventional Explanations of International Cooperation: Negotiation Analysis and the Case of Epistemic Communities." *International Organizations* 46, no. 1 (1992): 323–65.

Shaffer, Thomas. "Erastian and Sectarian Arguments in Religiously Affiliated American Law Schools." *Stanford Law Review* 45, no. 6 (1993): 1859–80.

Shepherd, George B., and William G. Shepherd. "Scholarly Restraints—ABA Accreditation and Legal Education." *Cardozo Law Review* 19 (1998): 2091–2257.

Silverstein, Gordon. 2009. *Law's Allure.* New York, NY: Cambridge University Press.

Skeel, David. "Making Sense of the New Financial Deal Essay." *Liberty University Law Review* 5 (2011): 181–200.

Sloan, Karen. 2018. "Future of Independent Law Schools Is in Peril." *Law.Com.* July 25, 2018. Retrieved at https://www.law.com/2018/07/25/future-of-stand-alone-law-schools-is-in-peril/ (accessed July 27, 2018).

Smith, Allan. 2018. "One of Trump's Lawyers Has Unexpectedly Become the Only Firewall between Him and Mueller." *Business Insider.* March 27, 2018. Retrieved from https://www.businessinsider.com/trump-lawyer-jay-sekulow-mueller-interview-2018-3 (accessed October 15, 2018).

Smith, J. Clay, Jr. 1999. *Emancipation: The Making of the Black Lawyer, 1844–1944.* Philadelphia: University of Pennsylvania Press.

Southworth, Ann. 2000. "The Rights Revolution and Support Structures for Rights Advocacy." In *Law and Society Review*, edited by Charles R. Epp, 34, no. 4: 1203–19.

———. "Conservative Lawyers and the Context over the Meaning of 'Public Interest Law.'" *UCLA Law Review* 52 (2004): 1223–78.

———. 2008. *Lawyers of the Right: Professionalizing the Conservative Coalition.* Chicago: University of Chicago Press.

Staszak, Sarah. 2015. *No Day in Court: Access to Justice and the Politics of Judicial Retrenchment.* Studies in Postwar American Political Development. New York, NY: Oxford University Press.

Stolberg, Sheryl Gay. 2011. "For Bachmann, God and Justice Were Intertwined." *The New York Times.* Politics | The Long Run. October 13, 2011.

Suhr, Jim. 2000. "Bankrolled by Pizza Mogul, New Catholic Law School to Begin Classes." *Associated Press.* August 25, 2000.

Swenson, Brady. 2007. "Phill Kline Goes after Planned Parenthood Again." October 18, 2007. *Rewire.com.* Retrieved from https://rewire.news/article/2007/10/18/realtime-phill-kline-goes-after-planned-parenthood-again/ (accessed October 22, 2018).

Tamanaha, Brian Z. 2012. *Failing Law Schools.* Chicago: University of Chicago Press.

Tarrow, Sidney. "Bridging the Quantitative-Qualitative Divide in Political Science." *American Political Science Review* 89, no. 2 (1995): 471–74.

Taylor, Kate. "The Domino's Pizza Founder Created a Catholic Town with No Birth Control or Pornography." *Business Insider.* January 11, 2016. Retrieved from https://www.businessinsider.com/dominos-founders-catholic-paradise-2016-1 (accessed July 28, 2018).

Teles, Steven. 2008. *The Rise of the Conservative Legal Movement: The Battle for Control of the Law.* Princeton, NJ: Princeton University Press.

Timothy 3:12, *Holy Bible: King James Version.*

Titus, Herbert W. 1994. *God, Man and Law: The Biblical Principles.* Oak Brook, IL: Institute in Basic Life Principles.

Titus, Herbert W., and Gerald R. Thompson. 1985. *CBN University Proposed School of Law Feasibility Study* (on file with authors).

Tocqueville, Alexis de. 1835. *Democracy in America.* New York: Bantam Classics.

Tomkins, Andrew, Min Zhang, and William D. Heavlin. "Reviewer Bias in Single- versus Double-Blind Peer Review." *Proceedings of the National Academy of Sciences of the United States of America* 114, no. 48 (2017): 12708–13.

Toobin, Jeffrey. 2017. "The Conservative Pipeline to the Supreme Court." *The New Yorker*, April 17, 2017. https://www.newyorker.com/magazine/2017/04/17/the-conservative-pipeline-to-the-supreme-court

Troy, Tom. 1999. "Domino's Founder to Open Catholic Law School." *Scripps Howard News Service.* April 8, 1999.

Trubek, Louise G. "Critical Lawyering: Toward a New Public Interest Practice." *Boston University Public Interest Law Journal* 1 (1991): 49–56.

Tubbs, Brett Wilson. 2017. "Regent University School of Law Ranks Highest Overall Bar Passage Rate in Virginia." *Regent University*. Retrieved from https://www.regent.edu/news-events/regent-university-school-law-ranks-highest-overall-bar-passage-rate-virginia/ (accessed September 18, 2018).

Tushnet, Mark. 1987. *The NAACP's Legal Strategy against Segregated Education, 1925–1950.* Durham: University of North Carolina Press.

United States Supreme Court. "The Justices' Caseload—Supreme Court of the United States." Retrieved from https://www.supremecourt.gov/about/justicecaseload.aspx (accessed May 14, 2019).

University of Iowa. "College of Law Tenure Standards and Procedures," March 13, 2008. Retrieved from https://uiowa.edu/conflictmanagement/sites/uiowa.edu.conflictmanagement/files/Law.pdf (accessed May 15, 2020).

University of Notre Dame. "FAQ // Core Curriculum // University of Notre Dame." Core Curriculum. Retrieved from https://corecurriculum.nd.edu/starting-fall-2018/faq/ (accessed June 28, 2018).

———. "Patricia—O'Hara // The Law School // University of Notre Dame." The Law School. Retrieved from https://law.nd.edu/directory/patricia-ohara/ (accessed May 3, 2018).

VanSickle-Ward, Rachel. 2014. *The Devil Is in the Details: Understanding the Causes of Policy Specificity and Ambiguity.* Buffalo, NY: SUNY Press.

Various. "Evangelicals & Catholics Together: The Christian Mission in the Third Millennium." First Things. May, 1994. https://www.firstthings.com/article/1994/05/evangelicals-catholics-together-the-christian-mission-in-the-third-millennium

Vegh, Steven G. 2007. "What Is the Real Face of Regent's Law School?" *The Virginian-Pilot*. June 18, 2007. Retrieved from https://www.pilotonline.com/news/education/article_9d34b584-551a-5d2d-9ceb-df619c41bcb6.html (accessed May 12, 2020).

Verges, Josh. 2016. "UMN law school losses expected to total $16M by 2018." *Twin Cities Pioneer Press.* February 11, 2016. Retrieved from https://www.twincities.com/2016/02/11/umn-law-school-losses-expected-to-total-16m-by-2018/ (accessed July 27, 2018).

Walker, Edward T. 2012. "Social Movements, Organzations, and Fields: a Decade of Theoretical Integration." *Contemporary Sociology* 41, no. 5: 576–87.

Walls, Dave. 2014. "Mat Staver Resigns as Dean of Liberty Law School." *WSET.com*. October 21, 2014. Retrieved from https://wset.com/archive/mat-staver-resigns-as-dean-of-liberty-school-of-law (accessed July 28, 2018).

Ward, Artemus, and David L. Weiden. 2006. *Sorcerers' Apprentices: 100 Years of Law Clerks at the United States Supreme Court.* New York: New York University Press.

Ward, Stephanie Francis. 2018. "ABA Removes Remedial Actions Requirements for Ave Maria School of Law." *ABA Journal.* February 15, 2018.

Weiss, Debra Cassens. 2016. "Two Law Schools Are Added to List of Universities Getting Greater Federal Scrutiny over Finances." *ABA Journal.* January 5, 2016. http://www.abajournal.com/news/article/two_law_schools_are_added_to_list_of_universities_getting_greater_federal_s

Wertheimer, Linda. 2006. "Evangelical: Religious Right Has Distorted the Faith." *NPR Morning Edition*. June 23, 2006. Retrieved from https://www.npr.org/templates/story/story.php?storyId=5502785 (accessed July 28, 2018).

Whitehead, Andrew L., Samuel L. Perry, and Joseph O. Baker. "Make America Christian Again: Christian Nationalism and Voting for Donald Trump in the 2016 Presidential Election." *Sociology of Religion* 79, no. 2 (May 19, 2018): 147–71.

Wilcox, Clyde, Mark J. Rozell, and Roland Gunn. "Religious Coalitions in the New Christian Right." *Social Science Quarterly* 77, no. 3 (1996): 543–58.

Williams, Daniel. 2010. *God's Own Party: The Making of the Christian Right*. New York: Oxford University Press.

Wilson, Joshua C. 2013. *The Street Politics of Abortion: Speech, Violence and America's Culture Wars*. Palo Alto, CA: Stanford University Press.

———. 2016. *The New States of Abortion Politics*. Palo Alto, CA: Stanford University Press.

Wilson, Joshua C., and Amanda Hollis-Brusky. 2014. "Lawyers for God and Neighbor: The Emergence of 'Law as a Calling' as a Mobilizing Frame for Christian Lawyers." *Law and Social Inquiry* 39, no. 2: 416–48.

———. "Higher Law: Can Christian Conservatives Transform Law through Legal Education?" *Law and Society Review* 52, no. 4 (2018.): 835–70.

Winkler, Adam. 2013. *Gunfight: The Battle over the Right to Bear Arms in America*. 1st ed. New York: W. W. Norton & Company.

Winter, Bill. 1981. "Oral Roberts University Wins Provisional Accreditation." *ABA Journal*. September 1981: 1095–96.

WVLT. "'My Father Voted for Trump:' Franklin Graham Responds to Anti-Trump Op-Ed," December 20, 2019. https://www.wvlt.tv/content/news/My-father-voted-for-Trump-Franklin-Graham-responds-to-Christianity-Todays-anti-Trump-op-ed-566374111.html

Yanow, Dvora. "Interpretive Empirical Political Science: What Makes This Not a Subfield of Qualitative Methods." *Qualitative Method Newsletter of the American Political Science Association Organized Section on Qualitative Methods* 1, no. 2 (2003.): 9–13.

Yee, Albert. "The Causal Effects of Ideas on Policies." *International Organizations* 50, no. 1 (1996): 69–108.

Cases Cited

Burwell v. Hobby Lobby, 573 U.S. 682 (2014)

Hicks v. State, 153 So. 3d 53 (2014)

Madsen v. Women's Health Center, Inc., 512 U.S. 753 (1994)

Masterpiece Cakeshop v. Colorado Civil Rights Commission, 584 U.S._____ (2018)

McCreary County, Kentucky v. ACLU of Kentucky, 545 U.S. 844 (2005)

Miller v. Davis, 667 Fed. Appx. 537 (6th Cir. 2016)

Obergefell v. Hodges, 576 U.S. 644 (2015)

Reed v. Town of Gilbert, 576 U.S. ____ (2015)

R.G. & G.R. Harris Funeral Homes v EEOC & Aimee Stephens (Docket No. 18-107) (6th Cir. 2019)

Town of Greece v. Galloway, 572 U.S. 565 (2014)

Trinity Lutheran Church v. Comer 582 U.S. ____ (2017)

Interviews Cited

Ave Maria Administrator 1. Ave Maria School of Law. Naples, FL. April 21, 2015.

Ave Maria Administrator 2. Ave Maria School of Law. Naples, FL. April 21, 2015.

Ave Maria Administrator 3. Ave Maria School of Law. Naples, FL. April 21, 2015.

Ave Maria Faculty 1. Ave Maria School of Law. Naples, FL. April 22, 2015.

Ave Maria Student 1. Ave Maria School of Law. Naples, FL. April 22, 2015.

Ave Maria Student 2. Ave Maria School of Law. Naples, FL. April 22, 2015.
Ave Maria Student 3. Ave Maria School of Law. Naples, FL April 22, 2015.
Ave Maria Student 4. Ave Maria School of Law. Naples, FL April 22, 2015.
Ave Maria Student 5. Ave Maria School of Law. Naples, FL April 22, 2015.
Blackstone Administrator 1. Alliance Defending Freedom. Scottsdale, AZ. December 16, 2015.
Blackstone Administrator 2. Alliance Defending Freedom. Scottsdale, AZ. December 16, 2015.
Blackstone Administrator 3. Alliance Defending Freedom. Scottsdale, AZ. December 16, 2018.
Blackstone Alum 1. Scottsdale, AZ. December 16, 2015.
Liberty Administrator 1. Liberty Law School. Lynchburg, VA. April 13, 2015.
Liberty Faculty 1. Liberty Law School. Lynchburg, VA. April 14, 2015.
Liberty Faculty 2. Liberty Law School. Lynchburg, VA. April 13, 2015.
Liberty Faculty 3. Liberty Law School. Lynchburg, VA. April 14, 2015.
Liberty Student 1. Liberty Law School. Lynchburg, VA. April 14, 2015
Liberty Student 2. Liberty Law School. Lynchburg, VA. April 14, 2015.
Liberty Student 3. Liberty Law School. Lynchburg, VA. April 14, 2015.
Notre Dame Faculty 1. Notre Dame Law School. South Bend, IN. September 23, 2016.
Notre Dame Faculty 2. Notre Dame Law School. South Bend, IN. September 23, 2016.
Notre Dame Faculty 3. Notre Dame Law School. South Bend, IN. September 22, 2016.
Notre Dame Faculty 4. Notre Dame Law School. South Bend, IN. September 22, 2016.
Notre Dame Faculty 5. Notre Dame Law School. South Bend, IN. September 22, 2016.
Notre Dame Student 1. Notre Dame Law School. South Bend, IN. September 22, 2016.
Notre Dame Student 2. Notre Dame Law School. South Bend, IN. September 23, 2016.
Notre Dame Student 3. Notre Dame Law School. South Bend, IN. September 23, 2016.
Regent Administrator 1. Regent Law School. Virginia Beach, VA. April 16, 2016.
Regent Faculty 1. Professor, Regent Law School. Virginia Beach, VA. April 16, 2016.
Regent Student 1. Regent Law School. Virginia Beach, VA. April 16, 2016.
Titus, Herbert. Founding Dean, Regent Law School. Virginia Beach, VA. April 12, 2016.

INDEX

For the benefit of digital users, indexed terms that span two pages (e.g., 52–53) may, on occasion, appear on only one of those pages.

Tables, and figures are indicated by *t* and *f* following the page number